# Reinventing the Warrior

LYDA CONLEY SERIES ON
TRAILBLAZING INDIGENOUS FUTURES

Farina King
Kiara M. Vigil
Tai S. Edwards
*Series Editors*

# Reinventing the Warrior

Masculinity in the
American Indian Movement,
1968–1973

Matthias André Voigt

University Press of Kansas

To Simon Wendt and Donald Fixico in gratitude.
To my parents, Jutta and Hartwig, and their support.
To the warriors of AIM whose tumultuous journey has left an enduring mark on Indian Country.

© 2024 by the University Press of Kansas
All rights reserved

Published by the University Press of Kansas (Lawrence, Kansas 66045), which was organized by the Kansas Board of Regents and is operated and funded by Emporia State University, Fort Hays State University, Kansas State University, Pittsburg State University, the University of Kansas, and Wichita State University.

This book will be made open access within three years of publication thanks to Path to Open, a program developed in partnership between JSTOR, the American Council of Learned Societies (ACLS), University of Michigan Press, and the University of North Carolina Press to bring about equitable access and impact for the entire scholarly community, including authors, researchers, libraries, and university presses around the world. Learn more at https://about.jstor.org/path-to-open/.

Library of Congress Cataloging-in-Publication Data
Names: Voigt, Matthias André, author.
Title: Reinventing the warrior : masculinity in the American Indian Movement, 1968-1973 / Matthias André Voigt.
Description: Lawrence : University Press of Kansas, 2024. | Series: Lyda Conley series on indigenous futures | Includes bibliographical references and index.
Identifiers: LCCN 2023049690 (print) | LCCN 2023049691 (ebook)
ISBN 9780700636976 (cloth)
ISBN 9780700636983 (ebook)
Subjects: LCSH: American Indian Movement. | Wounded Knee (S.D.)—History—Indian occupation, 1973—Influence. | Indigenous men—United States—Identity. | Masculinity—United States—History—20th century. | Red Power movement—United States—History. | Indians of North America—Ethnic identity. | Sovereignty.
Classification: LCC E93 .V835 2024 (print) | LCC E93 (ebook) | DDC 978.3/66033—dc23/eng/20240220
LC record available at https://lccn.loc.gov/2023049690.
LC ebook record available at https://lccn.loc.gov/2023049691.

British Library Cataloguing-in-Publication Data is available.

# Contents

Acknowledgments **vii**

A Note on Terminology **xi**

Abbreviations **xiii**

Introduction **1**

Chapter 1. Indigenous Men and Peoplehood under US Colonial Domination **28**

Chapter 2. From Powerlessness to Protest: Reinventing Indigenous Men in AIM, 1968–1972 **67**

Chapter 3. "We Became Warriors Again": Recasting Race, Gender, and Nation, 1970–1973 **102**

Chapter 4. Warriors for a Nation at Wounded Knee, 1973 **165**

Chapter 5. Reinventing Warriorhood and Nationalist Struggle after 1973 **225**

Conclusion **279**

Notes **297**

Bibliography **365**

Index **407**

# Acknowledgments

For this scholarly work, I am deeply indebted to numerous individuals and institutions, including universities, archives, libraries, and communities. Tremendous gratitude goes to history professors Simon Wendt and Donald Fixico for their insight, support, and time throughout this entire undertaking. *Reinventing the Warrior* would not have been possible without them. I am particularly grateful to Simon for discussing theoretical approaches and for his advice on academic writing. Donald has tremendously broadened my understandings of Indian Country as a whole; his ethnohistorian approach has greatly shaped my views. Thank you both so much for your unwavering aid throughout! This book has also greatly benefitted from the comments and questions of many colleagues. Parts of this work were discussed at the American Indian Workshop in Leiden and Odense; the DocLab at Free University of Berlin; the graduate sessions at the Goethe University of Frankfurt; the DFG conferences in Erfurt and Heidelberg; and in talks at the German Historical Institute in Washington, DC. A trimester at Arizona State University (ASU) offered fresh perspectives and new ideas and approaches to the project—aside from the opportunity to make friends with Dr. Farina King, Dr. Grace Hunt Watkinson, and Dr. William Kiser. Thanks also go to Prof. Katherine Osborne for offering valuable insights into this project. The American Studies graduate sessions at the University of Frankfurt have been particularly helpful in critically reexamining my work. Particular thanks go to the faculty of the American Studies Department: Profs. Opfermann, Herzogenrath, and Völz.

Friends and colleagues have been part of this long journey throughout, and they deserve an honorable mention here (in no particular order): Dr. Oliver Wehr and Sonja Kokorsky, Dr. Jürgen Fabian, Dr. Boaz Paz, Dr. Christian Müller, Prof. Dr. Mischa Honeck, and PD Dr. Christian Kuhn. Further thanks go to Dr. Philipp Dorestal, Prof. Paul Rosier, Dr. Sonja John, and Prof. Dr. Olaf Stieglitz for taking their time to discuss sections of this book. Further thanks go to Dr. Andrea Fischer-Tahir and Dr. Anne Saß for reading and commenting on sections of the book. I am deeply indebted to Dr. Peter Beylage for helping with the layout and to Dr. Ian Copestake for his language and editing skills. Thanks also go to the two anonymous reviewers whose feedback has made this a better piece of work. Numerous karate buddies and close friends have also helped me to keep things in perspective. You too deserve thanks!

Activists and veterans have shared their time in interviews on their personal recollections of the events in questions. A three-month trip in summer 2013 across Minnesota, South Dakota, North Dakota, Nebraska, and Montana made this project something of an adventure. Another follow-up field trip in summer 2019 added rich impressions of "things on the ground." In that sense, this book is also part of Indigenous interviewees' willingness to share their stories and their time. The staff of multiple archival collections—the National Archives, the Library of Congress, the Center for Southwest Research and Special Collections, the South Dakota Historical Society, the Minnesota Historical Society, the University of Utah collections, and others—also deserve thanks for their support.

This research has been made possible by a research grant from the German Research Foundation (Deutsche Forschungsgemeinschaft, DFG), which was obtained by Simon Wendt at the Goethe University Frankfurt, from 2013 through 2016 under the project title "Marginalized Masculinities and the American Nation—African and Native American Military Heroism, 1941–2001." This research was further supported by a three-month research and travel grant from the German-American Historical Institute (GHI) in Washington, DC, in 2013.

Portions of chapters 2 and 4 first appeared in a different form in the following publications and are used here with permission: "Between Powerlessness and Protest: Indigenous Men and Masculinities in the Twin Cities and the Emergence of the American Indian Movement," *Settler Colonial Studies* 11, no. 2 (2021): 221–241, © 2021 by Taylor & Francis, available online: https://www.tandfonline.com/doi/full/10.1080/2201473X.2021.1881330; "Warriors for a Nation: The American Indian Movement, Indigenous Men, and Nation-building at the Takeover at Wounded Knee in 1973," *American Indian Culture and Research Journal* 45, no. 2 (2021): 1–38, © 2022 by University of California, Los Angeles; and "Warrior Women: Indigenous Women, Gender Relations, and Sexual Politics Within the American Indian Movement and at Wounded Knee," *American Indian Culture and Research Journal* 46, no. 3 (2023): 101–130.

Finally, this work has been made possible by the support of my parents, Dr. Hartwig and Jutta Westphalen, as well as my brothers and sisters and their belief in what I am doing. Thanks!

# A Note on Terminology

Throughout the book, I have adhered to a terminology that reflects current scholarly debate. In gender discourse, the terms "masculinity," "manliness," and "male/masculine/manly subjectivity" imply the unsteady, mobile, fragmented, and varied construction of men; whereas terms such as "manhood," "male/masculine identity," or "male gender role" suggest a more stable construct of gender (or even a biologically based gender construct). The term "subjectivity" implies mobility and change, whereas "identity" signifies some stability.[1]

The words "American Indian," "Indian," "Native American," "Native," and "Indigenous" are often used interchangeably in the literature to refer to the original inhabitants of America. In general, I rely most often on the terms "Indigenous/Indigenous people," "Native/Native American," "Indigeneity," and "Indianness." However, I followed historical sources when they use terms such as "American Indian" or "Indian," as they occur in historical names and contexts—as in Bureau of Indian Affairs (BIA), Indian New Deal, or Indian Reorganization Act (IRA). When words such as "Indianness," "Indian," "urban Indian," or "urban Indian experience" are used in the sources, I employed the form that is articulated. Further, for lack of better wording, I have utilized terms such as "anti-Indian" or "anti-Indianism." It should be noted that there is no Indigenous term for Native American, thus pointing to colonial impositions, histories, and legacies. Whenever possible, I have used specific tribal names. However, some tribal names have their own pitfalls. For example, some tribal groups use words such as "Sioux" or "Navajo." While they admit that these names are colonial impositions—and instead prefer to use words such as Lakota, Dakota, Nakota, or, for that matter, Diné—they have named their nations with reference to the most common usage of the words, for example, the "Oglala Sioux Tribe," the "Rosebud Sioux Tribe," the "Cheyenne River Sioux Tribe," the "Standing Rock Sioux Tribe," and so on, or the "Navajo Nation." Admittedly, there is no umbrella term that captures the three subgroups of the Sioux (or Lakota, Dakota, Nakota), and Native Americans themselves utilize "Sioux" for lack of a better term.[2] Sometimes, tribal members give their tribal membership as Oglala, or Oglala Lakota (a certain subgroup within the Lakota), sometimes as Lakota or Lakota Sioux (signifying the larger subgroup of the Sioux), or simply as Sioux (a usage that is salient in particular in older documents). Sometimes historical sources are evasive when it comes to specific tribal groups or subgroups, only offering terms such as "Sioux" when referencing the tribal affiliation of a person; these are terms that I have adopted due to lack of better designations. Similarly, other terms such as Ojibwe (also spelled Ojibwa) or Anishinaabe are utilized interchangeably while other terms such as Chippewa (referring to the same tribal entity) are avoided due to a colonial past (unless they are still used in official names, e.g., Lac Courte Oreilles, Band of Lake Superior Chippewa Indians). The words "tribe" (sometimes clan or band) and "tribal nation" signify a historically grown relationship between tribal community and the federal government and point toward political expressions of peoplehood/nationhood.[3]

# Abbreviations

| | |
|---|---|
| ACLU | American Civil Liberties Union |
| AIM | American Indian Movement |
| APC | Armored Personnel Carrier |
| BIA | Bureau of Indian Affairs |
| BPP | Black Panther Party |
| COINTELPRO | Counter Intelligence Program |
| DMZ | demilitarized zone |
| FBI | Federal Bureau of Investigation |
| GSA | General Services Administration |
| IHS | Indian Health Service |
| ION | Independent Oglala Nation |
| IRA | Indian Reorganization Act |
| MAAC | Military Assistance and Advisory Command |
| NCAI | National Congress of American Indians |
| GOONs | Guardians of the Oglala Nation |
| RA | Rancher's Association |
| SOG | Special Operations Group |
| ToBT | Trail of Broken Treaties |
| UNA | United Native Americans |
| USMS | United States Marshal Service |
| WKLD/OC | Wounded Knee Legal Defense/Offense Committee |

# Introduction

On February 27, 1973, a group of roughly three hundred armed Indigenous men, women, and children seized the tiny hamlet of Wounded Knee, South Dakota, at gunpoint, took hostages, barricaded themselves in the hilltop church, and visibly displayed the upside-down American flag. Within hours, law enforcement agents sealed off the roads and brought in military equipment and personnel. What began as a symbolic confrontation to draw attention to local and national Indigenous hardships spearheaded by the American Indian Movement (AIM) ultimately evolved into a prolonged, seventy-one-day armed standoff between modern-day Indigenous warriors and law enforcement officers. Historically, in 1890, Wounded Knee had gained nationwide notoriety as the site of a massacre of 250 to 350 Lakota men, women, and children by the US Cavalry. But in 1973, it captured the spotlight once again in what many considered yet another Indian War refought in the twentieth century—this time with Vietnam-era equipment, weaponry, and veterans. News media footage showed Indigenous and non-Indigenous Vietnam veterans and activists alike clad in the revolutionary garb of the sixties and seventies engaging in what seemed like an anachronistic and retrograde standoff replete with symbolism of the nineteenth century. Halfway through the siege, the occupiers declared the Independent Oglala Nation (ION), a nation separate from the United States, and set up a modern-day warrior society.[1] A *Time* magazine article suggested quite fittingly that "history had been hijacked by a band of revolutionaries armed with a time machine."[2]

What is so remarkable about the takeover of Wounded Knee is that Indigenous activists reinvented themselves as modern-day warriors in defense of the newly proclaimed Independent Oglala Nation. These nationalists selectively adapted various elements of Indigeneity and connected them to the contemporary culture of the 1960s and 1970s, reinventing a warrior masculinity that was inherently hybridized. Traditionally, tribal communities continue to look upon their military veterans as warriors in a much older tradition. From World War I through World War II, Korea, and Vietnam, Indigenous men have joined the US military to defend both *their* homeland and *their* people against outside threats. In so doing, these veterans have continually reinvented their gendered subjectivities as warriors for their tribal nation(s). At the takeover of Wounded Knee, Indigenous men reinvented themselves as warriors through protest activism and in the face of overwhelming forces of US colonialism. Just like their ancestors before them, these Indigenous nationalists, too, considered themselves as warriors. And just like their ancestors, they saw themselves in a struggle to protect *their* lands, *their* people, and *their* rights. The occupation of Wounded Knee points to the inextricable linkage between warrior masculinity and the nationalist quest for self-determination, tribal sovereignty, nationhood, and decolonization.

The central project of this book is to describe and analyze the ways in which Indigenous men and masculinities reinvented themselves as men and as warriors in complex processes of gendered nation-building during the 1960s and 1970s. This reinvention was a specific product of its particular place, time, and circumstances and was short-lived. In this book, I take a special interest in describing and analyzing the cultural construction and social formation of Indigenous men and masculinities as they developed within a larger historical context in which forces such as colonial domination, race, gender, and culture have played major roles. More specifically, I explore particular constructions of nationalist and warrior masculinity that emerged within the context of the anti-colonial American Indian Movement.

During the Red Power era (ca. 1969–1978), Indigenous men vigorously confronted those conditions and institutions that kept them oppressed. Many shared similar feelings of being alienated, disempowered, and emasculated as a consequence of long-standing experiences of political marginalization, social estrangement, and cultural disconnect. Indigenous men reinvented their identities by protesting and turned toward their own cultural traditions, renewing, revitalizing, and remasculinizing themselves in the process. In doing so, they attempted to remake colonial formations of Indigenous manhood in order to feel reconnected and empowered. As Indigenous activists-turned-warriors embarked on their struggle for political rights and cultural reclamation, they were joined by many homecoming Indigenous Vietnam veterans. Together, they engaged in a far-reaching attempt to remake self and society.

## The American Indian Movement, Indigenous Masculinities, and Nationalism in Indian Country

The American Indian Movement boldly captured the public consciousness and renewed cultural pride during the 1970s, a time of considerable unrest as adherents of the Black civil rights movement, student activism, feminism, and anti-Vietnam war protests—in short, people of various ethnic, gender, and age groups—took to the streets. AIM's militant rhetoric, confrontational tactics, and larger-than-life leadership personalities somewhat overshadowed the entire Red Power movement. The fascination of scholars and journalists with this particular organization shows in the outpouring of numerous scholarly and journalistic books, articles, and documentaries. For one thing, these aggressive warriors for a nation would embody the aggressive posturing of identity that came out of the intertwined quest for political rights and cultural distinctiveness.

The American Indian Movement emerged in 1968 in the "red ghettoes" of the Twin Cities of Minneapolis/St. Paul as a local Indigenous community's response to persistent socioeconomic problems and a deep-seated racism and discrimination. Disempowered and disillusioned Indigenous activists, unwilling to submit to their subaltern status anymore, were devoted to bringing about social change with a classic civil rights program. By the early 1970s, AIM had expanded into a national organization with multiple chapters across the nation and gained considerable media attention. During this time, it became increasingly concerned with treaty rights, sovereignty, land reform, tribal governance and cultural revitalization. Between 1969 and 1973, AIM participated in or led numerous protests. Its members took part in the sustained occupation of Alcatraz Island (1969–71); they organized the transcontinental "Trail of Broken Treaties" and headed the subsequent weeklong takeover of the Bureau of Indian Affairs in Washington, DC, in early November 1972; and they instigated the two-and-a-half-months-long occupation of the hamlet of Wounded Knee in early 1973. After 1973, however, the protest organization disintegrated under a relentless onslaught of federal prosecution, FBI counterintelligence operations (COINTELPRO), and internal dissent. In 1975, members of the organization made headlines with a lethal shootout at the Jumping Bull compound in South Dakota. The "Longest Walk," a transcontinental demonstration to protest anti-Indigenous legislation in 1978, is widely considered the concluding event of the entire Red Power era.[3]

During this period of activism, Indigenous men, women, and children protested for a myriad of causes. They demanded the recognition of their civil and treaty rights, the acknowledgement of their religious freedoms, economic relief and political reform, a halting of the latest federal Indian policies of assimilation (commonly known as "termination") as well as and their cultural integrity and the right to be different. For themselves, they envisioned a form of non-assimilative inclusion into American society.[4] Unlike other minority movements, Indigenous people struggled against colonial rule, and they voiced their demands from within that very structure of colonial oppression.[5]

The Red Power movement was first and foremost a quest for Indigenous rights and cultural identity; yet, as this book shows, questions of gender were deeply embedded within that quest. From the onset, Indigenous men and women demanded the recognition of their particular political and cultural place as Natives within and/or alongside a larger encapsulating American society. In that sense, the demands for the recognition of Indigenous manhood were also calls for the recognition of Indigenous rights for both men *and* women. Yet men frequently dominated the public arenas in which the struggle for Indigenous rights took place through shaping much of the language, strategies, and objectives of the anti-colonial struggle. Indigenous women engaged in much grassroots work behind the scenes. While AIM activists were powerful advocates of the rights of Indigenous people(s), they were often unable to confront the male sexism and chauvinism from the rank and file to its leadership. Publicly AIM adhered to gender equality, yet behind the scenes Indigenous women often found their voices repressed in order to emphasize the struggle against settler colonialism. Throughout its existence, the organization frequently equated resistance with manhood, implicitly relegating women to positions of weakness.

Hitherto, historiography has not taken into account the cultural and gendered transformations that occurred within Indigenous men as they embarked upon their quest for rights in the anti-colonial struggle. Neither does it tell how and why these Indigenous men reinvented and reimagined themselves as men and as warriors. The stories of the American Indian Movement that are commonly told leave out a significant context that explains why and how Indigenous activists, seemingly out of nowhere, occupied the national spotlight when they commenced on the Trail of Broken Treaties and took over Wounded Knee a little later. When AIM gained momentum during the late 1960s and early 1970s, Indigenous men increasingly negotiated, challenged, and revised dominant notions manhood as well as their own. Initially, Indigenous activists did this peacefully through demonstrations, marches, and picketing. Later, they did so through increasingly confrontational tactics that involved the takeover of federal land and property, physical violence with police, and finally gunfights with various law enforcement officers. Paradoxically, news media focused its attention on these hypervirile images of (martial) Indigeneity and largely ignored Indigenous women. In yet another twist, historiography has focused much of its attention on women's activism and their significant contributions (while leaving out male perspectives). As a result, the experiences and perspectives of Indigenous male activists have been largely overlooked.

The American Indian Movement represented only one organization within the entire Red Power movement—which was made up of a wide spectrum of often disconnected organizations and endeavors; yet it is widely recognized for the central role it played in AIM due to its militancy and nationalism.[6] A comprehensive monograph-length study into this prominent masculinist and nationalist organization remains absent.

This is in large part due to AIM's multiple contradictions, internal fragmentation, and widespread controversy after 1973, as well as a relentless government campaign of repression.[7] There are only two main studies that shed light on various aspects regarding AIM. Historian Julie Davis's *Survival Schools* examines the emergence of two alternative schools in the Twin Cities urban Indigenous community as "part of the story of Indigenous colonization, resistance, survival, and revitalization in the United States."[8] Survival schools fostered a learning environment that provided Indigenous students with a cultural grounding, allowing them to remake their gendered identities. Davis's study provides valuable cultural and gendered perspectives into Indigenous community-organizing efforts and AIM's activism in the Twin Cities. Another study comes from scholars Paul Chaat Smith (Comanche) and Robert Allen Warrior (Osage). Their groundbreaking *Like A Hurricane: The Indian Movement from Alcatraz to Wounded Knee*, written with Indigenous voices, focuses on several pivotal events, shedding light on the organization's reception across Indian Country, yet offers few insights into the self-identified warrior society.[9]

Studies on the Red Power movement more generally focus on particular events, persons, women's activism and gender relations, transcultural or transnational alliances, or federal Indian policies and the Counter-Intelligence-Program (COINTELPRO), among other issues. These studies have largely overlooked the interplay between protest activism, identity politics, race, gender, and its interrelated political and cultural nationalist agendas.

More recently, scholars have begun to reevaluate the Red Power movement.[10] An early generation of scholars—Troy Johnson, Joane Nagel, and Duane Champagne—conceptualized Indigenous activism within a nine-year period of protest. They have identified the occupation of Alcatraz Island (1969–1971) as the starting point, the Wounded Knee takeover (1973) as the climax, and the Longest Walk (1978) as the culmination of that period of activism.[11] These scholars broadly contextualized the entire Red Power movement with a long line of Indigenous resistance movements to settler-colonial encroachment.[12] Red Power activism instigated a fundamental restructuring of Indigenous–settler-colonial relations, a limited degree of self-determination, and an ongoing cultural renewal across Indian Country.[13] The defining characteristics of this activism were a charismatic leadership, a legacy of resistance to settler-colonial encroachment, an emphasis on Pan-Indianism, national activist organizations, the tactic of property takeover to draw attention to Indigenous issues, and shared political goals.[14]

More recently, scholars have also begun to attach new meanings to the term "Red Power" and have started to push beyond the initial periodization. Historians Lucie Kýrová and György Ferenc Tóth have rightly pointed out that "Red Power can be considered a part of a larger movement for Native American rights and, at the same time, a movement in itself," thus broadening the meanings of the term "Red Power."[15] Historians Brad Shreve and Paul McKenzie Jones have argued that the Red Power movement began in the 1960s with the National Indian Youth Council (NIYC) and the fish-in movement in the Pacific Northwest that protested the restrictions on Indigenous fishing guaranteed by federal treaties.[16] Historian Daniel Cobb has made a compelling argument to extend the Red Power framework forward from 1953 in order to include early Indigenous intellectual traditions and the articulating of anti-colonial and decolonial thought.[17] Other scholars have further extended the Red Power movement timeframe backward into the 1980s to better capture how Indigenous activism turned international. According to historian Sam Hitchmough, the Red Power movement can be divided into three waves: an initial phase (roughly from World War II through the late 1960s) during which Indigenous activism focused on decolonization and sovereignty; a second phase of Pan-Indigenous protest (1969–1978); and a final phase (mid/late 1970s through 1980s) when protests became concerned with multiple issues (e.g., religious rights, environmentalism, decolonizing museums, repatriation, etc.).[18] This study falls into what can be regarded as the second wave of the Red Power struggle.

The study of Red Power nationalism has also attracted scholarly attention. Noted scholar Vine Deloria (Lakota) has pointed out in his famed *Behind the Trail of Broken Treaties, An Indian Declaration of Independence* (1974) that Indigenous nationalists made a compelling argument for reassessing the treaty-making era and for fundamentally restructuring Indigenous–settler colonial relations.[19] Sociologist Stephen Cornell's *The Return of the Native* examines Indigenous nationalism with regard to questions of political empowerment, tribal sovereignty, self-determination, and nationalism.[20] Another study comes from sociologist Joane Nagel, who has explored the ethnic renewal that paralleled and was closely intertwined with this period of political activism.[21]

Feminist scholars have explored some of Indigenous women's activism and gender dynamics within the larger context of the Red Power movement. M. Annette Jaimes (Juaneño/Yaqui) and Theresa Halsey (Standing Rock Sioux) have broadly contextualized Indigenous women's activism within a tradition of Indigenous resistance.[22] Historian Donna Hightower Langston (Cherokee) has examined Indigenous women's activism at key events such as the sustained Alcatraz occupation, the fish-in movement in the Pacific Northwest in Washington state, and the Wounded Knee siege, yet she does not offer an analysis into gender relations within AIM.[23] Historian Devon Abbott Mihesuah's (Choctaw) *Indigenous American Women, Decolonization, Empowerment, Activism* offers valuable insights into gender relations within AIM and the interplay between Indigenous women and feminism.[24] She covers some of the gendered and racialized dynamics surrounding the male-dominated AIM.[25] Both Mihesuah and historian Elizabeth Castle pay attention to particular AIM activists such as Madonna Thunder Hawk (Lakota) or Anna Mae Pictou-Aquash (Mi'kmaq); yet they largely focus their studies on women's activism after 1973.[26] Further insights come from Castle's comparative analysis of women of color's participation in two male-dominated organizations—the American Indian Movement and the Black Panther Party. Her findings suggest that the struggle by women of color for racial and sexual equality was dedicated to community.[27] Fresh perspectives into gender relations and sexual politics within AIM as well as Indigenous women at the Wounded Knee takeover come from historian Matthias Voigt.[28] Julie Davis has shown how women's community-organizing efforts in the Twin Cities led to the establishment of survival schools.[29] Historian Susan Applegate Krouse's examination of the contributions of women during the 1971 takeover of the US Coast Guard Station in Milwaukee, Wisconsin, has found that their activism has lasted much longer than the organization itself. Indigenous women supporters of AIM parlayed the takeover into a long-standing community organization. In turning the attention to their children, the women created the Indian Community School, a project that continues to serve the Indigenous Milwaukee community to the present day. The findings highlight that Indigenous women have been crucial as longtime community organizers and cultural leaders.[30] Indigenous women also led a successful campaign against coerced sterilization and child removal from their homes and communities, according to historian Meg Devlin O'Sullivan.[31]

In the public perception of its time, "the male gender was the 'power gender'"—in the words of historian Troy Johnson—yet scholars have left Indigenous male perspectives largely unexplored.[32] For one thing, news reporting has focused mainly on Indigenous men and their media-savvy tactics, contributing to the common perception of AIM as a male-identified organization. This rather one-sided public focus on Indigenous male activists—now figures epitomized in hypermasculine imagery—has left Indigenous women largely hidden from the media limelight. However, Indigenous women, who at the time carried out much of their grassroots-level activism behind the scenes, have drawn almost all scholarly attention. Indeed, the little research that has been conducted on gender relations within AIM focuses almost exclusively on women's perspectives, thus leaving out Indigenous male experiences as different, yet complimentary viewpoints. The obvious paradox to this historiographical trend is further aggravated by the fact that during protest events, expressions and performances of warrior masculinity made nationwide media headlines.[33] Additionally, the majority of published memoirs are written by male activists, a trend that further necessitates an inquiry into their experiences.

The little scholarship that pays attention to Indigenous men within AIM almost completely focuses on the inherent chauvinism, rampant sexism, and at times outright misogyny among the organization's male members.[34] While many Indigenous men in AIM publicly embraced a rhetoric of gender equality and liberation, they privately adhered to sexist language, practices, and behavior. To some extent, male AIM members were indeed a product of their times: some practiced a patriarchal culture of male domination that was conventional to America well into the 1960s and 1970s.[35] While this chauvinism was tempered through the arrival of the nascent women's liberation movement, the affirmation of male dominance behind the scenes remained always obvious. AIM's leadership was clearly male-dominated, despite the formidable efforts and activities of Indigenous women on the grassroots level. AIM's male leaders supported practices and notions that affirmed a cult of domesticity and traditional gender roles with men being the protectors and women being the purveyors of culture and tradition.[36] Through much of their upbringing and socialization, Indigenous men within AIM were caught in a cycle of dysfunction and toxicity that was harmful to themselves and others. In part this was because of their inculcation with and adherence to the ideals of hegemonic masculinity and male privilege, which, in turn, reinforced their own subordination.[37] AIM's male leaders and rank-and-file members were themselves products of a society where patriarchy was widely accepted. They had been fundamentally impacted through boarding school education, military service, the urban context, and correctional institutions—experiences with colonizing agents and with dominant society that fundamentally shaped their Indigenous and male identities.[38] The toxic masculinity internalized by many leaders and rank-and-file members stemmed from cultural loss, social alienation, and intergenerational experiences of repression that disconnected them from their own Indigeneity.[39]

This is also to recognize the intrinsic role that masculinity plays in nationalist and resistance movements and how it relegates women to positions of weakness. Anti-colonial movements such as AIM have a tendency to repress the voices of women in order to place the struggle against racial inequality and colonial domination first.[40] According to Devon Mihesuah (Choctaw), Indigenous women frequently equated their current state as one of "double colonization" in which both colonial domination and gender inequality kept them oppressed. Indigenous women in AIM thus found themselves in an inherent conflict over whether to prioritize the struggle against racial inequality or the struggle against gender inequality.[41] Within AIM, gender roles and sexism remained contested issues from the leadership to the rank and file. Indigenous women initially prioritized the struggle against colonial domination over gender equality; later they became more vocal in denouncing the sexism, chauvinism, and misogyny within AIM.[42] This should not obscure the fact that Indigenous men within AIM have received surprisingly little scholarly attention.[43]

The absence of studies on Indigenous men's activism is paralleled by a lack of studies on Indigenous Vietnam veterans and their active involvement with the Indigenous activism of the 1960s and 1970s. Historians Tom Holm (Cherokee/Muskogee) and Al Carroll (Apache) are the only scholars that devote some analysis to Indigenous Vietnam veterans' involvement with the Red Power movement; both have recognized their heavy participation at the takeover at Wounded Knee.[44] Carroll finds that the confluence of social protest and veteran activism has resulted in a "new direction for warrior societies and Native ideals on the right way to be a warrior" that occurred outside of the realm of military service.[45] However, Indigenous Vietnam veterans' participation in the American Indian Movement, the vanguard organization of Indigenous protest, has barely been scratched.[46] Hitherto, there has been no comparative analysis of AIM nationalists/warriors and Indigenous Vietnam veterans and (competing) notions of masculinity/warriorhood, nationalism, and male/martial virtues that would add another layer to this history.

Other studies have focused on the interplay of protest activism and gendered media imagery. In his "Modern Warriors," sociologist Timothy Baylor has noted the performance of hypervirile warrior masculinity at high-profile protest events. The news medias' framing of AIM's protests as militant dominated the news, yet it frequently overshadowed issues behind the protests and was not advantageous for the organization.[47] In building upon Tom Holm's findings, anthropologist Maureen Trudelle Schwarz has examined the (re)appropriation of popular stereotypes by Indigenous nationalists. AIM's use of what she calls "the savage reactionary image" points to the careful utilization of symbolic or racial/cultural capital in Indigenous protest politics. However, this analysis almost completely ignores the fact that many Indigenous nationalists not only (re-)appropriated stereotypes but also came to genuinely regard themselves as warriors, although they had not served in the US military.[48] Tom Holm's and Al Carroll's research aside, scholars have almost completely ignored Indigenous Vietnam veterans' involvement in protest politics during the Red Power era or have covered them in only a cursory manner.[49]

The lack of scholarly work on Indigenous male perspectives within AIM inhibits a deeper understanding of the social dynamics within this far-reaching social movement for change and of how Indigenous men and masculinities embody and perform their identities across Indian Country up to the present. The protest activism was paralleled and followed by a major cultural renaissance across Indian Country.[50] While the intertwined and parallel processes of identity construction and cultural renewal has been well-examined, the transformation of nationalist warrior masculinities, as well as their involvement in the parallel and intertwined cultural nationalist movement, has been overlooked. Finally, the remembrance and commemoration of certain events and persons is closely linked to hero-making processes that provide yet another perspective into the organization's commemorative activities and gendered interpretations of the struggle for Indigenous rights.

This study follows a shift in paradigm away from the Western-centric concepts of men and masculinities toward the analysis of marginalized masculinities within their own specific contexts. Dominant conceptualizations of masculinity continue to shape and reshape notions of masculinity across the globe. Hegemonic concepts of masculinity operate to suppress alternative versions of masculinity and leave the gendered "other" without agency and power. Numerous studies, images, or representations focus on either white masculinity as the performer of gender or, alternatively, on racialized constructions of the non-white "other" as the constructed of gender. This one-sided focus on the "white standard" of masculinity has prevented a better understanding of the formation of marginalized and/or subaltern masculinities within their own specific cultural contexts.[51] For example, there is very little scholarship on relations between colonizing and colonized men, on Indigenous men from colonized societies, and on how historical experiences have shaped nationalist, anti-colonial movements. Fresh insights into the interrelation between marginalized and hegemonic masculinities and nation-building processes have come from historians Simon Wendt and Pablo Dominguez Andersen.[52] In building upon this historiography, I explore the interrelationship between Indigenous masculinities and nation-building within the context of the Indigenous Rights Movement.

In their recent volume on *Indigenous Men and Masculinities*, Indigenous scholars Robert Alexander Innes (Plains Cree) and Kim Anderson (Cree/Métis) have called attention to the "lack of theoretical and applied scholarly work about Indigenous men and masculinities" in what is a largely overlooked academic field.[53] However, Indigenous masculinities studies are "one of the most important areas of research," according to anthropologist Ty Tengan (Native Hawaiian). Indigenous masculinity studies not only highlight the dynamics of race-, gender-, and class-based oppression and domination within particular colonial and nationalist contexts but, more generally, work to undermine cultural hegemony and white male privilege through alternative gender practices.[54] It is for this reason that Indigenous studies scholar Brendan Hokowhitu (Māori) considers the study of Indigenous men and masculinities "an untapped rubric for theorizing decolonization."[55]

Significant theoretical insights into Indigenous men and masculinities have emerged over the last two decades, laying important groundwork for future research. In their studies on Hawaii and New Zealand, Ty Tengan and Brendan Hokowhitu have pointed out the diversity and distinctiveness of Indigenous cultures, which inform culturally, temporally, and locally specific cosmologies of gender. Indigenous people share common historical experiences, yet their responses to settler-colonial incursions into their homelands, the dispossession of their natural resources, and the disruption of their gender systems are idiosyncratic.[56] Substantial influences on the transformation of Indigenous gender roles within settler-colonial contexts involve government policies and modernity (e.g., capitalism, urbanization). The primary sites for the construction of Indigenous men and masculinities include government-run boarding schools, the US military, and sports, among others.[57] Building upon these insights, Innes and Anderson have focused on the Canadian context, offering new pathways into the field of Indigenous masculinities studies with fresh theoretical insights.[58] Literary scholar Sam McKegney offers further important addition to ongoing scholarly debates in Indigenous studies. McKegney's *MasculIndians* draws attention to colonial imaginaries that reflect racialized and gendered notions of "masculinity" and "Indians." His more recent work *Carrying the Burden of Peace* seeks to counter "the perception that masculinity has been contaminated by settler heteropatriarchy as to be irredeemable" and sets out to explore "the potential generativity of Indigenous masculinities as rubrics for decolonial theorizing."[59] Finally, Martin J. Cannon's (Oneida Nation) critical examination of the Indian Act—the principal statue under which Canada administers the category "Indian" status—explores how racialized and sexualized legislation has severely undercut the gender identities of First

Nations men.[60] Within the US context, Indigenous masculinities remain a largely overlooked field of research.[61] The little research that has been conducted on Indigenous men and masculinities in the United States largely focuses on cultural and media representations.[62]

Within the last two decades, the field of Indigenous gender studies has been made up of feminist and queer studies. Queer studies have provided fresh perspectives into queer/Two-Spirit people's responses to the normalization of white settler-colonial heteropatriarchy. A central element of colonial regimes has been the violent control and replacement of Indigenous gender systems through whiteness and patriarchy. Queer studies have examined the gendered transformation of Indigenous people within the contexts of white settler-colonial societies. They have also pointed out ways to revitalize nonbinary Indigenous cosmologies of gender, queer, and Two-Spirit theories as decolonizing strategies.[63] Similarly, feminist scholars have theorized the implications of settler colonialism and heteropatriarchy for Indigenous women, their marginalization in settler-colonial societies, and their engagement in anti-colonialist struggles that address issues particular to them.[64] They have also emphasized new approaches to addressing women's empowerment and decolonization strategies in Indigenous contexts.[65]

This book contributes to a growing body of scholarly works on Indigenous men and masculinities across the globe, such as those in Hawaii, New Zealand, and Canada. It analytically and conceptually links the interrelated and overlapping fields of masculinity studies/nationalism, war and society, social movements, and cultural history. It follows a paradigm shift in describing and analyzing the history of "the other" through decidedly Indigenous perspectives and voices. It seeks to bridge several historiographical gaps.

First, this book seeks to make new sense of the American Indian Movement, a key player in the Red Power movement. Situated at the intersections of race, gender, and nation, *Reinventing the Warrior* seeks a deeper understanding of the social dynamics of this far-reaching social movement for change in what is an overall attempt to better understand Indian Country.

Second, it sheds new light on the gendered dimensions of nation-building. Scholars have long established the close linkage between gender and nationalism. What has been less well established, however, is the link between nationalism and masculinities, in particular the role of racially marginalized masculinities within these processes. Indigenous men within AIM reinvented their gendered subjectivities in relation to culturally based notions of warriorhood. *Reinventing the Warrior* calls attention to the myriad ways in which Indigenous men engaged in gendered nation-building processes, fundamentally altering meanings of Indigeneity and transforming settler-colonial–Indigenous relations.

## Theorizing Nationalism, Race, Gender, and Masculinities

Theoretical frameworks from various disciplines help in delineating the complex interconnections between (post)colonialism, nationalism, culture, and memory. They help to explore how Indigenous people have experienced oppression, domination, and discrimination through various intersecting structures of society along the lines of race, class, gender, and so on.[66] Postcolonial studies contain useful concepts for understanding and unwrapping the complexities surrounding Indigenous men's lives and the attendant masculinities; yet, to the present day, they have not been adequately considered.[67] The term "postcolonialism" suggests that there is neither a sociocultural, economic, and political colonization nor a decolonization in the purest sense of the word. Rather, the term suggests that the colonizers' impositions upon Indigenous people's lives cannot be separated from the colonial context and, at the same time, that the colonized have both the agency and independent identity to engage in postcolonial resistance.[68] This suggests that complicity and resistance exist in a fluctuating relation within the colonized subject; ambivalence, hybridity, and mimicry thus serve as viable weapons of the weak for challenging subalternity and speaking truth to power.

The term "Red Power" is historically distinct and rich in meaning but has defied a clear definition as it has continually evolved and relates to the overlapping and intertwined fields of political activism, cultural pride, and ethnic identification, among others.[69] A rather broad definition comes from historian Kent Blansett (Cherokee), who states, "Red Power was never about civil rights or equal integration into the colonial-state; rather, it was about protecting Indigenous human rights, especially as part of independent and sovereign nations."[70] He goes on to state that "Red Power advocated for Indigenous peoples to fight beyond colonial forms of recognition and to protect their Indigenous sovereignty."[71] Within its specific historical context(s), however, as historian Bradley Shreve has pointed out, the term "Red Power" carries multiple meanings and could mean different things at different times, depending on the context it was voiced in.[72] Frequently, the term "Red Power" refers to concepts such as self-determination, nationalism, sovereignty, and decolonization—interconnected terms that carry a range of meanings and that indicate varying kinds of power relations.[73] I follow Shreve's approach, as it better takes into account the particularities on the ground. Shreve's nuanced approach captures the meaning of Red Power as articulated in a specific context and helps to better follow the genesis in AIM's political agenda and its shift away from civil rights toward tribal governance, treaty rights and tribal sovereignty, nationhood, and finally global Indigenous rights.

In conceptualizing Indigenous expressions and constructions of sovereignty, I variously draw from both Indigenous epistemologies (e.g., the notion of peoplehood) and Western constructs (e.g., the notion of nationhood). Indigenous sovereignty is closely aligned with the concept of relationality—or what connects tribal nations, communities, families, individuals, spaces, places, and peoples altogether.[74] A basic ordering principle of Indigenous life—and thus sovereignty—is a communal understanding of peoplehood. Historians Tom Holm, Diane Pearson, and Ben Chavis have conceptualized peoplehood as the intertwining of four factors: language, sacred history, religion, and land, which serves as a model for the extension of sovereignty.[75] Historian Donald Fixico (Shawnee, Sac and Fox, Muscogee Creek and Seminole) has utilized what he calls "the medicine way" of understanding (a holistic worldview encompassing physical and metaphysical realities) to better conceptualize Indigenous ways of thinking and doing.[76] Peoplehood is self-contained and self-governing; it is an Indigenous concept of sovereignty, a structure of autonomy and practice of relation that predates colonization.[77] In building upon these considerations, I utilize a concept of "peoplehood" that encompasses the above elements while also acknowledging the complexities, ambiguities, and differences within Indigenous understandings of peoplehood/sovereignty and their layering through the forces of modernity, US colonial domination, and nationalism. During the Red Power era, Indigenous nationalists drew from both their own epistemologies and Western concepts of nationalism, frequently merging these concepts of self-governance.

Within the context of AIM's gendered anti-colonial endeavor, the connection between nationalism and masculinity requires some theoretical context. Nationalism and nation share a wide range of attributes. Benedict Anderson's *Imagined Communities* has made it commonplace to think of nations as imagined constructs in which individual identification along the lines of shared kinship and religion discursively produces and reproduces national identities and belongings.[78] At the center of the idea of a nation stands the notion that a collection of people are bound together through a common past and a common destiny.[79] While the nation is an imaginary construct, it is actively shaped and reshaped by nationalist discourse and practices and reinforced through nationalist ethnocentrism that stresses a common origin, a shared culture, or citizenship.[80] Further, ideas of nationalism are closely related to the physical existence of statehood.[81]

Nationalism can be defined as "both a goal—to achieve statehood, and a belief—in collective commonality," according to sociologist Joane Nagel.[82] Accordingly, nationalist movements have the express purpose of forming a nation (nationhood) and building a state (statehood). Within this gendered project, nationalism and militarism are closely intertwined.[83] The process of nation-building involves various elements that can be described, according to Nagel, as "'imagining' a national past and present, inventing traditions, and symbolically constructing community."[84] Nationalist ethnocentrism, the notion of a cultural and national identity, reinforces notions of "unity" among community members while simultaneously stressing the "otherness" of outsiders.[85] Conceptions of civic and ethnic nationalism continue to shape nations. Civic nationalism derives its political legitimacy from the active participation of its citizens in the legal-political community within a certain territory. Ethnic nationalism in turn is tied to notions of ancestry and kinship; a community that is linked through history, culture, anguage, customs, and traditions. In some nations, such as the United States, both forms exist side by side.[86] Within the United States, civic nationalism predominates the American settler nation, whereas ethnic nationalism mobilizes the anti-colonial American Indian Movement (or the Red Power movement, for that matter). The term "Indigenous nationalism" is non-exclusionary and alludes to an inherent sovereignty predating colonization.[87] According to Kent Blansett, tribes have employed Indigenous nationalism "to defend and promote their historic rights to maintain their distinct sovereignty from one another and to uphold their sovereign status apart from the interference of any colonial power or nation-state."[88]

Feminist studies have pioneered an understanding of the connection between gender and nation-building processes.[89] In nationalist movements, the domination of masculine interests and ideology has frequently overshadowed the active social and political participation of women. Women have frequently been included in rhetorical discourse, yet they largely have been excluded from political decision-making.[90] The scholarly focus on men's dominance and women's subjugation in nationalist struggles has reinforced an understanding of the gendered nature of nationalist struggles.[91] Nagel points out that "nationalist politics is a masculinist enterprise" and that "masculinity and nationalism articulate well with one another."[92] Nationalist constructions of gender tend to reinforce patriarchal systems, with men serving as gendered agents who are closely bound to the history of the nation-state and with women serving as keepers of family. Nationalist and anti-colonial movements encourage the participation of women, but they tend to relegate women to "traditional roles" and ignore their demands for gender equality.[93]

Historian Thembisa Waetjen argues that there is a need to look beyond the reality of men's shared dominance over women in nationalism in order to better comprehend the interplay between hegemonic masculinity and nationalism. Waetjen proposes to focus on the relations between dominant and marginalized constructions of masculinity.[94] A focus on the differences in and between men may shed light on hegemonic ideals of manliness and competing concepts and help in better understanding nationalism itself.[95]

In theorizing the construction of Indigenous men and masculinities in the American Indian Movement, I rely on sociologist Raewyn Connell's theoretical framework of hegemonic and marginalized masculinities. Connell defines hegemonic masculinity as a set of gender practices that embody the culturally exalted ideals of a nation and that work along the multiple lines of gender, race, and class to guarantee white male privilege. Hegemonic masculinities serve not only as a culture's model for what is perceived as ideal masculine behavior but also as a pivotal reference point against which others measure themselves.[96] In gender relations, hegemony is expressed through the subordination of women; in race relations, through the marginalization (or, in the colonial context, the subalternity) of the racialized "other," such as Indigenous men.[97] Connell identifies the most common patterns of masculinity as hegemonic, subordinated, marginalized (or subaltern), and complicit, a useful typology that can be applied to the cultural context of (post)colonial America.[98]

Critics of Connell's concept have pointed out that marginalized masculinities have a greater effect on the construction of hegemonic masculinities than has been recognized.[99] Demetrakis Z. Demetriou criticizes Connell's conceptualization of hegemonic and marginalized masculinities as dual blocs separated by distinct boundaries and configurations of practice.[100] Instead, he proposes the notion of a "hybrid bloc" that is "in constant process of negotiation, translation, hybridization, and reconfiguration," thus allowing for a hegemonic masculinity "to be capable of transforming itself in order to adapt to the specificities of new historical conjunctures" in an effort to maintain male privilege and dominance.[101] Another group of critics charge that marginalized masculinities have largely served as negative referents in relation and opposition to hegemonic masculinity and that this Western-centric focus on white American masculinity has neglected the active role of racially marginalized masculinities in shaping and reshaping the discourse over masculinity and nation.[102] In response to this criticism, Connell has acknowledged the power of hegemonic masculinities and the agency of marginalized masculinities in "the mutual conditioning of gender dynamics and other social dynamics."[103]

Closely intertwined with nationalism are the relational constructs of race and gender. Notions of race have been a fundamental ordering principle of colonialism, because nations tend to define themselves in relation and opposition to the racial constructs that they produce. Westerners have racialized Indigenous people by using the binary categories of "civilization" and "savagery." Concepts of race continue to play a significant function in shaping both social organization and cultural meaning in American life.[104] Categories of race (in terms of blood, identity, tribe, and land) remain pivotal in structuring Indigenous people's lived identities in relation to each other and in relation to dominant society.[105] Gender provides another useful analytic category, as it highlights the social and cultural construction of identities, showcases the fluctuating process through which dichotomous views of masculinities and femininities are produced, and signifies relationships of power.[106] Gender is performative and bodily enacted.[107] Performances and performative acts of Indigeneity occur through embodied speech and action and they open a window into the expression, assertion, and constitution of Indigenous identities.[108] Indigenous men have utilized cultural performances to remake their gendered identities.[109]

When Indigenous men and masculinities began to reimagine and reinvent themselves as warriors, they heavily relied on cultural traditions, memory work, and adaptation to contemporary realities. Colonialism and anti-colonial resistance involve cultural processes that include the construction and deconstruction of cultural traditions—cultural practices, customs, ceremonies, rituals, and belief systems—in what historian Eric Hobsbawm calls "the invention of tradition." According to Hobsbawm, cultural traditions generate social cohesion or group membership; they create and legitimize institutions, status, or authority relations; and they socialize, inculcate beliefs, value systems, and behaviors.[110] Similarly, "invented traditions" not only help in community survival but also aid as a mobilizing tool and instigate group cohesion. The concept of "invented traditions" also relates to cultural practices that can be revitalized, re-modified, and readapted to particular contexts.[111]

The notion of cultural reinvention also allows for innovative and subversive means—through hybridity, ambiguity, and colonial mimicry—that work to destabilize, disrupt, and counter dominant narratives. Indigenous men and women can engage in alternative gender practices to challenge hegemonic ideologies of gender and culture by drawing from their "cultural capital" (in this case deriving value from one's cultural knowledge, behaviors, and skills) and/or their "racial capital" (in this case deriving value from the strong racial coding of Indigenous people).[112] Historian Frank Usbeck speaks of a mutual process between the hegemonic attribution of cultural/racial qualities to Indigenous people for the benefit of settler-colonial society, on the one hand, and Indigenous people's conscious and strategic employment of these cultural/racial codings for their own benefit, on the other, for example, in efforts to maintain their cultural distinctiveness and assert their political sovereignty.[113] In *Playing Indian*, historian Philip Deloria (Yankton Dakota) explores white Americans' efforts to remake their gendered identities by appropriating notions of Indigeneity.[114] Conversely, Maureen Trudelle Schwarz has explored Indigenous efforts to appropriate Native stereotypes.[115] Tengan has examined how ceremonies foreground ideological dimensions of reclaiming Indigenous masculinity in the service of nation-building.[116]

The notion of gender as "performed" or "performative" offers pathways to understanding Indigenous efforts to remake their gendered subjectivities: whereas the "Indians playing Indian" theme or colonial mockery is performed, the continual recurrence of social and cultural practices is performative. In combining these approaches, I claim that dependent upon context, Indigenous nationalists sought to reappropriate notions of Indigeneity in order to reformulate their identities and/or to appropriate dominant stereotypes for the purpose of generating publicity and highlighting their cause. At times, these narrative and performative/performed enactments occurred in a hybrid space, making these distinctions less clear-cut and outright blurry.

Thematically and methodically, this book falls into the area of ethnohistory.[117] Ethnohistory emphasizes Indigenous meaning and agency in processes of cultural change. Ethnohistorians stress the various strategies that Indigenous people utilize to maintain their own cultural integrity—processes that variously involve innovation, change, continuity, and resilience as opposed to a complete loss of culture or outright assimilation.[118] I utilize an ethnohistorical approach that combines archival and oral history resources with personal fieldwork, as this approach offers the best possible evaluation of any phenomenon.[119] Further materials come from a broad range of archival sources, oral history collections, personal memoirs, Indigenous newspapers, documentaries, radio reports, and interviews.

Oral histories of Indigenous activists, veterans, and eyewitnesses bring nuance to narratives of Indigenous activism and nation-building. Oral history interviews give voice to those who might otherwise be "hidden from history"—those who are considered voiceless, invisible, and otherwise marginalized—to remember and reinterpret the past and enable them to include their own experiences and perspectives in the historical record. Oral history not only offers a more realistic and fair reconstruction of the past, but it challenges hegemonic discourse by empowering the voiceless to assert their own interpretation of historical events. Through the telling of memories and experiences, the narrator not only recalls the past but also offers a subjective interpretation of history, along with a personal meaning of that lived experience, making them both a historical source and a historian.[120]

This book relies on several oral interviews that I conducted firsthand during several ethnographic field trips to Minnesota, South Dakota, North Dakota, and elsewhere in 2013 and 2019. The plot or organizing theme of the interviews evolved around the interviewees' activist and/or military experiences and how these in turn related to their cultural identity. The majority of the interviews were narratively oriented interviews consisting of two parts, namely, a main narration period and a questioning period; the others were semi-structured interviews that were more like conversations.[121] The semi-structured interview method allowed a list of topics to be covered and gave the flexibility for interviewees to highlight the experiences that were salient for them.[122] In turn, narratively oriented interviews usually consisted of a first part wherein the interviewee narrated their personal experiences while the interviewer acted as an active listener and solely asked questions to encourage the continuation of the narrative and a second part wherein interviewee and interviewer actively engaged in a conversation about the topics covered in the narrative.[123]

*Reinventing the Warrior* follows Indigenous paradigms and research methodologies. Culturally appropriate research practices arise out of the epistemology and methodology of Indigenous people's survival struggles.[124] Historian Donald Fixico's research paradigm of a "Medicine Way" helps in understanding and reconstructing Indigenous history in a more comprehensive manner. Central to understanding an Indigenous ethos and reality is a holistic perception in which physical and nonphysical entities are in a reciprocal relationship and constitute a combined reality and a thinking in terms of well-being of community and homeland.[125] According to Fixico, a much deeper understanding of Indigenous culture and history is gained when the research paradigm is shifted away from a Western perspective (also called the First Dimension) or the interaction between Indigenous and non-Indigenous people (also called the Second Dimension) to an Indigenous point of view (the Third Dimension). Writing Indigenous history in the Third Dimension creates "a cross-cultural bridge of understanding" and is essential to understanding Indigenous reality and its changes.[126] This study is written to reconstruct how Indigenous men and masculinities have viewed and met historical change from their own cultural and historical reality; it is situated in the Third and Second Dimensions of this research paradigm.

## Summary of the Argument

In what follows, *Reinventing the Warrior* offers fresh insights into the interrelationship between masculinity and nationalism by examining how Indigenous men within the American Indian Movement remade their own gendered identities between 1968 and 1973, reinventing self and society in the process. Unlike their ancestors, who remade themselves into warriors through participation in intertribal warfare or through military service, these men reinvented themselves through protest activism to contest their subaltern status. In this book, I argue that the struggle for Indigenous rights—initially in urban areas, then in border towns and on reservations—transformed Indigenous subjectivities from a state of powerlessness into a state of empowerment, producing new constructions and expressions of Indigeneity in the process. From within the urban context, Indigenous men began to put forth a "protest masculinity" to contest their gendered position of powerlessness. The formation of Indigenous protest masculinities in itself marked a new way of thinking and of being Indigenous in the face of massive political and cultural turmoil underway in American society. As the anti-colonial struggle intensified, Indigenous men renewed, revitalized, and remasculinized by reaching out into their past (or through retraditionalizing) and through masculinized protest activism (or through radicalizing). In selectively drawing from shared cultural elements and engaging in militant protest, they reinvented themselves in new and imaginative ways as modern-day warriors. *Reinventing the Warrior* examines why and how Indigenous men within

AIM (re)invented new pathways and directions for being a man, being a warrior, and for warrior societies—recasting notions of race, gender, and nation in the process.

It might come as a paradox that many AIM activists were of Ojibwe descent (a woodland tribe), yet heavily referenced their identities to the Lakota (a Plains tribe), their hereditary archenemies of pre-reservation times. By the early 1970s, the urban activists turned to reservation traditionalists to make up for a lack of cultural grounding. Cultural borrowing aided AIM's urban members in their efforts to reclaim their Indigeneity and assert their right to difference. Over time, this cultural connection between reservation traditionalists and urban neo-traditionalists turned increasingly political as AIM became involved in border town racism and reservation politics. Key protest events were supported by local grassroots people, thus providing an additional link to Lakota and other Plains cultures.[127]

Indigenous understandings of being a warrior are different from what Westerners commonly associate with warriorhood. Westerners frequently restrict warriorhood to war, the battlefield, and the military, in short, to soldiering as a function within the (nation) state. Within this context, warriorhood is closely linked to territoriality, citizenship, and hegemonic gender practices.[128] By contrast, Indigenous views and concepts of warriorhood relate to family, kin community, and homeland. For example, the Lakota term *akíčita* refers, first, to warriors; second, to their responsibility as camp police; and third, to Lakota men in the US military.[129] The term *akíčita* points to the notion that being a warrior goes beyond war-related and martial abilities. It entails the notion of keeping peace by providing a moral example in tribal community and to providing for one's family, kinship, and community as a manly endeavor: in the past as hunter and in the present as wage earner or breadwinner, often through military service. The female equivalent to the *akíčita* of pre-reservation times was the *winoxtca* or woman warrior (that primarily related to the eastern Dakota), pointing to the fluidity of gender constructs.[130]

The warrior construct that Indigenous men in AIM emulated, expressed, and performed was both traditional and innovative. It was traditional in that it drew from traditional views and concepts that spoke of protecting Indigenous rights, tribal homeland, and people; providing for family, kin, and community; and keeping peace within the community; and that it alluded to a notion of service. More generally, the warrior construct signified a just cause and served as a unifier against outside threats. Indigenous nationalists drew from these traditional views and concepts of warriorhood and transplanted them into the present. The warrior construct was empowering as it helped AIM nationalists to assert cultural pride and it was innovative when emphasizing political demands. Through its hybridized nature, colonial ambivalence, and mimicry, the performance of warrior masculinity was heavily geared toward media attention: the uninformed American public widely regarded the Plains Indians (or more specifically the Lakota) with their bison-hunting warrior horsemen as the iconic, quintessential symbols of Indigeneity.[131]

The relational nature of gender allocates femininity with certain culturally specific attributes, definitions, and social functions. Within AIM, gender dynamics worked in numerous and ambiguous ways to construct, support, and reinforce the warrior construct and nationalist ideology, or, alternatively, to debunk the domination of masculine interests and ideology within movement politics. Indigenous women played a pivotal role in constructing and deconstructing nationalist warrior masculinity. Indigenous women actively participated in protest politics and often served as feminine reinforcements of Indigenous men, improving morale and masculine self-identification. However, as much as Indigenous women helped their male counterparts aspire to be manly, they also challenged male privilege. Paradoxically, Indigenous men were inculcated with the very ideals of dominant society that they struggled against. It is for this reason that Indigenous women frequently claimed that they privileged the struggle for Indigenous rights over the struggle against patriarchy and male privilege. After the occupation of Wounded Knee, they increasingly confronted gender inequality, male chauvinism, and the nationalist ideology with which these were intertwined, thus contributing to the demise of the AIM warrior construct.

## Chapter Outline

Chapter 1 examines Indigenous men's engagements with colonial domination, modernity, and their own cultural system. It describes and analyzes how Indigenous people have been impacted through the racial and gendered nature of US settler colonialism and also how they have sought to maintain their cultural integrity by reinvention. Indigenous men have reinvented their subjectivities, first, through the formation of Pan-Indianism and, second, through military service that has allowed them to be warriors once again. In tracing the warrior-to-soldier theme from World War I through World War II, Korea, and Vietnam, this part examines *how* Indigenous men have utilized the US military to *reinvent* themselves as warriors and *why* they have done so. The chapter asks whether these veterans interpreted their military service as a patriotic service for the American nation, or as a continuation of masculine cultural traditions, or as a combination of both. In addition, I seek to broaden an understanding of the Vietnam War experience and how/why it constituted a bridge to the protest activism of the Red Power movement. In tracing Indigenous responses to the government-driven move to urban centers, this part examines how the urban context opened new avenues for reinvention. The building of urban communities and the formation of a Pan-Indianian consciousness became significant factors for mobilization in the Red Power movement, laying the groundwork for Indigenous men to reinvent themselves as modern-day warriors during the 1960s and 1970s.

Chapters 2, 3, and 4 trace the emergence, evolution, and militarization of the self-proclaimed AIM warriors within the larger cultural and political unrest of the sixties and seventies. Chapter 2 traces the formative experiences of Indigenous men that led to the emergence of a "protest masculinity." Chapter 3 examines how AIM activists transformed their protest masculinities into warrior masculinities through identity politics—that is, by creating a revolutionary culture reaching out into this cultural heritage as well as through a radicalization in protest activism. Chapter 4 examines the gendered nature of the nation-building attempt at Wounded Knee that is perhaps best illustrated by the parallel declaration of the Independent Oglala Nation and the setting up of a warrior society. More specifically, this chapter describes and analyzes the merging of two different notions of warrior masculinity: one deriving from protest activism and the other from a tradition of military service.

Chapter 5 traces the winding down of protest activism and explores the memory of the activist years. It sketches how Indigenous nationalists reinvented themselves as cultural and political warriors after 1973 once again. It delves into the nationalist struggle's cultural and political legacy, touching upon internal controversy surrounding the ION warrior society, warriorhood, leadership, martial virtues, nationalism, and patriotism.

The conclusion sheds light on new pathways of Indigenous warriorhood after 1973 and new directions in warrior societies.

# Chapter 1

# Indigenous Men and Peoplehood under US Colonial Domination

On November 20, 1969, Gary Leach (Colville/Sioux), a recently returned Vietnam veteran, found himself among a group of Indigenous college students and urban Natives from the Bay Area, occupying Alcatraz Island in the San Francisco Bay. Once landed, the occupiers calling themselves Indians of All Tribes (IoT) released a press statement, demanding title to the island and the establishment of educational and cultural institutions.[1] The nineteen-months-long occupation hit the nerve of a nation already rocked by considerable unrest by a variety of race, gender, class, and age groups. The occupation was marked by proclamations, powwows, celebrations, negotiations with government officials, and the gathering of food and supplies on the mainland and their transport to the island.[2] The government's answer came with a policy of restraint, given the highly unpopular Vietnam War (with the recent massacre of Vietnamese civilians by US soldiers at My Lai in 1968); the shooting of college students at Kent State in 1970; and media attention highly favorable to the occupiers.[3] On June 11, 1971, the remaining occupiers were removed from the island by law enforcement officers.[4] A few months into the occupation, Gary Leach spoke about his motivation in taking part in the takeover and what he sought to gain from it for himself and Indigenous people in general: "It [Alcatraz] is just kind of a revolution to keep us from dying. . . . I am an Indian, I recognize myself as an Indian. . . . I was born on the reservation and I am very proud of it . . . and as an Indian I don't want to die and to me this is why I am on the island, I am trying to maintain not only my identity and my children's and their children's identity. . . . We still are prisoners of war literally."[5] In his statement the veteran-turned-activist echoed a prevailing sentiment among Indigenous people on the latest assimilationist government policies as a threat to their political sovereignty and their cultural identity. The prolonged takeover of Alcatraz Island is widely considered a transformative event that fundamentally altered the meaning and value of Indigeneity. Many Indigenous people, distanced from their respective tribal culture, religion, language, and custom, began to develop an ethnic pride in their Indigeneity and reinvented their gendered identities in relation to their own culture.[6] The Alcatraz takeover was a catalyst for cultural renewal and provided a springboard for the self-renewing power of further Indigenous activism.[7]

The formation of modern Indigenous masculinities occurred within a larger historical context in which colonialization and modernity (e.g., capitalism, urbanization) intersected with traditional forms of cultural and social organization. As a consequence, Indigenous men engaged in both hegemonic and marginalized gender practices that led to widely different consequences for their position of power or marginality within the United States.

As will be shown in what follows, throughout the twentieth century, Indigenous men repeatedly remade their Indigenous and male subjectivities in response to assimilationist settler-colonial policies. Paradoxically, Indigenous men utilized the US military, an essentially foreign institution, to reinvent self and society.[8] A new sense of being Indigenous emerged within urban contexts and would become a significant mobilizing tool in the Red Power movement.[9]

## Masculinity & Nationalism: Gender in the Making and Unmaking of Empire and Nation

United States settler colonialism has profoundly impacted the lives of Indigenous peoples. Settler colonialism is hegemonic in scope and normalizes the continuous occupation and exploitation of Indigenous lands, resources, and cultures. Historian Patrick Wolfe has theorized settler colonialism as a particular colonial formation that centers around land and a "logic of elimination." This logic entails eliminating the Native *as* Native through displacement, annihilation, or assimilation.[10] According to Wolfe, settler colonists impose structures that effectively work to eradicate Indigenous people in order to gain access to territory and naturalize their own status as Native to the land.[11] Wolfe's theoretical concept has drawn various criticism for its one-sided focus, its structuralist rigidity, and for reproducing a settler-Indigenous binary.[12] As much as settler colonialism is enduring, so is Indigeneity. As a counterpart analytic, Indigeneity holds out against settler colonialism—existing, persisting, and resisting.[13]

Empire-building and its dismantling through nationalist or anti-colonial movements involves particular notions of masculinity and femininity.[14] Nationalist projects require a reconfiguration of gender relations that resituate men and women in their relationship to each other and in relation to different ethnic/racial groups.[15] Nationalist projects and processes frequently tend to associate masculinity with the militarized defense and protection of nation and family (the smallest unit of the nation) and femininity with domesticated motherhood and support of their husbands, or, alternatively, as icons of nationhood.[16] Nationalism tends to be structured by a heteropatriarchy that subordinates women under a male privilege that leaves little or no place for unmanly or gay men.[17] Nationalist politics is essentially a masculinist enterprise. By its very definition, masculinity is at work not just in nation-making processes and colonialism but in the struggle for decolonization and the undoing of colonial empire and nation also.[18] Colonial rule and the shared experience of foreign domination may function as a unifying phenomenon for otherwise different marginalized groups in nationalist movements.[19]

From the beginning, the conflict between the United States and tribal nations has been not just about land but also about manhood. As Joan Nagel has pointed out, Indigenous-US relations can be seen as "a struggle over the definition and meaning of manhood and nationhood."[20] In this confrontation, dominant conceptualizations of masculinity and nation have suppressed and transformed Indigenous models of masculinity and tribal sovereignty/peoplehood.[21] While this process has been largely uneven and one-sided, alternative Indigenous gender practices and notions of tribal sovereignty/peoplehood have historically worked in ways that challenge, undermine, or otherwise subvert hegemonic notions of nation and gender.[22]

The very nature of US settler colonialism produces boundaries between colonizer and colonized that are never clear-cut. Gender relations between colonizer/colonized subjects are interdependent and mutually constitutive for subjectivities, yet they emerge in a contradictory and ambivalent space characterized by imbalance and inequality of power relations.[23] Indigenous men and women are complexly situated in multiple contexts and can access points of privilege or subalternity, based on their own positioning. As gendered social actors, they can draw upon hegemonic norms to produce and reproduce their gendered identities (e.g., through hybridity or syncretism), yet they may also draw from dominant norms, values, and group memberships for contradictory and even subversive purposes (e.g., through mimicry) in order to negotiate, resist, or transform those very systems.[24]

The interwoven projects of US settler colonialism and colonial masculinity found expression in the nationalist and imperialist projects of westward expansion and Manifest Destiny, endeavors that articulated well with middle-class American ideals of manliness.[25] Societal ideals defining American masculinity were rooted in Anglo-Protestant notions of "Muscular Christianity" (defined by virtues of Christianity and athleticism), a value system of rugged individualism and rationality, patriarchy, and landownership.[26] The cultural conceptualization of white, heterosexual masculinity has served to justify colonialism and maintain control over the image and definition of masculinity while at the same time disempowering alternative forms and expressions of masculinity. According to gender scholars Ronald Jackson and Murali Balaji, cultural imagery has depicted the colonized "other" as "the antithesis to how men and masculinity" should be.[27] Popular discourse frequently orbits around binary constructions of "other" men and masculinities as either hyper- or hypovirile. White masculinity is conveniently situated in the middle as neither too masculine nor too unmanly, allowing white men to masculinize themselves through analogy.[28] A case in point is historian

Mrinalini Sinha's study of *Colonial Masculinity* in British India that offers insights into the analogical concept between race and masculinity among colonizer and colonized, in this case the "manly Englishman" and the "effeminate Bengali."[29]

The gendered nature of US settler colonialism and the assertion of white supremacy rested on the hypermasculinity of white colonizers and the devirilization of colonized men.[30] Western men grounded their distinct race and gender bias in their belief in "Christianity" (as opposed to "heathenism"); a belief in the superiority of Western "civilization" over Indigenous "savagery" or "primitivism"; and a belief in the superiority of the white race over the "other," non-white races, to justify the building of a colonial empire or the settler nation.[31] Racialized and gendered coding denoted Western men as normal and Indigenous men as abnormal. Indigenous masculinity was associated with "savagery" (either noble or ignoble) or with notions of "primitivism" or being "civilized/uncivilized." In a similar fashion, Westerners made assumptions about Indigenous physicality and coded Indigenous men through their bodies. Indigenous studies scholar Brendan Hokowhitu (Māori) writes that common discourse tied Indigenous men to "a savage physiology and biological approach to gender"; this conflation of racial and gender stereotypes, in turn, has produced "a strongly coded masculinity" that is associated with the Native "other."[32]

The feminizing or devirilizing of Indigenous men resulted in images of Indigenous men as "effeminate" (i.e., someone who has become more like a woman) or "emasculated" (i.e., someone who has fallen from his status as man, e.g., through the loss of his homeland), or as "childlike" and (legally) "incompetent" (another form of emasculation/feminization); conversely, the cultural mindset also denoted Indigenous men as hypermasculine and warrior-like. These codings of Indigenous men as either hypovirile or hypervirile, produced and reproduced through media images, have worked to render the subaltern "other" as either invisible, without a voice, and inferior, or, alternatively, as a superior ideal to be emulated.[33] Within their specific contexts, settler-colonial discourses differed in their polarization of Indigenous men as hypermasculine or hypomasculine. For example, violent resistance of Indigenous men during the last Indian Wars (also known as Plains Wars, 1850s–1870s) and their subsequent participation in World War I and World War II promulgated different discourses of the Indigenous male violence as noble or ignoble. While the discourse of "ignoble savagery" justified Native subjugation, "noble savagery" served to assimilate Indigenous masculinity into settler-colonial society. The inherent tension between both concepts adjudicating Indigenous male violence has been naturalized through colonial ambivalence. Thus, each colonial discourse befitted its respective historical context.[34]

Colonial imagery was heavily dichotomous in its portrayal of Indigenous women also. Western-centric accounts either portrayed Indigenous women as objects of male sexual desire or disparaged them as "squaw-drudges," as beasts of burden worn down by overwork and spousal oppression.[35] Male explorers displaying manly courage as they conquered "virgin" lands established narratives of feminized lands and extended this metaphor to include its inhabitants. The feminization and infantilization of Indigenous lands and peoples facilitated settler-colonial encroachment on foreign lands and resources.[36]

The coding of Indigenous men in a gendered analogy (i.e., as lacking masculinity or as excessively masculine) has resulted in ambivalent colonial policies. First, white paternalism, that is, a persistent attitude of doing what was best for Indigenous people according to dominant norms, guided federal policymaking and gendered rhetoric from the eighteenth century until the mid-1970s. In racialized masculinity politics, notions of Indigenous men's "incompetence" constituted part of an effort to establish Western rule over Indigenous nations and people(s). "Incompetence" found its expression in notions of extreme government paternalism, on the one hand, and severe dependency, on the other. Throughout its existence, the Bureau of Indian Affairs (BIA)—the formulator and implementer of settler-colonial policies—has exercised near-complete control over its dependent subalterns, not allowing them to make choices affecting their own lives.[37] The BIA continues to make decisions over the very definition of Native American ethnicity: tribal membership is based on blood quantum or degree of Indigenous ancestry (in contrast to traditional Indigenous practices that include kinship structures and cultural criteria that did not utilize "race" to construct tribal membership).[38] Paternalistic thinking found its expression in the rhetorical image of the "Great White Father" (meaning the US president, who stood for the federal government) and his dependent children (meaning the various tribal nations). The adult/child opposition resembled a male/female dichotomy, with a dominating father, on the one end, and a child, who has not matured and attained manhood, on the other.[39] By the 1970s, much of this gendered rhetoric was gone. However, the paternalistic attitude persisted, coloring much of federal policymaking.

Second, martial race ideology, the belief that Native Americans were members of a "martial race" and imbued with certain warrior-like qualities, influenced American administrators and policymakers in recruiting Indigenous men into the US military. Apparently, centuries of fighting tribal warriors had left a deep imprint on Westerners who imagined Indigenous men as natural-born warriors belonging to the battlefield.[40] Historian Tom Holm (Cherokee/Muskogee) calls this phenomenon the "Indian scout syndrome"—a belief in the legendary racial predisposition of Indigenous men for combat, supposedly supernatural fighting and scouting abilities, and bravery beyond reason. The scout syndrome has followed Indigenous soldiers into World War I, World War II, Korea, and Vietnam and through to the present. Martial race ideology consciously and systematically geared colonial policies toward the recruitment of those believed to possess martial qualities.[41] It translated into the recruitment of those Indigenous men who primarily came from tribes with supposed warrior-like qualities.[42]

## Colonizing Indigenous Men in the United States, 1870s–1970s

A central tenet of settler-colonial policy was the transformation or elimination of Indigenous gender systems.[43] The reconfiguration of Indigenous family and gender practices according to settler-colonial norms, values, and Christian beliefs has been intrinsic to processes of colonization and the promulgation of modernity.[44] American masculinity evolved around US citizenship, individual property, and the nuclear family—tenets that included land, women, and children. The bourgeois family—the core unit of the nation—was constructed as a model to be emulated, was regulated by law, and rested upon male privilege and the gendered separation of private/public and home/work. The nuclear family model was constructed around a dominant patriarchal father, followed by a submissive wife, and, lastly, their immature children, a concept that replicated the colonial context as a whole.[45] United States settler colonialism imposed a capitalist economy, the gendered division of labor, individual property ownership, the patriarchal nuclear family model, and Christianity on Indigenous cultures and societies. These Western concepts stood in stark contrast to precolonial cultural practices of reciprocity, communalism, extended kinship-based, rather than nuclear, family units, and religious beliefs. The manipulation of Indigenous social and cultural practices, forms, and expressions of gender in effect constituted a fundamental element of dispossessive colonial policy.[46] According to gender scholar Mark Rifkin, Western-centric notions of gender were made "compulsory as a key part of breaking up indigenous landholdings, 'detribalizing' native peoples, [and] translating native territoriality and governance into the terms of . . . liberalism and legal geography."[47] The imposition of white settler colonialists' concepts of gender has led to what gender scholar Sam McKegney characterized as "[a] layering of racialized, patriarchal gender systems over preexisting, tribally specific cosmologies of gender."[48] A significant tenet of settler-colonial regimes lay in the transformation or elimination of Indigenous systems that Westerners considered as ambiguous and aberrant (such as Two-Spirit/LGBTQ people). This violent repression of non-binary and same-sex relationships has resulted in what has been called a "gendercide."[49]

The political and legal status of Indigenous people is more complex than that of any other minority in the United States, locating Indigenous people alternately outside or within the American nation, or somewhere in between, in what political scientist Kevin Bruyneel has called "the third space of sovereignty."[50] All racial minorities within the United States have a relationship that is characterized by civil rights and citizenship. However, Native Americans' special relationship to the American nation has historically been determined first through treaty rights and second through civil rights. Whereas civil rights determine a minority's status *within* the American nation, treaty rights determine Native Americans' distinct status vis-à-vis the American nation. From the 1830s, the political status of Indigenous tribes resembled that of "domestic dependent nations" and the quasi-colonial relationship between tribal nations and the US government evolved to one of federal guardian and Native ward.[51] In 1871, the US Congress unilaterally ended treaty-making processes on an equal nation-to-nation basis and began to impose modern colonial rule over Indigenous nations and tribes.[52] Historically, the Office of Indian Affairs (renamed the Bureau of Indian Affairs in 1947) has occupied a pivotal position in Indigenous–settler-colonial relations as the formulator and implementer of colonial policies, in effect acting as a quasi-colonial oversight agency for an entire population, their homeland, and their resources.[53] Since the imposition of citizenship on Native Americans—initially to Indigenous veterans of World War I in 1919, then extended to all Native Americans in 1924—civil rights have determined the legal status of Native Americans *within* the American nation-state as well. Accordingly, Native Americans' peculiar position in relation to the American settler nation carries transcultural and transnational elements that variously locate them somewhere *within*, *outside*, or *in between* the United States. Due to their unique history, culture, relationship to their homeland(s), and relationship to the settler nation, Indigenous people(s) have always considered themselves as entities different from mainstream America.[54]

According to anthropologist Sebastian Felix Braun, settler colonialists' efforts to fundamentally transform Indigeneity according to hegemonic ideals of culture and nation included ethnification (a strategy to make Native Americans appear as just another "ethnic group" within the American mosaic), denationalization (that is settler-colonial efforts to de-nationalize Native Americans as members of tribal nations and renationalize them as citizens of the United States), and de-territorialization (e.g., through dispossessive colonial policies that included the reservation system, allotment, and, finally, termination).[55] The fundamental prerequisite for the integration of Native Americans into American settler society was the breakup of Indigenous societies and their homeland(s), as well as the individualization of Indigenous people(s), because then their status as Indigenous nations could be ended.[56] Settler-colonial policies of assimilation represent part and parcel of an ongoing effort to detribalize, de-territorialize, individualize, and otherwise renaturalize and ethnicize Native American nations and people(s) in what is an overall effort to eliminate them as Natives.[57]

Reservation confinement established the situation of tribal communities as "colonized nations," over which the US settler nation exerts its colonial and hegemonic power.[58] The reservation—characterized by anthropologist Robert K. Thomas (Cherokee) as an "internal colony"—fundamentally compounded the subalternity of Indigenous masculinity.[59] On reservations, Indigenous men found themselves without much agency and power: The reservation system and its imposed political system of indirect colonial rule undermined traditional forms of tribal governance, widened sociocultural and sociopolitical divisions, and instigated severe political infighting between traditional and complicit masculinities.[60] The reservation system and colonial rule continually reinforced Native subalternity through land loss, government dependency, and misguided assimilationist policies. Sociologists Michael Omi and Howard Winant emphasize the ongoing legacy of racial oppression through "inequality, political disenfranchisement, territorial and institutional segregation, and cultural domination" of internal colonialism.[61]

Distant, off-reservation boarding schools—such as Carlisle Indian School in Pennsylvania (est. in 1878), Hampton Institute in Virginia (est. in 1878), and Haskell School in Kansas (est. in 1882)—sought to completely transform Indigenous children, inside and out, and to produce assimilated and compliant citizens.[62] As Richard Pratt, the founder of Carlisle, told US Congress about his civilizing and educational reform project in 1892: "A great general [Sherman] has said that the only good Indian is a dead one," Pratt said. "In a sense, I agree with the sentiment, but only in this: that all the Indian there is in the race should be dead. Kill the Indian in him, and save the man."[63] Pratt's statement is deeply revealing, as it succinctly sums up the gendered imperative behind the assimilationist onslaught: only through the undoing of all remaining vestiges of Indigeneity and their replacement through hegemonic gender practices could Natives be turned into Americans. Colonial discourse has frequently labeled boarding schools as a means to replace Native laziness, ignorance, and paganism with Western notions of industry, education and civilization, and Christianity.⁶⁴ This sentiment further translated into an educational philosophy of militarized education and institutional containment.⁶⁵

Modern American assimilationist policies include allotment (1887–1934), the Indian New Deal (1934–1945), and the World War II war effort (1940–1945). The allotment and citizenship era (1887–1934) included the breakup of tribal landholdings into individual allotments, compulsory boarding school education to produce assimilated and compliant citizens, and the bestowal of US citizenship on Indigenous people.⁶⁶ The Indian New Deal (1934–1945) marked a shift away from direct colonial rule toward indirect colonial rule.⁶⁷

Another assimilationist policy, commonly known under the name "termination" (1946–1975), sought to de-territorialize Indigenous nations, de-naturalize their tribal members, and renationalize them as Americans in modern capitalist society, turning them into just another ethnic group in American multicultural society.⁶⁸ The various policies constituting termination consisted of a tripartite effort—compensation, termination, and relocation—yet are known under the umbrella term "termination." First, compensation (through the Indian Claims Commission, set up in 1946) sought to settle all outstanding land claims and treaty disputes.⁶⁹ Second, termination (based on House Concurrent Resolution 108, passed in 1953) sought to end the trust relationship, thereby eliminating all government responsibilities once and for all. Termination called for the elimination of tribal nations and their landholdings in what amounted to an all-out settler-colonial effort to de-Indianize Native Americans.⁷⁰ Finally, urban relocation sought to transfer Native Americans from reservations to urban areas in what was another attempt to assimilate them into mainstream America, to denationalize them as members of tribal nations, and renationalize them as Americans.⁷¹ The paternalistic attitude behind the policies of compensation, termination, and relocation was to solve the Native problem once and for all. The thinking went that with the special trust relationship between tribal nations and the American nation terminated and with Native Americans finally relocated to urban areas, they would be assimilated into mainstream America.⁷² Termination constituted yet another attempt to detribalize Native Americans and eradicate tribal nations and their people as legal categories.

Termination was finally abandoned in 1973 with the introduction of a policy of self-determination.[73]

The relocation program of the 1950s and 1960s was a key factor in the urbanization of Native Americans. Relocation entailed a massive demographic shift, with more Native Americans living in urban areas than on reservations. Between 1950 and 1970—the start of the relocation program—the urban Indigenous population steadily increased. In 1950, the urban Indigenous population constituted 13.4 percent (or 56,000) of the overall Indigenous population, in 1960 it made up 27.9 percent (or 146,000), and in 1970 it stood at 44.4 percent (or 340,000).[74] Between 1952 and 1972, more than one hundred thousand Native Americans relocated to urban areas such Chicago, Cleveland, Dallas, Denver, Oklahoma City, Tulsa, San Jose (California), Los Angeles, Oakland, and San Francisco.[75] The BIA portrayed urban life as a golden opportunity for those who relocated to urban areas to escape their poverty-stricken reservation communities.[76] Once relocated, Native Americans found themselves trapped between government promises and the harsh realities of urban life. In the big cities, Native Americans became the poorest of the poor and settled in the red ghettoes of Chicago, Los Angeles, the Bay Area, Cleveland, and Minneapolis.[77]

Relocation and the urban experience impacted the gendered identities of Indigenous people tremendously. The move to a place such as the Twin Cities distanced Indigenous people from their relatives, extended families and familiar environments, and their traditional culture. Although traditional ways had been severely eroded, pockets of traditionalism had survived on Midwestern reservations; by contrast, they were virtually nonexistent in the Twin Cities urban context.[78] Indigenous relocatees also found that their move to the Twin Cities from reservations in Minnesota, South Dakota, North Dakota, or Wisconsin threatened their tribal citizenship and their special relationship with the federal government.[79] Yet urban Indigenous people were not entirely cut off from their reservation communities. They sought to preserve connections to ancestral homelands and kinship systems through occasional visits; the lived reality of urban life and deep-rooted connections to their tribal homelands also caused numerous Indigenous people to return.[80] Yet within the urban context, Indigenous people also sought to retain their tribal identity by maintaining traditional social structures and tribal relatedness to other urban Natives.[81] The urban experience is the major catalyst in the emergence of AIM.[82]

The urban context resulted in shared experiences of severe socioeconomic disparities, race and gender bias, unemployment, conflicts with white institutions (e.g., the criminal justice system, child welfare, and public schools), and severe cultural dissonance.[83] Some Native relocatees became disconnected from their Indigeneity and lost touch with their culture, value system, and language and in the process lost pride in their Native identity.[84] Negative external images strongly featured Indigenous maladjustment to urban lifestyle and connected Indigenous people with undereducation, crime, alcoholism, unemployment, and poverty. These racialized and gendered images of Indigeneity (that also create internal self-perception) have had lingering effects. Yet at the same time, Indigenous people have countered racial prejudice by formulating self-concepts that stress cultural values and traditions and promote an ethnic pride in their Indigeneity.[85]

More recently, new scholarship has begun to shifts its focus away from studying urban Indigenous maladjustment toward pursuing an agency-based approach and examining Indigenous contributions to urban life.[86] In *Indians on the Move*, historian Douglas K. Mills points out that urban spaces served as places of reinvention, both regenerative and degenerative.[87] Apparently, the move to the big cities was not only a consequence of settler-colonial displacement but at the same time something that Indigenous people pursued in spite of federal-sponsored programs.[88] In venturing beyond what he calls "a reductive assimilation–resistance binary that pits urban Indians against reservation Indians according to a divide-and-conquer strategy long practiced by the settler state," Miller arrives at a synthesis that interprets Indigenous urbanization neither as a policy-driven disaster nor as a precondition to Red Power activism.[89] Indigenous migration to the big cities not only produced Indigenous militancy and resistance "to being melted down" but also a new generation of Indigenous leaders who saw relocation as a way to survive in a hostile America and gain skills to bring back to their reservation communities.[90] Thus, mobility was a complicated choice for Indigenous people that provided socioeconomic opportunity and overwhelming uncertainty.

## Indigenous Men and Peoplehood under US Colonial Domination   41

Indigenous people sought to exercise agency over their lives; they insisted on exercising mobility and pursuing opportunities within and beyond the confines of settler colonialism, even against the backdrop of colonial pressures.[91]

The disruptive forces of US colonialism and modernity have impacted Indigenous men and masculinities in multiple and contradictory way, complexly situating them between dominant society and tribal communities. This has left Indigenous men struggling to find their gendered role and place in society.[92] Colonization has impacted Indigenous men through institutionalized containment (i.e., reservation confinement), institutional settings (e.g., boarding schools and incarceration), and colonial policies (e.g., allotment and termination), all of which ultimately served to enforce assimilation into a culture of whiteness through conformity, adaptation, and transformation.[93] In turn, Indigenous men and masculinities have adapted or internalized hegemonic perceptions of what men should be and how they should act.[94]

Indigenous men—more than other minority men—lead disturbing statistics in high suicide, incarceration, domestic, drug, and alcohol abuse, unemployment, low health and life expectancy, and poor educational and academic performance. They are continually confronted with the loss of land, culture, and beliefs, as well as a distinct racial and gender bias. Continual violations of treaty rights, civil rights, and religious freedoms and severe socioeconomic disparities have further worked to disempower them. Indigenous men culturally and socially construct their Indigenous and male identities in plural ways; as such they are also understood, enacted, and experienced according to cultural context.[95] In any given culture, time, and place, there are multiple masculinities. Indigenous masculinities, like other masculinities, are fluid, unstable, and continually in flux; they are varied, complex, ambiguous, and relative.[96] A cultural and spiritual connection to a particular land (sacred homeland) typically informs how Indigenous men defined themselves in the past and continue to define themselves in the present. While there are numerous tribal definitions of masculinity, Indigenous men continue to construct their gendered subjectivities within a host of relationships and contexts that are deeply intertwined, including a particular place/homeland, culture, community (reservation and/or urban), and gender.[97] Indigenous men's gendered identities continue to be shaped by their own cultural adjustment to white America as well as their retention of cultural values, belief systems, and languages, their connection to place, and their spirituality. What has undermined Indigenous masculinities is an almost complete exclusion from male hegemonic hierarchies and power as well as a severe erosion of cultural concepts of manliness that had anchored them in their place and role in society. It is exactly this perception of emasculation and powerlessness that works to mobilize colonized men in militant and nationalist endeavors.

## Reinventing Indigeneity through US Settler-Colonial Policies

The ideals of hegemonic whiteness have continually worked toward the assimilation and subordination of the Indigenous "other," yet not necessarily in the way that was intended. Instead, processes of assimilation have functioned as powerful tools for reinventing Indigeneity. Settler-colonial policies of assimilation have laid the groundwork for Indigenous ethnic resurgence, because they facilitated the emergence of a Pan-Indian consciousness, a key catalyst of the Red Power movement.[98]

Paradoxically, Indigenous people have utilized the very settler-colonial policies of assimilation intended to eradicate their cultural distinctiveness as resources for ethnic renewal.[99] From the turn of the century through the 1960s and 1970s onward, Indigenous people have responded to misguided assimilationist policies by building a sense of Pan-Indianism. For example, boarding school education facilitated English as a *lingua franca* among tribal members; the Indian New Deal eased intertribal contact; Indigenous participation in World War II led to a wider recognition of common problems and a novel sense of Indigenous rights; and termination policies had the unintended consequence of unifying and consolidating Indigenous people in resistance to settler-colonial coercion and control.[100]

The emergence of the nascent Red Power movement was a direct, yet unintended, result of settler-colonial policies of assimilation.[101] Urban relocation, Indigenous community-building efforts, and the generation of a Pan-Indian consciousness spoke not only of cultural loss but also of cultural persistence.¹⁰² Indigenous community-building efforts drew from shared notions of belonging (peoplehood). They began with the establishment of comfort zones and home spaces in an otherwise alien environment and involved a wide variety of inter- and supratribal organizations and communities that formed at urban Indian Centers—such as social clubs, bars, drumming and singing groups, athletic leagues, pow-wows, beauty contests, arts and crafts associations, political organizations, newsletters and newspapers, Christian churches, and charitable organizations, all of which began to serve the needs of a growing urban Indigenous population. What brought Native Americans of diverse regions, cultures, languages, and tribal nations together was a willingness to assert their own sense of Indigeneity and transplant their own sense of culture, identity, belonging, and rootedness into the urban context.¹⁰³

Scholarly discourses on relocation and urbanization frequently conceptualize urban Natives as being torn between the forces of assimilation and the retention of their own cultural values and practices. Social scholar Nancy Lucero (Mississippi Choctaw) has pointed out that many scholars regard urbanization as "a dynamic process in the evolution and development of distinctly urban Indian communities and identities that blend tribal practices and values with their own evolving traditions, cultural practices, and histories."¹⁰⁴ While urban Natives developed a larger sense of Indigeneity that transcended tribal differences, they also sought to maintain their tribal identities. Pan-Indian and tribal identities existed and developed side by side or together in complex and multiple layers.¹⁰⁵ However, the lived realities in the Twin Cities vividly indicate that by the 1960s and 1970s, Indigenous people had experienced considerable loss of tribal language and specific cultural knowledge; later generations saw a lessening of this devastating assimilation process.¹⁰⁶

The developing Pan-Indian consciousness heavily borrowed from Plains Indian cultural elements as models for contemporary Indigenous identity. Members of tribes that had sometimes considered each other foes began to think of themselves as sharing a larger sense of being Indigenous based on shared experiences. This Plains Indian culture continues to serve as an icon both for the general public and urban Indigenous people who are not Plains Indians but resituate various cultural elements into their specific contexts.¹⁰⁷ At the same time as AIM sought to foster a Pan-Indian consciousness, Indigenous people within the organization also maintained and continued their tribal identities.

In aligning with and expanding the concept of peoplehood, I maintain that peoplehood is portable and, just like the very people who practice it, selectively adapts to temporal, cultural, and geographical contexts.[108] Indigenous people constructed communities both through imagination (and a sense of commonality) and through practice (or interaction).[109] With the building of urban communities and the spread of a Pan-Indian consciousness, Native Americans built structures that facilitated their own empowerment. The social unrest, political upheaval, and cultural change taking place in American society in the 1960s and 1970s as different ethnic, gender, and age groups—the Black civil rights movement, student movement, anti-Vietnam War demonstrations, and women's liberation, just to name a few—provided a window of opportunity and served as a role model for protest activism.[110]

During the 1960s and 1970s, Indigenous people in the United States watched the civil rights struggle within the United States and decolonization efforts throughout the Third World. Both movements—one domestic, the other global—exercised a tremendous impact on the Indigenous rights' struggle. At home, various civil rights movements threatened existing social and political institutions and arrangements and instigated a shift in social and political culture (e.g., African Americans, Chicanos, women). The Black civil rights movement sought to break down the racial barriers that kept African Americans segregated and disenfranchised. Direct action and grassroots protests—protest marches, sit-ins, and other forms of civil disobedience—reconfigured politics and identity in America. Whereas the civil rights movement demanded inclusion into dominant society, racial solidarity, and full citizenship rights, Black nationalists advocated for autonomy and self-determination, cultivating pride in Blackness and celebrating territorial separatism.[111] Abroad, decolonization movements were instrumental in the undoing of overseas colonial empires after World War II. The Allied powers' efforts to characterize World War II as a conflict between democracy and fascism meant that independence movements began to press colonial powers to withdraw from their overseas possessions and grant self-determination to colonized peoples.[112] The unfolding Cold War and the ideological antagonism between the West and the East facilitated civil rights reform as the US government sought to polish its international image.[113] A similar logic can be extended to the Indigenous Rights Struggle and its international dimensions. While the struggle for Indigenous rights never received the same attention as the Black civil rights movement, the Soviet Union likewise sought to exploit failed federal policies toward its colonized subjects in its propaganda campaign.[114] Both the civil rights struggle and the decolonization movement advanced Indigenous understandings of their own subaltern status, informed their activism and their political ideas, and helped them to advance responses.[115]

The underlying causes of the Red Power movement cluster around three factors: first, the adversarial colonial policies of domination that unintentionally created the conditions for an urban-based Indigenous mobilization; second, American ethnic politics, that is, both the challenge to established social and political institutions and the federal government's response with massive federal programs; and third, the self-renewing Red Power protest activism itself, which served as a catalyst for cultural revival and restoration, inspiring further activism and offering Indigenous men and women an avenue to transform their own gendered subjectivities and their tribal communities.[116] Indigenous activists channeled their frustration and anger into a social movement for change that started in the urban centers and spilled over into reservation communities.[117]

## Reinventing Indigeneity through Military Service

Many indigenous men not only reinvented their masculinities in response to assimilationist settler-colonial policies but also chose the military to exercise some agency over their lives. As such, the military became significant for the production of modern Indigenous masculinities and a site where Indigenous men could contend with hegemonic notions of gender and culture. By focusing on Indigenous participation in the US military, my book highlights the intersection of American imperialism and colonialism with Indigenous systems of social organization.

During the Vietnam War era, an estimated forty-two thousand Indigenous men served in Southeast Asia. About 90 percent of them were volunteers, at a time when the military draft was in place, as was the case until 1973.[118] This means that during the Vietnam War period, one in four eligible Native Americans served in the military, as opposed to one in twelve of the general American population.[119] The high enlistment figure is somewhat in line with that of previous wars in which Indigenous men joined the US military in overwhelming numbers in relation to their relative population. During World War I, an estimated twelve thousand served at a time when they were not officially American citizens. During World War II, another forty-four thousand wore US uniforms.[120] In the Korean conflict, there were an estimated 29,700.[121] Indigenous participation in the US military is thus a complex narrative of ambiguous and competing loyalties, influences, and motivations.

Colonial attitudes toward Indigenous men were significantly shaped by racial assumptions and an ethnocentrism that mirrored American society in general. Martial race ideology found expression in a high admiration as well as a deep-seated fear. Colonial ambivalence translated into two contradictory agendas: first, attempts to emulate this manly race; and second, efforts to assimilate this worthy race into dominant society. Both boarding school education and military service were seen as pathways into white society. A highly regimented daily routine and highly patriotic procedures, the thinking went, would ensure Indigenous loyalty. Boarding school education preconditioned Indigenous men for military service and turned them into well-qualified recruits in comparison to their non-Indigenous counterparts.[122]

Indigenous militarization and masculinization are closely linked to empire-building and the racialized and gendered legacies of colonialism. In striking parallels to US expansion over Native America, the building of a US overseas empire (with bases in the Philippines, Hawai'i, Guam, and other countries) also advanced a discourse of civilization, nationhood, and race. United States colonial institutions—schools, clinics, and public administration—spread an ideology of empire with racialized and gendered constructions of the non-white "other." Colonial society established an Indigenous elite and a collaborator class and marginalized the majority of the Indigenous population.[123] In that sense, the formation of Indigenous militarized masculinities has aided in upholding US military and political hegemony.

However, the gendered dynamics of Indigenous militarization are deeply contradictory and produce unexpected forms of anti-colonial resistance also. Undoubtedly, the recruitment of Indigenous men illustrates that the US military has been a prime force not only in nation-building but also in multiethnic integration. In absorbing certain ethnic groups into its military, the United States has diverted attention from anti-colonial struggles or quests for self-determination. However, from a military perspective, subjects in colonial armies have been rarely treated as equals but rather as expendable pawns in nationalist endeavors.[124]

Few scholars have examined how colonized masculinities negotiate their gendered incorporation into the US military and how they struggle against and with their subordinated status in relation to white hegemonic manhood along the lines of race, gender, and nation. A rare exception are anthropologists Keith L. Camacho (Chamorro) and Laurel A. Monnig, who have explored the experiences of Chamorro men of Guam within the US military.[125] The reasons for Chamorro men joining the US military revolve around cultural traditions, economic opportunity, educational advancement, patriotism, and efforts to utilize the US military to redefine the emasculated image that Western colonization has imprinted upon Chamorro society. Chamorro men can remake their emasculated image by reappropriating Pacific "savagery" and "warriorhood" into their service and by reshaping their bodies.[126] However, Chamorro participation in the US military also produces unexpected forms of resistance through colonial ambivalence. The experiences of these men within the US military involve their continual emasculation and exclusion from white-based notions of masculinity, contradictory experiences with their own marginality and colonial politics and practices, and racialized and gendered bias. Many Indigenous veterans have turned into advocates for Indigenous rights and see no contradiction between their military service and struggles for decolonization. Processes of Indigenous militarization and masculinization are inherently contradictory, and have shaped anti-colonialist movements.[127]

Recently, historiography has turned away from considering Indigenous military service in the colonizer's army as evidence of dependency.[128] Tom Holm, William Meadows, and Al Carroll have dismissed interpretations of adherents of dependency theory, who considered Indigenous entrance into the US military primarily an effort on the part of Indigenous men to legitimize themselves in the eyes of the American nation as loyal citizens and assimilate into dominant society, or, alternatively, to gain economic incentives. The US military has frequently served as an entry point into American society; yet while the above motives may hold true for other marginalized minorities, they do not necessarily apply to Indigenous people. Recent historiography has taken into account Indigenous agency and cultural persistence, considering Indigenous veterans as cultural navigators at the intersection of colonial domination and modernity as well as their own cultural systems, practices, and beliefs.

Indigenous motivations for enlistment during the Vietnam War are manifold, yet they are largely culturally based. Historically, Native Americans have utilized the US military for reasons of their own and not necessarily those imagined for them. In building upon previous insights and combining them with my own findings, Indigenous motivations include: first, a hybrid patriotism that is both Native and American; second, cultural motivations around warrior-based themes (e.g., the continuation of tribal and family traditions; honoring by tribal members and communities, etc.); third, economic considerations (e.g., employment opportunities); and fourth, acculturative and assimilationist influences (e.g., boarding schools).[129]

First, Indigenous Vietnam veterans embrace what historian Paul Rosier has called a "hybrid patriotism."[130] Indigenous veterans consider themselves as members of their sovereign tribal nations first and the American nation second. The dual allegiance to these different entities has translated into a patriotism that is both Native (that is for *their* homeland and for *their* people) and American (for the American nation and its people).[131] Most importantly, many Indigenous veterans feel that by joining the US military, they can defend their ancestral homelands and their people, as well as the United States and its citizens. For example, Ed Charging Elk (Lakota), a Vietnam combat veteran, joined the US military because, as he put it:

> I think the basic thought of we as Lakota people is: we defend our families first, we defend our nation, our traditional way of life and our spirituality. And whether it's a government like the United States . . . we still take that

same philosophy and that same thought. . . . You know, we were a nation here first. . . . You gotta keep in mind that our heart is with our people. Our heart is with our traditional way of life, our heart is with spirituality. Then, second, we're defending the United States.[132]

It follows that Indigenous patriotism is based on an entirely different understanding of warrior and nation from its Western counterpart. While non-Indigenous veterans regard themselves as citizen soldiers who fight on behalf of the US nation (or in the case of marginalized minorities seek to validate through heroic soldiering to gain entry into American society), Native Americans continue to understand themselves as defenders and protectors of what was originally theirs. Accordingly, Indigenous people regard military service as a way to defend their country and protect their people; and they continue to consider a war against foreign enemies as a potential threat.[133]

Second, many Indigenous Vietnam veterans see themselves as carrying on a long line of cultural and warrior traditions that have turned into family or veteran traditions through service in the US military. No other racial/ethnic group within the United States shares Indigenous people's cultural traditions, a central element that explains their unique war experience, as historian Al Carrol (Apache) has pointed out.[134] Indigenous veterans see themselves as in line with a much older tradition. For example, Thomas Roubideaux (Lakota) from Rosebud, South Dakota, enlisted in the US Army in 1965 at age seventeen. When reflecting on his reasons for enlisting in the US Army, he recounted his family's long tradition of military service:

> Well, I think I chose the Army primarily because it's a family heritage, you know. My ancestors fought against the Army in the Indian Wars, one of my great grandfathers was a scout with a scout detachment with the Cavalry during the early 1890's. My grandfather fought in World War I with [General] Pershing, and my father fought with the Rangers in North Africa and Italy and then in Normandy [during World War II]. . . . My uncles fought in Korea as Airborne Rangers and my brother was in the Army [during the Vietnam War], so I decided to follow the line and become a Ranger.[135]

Highly decorated, Roubideaux was discharged from the US Army in 1976 after eleven years of military service and what amounted to a total of 52 months in Vietnam, all in combat roles. As the above example illustrates, military service not only offered Indigenous men a way to protect their homeland and their tribal nation but also provided a vital link to the manly roles of pre-reservation times. Military service resonates with Indigenous value systems and continues to be seen as a way to earn respect among other Indigenous people. According to Tom Holm (Cherokee/Muskogee), Indigenous men have joined the US military because "they were patriots in the tribal sense of the world." They considered military service as an honorable activity and as a way to continue their family and/or tribal tradition. Perhaps most importantly, "they wanted to be warriors—to protect their land and their people. And, in the tribal tradition of reciprocity, they wanted to gain respect from other Native Americans."[136] In joining the US military—an essentially foreign institution—Indigenous men (and more recently also women) have syncretized two different military systems, thus mainlining a sense of their Indigeneity.[137]

Third, economic opportunity (employment, status, income) played a major role in prompting Indigenous enlistment. Military service offered veterans an opportunity to serve as breadwinners for their families and relatives by sending home paychecks and bringing their military pensions and retirement benefits back into their tribal communities.[138] Political scientist Sonja John suggests that economic motives and educational advancement have a much higher significance for Indigenous men and women entering the US military than hitherto acknowledged. These motivations to enter the service trump all other motivations, she claims, and are based on cultural understandings of warriorhood that entail the notion of providing for family, relatives, and tribal community.[139]

Fourth, assimilationist and acculturative influences such as boarding school education, the draft, and American consumerism certainly also played a significant role in Indigenous recruitment. Indigenous militarization can therefore also be described as a twofold historical process.[140] For example, Wes Studi (Cherokee), a Chilocco Indian School graduate and National Guard reservist from Oklahoma, reflected upon his motivations for service in the US Army as follows:

Well, I have to tell you that at about in the late 20s or early 30s, a young man begins to think of what in the world is it that I am here for? And I began to think, well am I a real man? Am I a warrior? . . .

My father was in Korea and . . . my father before him was in World War II. What about me? Can I do that kind of stuff? . . . It's a question of am I capable of actually doing what it is that people do in the world as warriors? So I had to find out.[141]

Studi decided to volunteer to go to Vietnam to find out about himself. In an interview, he reflected that "I really didn't care about the political, the social issue of the whole thing. I simply wanted to find out about myself." Following a year in Vietnam, he found out: "Yes I can do that. I don't like it. I think it's an awful freakin' thing that people do to one another in warfare. The process of war is the ugliest thing that a person can ever see in their goddamn life."[142] As his personal recollections indicate, Studi volunteered for service in Vietnam for a number of interrelated reasons: warrior/veteran traditions in his family, adventurism, and a desire to prove himself as a man/warrior and follow in the footsteps of his ancestors.

Indigenous military service during the Vietnam War era can thus be explained through a combination of culturally rooted motives: a hybrid patriotism (dual allegiance to different entities); aspects of cultural continuity (the continuation of cultural and warrior traditions in the form of family and veteran traditions); and military syncretism (a blending of Indigenous and non-Indigenous martial traditions) that, in combination, allow Indigenous people to maintain a strong sense of their own tribal/ethnic/cultural identities. For many, joining the military has been a pathway to better themselves, escape the poverty and remoteness of reservation life, see the world, and have adventures. Whatever their motives, Indigenous veterans have utilized the US military, an essentially foreign institution, for their own benefit. There is wide consensus that Indigenous participation in the military is closely linked and intertwined with cultural practices, ceremonies, and rituals. Cultural practices (e.g., giveaways), ceremonies (e.g., powwows), and rituals (e.g., sweat lodges), are tribal-culture specific and community-based and involve song, dance, and tribal language; they are all part of a larger, complex cultural system and inextricably intertwined. Ceremony is a larger reflection of Native worldviews, reality, and ways of thinking and doing.[143] Ceremony continually reaffirmed the mutual and reciprocal relationship between warrior (now called veteran) and tribal community.[144]

By joining the military, Indigenous men have thus also been able to maintain a strong sense of their own identity. From World War I through World War II, Korea, and Vietnam, each generation of outgoing or homecoming veterans (also called warriors) has necessitated a need among tribal communities to ceremonially protect, pray, send off, welcome home, cleanse, or honor their service members through cultural practices and ceremonies, thus instigating a major cultural revitalization and renewal across Indian Country.[145] Through military service, Indigenous veterans have carried on old cultural and warrior traditions, revitalizing some, modifying others, and reinventing new ones, continually remaking themselves as warriors. In joining the military, Indigenous men have maintained their own distinct tribal identities and instigated a cultural renewal of tribal societies.[146]

## The Military Experiences of World War I, World War II, and Korea

During each twentieth-century war, Indigenous people served as a model minority, fully throwing themselves into the war effort. The outpouring of red patriotism, however, should not obscure the fact that Indigenous responses to each war were highly diverse. In a society in which citizenship and national belonging went hand in hand, military heroism offered marginalized minorities such as Japanese Americans and African Americans an avenue to prove their loyalty in order to become fully-fledged US citizens; yet Native Americans largely enlisted out of a hybrid sense of patriotism.[147] Indigenous enlistment figures, while relatively small in actual numbers, were larger in proportion to the overall population than that of any other racial/ethnic group in America during each war.[148] As a whole, Indigenous participation in the US military has received comparatively little scholarly attention.[149]

During World War I and World War II, the question over whether to integrate Indigenous soldiers into the military or segregate them in separate units triggered a national debate. The national debate touched upon questions of citizenship, nationhood, and the position of Native Americans in the nation-state. Like other colonial and imperial powers, the United States faced similar questions over the military usage of their colonized Indigenous people.[150] At the center of the national debate surrounding Indigenous participation in the US military stood the identification of Native Americans as a martial race. Advocates of the inclusion of Indigenous soldiers into the military were divided along the lines of preserving Indigenous culture (through segregated units) or furthering assimilation (through integrated units). At the advent of World War I, the proponents of racially integrated military service ultimately won out, not least because this approach was consistent with assimilationist colonial policies.[151] During World War II, the national debate resurfaced, was debated with similar arguments, and produced the same result.[152]

Throughout all twentieth-century wars, Indigenous resistance to the draft has been negligible. Few Indigenous men attempted to avoid military service on grounds that it was "a white man's war." Instead, most resistance stemmed from controversy over treaty rights and tribal sovereignty, unsettled citizenship status, draft registration (which compromised tribal sovereignty), or religious reasons.[153] As a supposed reward for their loyal service during World War I, Indigenous veterans were given US citizenship in 1919 (which was extended to all non-citizen Native Americans in 1924 through the Snyder Act). The Nationality Act of 1940 reinforced the Citizenship Act and stipulated that all Native Americans, including those born after 1924, were American citizens. The *Ex Parte Green* court ruling of November 25, 1941, decided that Indigenous citizenship and wardship were compatible, thus becoming the authoritative decision on compulsory military service for Native Americans.[154] During subsequent wars in Korea and Vietnam, Indigenous draft resistance remained unheard of across Indian Country.[155]

The Indigenous war experience in twentieth-century wars was predominantly that of the foot soldier on the frontlines. Evidence suggests that the highest percentage of Indigenous soldiers served on the ground where they saw the heaviest fighting.[156] In each of these wars, Indigenous men found themselves acting as scouts, runners, snipers, or point men, and in some cases also as code talkers—precarious assignments that reflected dominant notions of the "Indian scout syndrome," as well as Indigenous veterans' own choices. The "Indian scout syndrome" has followed Indigenous service members into each war from World War I through the present.[157] During World War I, the US Army pioneered the use of Indigenous code talkers, a concept that continued in World War II. Indigenous code talkers serving in either war came from more than twenty different tribes. They utilized their tribal language in coded form to transmit messages at a time when the very usage of their languages was officially prohibited by that same government.[158]

World War I and World War II propaganda efforts featured hypermasculine warrior imagery in US news media. When reporting about Native Americans, newspaper captions built on the legendary racial predisposition of Indigenous men for combat and frequently featured words such as "warrior," "brave," and "fighter." The warrior image was the embodiment of militant Americanism: just as the Indigenous warrior had defended his land, people, and way of life centuries before, so now he defended Americanism in the name of freedom and democracy with a "savagery" that matched or surpassed barbarism at the hands of the German "Huns" or, later, the Nazis.[159] For example, during the Great War, the *Indian's Friend* reported that "Indians in the regiments are being used for scouting and patrol duty because of the natural instinct that fits them for this kind of work."[160] During World War II, American newspapers depicted Native Americans as loyal, brave, and fierce fighters who wholeheartedly threw themselves into the war effort, giving legitimacy to the American cause. In a *Collier's* article of 1944, Secretary of the Interior Harold Ickes pointed to the "inherited talents" that made Indigenous soldiers so valuable in the ranks of the US Army:

> There is no denying the fact that he is one of our best fighters. The inherited talents of the Indian make him uniquely valuable. He has endurance, rhythm, a feeling for timing, co-ordination, sense perception, an uncanny ability to get over any sort of terrain at night, and, better than all else, an enthusiasm for fighting. He takes a rough job and makes a game of it. Rigors of combat hold no terrors from him; severe discipline and hard duties do not deter him.[161]

The World War I and World War II propaganda efforts stand in stark contrast to the Korean and Vietnam experience, where Indigenous soldiers received little if any media attention at all.[162] Indeed, different recruitment practices make it hard to find any sources on Indigenous soldiers during these wars, suggesting that, within the American nation, the Indigenous subaltern was largely invisible.[163] However, as much as the Korean and Vietnam War wars were marked by a conspicuous absence of warrior imagery in the national media discourse, Indigenous soldiers encountered the "Indian scout syndrome" on a regular basis in their military outfits.[164]

The homecoming experience of each war generation was similar in that Indigenous soldiers returned into a situation of domestic colonialism characterized by government indifference, subalternity, and racial bias that in many regards paralleled the return of Black veterans into segregation, discrimination, and poverty. The bestowal of US citizenship meant the forced inclusion of Indigenous people into dominant society and the further erosion of treaty rights.[165] After World War II, homecoming Indigenous veterans once again saw themselves confronted with their own subalternity and second-class citizenship status. In a 1948 speech, tribal leader Robert Yellowtail (Crow) voiced the sentiment of many: "We [Indigenous people] are forgotten men in the land of plenty," he stated. "We are prisoners in the land of our birth."[166] Homecoming Korean War veterans fared little better than previous generations. The national controversy over the burial of Sergeant John Rice (Ho Chunk), a decorated World War II veteran and Korean War casualty, best encapsulates the prevalent anti-Indian sentiment in American society of the 1950s. In August 1951, halfway through the burial service at a Sioux City, Iowa cemetery officials realized Rice was not white, informed the funeral party of the "Caucasian only" policy, and refused burial. The event provoked national disbelief and outrage and required the personal intervention of President Harry Truman, who offered Rice's family a burial plot at Arlington National Cemetery. Public reference to the embarrassing incident quickly diminished, but racial prejudice in border town communities close to reservations continued.[167] The 1950s were also remembered for the tragic death of World War II war hero Ira Hayes, one of the iconic flag raisers on Mount Suribachi on Iwo Jima. In 1955, Hayes's premature death at age 32 due to drinking and exposure came to symbolize Indigenous disillusionment about the harsh realities of anti-Indianism in postwar America.[168]

During and after each war, Indigenous veterans became politically active at home, contesting their subaltern position vis-à-vis the American nation-state. Indigenous participation in overseas wars broadened their horizons, brought them into contact with other colonized or marginalized people across the globe, and empowered them in their struggle for Indigenous rights. The Great War was a precursor to the Pan-Indian sentiment that emerged during subsequent wars. Military service in Uncle Sam's army brought together Indigenous men from different tribes across the United States and resulted in the development of "a limited form of Pan-Indianism among veterans," as historian Thomas Britten states.[169] Indigenous World War I veterans set a precedent for organizing and lobbying for Indigenous rights.[170] During World War II, more than in the previous war, red patriots developed a sense of their shared Indigeneity. If not in rhetoric, then in spirit, they embarked on a "double victory" campaign, assuming that victory over fascism abroad would also bring an end to their subaltern status at home. Indigenous veterans also connected their own struggle against oppression at home with foreign people's struggles against colonial domination abroad. In 1944, they founded the National Congress of American Indians (NCAI), an organization that lobbied for both civil rights and treaty rights.[171] The World War II and Korean War experiences empowered Indigenous veterans in their struggle for postwar civil rights (e.g., against the ban of alcohol on reservations and for voting rights), leading to a reassertion of their cultural identity and claims for self-determination claims—in this regard, they foreshadowed the Red Power movement.[172]

### The Vietnam Experience and Indigenous Veterans' Participation in Sixties Movements

Indigenous soldiers who served in Vietnam were highly likely to be in an infantry unit, walk point, and be called "chief" or "Geronimo" by their non-Native counterparts.[173] Many Indigenous veterans observed that their non-Indigenous counterparts recast the Vietnam War in a gendered and racialized language replete with rhetoric of the American West. For example, Vietnamese people were referred to as hostile "Indians," enemy-held territory was called "Indian Country," US bases were turned into "Fort Apaches," and Vietnamese defectors were named "Kit Carson scouts." Hollywood exploited Indigenous-Vietnamese parallels in the movie *The Green Berets* (1968) in which the war in Vietnam resembled a frontier conflict between cowboys and tribal warriors.[174]

Among Native Americans, the Vietnam War was every bit as controversial as it was for other Americans, but unlike their non-Indigenous counterparts, Native Americans did not engage in any major reported anti-war protest or draft resistance. Tribal communities did not view their veterans as political pawns; instead, they continued to view their veterans in the tribal sense—as men, proven warriors, defenders of their homeland and their people, and guardians of old-standing traditions. Madonna Thunder Hawk (Lakota), sister of AIM leader Russell Means, recalled: "There was this anti-war movement going on across the country. But in Indian Country, on any reservation anywhere in the country, our servicemen were treated with respect. We didn't agree with the war, I was against the war, but I wasn't against the soldiers. They were drafted. . . . We come from a society where the men were the protectors or providers. So it was just automatic respect."[175]

During their tour in Vietnam, Indigenous veterans became aware of the racial dimensions of the war. They realized that what was done to the Vietnamese people in many ways paralleled their own historical experience and treatment at home. Wes Studi (Cherokee) spent 1968/69 with the Marines in Vietnam. As a "grunt," he shared experiences that made him question what he was doing as a colonial soldier in a white man's army engaged in a conflict in a faraway country. For one, the disturbing Vietnam War experience altered his outlook on life tremendously, as he stated, "Well, there's truth to the fact that war is hell. And I think I saw the worst in men and the best in men. It [the war] certainly changed my view of life in the USA."[176]

For him, both his own resemblance to the Vietnamese and the Vietnamese situation of fighting off foreign invaders reminded him of that of his own people. What also got to him was the ambiguous relationship with Viet Cong soldiers-turned-US scouts. Indigenous scouts played a significant role in subduing the last resisting tribal nations during the Indian Wars and were highly complicit in colonizing processes, yet at the same time they allowed Indigenous people to meet their future at least partially on their own terms.[177] Many Vietnamese did not look that much different from Indigenous people. Quite often, captured North Vietnamese soldiers turned into scouts for the US Army. As Studi put it, "One of the things that I remember: many of those Vietnamese looking at me. And I began thinking that, yeah it wasn't that long ago that we, as Cherokee people, as American Indian people, we were on the other end of that rifle that I was holding. So, it was kind of an awakening."[178] Studi also recalled that captured North Vietnamese soldiers would look at him and say, "I, you: same, same." And he thought: "you're right. . . . I same, same like you. And because only 150 years ago my people were fighting the same people that I am hooked up with now." Not just the physical resemblance but also the larger dimensions of the war played a significant part in Indigenous soldiers' alienation within American politics and society. Studi, like many other Indigenous veterans, felt that they had been used as pawns in the white man's colonial army.[179]

For many, the homecoming experience proved to be a severe culture shock. After a tour in Vietnam and experiencing the Tet Offensive as a grunt, Studi returned to the United States in 1969 from a highly unpopular war. Once there, he recalled being told to change from his uniform into civilian clothes: "When I first came back, the army actually told me to go to the PX [= Post Exchange/US Army base retail store] there and get yourself some civilian clothes. Don't go home in your uniform, because everybody is spitting and throwing at you. Anyway, you know it was not a good time to be a soldier. So that's what I did: I got civilian clothes and went home."[180]

The homecoming experience left him with deep-seated feelings of alienation, disillusionment, and deceit. As he recalled, "We were not appreciated, we were degraded actually. Not a pleasant homecoming. I didn't really dwell on the relation between my [Cherokee/Indigenous] people with the United States government at that point of time."[181] Indigenous veterans not only shared a sense of betrayal for serving as helpful hands in yet another imperialist conflict but, just as the Vietnam War generation as a whole, harbored a sense of being let down by politicians and the military in a struggle against an enemy that could have been subdued. Like other veterans, Wes Studi had a hard time readapting to

An Indigenous Vietnam veteran at the Crow Dog Sun Dance, 1971. Indigenous Vietnam veterans considered themselves as warriors in line with a much older tradition. Homecoming Indigenous veterans returned to an intolerable situation in the United States. Many became strong advocates for Indigenous rights and joined the American Indian Movement, adding a new element of radicalism and militancy. (Richard Erdoes Papers, Yale Collection of Western Americana, Beinecke Rare Book and Manuscript Library)

civilian life. Following years of drifting around, Studi enrolled as a college student in Tulsa, Oklahoma, and joined AIM in 1972. As he recalled: "I made it through the year in Vietnam, came home and actually wanted to go to war with the USA. So, I joined up with the American Indian Movement, AIM."[182]

Homecoming Indigenous Vietnam veterans returned to a situation of heightened upheaval, as well as one of domestic colonialism. They brought with them a sense of betrayal for serving in the white man's army and for perpetuating US colonial and imperial domination. They were at odds as to why they had put their lives on the line for a government that continued to impose its colonial policies and practices upon "other" people abroad in Southeast Asia and its own people at home in America. They felt they had been used as pawns in the colonial army to further US domination abroad and fight in what seemed a questionable conflict at best.[183]

As Indigenous Vietnam veterans returned home, they encountered a "double discrimination" from mainstream society: first, as Indigenous soldiers, they were confronted with the ongoing bias directed against them as subaltern people; second, as participants and returnees from a war that was highly unpopular, they endured the same discrimination as other veterans.[184] Upon their return home, many Indigenous Vietnam veterans found themselves denied their basic civil rights; worse, they found themselves in the midst of yet another war against a quasi-colonial bureaucracy that regulated their lives socially, politically, economically, and culturally. Many veterans felt that instead of fighting in a faraway country for the US government, they should have taken up arms against their own government at home.[185] More than any previous generation, Indigenous Vietnam veterans recognized a joint historical experience and shared a sense of Indigeneity that transcended tribal affiliations. Indigenous Vietnam veterans joined a social movement for change, the Red Power movement, adding a new element of radicalism and militancy.[186]

A precursor of the surging Indigenous activism occurred in the fishing rights struggle of the Pacific Northwest. There, a number of local tribes around Puget Sound and the Columbia River sought to uphold their traditional fishing rights, which were guaranteed by treaties but challenged by state and local authorities. In a series of fish-ins, Indigenous activists brought international attention to their struggle. The battle over fishing rights encouraged Indigenous activists to utilize tactics of direct action and civil disobedience, a precursor to Indigenous militancy during later years. In 1968, Sidney Mills (Yakama/Cherokee), a wounded combat soldier recently returned from Vietnam, found himself in the midst of the ongoing fishing rights struggle. He was arrested on October 13, 1968, at Frank's Landing on the Nisqually River. In his court testimony, he articulated a growing bitterness shared by many Indigenous veterans who regarded themselves as warriors fighting for a country in which their own people were treated unjustly. In his testimony, Mills related the story of Sergeant Sohappy—a combat veteran with three tours in Vietnam and a distinguished service record—who was arrested for (supposedly) illegal fishing, by which he was attempting to provide for his family while at home recuperating from yet another series of combat wounds.[187] In a 1971 interview for a *Ramparts* article, Mills reflected on the parallels between America and Vietnam: "It dawned on me that I had been out there in the jungle killing natives. I mean natives in the way we're natives. And when I thought it over, it seemed to me that they were a lot like us. They don't want whites conquering them."[188]

## The Red Power Era: Political Protest and Cultural Renewal, 1969–1978

The sustained takeover of Alcatraz Island is what Donald Fixico (Shawnee, Sac and Fox, Muscogee Creek, and Seminole) calls "one of the cornerstone events in modern Indian history" and a "symbol for Native Americans today."[189] The Alcatraz takeover stimulated a profound reclamation of Indigenous identities, inspired cultural renewal, provided a catalyst for protest activism, and had a wide-ranging transformative impact across Indian Country.[190] The Alcatraz occupation was a focal point of Indigenous activism and became a role model for future Red Power activism, touching off a series of takeovers and demonstrations that lasted well into the late 1970s.[191] Between 1969 and 1978 there were more than seventy protest events.[192] The incoming Nixon administration, which made the reversal of termination and the endorsement of self-determination the centerpiece of its federal Indian policy, responded with a policy of restraint to Indigenous rights activism.[193]

The American Indian Movement is widely recognized as a key political actor of the Red Power movement, leading, organizing, or participating in all major protests of the era.[194] From its inception, AIM was a male-identified activist organization, although women played an integral, much overlooked role in the organization.[195] AIM's origin in 1968, its peak as a national organization in 1973, and its final demise after 1978 roughly paralleled the history of the entire Red Power movement. AIM never represented the entire spectrum of Native protest activism, yet its spectacular protests and demonstrations attracted widespread media attention, in turn overshadowing other Native groups, organizations, and endeavors. For the uninformed onlooker, the organization thus became synonymous with the entire Indigenous struggle.[196]

The American Indian Movement originated as a local community's response to pressing socioeconomic and political problems. By the early 1970s, AIM had expanded nationally, gained considerable media attention, and begun to reach out to reservation communities. This was paralleled by a shift in focus from urban Indigenous issues and civil rights toward treaty rights, sovereignty, land reform, tribal governance, and cultural revitalization. In the wake of the Alcatraz takeover, AIM embarked on the militant advocacy of self-determination and considerably shaped, launched, and sustained protest activism.[197] Historian Donald Fixico considers this generation of Indigenous activists "a new warrior prototype." What set this generation of Indigenous nationalists apart was their desire to instigate change, their intrepid desire to speak out for Indigenous rights regardless of the consequences, and their oratory skills. Red Power movement leaders were articulate, visionary, intelligent, and proactive. At a time when a myriad of protest movements challenged old, conservative thinking, this modern Indigenous leadership realized that it was the right time to take action against a colonial US government and often became disenchanted with established tribal leaders for their radicalism in the process.[198]

Early national reform movements such as the Society of American Indians (SAI, est. 1911) were composed of educated Native professionals who resisted government paternalism, sought the abolition of the Bureau of Indian Affairs, and pursued the protection of Indigenous rights until the organization fell in disarray in the 1930s.[199] Following World War II, the National Congress of American Indians, another Pan-Indian organization, originated as a national policy and legislative lobbying force in American politics.[200]

The 1960s and 1970s bore witness to the forging of a new Indigenous leadership that utilized social protest rather than established political procedures to represent the issues and concerns of Indigenous people from urban areas as well as from reservations who often found themselves at odds with tribal governments and their leaders. In 1961, the National Indian Youth Council (NIYC), organized by college-educated activists, adopted some ideas of the civil rights movement, became involved in the Poor People's March in 1968, and during the 1960s staged numerous fish-ins in the Pacific Northwest where Washington state sought to infringe upon Indigenous fishing rights guaranteed by federal treaties.[201]

The term "Red Power" carries a large range of political and cultural meanings.[202] As a political term, "Red Power" touches upon self-determination but is unlike nationalism. According to literary scholar Leah Sneider, self-determination depends on "a complementary relationship between independence and interdependence."[203] Across Indian Country, "self-determination is distinctly different from nationalism, which focuses exclusively on independence, rather than interdependence and relationship."[204] Nationalism requires both statehood and nationhood.[205] Sovereignty encompasses a people's right to self-government independent of outside influence.[206] Decolonization is a far-reaching attempt to reclaim epistemologies and social structures.[207] Sovereignty and self-determination are prerequisites to decolonization, and they are dependent upon "the will of the people to establish themselves as a nation in culturally appropriate ways and as demonstrated through the people's stories and histories."[208]

The term "Red Power" also carries cultural meanings. The Indigenous cultural nationalist movement that began in the late 1960s closely paralleled and intertwined with the political Red Power activism. Political scientist John Hutchinson distinguishes between political nationalism, which aims to establish a sovereign nation-state or citizenship within a nation-state, and cultural nationalism, which primarily seeks to form national communities.[209] According to Hutchinson, political nationalists center on establishing a modern nation-state from the top down; cultural nationalists in turn seek to re-create or renew a distinctive "historic community" from the bottom up.[210] Cultural nationalism plays a distinctive role in nation-building endeavors through its reference to a unique history, culture, and geography that helps to create a sense of belonging within the community.[211] Hutchinson shows that cultural nationalism functions through recourse to historical memory, which provides links to a distinct homeland and specific social, cultural, and political forms of expression and organization, and through cultural revival, such as the revitalization of languages, arts, common cultural rituals, ceremonies, and practices, in efforts to form "a moral community."[212] Cultural nationalists employ the term "moral regeneration" and utilize history to validate their nation-building enterprise.[213] In so doing, they also enable reconciliation between potentially conflicting aspects such as tradition and modernity, or "authenticity" to the nationalist cause.[214] Their project of pursuing reform from within makes cultural nationalists what Hutchinson describes as "moral innovators."[215]

Red Power was influenced by the principles of Black Power, but it was not a mere imitation. Rather, as literary scholar Casey Ryan Kelly has pointed out, Red Power consisted of "a set of cultural specific expressions that reflect Indigenous experiences and struggles."[216] Indigenous nationalists commonly found themselves caught between a civil rights framework within the United States and a nationalist decolonization framework common to Third World struggles after World War II—all of which made it harder for Indigenous people to articulate their demands in a third space of sovereignty in the settler nation-state.[217] Vine Deloria Jr. (Yankton Dakota), one of the preeminent Indigenous intellectuals of that time, argues that the advent of Black Power helped Red Power activists to better articulate their demands for self-determination, tribal sovereignty, and nationhood due to their distinct political status.[218]

Black Power and Red Power movements shared some similarities but also had their differences.[219] According to political scientist Kevin Bruyneel, "both Black Power and Red Power referred to respective experiences of political inequality and domination as consequences of American colonialism rather than to internal prejudice or racism alone." In doing so, they both sought "to articulate a stronger sense of collective identity for their people and make a non-integrationist national claim to and against the U.S. government."²²⁰ However, there were also key distinctions between the power movements, as Bruyneel points out in his discussion of Deloria's ideas.²²¹ For example, Black nationalist discourse could not provide the language and ideas to articulate Indigenous concerns. Perhaps most importantly, Deloria viewed Black nationalism, correctly or not, as caught in a Black–white binary and as demanding economic concessions and political rights from the white power structure. To him, the Black demand for individual equality meant an affirmation of the racial, cultural, and gendered political norms of the dominant American citizen. It meant the imposition of that sameness on the marginalized and colonized subjects within larger encapsulating American society—or so Deloria saw it. In turn, Indigenous nationalists sought to preserve their cultural distinctiveness through political autonomy (or self-determination).²²²

Similarly to the Black example, Red Power affirmed and empowered Indian Country with messages praising the nobility, beauty, and richness of Indigenous life. Black Power activists adhered to Marxist principles and the international leftist thought of Karl Marx, Frantz Fanon, Ho Chi Minh, Che Guevara, and Mao Tse-Tung; they sought communal empowerment and endorsed the revolutionary potential of the dispossessed and lower class, the *lumpenproletariat*.²²³ Akin to the Black example, Red Power activists were concerned with community empowerment and direct action. However, Native Americans were primarily influenced by traditional Indigenous philosophers and spirituality, rather than modern political thought and liberation theories.²²⁴ Black Power meant the rebuttal of integration in favor of separatism.²²⁵ In turn, Indigenous activists endorsed the concept of an inherent sovereignty—the notion that tribal nations possessed the right to self-governance prior to settler-colonial encroachment—and called for self-determination and tribal sovereignty, akin to yet different from Black concepts of territorial separatism and/or racial exclusivity.²²⁶

## Conclusion

To a large extent, Indigenous–settler-colonial relations can be interpreted as a conflict over competing meanings of masculinity and nationhood.²²⁷

The imposition of dominant notions of race, gender, and nation has led to the subalternity, marginalization, and disempowerment of Indigenous men. Cultural imagery has depicted Indigenous manliness in terms of hypomasculinity or hypermasculinity in order to shape and reshape masculine and nationalist notions of Americanness.[228] In response, Indigenous men have continually reinvented their Indigeneity and manliness by rejecting settler impositions and through cultural retention, adaptation, and incorporation.

While the gendered policies of US settler colonialism have served to alienate Indigenous people from their traditional epistemologies, they also had an unintended effect, functioning as a source of empowerment. Participation in the US military has allowed Indigenous men to maintain their cultural integrity and remake themselves into warriors once again. At the same time, military service has provided a bridge to the widespread revitalization, renewal, and reinvention of cultural practices and language through songs, dances, ceremonies, and rituals across Indian Country. During the 1960s and 1970s, Indigenous men and women renewed their sense of identity and what it meant to be Indigenous, most notably through the formation of urban Indigenous communities and the emergence of a Pan-Indian consciousness. The building of urban Indigenous communities and the formation of Pan-Indianism became significant mobilizing tools in the Red Power movement.

## Chapter 2

# From Powerlessness to Protest
## Reinventing Indigenous Men in AIM, 1968–1972

In June 2010, Bill Means (Lakota), a paratrooper and Vietnam combat veteran, reflected on how he became involved with the American Indian Movement. While sitting in a bunker in Vietnam, he came across an issue of *Stars and Stripes* with a picture of his brother Russell Means standing on a statue of Chief Massasoit near Plymouth Rock, Massachusetts, protesting Thanksgiving Day in 1970. The article read that AIM was announcing a national day of mourning for Native Americans because they had nothing to be thankful for with regard to government policies and severe socioeconomic disparities. As he put it, "So it was pretty amazing. . . . I kinda felt like "Wow. I'm really missing something," you know. And unfortunately I was in Vietnam and [there was] really nothin' I could do at that time other than finish my time and survive. So [it] made me aware of a new movement that was taking place."[1]

Upon his return from Vietnam, Means finished the last five months of his military service in Fort Lewis, Washington, where he was trained in riot control—how to control, disperse, and arrest people involved in the demonstrations, protests, or riots that became increasingly commonplace during the 1960s and 1970s. His overseas tour made Means aware of the highly ambiguous role Indigenous veterans played in US imperialist and colonialist endeavors and of his own complicity in this. However, his personal turning point came when he had to face his own people at home. One night, his unit was put on alert and was waiting to be deployed. He recalled:

> And we were sitting on the runway with all our gear on, rifles and bayonets, and a sergeant comes walking by and I said, "Hey, Sarge, what's the deal? What's going on? Protests?" He says, "Some Indian people have taken over a military base that's abandoned in Seattle [Fort Lawson] and we might have to go get them outta there." I said, "Hey, Sarge, man, I'm not going over there. I just came back from the war in Vietnam and I'm not gonna start killing my own people."[2]

For his action, Means was confined to barrack duty. This was a relatively mild form of punishment, yet given the heightened interracial tensions within his unit and the solidarity of a number of Black servicemen, quite a reasonable one. When his military service was completed, Bill Means became a college student and, like many other Indigenous veterans, later joined AIM.[3]

The start of the American Indian Movement is widely associated with the emergence of an Indigenous protest masculinity, a forerunner of a new Indigenous warrior prototype that would emerge later on. The emergence of this "protest masculinity" can be traced to the severe existential crisis faced by the Indigenous community in the Twin Cities. The Indigenous protest masculinity arose from within the urban context and shared cross-cultural experiences of alienation and powerlessness. The personal life stories of boys and men in AIM reflect that this form of protest masculinity was expressed through violence, crime, resistance to school, and substance abuse, as well as short-lived, exploitative heterosexual relationships.[4] The Twin Cities case study provides hitherto unexplored perspectives into the ways Indigenous men were affected by boarding schools, military service, penitentiaries, and the urban context—profoundly alienating experiences that influenced their subjectivities in multiple, complex, and contradictory ways.

In society, social classes are closely associated with the construction of masculinities. The very idea of providing for the family is a major part of constructing masculine identity.[5] Men in low-level classes wield little power in their workplace and as a consequence will adopt macho identities to disguise their powerlessness and compensate for dominating at home.[6] It is for this reason that lower-class men produce hypermasculinity as a compensatory mechanism.[7] In displaying exaggerated masculinity—through physicality, aggression, domination, as well as violence, sexual prowess, spousal abuse, and misogyny—lower-class men attempt to make up for their subordinated status.[8]

Sociologist R. W. Connell has noted that "a protest masculinity" is frequently a marginalized masculinity that is actively constructed, just like other masculinities. A "protest masculinity" is built through defiance of authority, toughness, and confrontation—gendered practices that stem from experiences of powerlessness.[9] This gendered practice appears in urban street gangs and among ethnic minorities, often "in defiance of authority," as Connell writes.[10] According to political scientist Thokozani Xaba, "protest masculinity" can also be found among diasporic and migrant men, as well as formerly colonized men who engage in armed liberation struggles within a larger context of poverty and racism.[11] "Protest masculinity" is concerned with saving face and keeping up a front,[12] and it is situational and context-dependent.[13] Examples of marginalized men developing their own forms of machismo can be found within the Chicano movement, the Black Panther Party, and Puerto Rican Young Lords.[14] Yet another example of exaggerated masculinity can be found in Indigenous men in AIM.

Indigenous scholars have repeatedly cautioned against the recovery of a "traditional" or "authentic" Indigenous masculinity.[15] The concept of authenticity—the notion of a fixed, already predetermined, essential or core quality or characteristic of being—is probably among the most pervasive of settler imaginings. To the present day, essentialist concepts of Indigeneity influence the construction of settler and Indigenous identities and their relations alike.[16] In aligning with the claim that colonial hybridization makes it impossible to recover the essence of subaltern subjectivities, Indigenous studies scholar Brendan Hokowhitu (Māori) suggests that "any conceptualization of an 'authentic' or 'traditional' [Indigenous] man is an illusion."[17] He goes on to note that "to buy into the notion that [Indigenous] culture can be 'authenticated' is to align with the colonizer."[18] Rather, researchers have to disentangle the processes that explain the hybridization of Indigenous masculinities in the first place.[19] In turn, research has to balance a necessity to identify and reaffirm Indigenous masculinity, on the one hand, and acknowledge contingency, indeterminacy, and gender fluidity, on the other.[20] Scholars have thus repeatedly emphasized the need to uncover Indigenous epistemologies and regenerate positive masculinities in order to facilitate processes of empowerment and decolonization.[21]

In following this paradigm, I do not attempt to delineate the pathway through which "traditional" Indigenous masculinities (of Ojibwe or Sioux descent) became obfuscated by settler colonialism and then refractured through protest politics. Rather, I track the series of influences that made possible the specific performances of masculinity in which AIM members chose to engage. In so doing, I examine how expressions of Indigenous masculinity have been influenced by historical conditions of power and the violence of settler colonialism in order to delimit the range of viable expressions of masculinity available to those urban Indigenous men confronting colonial power in the Twin Cities and elsewhere.

## Experiences of Powerlessness and the Founding of the American Indian Movement

On July 28, 1968, about two hundred Indigenous people formed the American Indian Movement to confront and alleviate the persistent racism, discrimination, and socioeconomic disparities in the Twin Cities of Minneapolis/St. Paul.[22] When reflecting on the origins of AIM, Clyde Bellecourt (Ojibwe) stated: "Nobody was dealing with the racism, the police brutality, the dual system of justice, the poor housing conditions . . . Nobody was dealing with those kinds of issues; they just were too scared to stand up to the system."[23] An unidentified early member of AIM reflected, "I was fueled by anger and rage at the poor condition of the lives of Indians in the community. I began to see things that were happening to my people here in Minneapolis."[24] For a name, the organization first called itself "Concerned Indian Americans," but when someone pointed out the acronym CIA, they changed it to "American Indian Movement" or AIM.[25]

The American Indian Movement built upon an Indigenous history of urban migration, community organizing, and activism that reached back to the early twentieth century.[26] By 1968, Minneapolis boasted an estimated eight to ten thousand Indigenous residents (in a city of 489,000) and St. Paul an estimated four thousand (in a city of 309,000), who resided in red ghettoes.[27] A 1968 report by the League of Women Voters (LWV), a liberal civil rights organization, revealed long-standing grievances in the Indigenous community in Minneapolis: socioeconomic disparities, unemployment, substandard housing, poor health, a lack of access to social services, low education, a pervasive gender and racial discrimination, institutional bias, and a troubled relationship with the judicial system, including the police, the courts, and prisons. In addition, there was widespread confusion about bureaucratic procedures, competences, and services between the BIA (which offered services on reservations) and city and county agencies in the metropolitan area (which served all citizens).[28] LWV's report touched upon the intersections of gendered power structures, mechanisms of social control, and race. The report stated that Indigenous people received indifferent, difficult, and sometimes even prejudiced or hostile treatment from white bureaucrats in social service agencies and local state/city institutions in the Twin Cities, landlords, and employers.[29]

While AIM built on existent structures and a legacy of Indigenous activism in the Twin Cities, it was more confrontational in challenging racial discrimination and socioeconomic disparities than were existing Indigenous organizations.[30] Similarly to the Black Panthers, AIM considered community organizing as a tool of empowerment from hegemonic society.[31] AIM modelled two of its projects—the Indian Patrol and survival schools—after Black inventions. The American Indian Movement utilized the Panthers' Black Patrol as a role model to borrow forms of Black protest forms and resituate them into the particular Twin Cities context.[32] The organization also drew from the example of Black Freedom Schools and established two survival schools in the Twin Cities to empower local Indigenous people.[33]

The new organization attracted men and women alike, in particular from the younger and better-educated segment of the Indigenous community. The organization's membership—predominantly Ojibwe and some Sioux—was fairly representative of the Indigenous population of Minneapolis as a whole.[34] The multitribal, multiracial makeup was a reflection of the organization's early supratribal outlook and its efforts to instill its members with a sense of cultural pride in being Indigenous.[35] An early statement by the organization read, "The American Indian Movement is Indian and thinks Indian."[36]

The creation of a self-help organization such as AIM was in itself a radical departure from past Indigenous organizations that were controlled by non-Indigenous people.[37] The Indigenous activists in Minneapolis and St. Paul sought to respond to and alleviate persistent racism and socioeconomic disparities through a classical civil rights program. An objectives sheet stated that the organization sought "to upgrade the conditions in which the urban Indian lives, and to improve the image of the urban Indian." The paper continued: "Our main objective is to solicit and broaden opportunities for the urban Indian in order that he may enjoy his full rights as a citizen of these United States." Significant short-range steps into that direction involved the creation of programs that dealt with housing, youth, employment, and sensitizing industry to Indigenous culture(s), communication between the Indigenous and non-Indigenous community, and education. AIM's long-range objectives were to generate unity within the Indigenous community, to keep the community informed, to encourage community building, and to improve economic conditions.[38] According to participant-observer Fay Cohen, AIM functioned as an informal aid assistance network.[39]

The personal life stories of the male founders of AIM—mostly Ojibwe, like Dennis Banks (from Leech Lake, MN), George Mitchell (from Lac Courte Oreilles, WI), Harold GoodSky (from Nett Lake, MN), Clyde Bellecourt and Charles Deegan (both White Earth, MN), and Eddie Benton-Benai (from Lac Courtes Oreilles, WI)—paralleled that of many Indigenous men in the Twin Cities and elsewhere around the nation.[40] Their cross-cultural experiences involved cultural loss, social alienation, and self-destructive behavior that arose from their shared experience with colonial domination and assimilationist policies at the intersection of urban and reservation life.⁴¹ Although conditional and contextual, their personal life stories reflect a number of social institutions and experiences that were both gendered and (en)gendering in that they promoted conformity, adaptation, and assimilation into white settler society.

Dennis Banks, Clyde Bellecourt, and Russell Means (Lakota), who joined later, became AIM's most prominent leaders. Carter Camp (Ponca) and Vernon Bellecourt (Ojibwe), Clyde's brother, joined afterward. Banks grew up on the Leech Lake reservation in Northern Minnesota from the late 1930s through the early 1940s and was largely raised by his maternal grandparents, who practiced some of the traditional Ojibwe ways. From age five onward, he was forced to spend eleven years at various boarding schools without seeing his family. "At age sixteen," he later reflected, following years away from his relatives, "I considered myself a man."⁴² Following a four-year tour in the US Air Force, parts of which he served overseas in Korea and Japan, he finally ended up in Minneapolis. There, he spent several years drifting without direction, working a number of odd jobs, drinking, partying, turning to petty crime, and finding himself in and out of prison.⁴³ Clyde Bellecourt's childhood on White Earth reservation in Minnesota during the late 1930s and early 1940s lacked any cultural grounding in Ojibwe ways. Bellecourt traced that lack of cultural awareness to his parents' own traumatic boarding school experiences.⁴⁴ His early childhood and educational experiences involved three different schools during his five years of schooling, each of them more rigorous than the last in their enforcement of discipline and punishment. His increasing defiance and rebellion set him on a course that led him to spend the rest of his youth and early adult life in correctional facilities and prison for various felonies, including robbery, burglary, and parole violations.⁴⁵

The personal accounts of AIM's leaders highlight the significance of various agents of assimilation with dominant society in shaping their masculine and Indigenous subjectivities. Gender is built into society and produces and reproduces identities, practices, and institutions, replicating hegemonic conceptions about femininity and masculinity, as well as differences and inequalities with regard to race, gender, class, and sexuality.⁴⁶ Sociologist Joane Nagel has identified the very settler-colonial policies that were intended to eradicate Indigeneity as *the* underlying factors creating an English-speaking, educated, urban Indigenous population

Dennis Banks (Leech Lake Ojibwe) helped organize the meeting that led to the founding of the American Indian Movement in Minneapolis in July 1968. Dennis Banks and many other Indigenous men shared disorienting experiences—boarding schooling, military service, the urban experience, and correctional facilities—that led to the emergence of a "protest masculinity." The newly established organization sought to challenge racial discrimination, improve the conditions of urban Natives in the Twin Cities, and help its members overcome a sense of powerlessness. The organization's evolving ideology stressed its "Indianness," a sense of cultural pride, and dignity and opposition to whiteness. Photo taken at the takeover of the BIA headquarters in Washington, DC, in 1972. (Richard Erdoes Papers, Yale Collection of Western Americana, Beinecke Rare Book and Manuscript Library)

*Opposite:* Clyde Bellecourt (White Earth Ojibwe), cofounder of the American Indian Movement, rediscovered his Indigenous identity at Stillwater State Prison and became an effective activist in the Twin Cities. Bellecourt and other AIM leaders embraced an appearance and style that included elements of Indigenous culture, the counterculture, as well as mainstream fashion. This outlook reflected the newfound pride, showed cultural dignity, and commanded respect from whites. (Richard Erdoes Papers, Yale Collection of Western Americana, Beinecke Rare Book and Manuscript Library)

Eddie Benton-Benai (Lac Courte Oreilles Ojibwe) was raised in Ojibwe history, language, and traditions, giving him a firm cultural grounding. He worked at Stillwater State Prison during the early 1960s and recruited Clyde Bellecourt to organize the American Indian Folklore Group for Indigenous inmates in 1962. Benton-Benai was a cofounder of AIM and led the St. Paul chapter. In 1972, he became a founding director of the Red School House, a survival school in St. Paul. Photo taken in 1973 in New York City in front of the United Nations building during a rally to support the Wounded Knee occupation. (Richard Erdoes Papers, Yale Collection of Western Americana, Beinecke Rare Book and Manuscript Library)

Russell Means (Lakota) joined AIM in 1969. He became a prominent leader and helped organize notable events that drew widespread media coverage. Russell Means and Dennis Banks are probably the most photographed Native Americans in the twentieth century. During protest events, they frequently engaged in "Indians playing Indian" themes through appearance, rhetoric, street theatrics, and confrontational protests, thereby tapping into popular images of hypermasculine Indigeneity. In response, the news media often focused its attention on stereotypical imagery in order to sell the news story rather than the underlying issues. Photo taken at the occupation of the BIA headquarters in Washington, DC, in 1972. (Richard Erdoes Papers, Yale Collection of Western Americana, Beinecke Rare Book and Manuscript Library)

that was discontented and ready for mobilization in the 1960s and 1970s. Building on these findings, I argue that the emergence of an Indigenous "protest masculinity"—just as the entire Red Power movement itself—did not occur *despite* but rather *because of* assimilative US settler colonial policies.[47] Thus, the very colonial policies and dominant institutions intended to produce and reproduce Western ideals of hegemonic manliness ironically became the very forces that renewed, reinvigorated, and reinvented Indigenous masculinity.[48]

Autobiographical accounts indicate that four cross-cultural experiences profoundly impacted the identities of Indigenous men in AIM: boarding school education, the military, the urban experience, and correctional facilities. Gender scholar Scott Lauria Morgensen calls boarding schools, the military, and correctional institutions—which, in one way or another, have worked toward the subordination of Indigenous people—"militarized, incarcerating and other[wise] institutional[ized] forms of containment."[49] Through their gendered and engendering practices, these hypermasculine institutions continue to perpetuate hierarchical relations and hegemonic practices in terms of domination and subordination.[50] The urban context has also fundamentally transformed Indigenous men and masculinities.

First, boarding schools were set up with the express purpose of transforming Natives into Americans. Boarding schools were a continuous effort to take away Indigenous identities by repressing their language, eroding their values, beliefs, and spiritual systems, and instead

---

*Opposite:* Leonard Crow Dog (Lakota) from Rosebud Reservation, South Dakota, was a spiritual advisor to AIM and joined its numerous protests. By the early 1970s, Indigenous activists from the Twin Cities (overwhelmingly Ojibwe) had reached out to reservation traditionalists like Crow Dog (Lakota) to reconnect to their cultural heritage. Cultural borrowing aided many AIM members to reclaim their Indigeneity and assert their right to difference. Over time, this cultural alliance between reservation traditionalists and urban neo-traditionalists turned political, and AIM began to shift its focus away from urban issues and civil rights toward treaty rights, sovereignty, and self-determination. (Richard Erdoes Papers, Yale Collection of Western Americana, Beinecke Rare Book and Manuscript Library)

indoctrinating Indigenous children with the ideas, values, and behavior of dominant white society, along with Christianity.[51]

As institutional agents, schools are instrumental in the formation of gendered identities and in perpetuating hierarchical relations in terms of domination and subordination.[52] The express purpose of boarding schools was less to "civilize" Indigenous "savages" and to turn them into fully-fledged citizens than to keep them the subaltern, preparing Indigenous children for work in agriculture/industry (for boys) or domestics (for girls).[53] Faraway boarding schools distanced Indigenous children from their cultural and familiar ties and exposed them to a highly regimented school regime. Historian David Wallace Adam labels boarding schools as "total institutions" with a highly regimented military-style education involving uniforms, drills, marches, daily routine, strict discipline, a demerit system, and harsh corporal punishment to coerce Indigenous children into obedience.[54] Dennis Banks recalled the way his former teacher, a drill sergeant in the US Army, treated him and his classmates: "He had a harsh, grating voice and he never talked—he barked. He was always talking about the army, which made men out of dumb boys. He lectured us on how the army built character and how a soldier stood as high above a civilian as a human being stood above a chimp."[55]

As the above account illustrates, Indigenous children experienced boarding schools as disorienting, humiliating places of cultural alienation. The continuous repression of their language and the erosion of their beliefs and spiritual systems severely undermined their senses of self-worth. Frequent experiences included shame and punishment, extended absence from their families, runaway attempts, physical and mental abuse, and rotations to other boarding schools. Indigenous children's formative years were fundamentally shaped by this disconnect from their family and cultural ties and by an ongoing exposure to a racialized predicament that instilled in them a belief in Americans' superiority to Native peoples. When they returned to their relatives on the reservation, they had lost their own cultural grounding and found themselves trapped in a "cultural chasm" between two completely alien cultural systems.[56] Clyde Bellecourt attended a number of boarding schools and finally ended up at Red Wing State Training School, a harsh environment for juvenile offenders much like a military academy.

I found out that it was a strict, institutional environment—a kind of military academy. We wore uniforms. We marched to church. We shined our boots. . . . I was three hundred miles away from home in an environment where they housed some inmates with long criminal records. It was a transformative experience. . . . I faced a lot of racism. . . . It was a tremendous culture shock to get into that kind of setting.[57]

A major effect of the boarding school experience was Indigenous boys' internalization of racial oppression. In masculinity studies, the concept of internalized oppression can be utilized to explain the subtle mechanism of hegemonic manhood to sustain white privilege by inculcating an oppressed racial group with dominant stereotypes, values, and ideologies; in turn, internalized oppression perpetuates and reproduces white supremacy and racial subordination.[58] A case in point is Dennis Banks, who recounted that he came to believe in the version of history as taught by his white teachers. He began to hate himself for being Indigenous and to despise his own people. As he expressed the detrimental effects of his school experience,

When they took us once a week to the movies—the twelve-cent matinee—I cheered for Davy Crockett, Daniel Boone, and General Custer. I sided with the cavalry cutting down Indians. In my fantasies I was John Wayne rescuing the settlers from "red friends." I dreamed of being a cowboy. My teachers had done a great job of brainwashing me. They had made me into an "apple"—red outside but white inside.[59]

The impact of boarding schooling on Indigenous men came with a severe cognitive dissonance that instilled in them a sense of inferiority, disrespect for their own Indigenous culture and themselves, and also a "defensive othering," that is, an effort—often by children with mixed heritage—to distance themselves from the supposedly inferior group, the traditional reservation people, often "full-bloods."[60] During the 1960s, metaphors such as being an "apple," a "Hang-around-the-fort-Indian," or "Uncle Tomahawk" were widely used to refer to those Native Americans who were less willing to commit to social change and to "other" them as being internally colonized.

Second, the US military fundamentally impacted Indigenous men in AIM through its ideology of hegemonic masculinity and set of embodied practices.[61] Boarding schools and their militarized pedagogy for citizenship instilled a sense of duty in flag and country and directly channeled Indigenous men into the US military.[62] For many boarding school graduates, joining the US military represented a natural choice. "I found myself in the military after getting out of high school," Dennis Banks reflected, "and to me it was the only way to really express your manhood was to go into the U.S. military."[63] A high number of AIM's male activists were veterans of peacetime service at home or wartime service in Korea or, more frequently, Vietnam.

The US military introduced Indigenous men to a contradictory culture of toughness that stressed rugged individualism and autonomy, on the one hand, and subordination and surveillance, on the other.[64] As such, it promoted a masculine culture that involved constant validation of what it meant to be a man—through masculinized and masculinizing practices that involved a culture of conformity (via displays of power and dominance and, for that matter, obedience and oppression) as well as through a culture of non-conformity, which included drinking, fighting, and frequently changing sexual relationships.[65] Marine veteran Woody Kipp (Blackfeet) from Montana remembered that "the Marine Corps in my experience promoted an environment that glamorized drinking and made it integral to the persona of a Marine—drinking and toughness were twins I came to know well."[66]

Serving in the colonizer's army highlighted injustices at home and abroad. In 1956, while stationed in Japan, Dennis Banks witnessed police violence against nonviolent demonstrators—local farmers, students, monks and nuns—who protested against the expansion of the Tachikawa Airfield, a US base near Tokyo. "I felt sick at what I had seen and ashamed of the uniform I was wearing."[67] In the end, the US military halted the effort to expand the base; however the terrible image of "Native people fighting for their land" remained with him during his activist years.[68] His time in the service also led to another realization: "I had been guarding the ramparts of the American Empire, but now felt like those Crow and Arikara Indians who, after scouting for Custer and fighting on behalf of the whites, were pitted against their own brothers, the Cheyenne and

Lakota." He recalled that the Japanese were called "gooks," "slopes," and "slant-eyes" by his fellow American soldiers. Yet those insulted were not much different from himself. After all, Banks reflected, "was I not a 'slant eye,' as all American Indians are? The American Air Force, which I had thought of as a friend, turned out to be an enemy."[69]

During the Vietnam War era, Indigenous soldiers increasingly questioned why they should put their lives on the line for a government that continued to impose its colonial policies and practices on "other" people abroad and Native people at home in America. On his tour in Vietnam (1964–1968) with the Marine Corps, Woody Kipp (Blackfeet) remembered that "the white marines often saw me as a historical oddity" and confronted him with stereotypical images, asking whether he still lived in a tipi, rode horses, and hunted buffalo.[70] "I was the only Indian in our outfit, and I went by the generic name of Chief," he recalled.[71] At the same time, local Vietnamese people noted his physical resemblance to them.[72] Kipp also had firsthand experiences with racism and, while riding a truck, observed a fellow Marine hurl a block of concrete at an elderly Vietnamese. It was then, he realized, "that what I had seen had in fact taken place over and over as the Europeans stormed into a so-called New World and into the American West. Other old men—my grandfathers—had suffered similar treatment at the hands of American soldiers."[73]

Soon, Kipp began to draw parallels between the treatment of the Vietnamese and his Blackfeet people at the hands of the Americans. He realized that during both colonial and imperialist endeavors, "other" people had suffered from "the same hatred and contempt" that was an assertion of racial and national superiority.[74] These and many other comparable experiences reshaped the perception Indigenous men had of themselves and their place in American society. As a consequence, many homecoming Indigenous Vietnam veterans turned into advocates for Indigenous rights at home.[75]

Third, urban relocation and the urban experience played another major factor in the emergence of an Indigenous "protest masculinity." For Indigenous men and women, the urban context entailed many similar, yet distinct experiences. For Indigenous men, the Twin Cities urban context fostered experiences of powerlessness, alienation, and emasculation. Indigenous men frequently found themselves economically, socially, and culturally marginalized. According to an article by sociologist Joseph C. Westermeyer titled "Indian Powerlessness in Minnesota," published in *Society* in 1973, Indigenous men stood at the very bottom of the gendered and racialized order in the state of Minnesota in terms of education, jobs, and employment: they were the least educated, occupied lower status jobs, and could find less employment than their female counterparts who worked in slightly higher status positions.[76] Indigenous men's marginal position was partly due to "a subtle bias" in education "to keep Indian males in a socioeconomic position not only inferior to non-Indian males, but often inferior to Indian women as well," which accounted for the fact that Indigenous men tended to be less educated than Indigenous women and deprived of their role as breadwinners.[77]

The overwhelming evidence suggests that within the urban context of the Twin Cities, Indigenous men experienced an erosion of their role as family breadwinners and a reversal of gender roles. To a large extent, 1960s and 1970s American male identity revolved around notions of male breadwinning and female homemaking. Women's paid employment and the relative loss of men's position as breadwinners undermined their position as head of the household.[78] The fact that social workers "wielded great power" over Indigenous families, ranging from personal decision-making over the finances of their Indigenous clients to the power to place Indigenous children in white foster homes, further eroded male positions of power.[79] From the 1950s through 1970s, the removal of Indigenous children and their adopting out to non-Indigenous parents reached endemic proportions; this concerted, genocidal effort severely undermined the integrity of Indigenous family structures.[80]

In addition, social institutions practiced gross racial bias against Indigenous people in Minnesota.[81] Most social agencies having the greatest contact to Indigenous people or serving their needs—the courts, police, welfare agencies, schools, clinics, social agencies, and so on—were almost exclusively occupied by non-Indigenous personnel. Indigenous women occupied higher status positions (nurses, secretaries) than did Indigenous men, who were in the lowest positions (janitors, maintenance).[82] According to Westermeyer social institutions were "exclusively white-dominated and white oriented in their services."[83] The needs of Indigenous people were either "blatantly ignored or poorly handled."[84] Paternalistic attitudes pervaded federal, state, county, and local institutions from top to bottom. The overall structure of this institutional framework "tacitly implied that Indian people are incapable of assuming responsibility for their education, health services, social welfare, religious needs and so forth," according to Westermeyer.[85] The bureaucracy operated under guidelines to treat everybody the same despite obvious cultural differences, the article elaborated. This pseudo-egalitarianism of "forcing . . . foreign social values on a minority people" resulted in a "gross inequality in services" and amounted to "ethnocide," Westermeyer claimed.[86]

Perhaps more than any other ethnic minority, Indigenous men felt the brunt of assimilationist federal policies and mainstream pressures to conform to dominant norms and ideals that expected the man to be the wage earner and head of the family. Away from their tribal community, such men were no longer the traditional providers and protectors of their families and—in the words of Donald Fixico—"lacked the opportunity to gain respect in a traditional manner."[87] Many could not cope with their paternal responsibilities and absented themselves from their families, leaving their family without a provider and a male role model. "The men in our community were defeated by unemployment and alcohol. The men didn't see a future," Clyde Bellecourt said of the impact this collective experience had upon Indigenous men.[88] This was somewhat different to how Indigenous women handled their experiences: "The women were raising the kids; they looked the future in the eye every day," as Bellecourt put it.[89]

In the Twin Cities, social hierarchies and work impacted the marginal position of Indigenous men and the way they performed their manhood. Undereducated and often unemployed, Indigenous men wielded no institutional power, as middle-class men did; in response, many compensated for the inequalities in power relations with physical ability, similar to working-class men. For younger Indigenous men, this involved fighting, drinking, machismo, and displays of sexual prowess. Older men—who could no longer assert dominance over younger men—sometimes adopted macho identities. In so doing, they masked their own formal disempowerment and asserted their dominance at home over their family. Also, whereas younger men actively sought out sex, older men sought companionship in interpersonal relations.[90] Drinking can be seen as a survival mechanism of urban Indigenous men to escape the pressures of mainstream society.[91]

As a consequence of the severe socioeconomic disparities and anti-Indian sentiment, Indigenous men in the Twin Cities found it hard to find their place and position in society. The inability to provide for their families left many with feelings of powerlessness and dependency, rejection and cultural dissonance, as well as negative self-image and a lack of self-respect. The image of the emasculated Indigenous male unable to survive in modern America was also reflected in the attitudes of Minneapolis's (white-dominated) agency personnel, as a 1968 survey by the University of Minnesota revealed.[92] Popular notions of Indigenous men trapped in a cycle of dependency and emasculation contrasted sharply with white, middle-class expectations of relative prosperity, upward mobility, competition, and social and economic stability in suburban Minneapolis.[93] Navigating between these conflicting cultural notions of manhood created cultural confusion, alienation, anger, and cognitive dissonance among Indigenous men. Feelings of alienation and powerlessness frequently found expression in alcoholism.[94]

Finally, the judicial system—police, courts, and correctional facilities—constituted another element in Indigenous men's formative experiences.[95] In the Twin Cities, much of Indigenous men's collective experiences with the criminal justice system stemmed from institutionalized racism, a biased application of law, and a deep-rooted "historic distrust."[96]

A report by the Minnesota Advisory Committee to the US Commission on Civil Rights revealed severe disparities in local law enforcement, courts, and corrections in the Minneapolis Indigenous community. The report read that between 1970 and mid-1971, Indigenous people accounted for one-third of all arrests made for drunkenness in Minneapolis; yet only half of those were made because of disorderly conduct.[97] It also revealed that Indigenous people were "grossly underrepresented as employees [and] significantly overrepresented in the numbers of convicts and arrests."[98] According to the committee's findings, Native Americans accounted for roughly 10 percent of all inmate admissions to state penal institutions but only about 2 percent of employees in corrections.[99] The report also included strong testimony alleging the Minnesota Police Department was "unequal in its application of law in Native and white communities."[100] Native Americans stated that they were frequently stopped and searched by police.[101] Common Indigenous experiences with law enforcement officers included indifference, harassment, or brutality that ranged from abusive language to excessive force in outright violation of their civil rights.[102] It is for these reasons that in his autobiography Dennis Banks claimed "for Indians, doing time in jail is almost a traditional rite of passage.... We wind up in the slammer because we cannot pay for an attorney. We have to deal with a public defender who, in most cases, persuades us to make a quick plea-bargain deal."[103] Public data confirmed Banks's assertion.[104]

During the 1960s and 1970s, many Indigenous prison inmates came to see themselves as political prisoners in the struggle for self-determination. They drew direct connections between their racial/cultural heritage, US colonialism, and the criminal justice system.[105] To the present day, Indigenous people assert that the high incarceration rate of their men is a reflection of their disempowered and emasculated status within US colonial society.[106] They claim that the imprisonment of Indigenous men, defenders of their tribal nations, stands for the gendered influence and control of dominant society over their lives. Indigenous women's calls of "Where are our men? Where are our warriors?" can be understood within this larger colonial context of occupation, imprisonment, and policing. The abnormally high rate of incarceration among Indigenous men within the settler nation-state is caused by gendered racism, as well as the fact that Indigenous activists are commonly seen as a threat to the very existence of the settler nation.[107] Exposure to militarized and incarcerating forms of institutional containment has worked toward the denial or erasure of Indigenous identities.[108]

When reflecting on the birthplace of the American Indian Movement, its founders alternatively name Stillwater Prison, or the bar culture in Minneapolis, not a community meeting that started AIM.[109] There is ample evidence that the new organization was "cooked up in the Minnesota penitentiary," as Clyde's brother Vernon put it.[110] According to sociologist James W. Messerschmidt, "crime by men is a form of social practice invoked as a resource, when other resources are unavailable, for accomplishing masculinity."[111] While "doing time," Dennis Banks and Clyde Bellecourt underwent significant changes and reinvented their subjectivities. Anthropologist Rachel Bonney has found that while in prison, AIM leaders underwent a "conversion experience" and developed an ideology that allowed them "to accept their Indianness, to be proud of their Indian heritage, and to communicate this newly-developed pride to other Indians and to non-Indians to create a positive image."[112]

During his imprisonment at Stillwater penitentiary, Bellecourt remembered: "I knew I was Indian, but I didn't know anything about 'Indian,' absolutely nothing—language, culture, tradition . . . I would fight anybody that said bad about Indian people, but many times, I didn't know why I was fightin'."[113] Internalized oppression meant, Bellecourt said, that "I was convinced that I was an ignorant, dirty savage—so I just gave up."[114] This changed as Eddie Benton-Banai (Ojibwe), a cultural instructor and James Donahue, a white caseworker, persuaded him to start the American Indian Cultural Folklore Group. Benton-Benai and Donahue both believed that teaching Native inmates about their culture and traditions would allow them to reformulate their Indigenous and masculine identities and to break the vicious cycle that brought them into prison in the first place. Enlisting the aid of Clyde Bellecourt was essential for the formation of a cultural study group, because his bond with other Native inmates reached back into childhood.[115] Other than Bellecourt and Banks, Benton-Benai's (Ojibwe) personal history involved a full immersion in Ojibwe language and the Midewiwin traditions of his ancestors, giving him a strong sense of cultural identity that many of his Indigenous counterparts lacked.[116]

During his years in Stillwater Prison, Bellecourt had a life-changing experience. While in solitary confinement for disciplinary infractions and realizing that living the life of a criminal no longer constituted a resource for achieving masculinity, Clyde Bellecourt set out to reinvent his identity by drawing from various elements of Indigeneity such as Ojibwe and Sioux culture.[117] This transformative experience led to a renewed sense of identity, self-worth, and pride. "For the first time in my life," he explained, "I realized that I wasn't a savage. I wasn't filthy and I wasn't ignorant. I was smart and capable."[118] This transformative experience instilled him with a newfound commitment to his people and ultimately helped him launch an organization for reform to help other Indigenous people in a similar situation.[119]

"Doing time" in prison was also one in a series of many life-changing experiences for Dennis Banks and eventually led him to reconsider his masculinity and participate in a larger social movement for change. Between 1964 and 1968, he served what amounted to a total of two and a half years for burglary, forgery, and parole violation.[120] Yet it was the Stillwater experience that "politicized" him. The political protest and social change underway in American society tremendously impacted him. Realizing "all these different kinds of people trying so hard to straighten this country out," Banks recognized the need for an Indigenous movement for change, as otherwise Indian Country would be passed over once again:

> It had a tremendous impact on me, what was going on right here in the United States; and I began to realize that there was a hell of a situation in this country—all these different kinds of people trying so hard to straighten this country out. It was inside the jug that I thought there has to be an Indian movement, too. Otherwise, it'll pass us by again. And realizing then what was really going on, I made a commitment that there would be an Indian movement.... When I got out of prison, I called George Mitchell ... to get together the whole Indian community in Minneapolis behind a new effort to fight the government, a new effort to begin making some of the changes that we needed.[121]

The drinking culture that emerged along Franklin Avenue attracted many Indigenous residents, especially young men. There, they could socialize and share their daily frustrations with others, drown their sorrows, and, for a time, forget their problems, engage in a manly activity, strengthen male friendships, experience romantic success with women, and overcome feelings of inferiority. Some drinking circles were composed of veterans that shared memories of their service days. Banks remembered,

> We [Fred Morgan, Bojack, George Mitchell, and Floyd Westerman] were all drinking in those years, ... sometimes going on binges for days and

even weeks. But when we were together, we had good times. Often we spent the night talking of the old days, laughing and remembering all the crazy things we used to do. We had all served in the military, and during our get-togethers, would talk about our boarding school buddies who had never come back from the wars in Korea and Vietnam. Many times we cried. We eventually all lived on Fourth Avenue, the center of Indian life in Minneapolis.[122]

The bar culture instilled Banks with a sense of belonging and made him familiar with the Twin Cities Indigenous community. Neither Banks nor Bellecourt hid the fact that their lives involved alcohol, crime, and prison—all of which in turn explained their aura of authenticity and enabled their followers to identify more easily with them.[123]

The cumulative effects of prolonged exposure to dominant institutions—boarding schools, the military, the judicial system, and the way gender was built into those experiences—together with the urban experience, severely impacted Indigenous men and masculinities. During much of their lives, Indigenous men in AIM were exposed to a setting typified by hierarchical relations, sex segregation, male culture, and race and gender bias.[124] Each of these patriarchal institutions was guided by another impulse to transform men and masculinities according to hegemonic ideals—whether it was to turn "savages" into citizens and converts or civilians into soldiers and "build men" or involved a penal system bent on "correcting" them.[125] Each social institution in one way or another had the ultimate purpose of transforming marginalized masculinities to meet hegemonic norms and ideals. Accordingly, the federal Indian policies of termination and relocation served the express purpose of making Native Americans less Native and more American, rendering them invisible in the melting pot of urban America.[126]

The shared historical conditions of subalternity and sustained exposure to dominant ideals of gender affected Indigenous men in complex and ambiguous ways. This showed, first, in gender relations (and the replication of hegemonic gender norms); second, in cultural alienation (and efforts to overcome a severance from traditional life while struggling against marginalization from hegemonic society); and third, in efforts to challenge racial discrimination and their own powerlessness in the Twin Cities through exaggerated claims to masculine power.

First, for many male AIM activists, sustained interaction with institutional agents and hegemonic society channeled the ways they conceptualized and practiced their masculinities. They did so in accordance with dominant gender norms and the way these in turn produced and reproduced male privilege and power inequalities.[127] Reflecting on his experiences with institutional agents—eleven years in boarding schools, four years in the US Air Force, more than two years in Stillwater Prison—Dennis Banks remembered, "I had been institutionalized for a long time, so it became very easy for me to fall into a routine."[128] Robert Alexander Innes (Plains Cree) and Kim Anderson (Cree/Métis) have drawn attention to the ways Indigenous men's conforming to hegemonic ideals has contributed to their subordination as a group. Indigenous men's adherence to hegemonic cultural ideals has subordinated them to white male privilege, and they receive male privilege through the oppression of those who are perceived as weaker.[129]

Male sexism and chauvinism would come under frequent attack from Indigenous women. Historian Devon Abbott Mihesuah (Choctaw) pointed out that Indigenous women within the Red Power movement frequently considered themselves in a condition of "double colonization." They felt oppressed, first, through racial inequality and colonial domination and, second, via male privilege and female subordination.[130] Indigenous women spoke of a cultural disarmament of their men, who had lost their connection with traditional notions of manhood. They also highlighted the dynamics of internalized colonialism that sustained patriarchal power, hierarchal relations, and hegemonic practices that kept Native Americans oppressed in the first place.[131]

Second, the life stories of Indigenous men in AIM involved the disorienting experiences of cultural loss, social alienation, and self-destructive behavior at the intersection of urban and reservation life. This generation of Indigenous male activists had firsthand experienced the assimilationist pressures to conform to notions of hegemonic colonial masculinity while seeking to retain their Indigeneity. AIM's male leaders struggled with what historian Julie Davis calls a "legacy of multigenerational cultural alienation."[132] Raised at the intersection of urban and reservation life, many AIM members had spent much of their lives in a cultural and spiritual void that led them to "become alienated from their tribal traditions, ashamed of their Indianness, while simultaneously rejecting the dominant society as well," according to sociologist Rachel Bonney.[133] Her study found that these firsthand experiences of alienation, discrimination, and maladjustment were among "the primary factors leading to the establishment of AIM."[134] AIM members' heightened awareness translated into an effort to bridge their cultural chasm. Thus, AIM's ideology sought to engender its members with ethnic pride in their Indigeneity and to strengthen their sense of personal empowerment and community membership through the concept of Pan-Indianism.

Finally, Indigenous men in the Twin Cities—just like other young men from minority communities elsewhere—reacted to pervasive conditions of alienation and powerlessness. In circumstances like these, typical responses involve exhibiting a version of protest masculinity and involvement in urban unrest.[135] The disruptive forces of settler colonialism and modernity continue to disadvantage Indigenous men through a rampant racial and gender bias.[136] The urban conditions of the Twin Cities have thus delimited the range of viable expressions of masculinity available to urban Indigenous men.

However, as much as these disorienting experiences served to alienate and disadvantage Indigenous men, they also provided them with the tools for their own empowerment. Boarding school allowed for an educated, eloquent Indigenous leadership.[137] Military service, and the way discipline, perseverance, and toughness was built into it, was another source of empowerment. "Being a military person—we gained experience and discipline and determination in terms of what we needed to do when we get out of the military. A lot of what I learned in the military—discipline as a way to control our anger and direct it in a very positive way to make changes," Dennis Banks reflected.[138] Prisons, the most oppressive patriarchal institutions of all, were also key sites for reinventing Indigenous masculine identities, as the life-changing experiences of Clyde Bellecourt and Dennis Banks show.[139] Finally, the urban experience led to the recognition of shared problems and sparked the emergence of a generic Indigeneity that helped in the formation of AIM itself.[140] In combination, these shared experiences among Indigenous men instigated the emergence of a "protest masculinity" that coincided with the founding of AIM. The right timing and the larger social change underway in American society enabled AIM to come about and be effective.[141]

## The Indian Patrol and the Emergence of an Indigenous "Protest Masculinity"

The emergence of the "protest masculinity" can be traced to the severe existential crisis faced by the urban Indigenous community of Minneapolis. From early on, Indigenous men and women within AIM defined much of their gendered subjectivities through confronting the white institutions they held accountable for their powerlessness and emasculation. Within the urban context of Minneapolis, representatives of the bureaucracy were overwhelmingly coded as white, with an upper- and middle-class background. These included social service workers and welfare bureaucrats, teachers and school officials, police officers, and lawyers and judges, the representatives of the city's white power structure. Minneapolis Natives encountered them on a daily basis in welfare agencies, schools, police, courts, and prisons. To them, they impersonated white male supremacy and the exercising of power inequalities. It is perhaps no coincidence that, from its inception, much of AIM's protest activism was directed against those agents of colonialism that the Indigenous community associated with its powerlessness: the police and the Twin City's white bureaucracy, in particular the BIA, schoolteachers and administrators, and Christian churches.[142]

The Indian Patrol was an initial effort to combat the gendered racism of the Minneapolis Police. Minneapolis showed a distinct racial bias against Indigenous men and women in the Phillips community south of downtown Minneapolis. Across the urban Indigenous community, there was a widespread belief that Indigenous people were targeted and arrested in situations where a white person would not be, principally when it came to drunkenness and misdemeanors.[143] There were rampant complaints that police applied the law unequally within the Indigenous community.[144] Complaints against police involved the unnecessary use of physical force, derogatory language, and lengthy bureaucratic procedures for complaints.[145]

Apparently, police officers parked paddy wagons behind a bar, then walked in through the front doors. As they made arrests, they caught those who attempted to escape through the back exit in the opened doors of the paddy wagon.[146] Jay White Crow (Seneca) remembered a typical raid: "They'd take their nightsticks and bang on the counters and say—'all right you sons-of-bitches, you're all under arrest. Get out there and get in that paddy wagon.'"[147] Indigenous men were arrested by police officers in disproportionately high numbers in a calculated effort to supply the city's correctional system with unpaid labor.[148]

Most arrests were made on Fridays and Saturdays, and those arrested could not get out until the courts opened on Mondays.[149] Pat Bellanger (Ojibwe) alleged that young men were regularly beat up by police and that the arrests put Indigenous families in jeopardy, because men were laid off work.[150] Studies of the League of Women Voters, a nonpartisan grassroots organization lobbying for reform legislation, partially confirmed these law enforcement practices.[151] These incidents had led to a feeling of embattlement in the urban community in Minneapolis and polarized the relationship between Indigenous residents and local police. The Twin Cities Indigenous community began to see police as "the representative of an unjust and oppressive establishment," as one report by LVW put it.[152]

The idea of the Indian Patrol drew from the example of the Black Patrol that operated out of Oakland in 1966, the local Panther's Patrol in northern Minneapolis, and a previous, unsuccessful attempt by local Indigenous students to set up a patrol.[153] Bonnie Wallace (Ojibwe) and Pat Bellanger (Ojibwe)—who later organized an Indian Patrol in St. Paul—accompanied Dennis Banks and Clyde Bellecourt to meetings with the Black Panthers in North Minneapolis.[154] Bellecourt formed a close connection with Matthew Eubanks, a Black Panther who had organized civil disobedience campaigns in the South.[155] "The Black Panther Movement, well, they were beyond radical," Bellanger recalled. "They were militant. Their rhetoric was interesting and very powerful."[156] The local Minneapolis Black Panther chapter influenced AIM profoundly.

"The next thing I knew Dennis and Clyde and those guys were all wearing red berets and speaking some of the same language of the Black Panthers," she remembered.[157]

Apparently, the Black Panther Party (BPP) model of manhood and militancy strongly resonated with Banks and Bellecourt. The BPP's ideology insisted on calls for self-determination and demands for a revolutionary international socialism. The BPP called attention to police brutality, poverty, and racial discrimination that plagued the Black community. The Panthers considered the Black ghetto a colonized nation at war with oppressive police forces and embraced community control and self-help. The Panthers' masculinist liberation ideology encouraged its most strident message through the Panthers' stress on manhood and armed self-defense.[158] The Panthers' stance at the steps of California's State Capitol in Sacramento in May 1967 to protest a gun bill to prohibit armed Panthers from policing the police drew national attention. News media coverage overwhelmingly focused on Black men, rather than women.[159] Media images of the Black masculine militancy—brash, gun-toting, profanity-speaking, in black uniforms and with clenched fists and guns—projected manly pride and generated fear among white people.[160] The Black Panther Party endorsed the gun as a symbol of empowerment and a tool for liberation; to others, it became an extension of manhood.[161] The BPP's self-representation communicated to America a powerful image of Black masculinity, debunking stereotypes of Black emasculation and powerlessness, projecting defiance to white America, and instilling self-respect and pride into Black men.[162]

The Panthers addressed an immediate and common concern of the urban Indigenous community of the Twin Cities—police brutality. The Panthers' paramilitary character reflected their attempt to halt police harassment. The Panthers publicly stressed their right to armed self-defense against so-called legalized forms of state violence. Black Patrols shadowed squad cars and monitored police behavior in order to discourage derogatory language and unnecessary violence from police and to protect Black neighborhoods. The Oakland Panthers conducted armed citizens' patrols, and when they observed a police patrol, they displayed their weapons openly in accordance with California law. Panthers utilized the gun to defend themselves from police, to challenge and intimidate white authority, and to empower the Black community via individual acts of defiance. Frequently, Black Patrols carried with them a "pocket lawyer" on basic legal rights. Panthers documented police behavior, followed police arrests, and posted bail for the release of those taken into custody.[163]

The Indian Patrol drew on the Black example. Beginning on August 23, 1968, about twenty men, women, and teenagers, primarily Indigenous people but also some Black and white people, began to monitor police relations on the streets, initially on foot and later using red cars, two-way radios, tape recorders, and cameras.[164] They utilized observation, documentation, and their physical presence to combat police misconduct within the larger East Franklin Area, followed squad cars, and organized lawyers and bail.[165] Akin to the Panthers, AIM considered police as the armed guardians of white oppression.[166] Yet, other than the Panthers' emphasis on armed self-defense as a tool for masculine empowerment, AIM stressed nonviolent methods.[167] AIM understood the implications of projecting a distinct image. The Black example proved that visual self-representation and police monitoring could act as a deterrent to police brutality and function as a source of self-identification.[168] On their patrols along Franklin Avenue, AIM activists sent a powerful message to the Indigenous community that they would not back down under white pressure but rather would confront police, the arm of the white establishment, head on.[169]

The Indian Patrol was among the first visible signs of an Indigenous protest masculinity.[170] The state of crisis in the East Franklin neighborhood, exemplified by the image of the paddy wagon rounding up Indigenous men, offered a context in which men could stand up and confront white police officers, the very embodiment of white oppression in Minneapolis. Apparently, Bellecourt stopped numerous fights on Franklin Avenue.[171] He provided a role model for many, particularly young Indigenous men. The *Minneapolis Tribune* stated, "Indians recall specific instances of Bellecourt's courage on the streets with awe—Bellecourt walking into a gunfight . . . , Bellecourt cooling down belligerents, Bellecourt taking on troublemakers himself and Bellecourt gently escorting drunks home."[172] Street occurrences like these offered Indigenous men opportunities to step forward, to prove themselves, and to demonstrate their commitment to community and the new organization. According to participant-observer Fay Cohen, the Indian Patrol served as a "proving ground out of which emerged the men who were to become the leaders of AIM."[173] The Indian Patrol operated with the tacit approval of the city's mayor.[174] Initially, police officers welcomed the establishment of the Indian Patrol.[175] Many police officers saw the removal of drunks as a positive contribution.[176] Soon, however, police officers claimed that Indian Patrollers made arrests difficult and that their presence frequently came close to interference, often resulting in "verbal hassles."[177] There was also a pattern of conflict between police and Bellecourt, who found himself particularly targeted by police.[178] Police officers also grew increasingly disturbed about AIM's anti-white, anti-police attitude.[179]

The significance of the Indian Patrol, however, lay in its symbolic role vis-à-vis police, rather than its actual intervention with police, which was quite minimal and has been overstated.[180] Sociologist Fay Cohen characterized the Indian Patrol as "a quiet, but recurrent protest demonstration."[181] By maintaining high visibility and physical presence in the Native community, AIM demonstrated organizational unity and established itself as an advocacy group for Native people that would not shy away from confronting white institutions. Indeed, much of AIM's early appeal stemmed from its claim that the Indian Patrol was effective in halting the brutalization and harassment of Indigenous people, whereas in fact there was no conclusive evidence to back this claim up. The immediate effect of the Indian Patrol upon police practices is inconclusive, in part due to its short existence and a lack of data.[182]

The Indian Patrol provided a striking expression of ideological belief and challenge to police authority, which many within the urban Native community viewed as "militant."[183] AIM's self-proclaimed outlook as an advocate for Native people foreshadowed its later outlook as a warrior society.[184] At the same time, the organization's evolving ideology stressed its "Indianness"—pride in Native culture and heritage—and opposition to whiteness.[185] In endorsing a generic Indigeneity that served as a tool of identification, AIM activists ultimately forecast a gendered transformation of Native peoples, a prerequisite to their decolonization.

The American Indian Movement identified Christian churches as another main enemy. Christian churches severely impacted Native people through the dispossession of their lands, the weakening and disruption of traditional economies and sociopolitical structures, and cultural repression and assimilation. Christianity was a powerful weapon in US colonialism, as is evident in its collective, cross-generational impact. At a variety of national church meetings, members of AIM successfully confronted Christian clergy with demands for support. Through a combination of, alternatively, charm and persuasion, or moral pressure and physical intimidation, Dennis Banks and Clyde Bellecourt confronted the Lutheran churches and ultimately won their support.[186] In general, Christian church groups such as the Lutherans were sympathetic to Native activism. A number of factors—a belief in social justice (as shown in churches' support of the Black civil rights struggle in the Deep South); a deep sense of guilt in churches' complicity in US colonialism; and AIM's willingness to extort guilt money—all came into play.[187] The substantial support by Christian churches was a viable resource for AIM to expand its increasingly radical road of activism.[188]

In the early 1970s, the Indigenous community of the Twin Cities established survival schools in a far-reaching effort to remake their children's Indigenous and gendered identities vis-à-vis settler society. The educational alternative came in response to the Twin Cities Public School system, which massively failed Indigenous students.[189] Two survival schools emerged in 1972, one in Minneapolis (AIM Survival School, later renamed the Heart of the Earth Survival School) and another in St. Paul (Red School House).[190]

## Survival Schools and Recasting Race, Gender, and Memory

Survival schools capitulated a conscious decolonization effort through cultural revitalization, political consciousness-raising, and academic performance.[191] The three-pronged school curriculum—consisting of academic, cultural, and political components—sought to provide students with basic academic skills, positive self-image and pride in their cultural heritage, and a heightened political consciousness.[192] Survival school educators encouraged their students to understand their cultural and racial identities not only as members of specific tribes but also in terms of a broader, more general sense of Indigeneity.[193]

Survival schools constituted an innovative educational concept and learning environment that would allow for the (re)generation of positive identities.[194] To a large extent, these mental decolonization efforts were facilitated by various dynamically interrelated mnemonic practices of cultural remembering and, for that matter, forgetting.[195] Survival school educators promoted a sense of Indigeneity by teaching their students about the collective history and shared historical experience of Indigenous people with US settler colonialism, a common belief system, and current political realities that connected them to other Native people.[196] While Native children retained their specific tribal identities, they also began to see themselves as Native people in a more general sense.[197] History and politics classes were taught from a decidedly Indigenous perspective, which was both empowering and liberating. In response to a dominant discourse in which Native Americans were either absent, distorted, or denigrated, survival school educators provided a counternarrative that stressed a commanding presence, rich cultural heritage, and pride in "Indianness." These classes emphasized Indigenous people's contributions to American culture, history, and politics.[198] "We wanted to teach our kids the truth about Indian people," Clyde Bellecourt explained, "who our real leaders were and what they said and did, and also the contributions that they made, and that some old white man in lace shirt and powdered wig was not our 'Great White Father.'"[199]

This new teaching approach involved a gendered reconfiguration of Indigenous masculinity and femininity as part of the mental decolonization process. There were lessons about men's and women's gendered roles, responsibilities, and spheres of life.[200] When reflecting on his own boarding school experience, Dennis Banks remembered that "there were no pictures on the walls of Native Americans or Indian heroes such as Sitting Bull or Geronimo. Instead, there were pictures and posters of white presidents and generals. Nothing could be seen that would indicate that we were in a school for Indian children."[201] In response, survival schools constituted part of a larger effort to reclaim, revitalize, and reinvent the cultural heritage of Native America. Cultural and history classes recounted the lives of notable Indigenous women, as well as the political and military exploits of visionary chiefs and warriors such as Tecumseh, Sitting Bull, Red Cloud, and Geronimo, who confronted

US settler colonialists through diplomacy and war.[202] Educational efforts worked toward the regeneration of positive Indigenous masculinities and femininities. The recasting of the memory of a past Native America from one associated with defeat and surrender into one highlighting victory and triumph involved the notion of defiant nationalism.[203]

However, external criticisms that survival schools lacked academic standards and promoted anti-white attitudes among Native students were not easy to dismiss.[204] Historian Julie Davis and anthropologist Sonja Schierle have defused claims that survival schools were used as "revolutionary indoctrination camps" or "AIM training grounds," yet they independently confirmed that there was ample evidence that survival schools supported anti-white attitudes.[205] Schierle, a German Fulbright scholar and visiting student at the University of Minneapolis, Minnesota, who spent the first half of 1978 at the Heart of the Earth Survival School as a participant-observer, recalled that male AIM leaders frequently dropped by at the Heart of the Earth Survival School and promoted anti-white attitudes.[206] In-depth research by Julie Davis revealed widespread negative generalizations among teachers about whiteness, some of which were internalized by Native students.[207] Survival schools were an ideal vehicle for the dissemination of ideas about the newly developed pride in Indigeneity. The negative portrayal of whiteness stemmed in part from a desire to reaffirm and reinvent positive notions of Indigeneity.[208] In part, it also served to counter degrading images of Indigenous history and culture perpetuated by dominant society.[209]

## Conclusion

In the Twin Cities and elsewhere across the nation, Indigenous men were confronted with their own alienation, powerlessness, and emasculation on a daily basis. Their hypomasculinity was reflected in abysmal socioeconomic disparities and gendered racism encompassing figures from the entire spectrum of urban life: landlords, employers, agency personnel, city administrators, police, and teachers. Indigenous men's complex situatedness in hegemonic society involved a number of formative influences that inculcated them with hegemonic ideals of manliness while also exposing them to cultural alienation. Together, these conflictual experiences provided Indigenous men with a strong foundation from which they could relate to each other and as a source of empowerment that came in the formation of a "protest masculinity." The cross-cultural experiences provided Indigenous men with a keen awareness of past and present injustices, anger about the slow pace of change, rhetorical skills, and the boldness to back up their demands with confrontational actions. Settler-colonial policies have consistently worked toward the assimilation and/or subordination of Indigenous people, yet, as the Twin Cities case study reveals, they have also led to an unintended outcome, namely, the emergence of an Indigenous "protest masculinity."

AIM members confronted those institutions they felt fostered racial bias and socioeconomic disparities and outright hindered Indigenous people from exercising their civil rights and maintaining their cultural integrity. The establishment of the Indian Patrol and of alternative, all-Native institutions challenged the white power structure of the Twin Cities. The Indian Patrol confronted police brutality and was an expression of AIM's evolving nationalism. Survival schools constituted a conscious decolonization effort to allow Indigenous children to remake their gendered and cultural identities. Survival schools were instrumental in renewing cultural pride and political consciousness as well as reclaiming and revitalizing the memory of Native America. Christian churches, eager to right a past wrong, often became significant supporters of the rising American Indian Movement. AIM's founding years show an absence of a public discourse on gender-related themes. Yet they indicate that from early on, the organization sought to recast notions of Indigeneity, most notably through increasingly hypermasculine practices and confrontations with hegemonic whiteness.

# Chapter 3

# "We Became Warriors Again"

Recasting Race, Gender, and Nation, 1970–1973

Between November 2 and November 8, 1972, Woody Kipp (Blackfoot) found himself in the midst of the belligerent standoff between Indigenous activists and law enforcement officers that occurred during the weeklong occupation of the BIA headquarters in Washington, DC, at the conclusion of the Trail of Broken Treaties caravan.[1] A former Vietnam combat veteran, present-day college student, and Trail of Broken Treaties participant, Woody Kipp was among the roughly five hundred Indigenous occupiers of the BIA building—among them women, children, elderly, college students, and veterans.[2] The gendered nature of the numerous confrontations between Indigenous activists and law enforcement officers that occurred during the occupation made national news headlines.[3] Outside the BIA building, rows of helmeted police in riot gear, armed with sticks and shields, cordoned off the edifice and prepared to oust the occupiers. Inside, the Indigenous occupiers fortified the building's entrance with furniture and armed themselves with makeshift weapons—clubs, spears, tomahawks—made of office equipment in anticipation of the ensuing violence.[4] Like many others, Woody Kipp armed himself with a makeshift weapon and prepared for an imminent attack that never came.[5] The original intention behind the transcontinental Trail of Broken Treaties (ToBT) caravan had been a peaceful demonstration to highlight pressing Indigenous concerns and to bring America into a new paradigm of Indigenous-settler relations. However, the protest event eventually turned into a violent confrontation in which Indigenous protesters battled with law enforcement officers for control over the BIA, the quasi-colonial agency that oversaw Indigenous people.[6]

The anti-colonial struggle of the American Indian Movement instigated new forms and expressions of masculinity and nationalism. Indigenous nationalists drew from a wide range of cultural elements such as their own heritage, the Black civil rights movement, the counterculture, and the anti-war movement as sources of inspiration. For AIM—as for many other ethnic movements of people of color—it was particularly the Panthers' form of Black nationalism, revolutionary struggle, and radical chic that represented a model to be emulated and transplanted into their specific cultural and political contexts. Red Power nationalism had enormous potential for political mobilization, and cultural renewal. Red Power activism allowed Indigenous men and women to remake their identities and rebuild their communities.

The Indigenous nationalist struggle highlighted new pathways to be a warrior in defense of Indigenous land, people, and rights. In the struggle against colonial oppression, Indigenous men sought to emulate a warrior ideal and resituate it in their own specific context. Many Ojibwe men and women active in the Twin Cities reached out to Sioux culture—language, customs, and traditions—as well as the revolutionary culture of other social movements for change in an overall effort to reinvent self and society. This went hand in hand with a rising militancy in protest politics. Between 1969 and 1972, Indigenous men continually renewed, revitalized, and remasculinized in dual efforts to challenge white supremacy and to reconnect to their own cultural heritage. By late 1972, they had fundamentally reinvented themselves as men and imagined themselves as modern-day warriors.

## Transforming Indigenous Men Through Cultural Retraditionalization and Political Radicalization

Nationalist struggles, such as decolonization and independence movements in the Third World as well as anti-colonial struggles in settler states, are highly gendered endeavors requiring remasculinization.[7] The renewal, revitalization, and remasculinization of Indigenous movement masculinities prior to the occupation of Wounded Knee is closely related to two parallel and intertwined developments: a cultural retraditionalization (that is, the return of Indigenous activists to cultural traditions) and a radicalization of masculinized protest politics.[8] Together, these formative processes account for the emergence of a modern-day warrior masculinity. The anti-colonial struggle can be understood as a power struggle between competing masculinities in which Indigenous men sought to become "more manly" in order to challenge hegemonic masculinities and, by implication, colonialism.[9]

The radicalization in protest events made AIM the leading Indigenous advocacy group for a new militancy within the Red Power movement. By 1970, AIM had become active in a wide variety of demonstrations, takeovers, and property seizures and confrontations. These protest events included the takeover of a dormitory at Augustana College, Sioux Falls, South Dakota, in July 1970; protests at the Sheep Mountain, North Dakota, gunnery range in 1970; the seizure of the Mayflower II replica on Thanksgiving Day 1970; the takeover of the Twin Cities Naval Air Station in Minneapolis, Minnesota, from May 17 to May 21, 1971; the Winter Dam, Lac Courte Oreilles, Wisconsin, takeover in August 1971; an abortive attempt to invade the Washington, DC, BIA offices in September 1971; the Mount Rushmore, South Dakota, occupations in the summers of 1970 and 1971; as well as the transcontinental Trail of Broken Treaties caravan and the subsequent BIA takeover in Washington, DC, from November 2 to November 8, 1972. Additionally, AIM was involved in significant activism in border towns, for example, in Gordon and Alliance, Nebraska, as well as in Custer, Rapid City, Sturgis, and Hot Springs, South Dakota, that took place through much of 1972 and early 1973 prior and up to the takeover of Wounded Knee, South Dakota, in late February 1973. The radicalization of protest politics and aggressive posturing of identity for Indigenous rights went hand in hand with a retraditionalization in identity politics.

The retraditionalization that took place in Indigenous men and women came through the affirmation of Indigeneity, the development of revolutionary culture, and nationalist symbolism. The turn toward tribal traditions and ceremonial practices attracted those who sought to bridge their cultural disconnect and embrace their Indigeneity. Powerful messages of cultural pride, the advocacy of armed self-defense, and anti-white rhetoric resonated among those Indigenous men who knew the disempowering nature of white supremacy.

Together, the dual processes of radicalization and retraditionalization led to the assertion of a warrior masculinity. This modern-day warrior construct was itself the product of a particular time, place, and set of circumstances: an inherently hybridized masculinity that exhibited cultural pride, expressed political radicalism, and showcased militancy at a time of great social unrest in American society.

From the onset, a central tenet of AIM's agenda was to reconnect its members to cultural traditions and renew their cultural pride and dignity.[10] The revitalization of Indigenous culture and a pride in "being Native" were part of a larger attempt to overcome severe feelings of social alienation and cultural disconnection.[11] Much of AIM's early activism in the Twin Cities was directed against negative stereotyping of Native Americans: This involved the cancellation of a Thanksgiving play at a local elementary school; the disruption of a public parade; and protests against school textbooks that drew on stereotypes or inaccurate information. Further activism included the disruption of the 1972 Thanksgiving celebration at Plymouth, Massachusetts, and the seizure of Indigenous artifacts by archeologists, all of which, in one way or another, damaged Indigenous cultural identity.[12]

Russell Means (Lakota), a future leader of AIM who would take confrontation politics to the edge, joined AIM in late 1969.[13] Means had been involved in the first, short-lived occupation of Alcatraz Island in 1964. He was a college dropout and said that he had been "a thief, a drunk, a computer operator, a rodeo hand, a junkie, a ballroom dance instructor, a janitor, [and] a farmhand" before joining AIM.[14] He described his first encounter with Dennis Banks and Clyde Bellecourt in 1969 as follows: "When I saw them, I thought they were clowns, you know, trying to prove they were Indians."[15] He recounted: "They wore beaded belts, sashes, chokers, moccasins, headbands, and lots of Indian jewelry. I thought, what are they trying to prove? There I was, in the swing of things, accepted by the white man, wearing his stylish clothes. Those guys looked ridiculous, all dressed up like Indians."[16] He also noticed that "they were so full of pride . . . and self-dignity, and they were so well prepared; they knew what they were talking about."[17] Russell Means's observations reflect contradictory feelings about how AIM leaders had reinvented their Indigenous masculinities: an admiration of their cultural pride in being Native as well as a skepticism of their expressions of Indigeneity. However, the encounter with AIM leaders made a lasting impact on Means:

> Now there was no way to be real Indian, and AIM had shown it to me. No longer would I be content to "work within the system." Never again would I seek personal approval from white society on white terms. Instead, . . . I would get in the white man's face until he gave me and my people our just due. With that decision, my whole life existence suddenly came into focus. For the first time, I knew the purpose of my life and the path I must follow to fulfill it. At the age of thirty I became a full-time Indian.[18]

The way AIM members expressed their gendered identities was also a reflection of their cross-cultural rootedness and their efforts to bridge their cultural disconnect, which they would never entirely overcome. From early on, Dennis Banks felt that AIM needed a cultural and spiritual foundation. "Spirituality is the heart and soul of Indian life, but we AIM people had been raised in white boarding schools, had lived in the Indian ghettos of big cities, had done time in prison. We did not know what we should believe in or how we could find sacredness."[19]

In the early 1970s, Dennis Banks sought out Leonard Crow Dog (Lakota), a traditional Lakota medicine man on the Rosebud Reservation, South Dakota.[20] Crow Dog became a spiritual instructor and familiarized activists with Lakota culture, such as the use of the pipe and drum, songs, language, and ceremonies.[21] For Crow Dog, an active participant in many protest events, AIM was both "something new" and also "something very old." He clearly saw the organization within the context of a long line of Pan-Indian resistance movements against settler colonialism.[22] To him, AIM was born "when the white man killed the first Indian and stole some of his land," and he believed in a cultural nationalist movement that could overcome colonial fragmentation and "unite all the Native Americans in the United States."[23] Vernon Bellecourt (Ojibwe) reflected how a visit with the medicine man impacted Indigenous men: "They heard about Leonard Crow Dog, a medicine man who was maybe twenty-five. They were curious, and they went to visit him and his dad. . . . Well, they went there for advice, and one of the first questions they asked was, 'What is an Indian?'—They wanted to redefine what they were. And they were told that to be an Indian is to be spiritual." To Bellecourt, the newfound identity established a direct connection between spirituality and warriorhood: "We have the spirituality, yet we are warriors. We'll stand up and fight for our people. We haven't had that for many years." He ultimately considered AIM "the warrior class of this century"—a Pan-Indian alliance with a common cultural belief (in the drum and the circle), a shared song, and a political agenda as expressed through the bumper sticker: "AIM for Sovereignty."[24]

The meeting between reservation traditionalists and urban neo-traditionalists translated into a cultural alliance that soon turned political.[25] Reservation elders offered the younger urban activists a viable link into Lakota culture, allowing AIM members urban activists to authenticate themselves and their organization.[26] To AIM's leaders, who were overwhelmingly Ojibwe, it did not seem to matter that they turned to the Oglala Lakota from Pine Ridge, who had been the traditional enemies during previous centuries, practiced a different religion, and spoke an tribal language entirely unrelated to their own. As historian Akim Reinhardt puts it, "through the lens of AIM's intertribal ideology, the full-bloods of Pine Ridge offered a connection to their Native roots to achieve what Dennis Banks referred to as 're-identity.'"[27] As Indigenous activists reached into their cultural heritage, they became increasingly involved with border town and reservation issues.[28] This was mirrored by a shift in the organization's agenda toward treaty rights, sovereignty, and self-determination.[29]

By gaining advice from Leonard Crow Dog, Indigenous activists filled a cultural and spiritual void in their lives and gained a renewed sense of Indigeneity. The cultural alliance also carried some intergenerational elements. Mary Crow Dog (Lakota) observed that at the 1971 Sun Dance on Pine Ridge, "something strange happened then. The traditional old, full-blooded medicine men joined with our kids," she remembered. "It was the real old folks . . . who still remembered a time when Indians were Indians, whose own grandparents or even parents had fought Custer, gun in hand, people who for us were living links with the great past."[30] Reservation traditionalists saw themselves as part of an ongoing resistance against US settler colonialism. For them, the cultural alliance became a political alliance in the simmering conflict with Tribal Chairman Richard Wilson, which would soon come to a climax at Wounded Knee.[31]

Indigenous men within AIM found the renewed discovery of their Native identity both liberating and empowering. Leonard Crow Dog (Lakota) described the meeting of the two groups as follows:

> When the traditional Lakota and the urban militants got together, that was the moment AIM took off. Suddenly men wore their hair long or in braids. They threw away their neckties. Everybody started wearing bead or bone chokers. They began wearing ribbon shirts. They wore Levi jackets with AIM patches and buttons reading, INDIAN POWER or INDIAN AND PROUD. They had eagle feathers tied to their hair or stuck into their hatbands. We became warriors again.[32]

Quite tellingly, Leonard Crow Dog regarded AIM as "a rebirth of our nation."[33] Given the masculine gendering of nationalism, such a development was not entirely unexpected; however, what was unexpected was the relatively short span of time in which it occurred.

The radicalization of Indigenous protest activism was epitomized by the "getting in your face" approach, a considerably more confrontational, serious, and violent approach than the festive Alcatraz occupation. In the early 1970s, AIM developed a symbolism, language, and activities that mirrored their nationalist endeavor and directly challenged US settler colonial society.[34] AIM nationalists sought to address Indigenous concerns through what Clyde Bellecourt called "confrontation politics." These tactics worked as follows:

You go knock on the door of the mayor's office, and if he doesn't let you in, you knock a little louder. If he doesn't hear you, . . . you kick the damn door down. But when you go in there, you better have your shit together. You got to know exactly what you want, and why you want it, and be able to prove to the mayor, the chief of police, the city council, the superintendent of schools, the Bureau of Indian Affairs that discrimination is occurring.[35]

These protest politics became "the blueprint" of AIM's long-term struggle against Western education, the BIA, and organized religion.[36]

A key feature of AIM's protest tactics was the occupation of federal property or unsettled land in order to draw the attention of the news media toward Indigenous issues.[37] For example, at Mount Rushmore, the shrine of American democracy, Indigenous activists contested dominant narratives of history that defined America and put forth a counter-narrative stressing Indigenous perspectives. Indigenous people consider Mount Rushmore, South Dakota, which is located in the heart of the sacred Black Hills that were illegally taken by the US government in 1877 and then defaced by the visages of US presidents, a serious insult.[38] In a telling analogy, John Lame Deer (Lakota), a World War II veteran and noted medicine man, compared the four carved heads to "a huge cavalry boot standing on a dead Indian."[39] In August 1970, Indigenous protesters painted "Red Power—Indian Land" on a huge rock and hung a flag bearing the words "SIOUX INDIAN POWER" over the presidents' heads.[40] Following a brief ceremony, they renamed the location Crazy Horse Mountain in honor of Crazy Horse (1849–1876), the Lakota visionary and warrior, noted for his continual efforts to protect his people and way of life.[41] A CBS News segment showed an angry Lehman Brightman (Lakota), a Korean war veteran and doctoral student from United Native Americans (UNA), an activist group from the Bay Area that occasionally joined AIM protests. "We're sick and tired of sitting back and turning the other cheek," he said. "You gonna see some wide-awake educated Indians. We got some new Indians coming up, new warriors. This is a breeding ground, right here. You're gonna a see a lot of spark."[42] In November 1970, Indigenous activists challenged the annual commemoration of Thanksgiving, the first harvest by settler colonialists and celebration of the national origin myth of America. A group of Indigenous activists covered Plymouth Rock, Massachusetts, with sand, boarded the Mayflower II replica, and disrupted a feast.[43]

"Confrontation politics"—as encapsulated by the tactic of the takeover—was an empowering experience. As Clyde Bellecourt elaborated, "Winter Dam and the other takeovers empowered Indian people across North America. It made them see they could do something to improve their lives; they could take action, take back the things that belonged to them, and that were being used illegally to oppress us. Native people saw that confrontation politics was the only way we could get things done. We had to take control, occupy, and fight—whatever it took to bring our grievances to the forefront."[44]

The dual processes of cultural re-traditionalization and political radicalization described above were intricately connected. Participation in cultural practices, traditions, and ceremonies inspired a renewed sense of ethnic pride that allowed Indigenous activists to reconnect to their cultural heritage. Indigenous activists found a new meaning in the search for tribal traditions and the rebuilding of their communities. Protest activism fueled a resurgence in ethnic pride and catalyzed further activism, testifying to the self-renewing protest and cultural renewal of Red Power activism.[45] Wes Studi (Cherokee) remembered the empowering experience of meeting AIM. "AIM was a group of people who said . . . : 'we have had enough of this shit.' . . . Yes, we are a dying race . . . and . . . we will soon be gone and people don't know who in the world we are anyway.'" More importantly, AIM instilled a cultural pride in him of being Indigenous and a righteous anger about the current state of affairs. "I said: 'wait a minute. These freakin' Americans can't be—excuse my language—running over us for . . . forever. We have to at least make a stand that we will no longer be your goddamn matt and lap dog and you will not run over us anymore.'"[46]

The radicalization of protest activism went hand in hand with the aggressive assertion of masculine warriorhood. Indigenous men's efforts to reinvent themselves relied heavily on both cultural memory and contemporary realities.[47] Indigenous men's radicalization and aggressive posturing was both overcompensation for their obvious cultural void and an effort to gain legitimacy in the eyes of reservation traditionalists. As much as they publicly indulged in their newfound Indigeneity, they privately lacked substantial knowledge of any cultural traditions.[48] In combination, the return to cultural traditions and the radicalization of protest activism accounted for a renewal, revitalization, and remasculinization within Indigenous men.

## Nationalist Symbolism and Revolutionary Culture

The gendered and cultural transformation of Indigenous men and women took place against the backdrop of greater changes underway in American society—the civil rights, student, anti-Vietnam war, feminist, gay/lesbian, and environmental movements. During the 1960s and 1970s, there was a growing visible presence of Native Americans in academia, media, literature, and music. The establishment of the first college and university courses in Native American studies and of American Indian studies departments and programs occurred during this time. A series of books—*The New Indians* (1968) by Stan Steiner, *Custer Died for Your Sins* (1969) by Vine Deloria Jr. (Yankton Dakota), Dee Brown's *Bury my Heart at Wounded Knee* (1970), N. Scott Momady's *House Made of Dawn* (winner of the Pulitzer Prize in 1969)—and films—*A Man Called Horse* (1970), *Soldier Blue* (1970), and *Little Big Man* (1970)—raised public awareness of Indigenous issues. The rise of Indigenous news media such as *Indian Voices*, *Akwesasne Notes*, and *Wassaja* gave Indigenous people a voice to purposefully engage with the public.[49] Similarly, the songs of Indigenous folk and rock singers and bands such as Peter La Farge (Narragansett), Floyd Crow Westerman (Dakota), Redbone, the first Indigenous rock band of the Red Power era, and XIT carried messages of the oppression and the struggles Indigenous peopled faced to the American public, singing out for social and political justice, fair treatment, and the righting of wrongs. Among the most popular songs were LaFarge's "Ballad of Ira Hayes" (1962), also recorded and covered by Johnny Cash; Westerman's "Custer Died For Your Sins" (1969), named for and based on Vine Deloria's (Lakota) first book; Redbone's album "Redbone" (1970); and XIT's song "Plight of the Redman" (1972).[50] Singer-songwriter Buffy Sainte-Marie (claiming Cree heritage) gained widespread popularity with songs such "Now That the Buffalo's Gone" (1964), "The Universal Soldier" (1964), and "Soldier Blue" (1971); however recent revelations by

CBS News have exposed her as a "Pretendian," falsely claiming Indigenous ancestry.[51] Through "aesthetic activism"—writing, singing, and performance—Indigenous activists engaged both Native and American realities as a mode of reclaiming their cultural identity that literary scholar Dean Rader has called "engaged resistance."[52]

AIM ideology stressed pride in a generic sense of Indigeneity (or Indianness), spirituality and an affinity with nature, unity, political sovereignty, and militancy.[53] The organization's banner portrayed a fist with the slogan "United We Are One Powerful Fist—Dignity, Pride, Unity." Participant-observer and anthropologist Fay Cohen found that AIM hoped "to engender in its members a pride in being Indian," as exemplified through the color red.[54] AIM's emphasis on ethnic pride attracted Native Americans who sought bridge their cultural chasm and to reestablish a sense of their Indigenous identity.[55] The newfound cultural pride was also expressed in the organization's acronym A-I-M, which, written vertically and stylized, resembled an arrow and expressed the organization's determination.[56] The concept of unity was based on the notion that resistance required the blurring of tribal affiliations, or Pan-Indianism, to overcome Western divide-and-conquer tactics, as well as the notion that there is something akin to a shared historical experience and set of values among Indigenous peoples.[57] Vietnam veteran Woody Kipp (Blackfoot) observed on how cultural pride gave strength and confidence to AIM's leaders: "They carried themselves with a certain confidence, a pronounced arrogance that one recognized as having come from pushing themselves forward into the world as Native men battling for something that was theirs. That confidence galvanized and lent strength to protests."[58]

The American Indian Movement soon adopted national symbols, indicating its rising ethnic nationalism. National symbols—flags, songs, and cultural dress—invoke unity, solidarity, and group coherency.[59] In social movements for change, these symbols also empower participants against hegemonic notions of manhood and nation.[60] AIM adopted a logo that resembled a warrior with feathers: the nationalist symbol featured the (red) profile of an Indigenous man with a hand forming a peace or "V" sign. A 1971 *Minneapolis Tribune* article featuring the AIM logo stated that the "V" sign stood for "victory over the white man."[61] By 1973, AIM also had adopted a flag with the four color bands representing the cardinal directions—black (west), yellow (east), white (north), and red (south)—that were shared among the Lakota and Ojibwe people.

In late February 1972, during the Gordon, Nebraska, protests over the racially motivated murder of an Indigenous man, Raymond Yellow Thunder (Lakota), AIM adopted the upside-down American flag, a song, and other nationalist symbols and expressions of a rising militancy.[62] The inverted flag—an international distress signal—became a central piece of AIM's appropriation of symbols. The upside-down flag highlighted the plight of Indigenous people in the United States and called for justice.[63] The adversary nature of the flag use was intended to upset white Americans and their sense of patriotism. According to Means,

> Now this is 1972 in virgin America and they'd seen on TV how hippies had desecrated the American flag in the anti-war movement but they hadn't seen it in South Dakota or Nebraska; it was revolutionary in those days when hippies wore the flag on the seat of their pants, and white people would beat up white kids as traitors for doing that! . . . In fact, that's what the hippies of the United States were proclaiming in those days; the youth were telling their fathers and mothers and the rest of the world that this U.S. flag is a piece of shit.[64]

At each major protest event, the use of the American flag, either flown upside down or draped around the body in the same manner, attracted considerable media attention. The desecration of the American flag, however, did not sit well with some Indigenous veterans not affiliated with AIM, drawing condemnation and outrage that was never quite resolved.[65]

The AIM song was originally a powwow song without words.[66] Severt Young Bear (Lakota) described it as "an emotional song of pain and of protest and of eventual victory over many years of oppression and racism."[67] AIM officially adopted the song as its national anthem in May 1972.[68] Another well-known protest song is Floyd Crow Westerman's "BIA" with its powerful lyrics "I'm Not Your Indian Anymore." The protest song was a reinvention of a 49ers song sung by World War I veterans and voiced resistance to US colonialism. Westerman (Dakota) attended the same boarding school as Dennis Banks and, prior to his singing career, served two years with the US Marines.

Movement culture and fashion reflected the newfound pride in Indigeneity and the cultural revolution of the 1960s and 1970s. Appearance and style included elements of hippie and counterculture, military, and Indigenous culture, as well as mainstream fashion. As a show of cultural pride and as a political statement of resistance, Indigenous men and women let their hair grow long.[69] Culturally, Indigenous people believe that long hair carries symbolic significance as the extension of the soul; hair is only cut as part of tribal mourning customs and the loss of a close relative. The growing of braids was a political statement as it stood in direct opposition to colonial policies that enforced the cutting of hair according to dominant norms and practices.[70] Among Native Americans, the wearing of long hair thus signified both a newfound cultural pride as well as a spirit of defiance.[71] In the Red Power era, slogans of ethnic pride—often put on bumper stickers and buttons—included "Custer Had It Coming"; "Custer Died for Your Sins"; "Custer Wore Arrow Shirts"; "BIA—I'm Not Your Indian Anymore"; "Red Power"; "Geronimo for President"; "Indians Aren't a Minority—They Are a Chosen Few"; and "Remember Wounded Knee."[72]

Revolutionary culture was influenced by the mores of the cultural changes underway in larger American society. Vietnam veteran Woody Kipp (Blackfoot), a Trail of Broken Treaties participant, recalled: "I was having a good time and had taken on the euphoric air of revolutionary-near-tantric sex, good smoke, an occasional sneaked beer, and a purpose in life. Our car, filled with my fellow revolutionaries, was running well. I was learning a new way of being an American, a new way of being Indian."[73]

The AIM uniform became the symbol of militant Indigenous manliness. It contained numerous elements that were genuine to Lakota culture and iconic to the general public. Mary Crow Dog (Lakota) describes its outlook as follows:

> The AIM uniform was Sioux all the way, the black "angry hats" with the feathers stuck in the hatband, the bone chokers, the medicine pouches

worn on our breasts, the Levi's jackets on which we embroidered our battle honors—Alcatraz, Trail of Broken Treaties, Wounded Knee. Some dudes wore a third, extra-thin braid as scalp lock. We made up our own songs—forty-niners, honoring songs, songs for a warrior behind bars in the slammer.[74]

Movement culture was expressed in wearing jeans with patches and ribbons of the protest events as "battle honors" or wearing braids as "scalp locks." The AIM uniform was an affirmation of ethnic pride and dignity in the face of rampant racism. At the same time, the AIM uniform would become a symbol of militant Indigenous manhood. Since 1972, the hypermasculine image of gun-toting warriors not only came to represent the right to self-defense and a willingness to use defensive violence against racist attacks when necessary but also countered images of powerlessness and emasculation. The high visibility of the AIM uniform indicates that it was an expression of cultural pride and that it instilled a positive identity in many Indigenous activists.[75]

AIM cemented its confrontational image by utilizing derogatory designations to delineate allies from enemies. An "us" versus "them" dichotomy helped to distinguish between AIM members, supporters, and sympathizers, on the one hand, and those who cooperated with the BIA, the government, or were considered non-Indigenous, on the other. Derisive terms included "apple" (as in, red on the outside, white on the inside) to refer to colonial complicity; "Uncle Tomahawks" to signal complacency and apathy; and "Hang-around-the-fort-Indian" to describe governmental dependency.[76] Significantly, these character types were antithetical to AIM's nationalist agenda and its cultural pride.[77] At times, AIM ideology found its expression in a reverse racism. "I truly believed the white race was the devil incarnate," Woody Kip expressed of the hate-whitey attitude that he harbored during his involvement with AIM, even though he had grown up among white people.[78]

The Black Panther Party (BPP) played some part in influencing AIM's revolutionary culture and nationalist agenda.[79] Red Power borrowed from Black organizational forms, rhetoric, and tactics and transplanted them into their specific circumstances.[80] Both the Indian Patrol and AIM Survival Schools were patterned after Black inventions, as were direct action tactics. Similarly, the "power to the people" theme resonated with AIM members, and AIM's Ten-Point Program closely resembled the Panthers' Ten Point Program. The targets of the Indigenous nationalist struggle—police, schools, and colleges, along with white racism—were reminiscent of those of African Americans. African-inspired clothes enjoyed great popularity among Black civil rights activists. The Panthers donned revolutionary chic: a black uniform with black shoes, pants, shirt, leather jacket, and a black beret. The black beret, inspired by the French resistance movement during World War II, signaled militancy. AIM members selectively adopted elements from the iconic Panther uniform. They drew from Indigenous-inspired fashion, sometimes with a red beret. Occasionally, they would use a power salute with the fist, similar to the Black Panthers.[81]

The Black Panther Party and the American Indian Movement both highlighted the parallels of the Black and the Indigenous experience, emphasizing their intersectional oppression and a shared history of resistance.[82] The *Black Panther* newsletter, printed out of Oakland, California, and distributed worldwide, stressed shared impacts of colonialism and its underlying ideology of white supremacy and structural inequality—from high incarceration rates to sexual violence and housing segregation. *Akwesasne Notes*, an alternative Indigenous newspaper outlet, also took notice of the intersectional structures of Indigenous and Black oppression.[83] During the Alcatraz occupation, AIM leaders met with Stokely Carmichael, leader of the Black Panther Party in Oakland, California.[84] Carmichael visited the BIA takeover; and Angela Davis made a visit to Wounded Knee to show Black solidarity.[85] Scholars have repeatedly noted the differences in historical experiences of Black and Indigenous people(s) and their potential for coalition-building.[86]

However, as much as AIM borrowed from the Panthers' rhetoric, protest tactics, and revolutionary culture, the organization soon sought to establish itself as distinctly Indigenous. Clyde Bellecourt recalled that initially, some people regarded AIM as little more than a replica of the BPP. As he recalled, "While we had done a lot of work in the Black community and wholeheartedly supported the Panthers' struggle for equality, we were after something much different."[87] He also noted that Indigenous political activism was not only complicated by the dual nature of the Indigenous struggle (both for civil and treaty rights) but also because race relations in the United States were predominantly viewed as a Black and white issue.[88]

Throughout much of their lives, Indigenous activists sought to bridge the cultural chasm that distanced them from their relatives on reservations but never quite managed to regenerate culturally and spiritually from intergenerational experiences of colonialism, political repression, and cultural loss.[89] The neo-traditionalists were continually criticized across Indian Country for their lack of cultural knowledge and their confrontational protest politics.[90] Robert Burnette (Lakota), a former Rosebud chairman, recalled that during the BIA takeover AIM members attached little preprinted cards to their buttonholes reading "I Am a Grass Roots Person" in what constituted an effort to legitimize themselves in the eyes of those Indigenous people who were culturally immersed.[91] Often AIM activists went to extremes to prove to themselves and others that they were Indigenous, inspiring the term "seventies superskins" (shorthand for "super redskin"), a derisive term embodying the notion that Indigenous youth wanted to be militant when it was fashionable or profitable for them.[92] Much of AIM's militancy may thus be explained as an effort to (over)compensate for their lack of cultural grounding and gain some recognition among reservation people—something they never achieved.[93] It was not without reason that critics claimed that AIM stood for "Assholes In Moccasins."[94] Others denounced AIM members as "poseurs from the city, charlatans, felons, and freebooters of racism."[95]

Many reservation people viewed AIM quite ambivalently, given their reverence for veterans and the organization's sympathy for the anti-war movement that was widely regarded as unpatriotic across Indian Country. Historian Rolland Dewing has pointed out that to many reservation residents, "AIM seemed to belong to the hippie fringe element and express an urban flippancy alien to traditional Indian values." Hence, AIM always ran into problems when trying to establish its credibility as an organization that sought to serve Indigenous people in urban and in reservation areas.[96] Local reservation residents frequently recognized the "un-Indigenous" behavior of the urban nationalists. For example, Walter Littlemoon (Lakota), a local resident, remembered when AIM nationalists took over Wounded Knee:

> They came from a lot of different nationalities and some were mixed with Indian. I don't think any of them cared or realized what life was all about. I saw them imitate and copy what they thought a Lakota was to be, but they had a complete lack of respect and they spoke in city street slang, which had no pride. It was embarrassing to watch and listen. None showed any Lakota behavior that we were familiar with. Their actions were more those of gangsters. They always hollered about "The Cause! We're doing this for The Cause!" They dressed with feathers and a little beadwork here and there. Their hair was braided and held into place with headbands, whereas the men in our community wore more of a casual, everyday western style, which fit the weather conditions. They screamed and hollered about being Indian, yet, here we Lakota were living right in front of them in a quiet respectful manner; they didn't seem to see us.[97]

As these observations reveal, AIM members inhabited little or no culturally appropriate behavior. Their street slang, use of gang signs, and handshakes alienated local reservation people. They rarely shared food, cigarettes, or other items with others; and they intimidated and bullied reservation residents.[98] Traditional reservation residents favored tribal values of generosity and sharing, rather than those of material consumption and accumulation. They also prioritized values of communalism over those of individualism, and they favored the extended family and kinship over that of the more close-knit movement community. Indigenous people from urban and reservation contexts departed when it came to a grounding in traditional knowledge and their anchoring to family, kin, and community. Local Wounded Knee residents took notice that when the smoke cleared after the siege, AIM members were less concerned with rebuilding their devastated community than with movement struggles.[99]

The condescending treatment of reservation residents indicated that many urban Natives considered their reservation counterparts as somewhat backward, did not understand the viability of traditional ways, or/and engaged in "defensive othering." This somewhat contradictory and ambiguous behavior—after all, urban Natives sought to reconnect to their Indigeneity—stemmed from cultural confusion and identity conflicts.[100] While AIM's militancy drew criticism from across Indian Country, many were in favor of the purpose of the organization, its dramatizing of Indigenous grievances, and its goal of making a change in the lives of Native Americans.¹⁰¹

### Nonviolence and Armed Self-Defense in AIM and the Black Panthers

Oral histories and autobiographies provide some glimpses into the intricate relationship between nonviolence, violence, and manhood within the American Indian Movement. The Black Panthers were an important inspiration for AIM when it came to addressing police brutality. AIM utilized some of the same tactics to confront police abuse (e.g., monitoring police radios, observing and documenting police behavior, providing a uniform outlook, etc.). The Panthers in Oakland utilized the gun to exhibit courage, militancy, and manhood or as a recruiting device for new members. Unlike the Panthers, however, AIM was committed to a philosophy of nonviolence—at least during its early years. Dennis Banks felt uneasy about the use of violence and rejected some of the Panthers' militant methods.¹⁰² Members of the Indian Patrol would utilize nonviolent methods to settle a dispute; no guns were reported as seen on any patrol.¹⁰³

The setup of the Indian Patrol sparked internal debates within AIM about the use of nonviolence (and civil disobedience) and violence (or armed self-defense) that would continue throughout the early 1970s. "I didn't want AIM to be seen as a group that advocated violence," Banks stated his position. "But, on the other hand, I felt that our people should not face heavily armed, racist cops empty-handed."¹⁰⁴ Initially, AIM adhered to principles of nonviolence. Yet at the same time, AIM was eager to put forth an image of unity and militancy. Its tactics—monitoring police behavior, documenting arrests, reciting relevant portions of the penal code, following police, and posting bail at the police station—and militaristic rhetoric closely mirrored that of the Black Panthers, thus making the parallels between the BBP and AIM apparent to police and the wider public.¹⁰⁵ By 1972, Indigenous nationalists were bringing guns to protests, and debates over the use of guns for armed self-defense did indeed occur.¹⁰⁶

Throughout, AIM was decidedly anti-intellectual. Unlike the Panthers, who developed their own philosophy of liberation, AIM did not draw from a particular set of philosophies or doctrines of Indigenous liberation. While AIM members were certainly inspired by nationalist thought, there was no major intellectual discourse with messages of militant masculinity and liberation from oppression. Accordingly, activist voices can only offer some limited and fragmentary insights into the gendered dimensions of armed self-defense and manhood while leaving much room for speculation.

The Black freedom struggle, forms of Black masculinity, and gendered protest influenced the Red Power movement. The Black civil rights movement was overwhelmingly committed to a philosophy of nonviolence, yet these Gandhian principles were frequently challenged by those who viewed it as an obligation of Black men to protect their women and themselves from white supremacist violence. Historian Simon Wendt has conducted a comparative analysis of armed self-defense efforts in the Southern civil rights movement and in post-1965 Black Power groups in order to highlight the intricate relationship between self-defense and gender. His findings indicate that both groups considered armed self-defense "as an affirmation of black manliness"—no matter whether this meant facing extralegal white terrorists in the South or legalized state violence from the hands of police as in the case of the Black Panthers.[107] In the South, armed self-defense as a source of manly pride was largely a by-product to the physical necessity to protect Black lives. Compared to the Southern freedom struggle, the Panthers' decision to arm themselves was not instigated by the need to repel extralegal attacks. Rather, the Panthers sought to stop legalized state violence at the hands of police. The Black Panthers dismissed the integrationist and nonviolent stance of earlier Black activism though their adherence to a philosophy of armed self-defense. The Black Panthers' visual self-representation of militarized manhood—through the organization's paramilitary character, the brandishing of guns, and its militant rhetoric—was largely "a symbolic form of defiance," according to Wendt.[108]

The Panthers' high visibility sought to affirm Black manliness and the right to self-defense and by implication all other rights of manhood, including the right to protect woman and child. The Black Panther uniform consisted of a beret, a leather jacket, gloves, and sunglasses—all in black. The uniform was meant to generate pride and dignity in Blackness and generate fear and respect among white people. The organization's Ten-Point program explicitly called for the right to self-defense in order to defend the Black community.[109] Guns allowed the Panthers to defend themselves from police brutality, to intimidate police, and to empower the Black community by individual acts of defiance.

By 1972, AIM nationalists changed their position from adhering to a concept of non-violence to embracing armed self-defense. Similarly to the Black Panthers, they believed that armed self-defense represented an affirmation of Indigenous manhood. In their public speeches, AIM leaders often threatened to counter racist violence with armed force. In an interview, Russell Means described himself as "a staunch believer in self-defense."[110] Means further elaborated that "one of our axioms was self-defense. If we were attacked, we would not turn the other cheek, nor would we bend over to get the other two kicked. We fought."[111] Means did not distinguish between legalized state violence (from police) and violence from extra-legal terrorists, but he considered defensive violence against racist aggression a physical necessity. While Means did not frame this short statement in terms of claiming or defending Indigenous manhood, he clearly sought to counter dominant stereotypes of Indigenous powerlessness, express his defiance to white America, and (re)generate AIM's members with ethnic pride and a positive identity. In the same breath, Means stated that "we were the vanguard of the renaissance of Indian pride and self-dignity. . . . Our primary focus was to fight racism and also to fight for independence, complete independence and freedom from the United States of America."[112] From Means's perspective, armed self-defense represented a vital affirmation of Indigenous manhood. Around this time, AIM got in touch with other militant dissident groups around the nation such as the Weather Underground, the Black Panthers, the Young Lords, and the Brown Berets.[113] AIM built alliances with "other" movements, in particular when their parallel and otherwise disparate struggles intersected.[114]

Akin to the Black Panthers, AIM members embraced masculine militancy. Initially, the Indian Patrollers sported red berets and red jackets, symbolic of their pride in Indigeneity.[115] AIM's visual self-representation—red jackets and red berets—commanded respect and instilled a sense of pride in those who wore them. Pat Bellanger (Ojibwe) recalled that the outlook had an immediate impact on police: "They were seeing all these red berets . . . the police would start getting nervous. And we liked them nervous."[116] Later, the AIM look involved either a beret, hat, or a headband with feathers, bone necklaces and bone chokers, medicine pouches, Levi's jeans, and military jackets—all of which sought to generate manly pride and command respect from white people. At Wounded Knee, AIM's powerful image of warrior masculinity—warrior poses, brandished weapons, and militant rhetoric—also served to affirm Indigenous masculinity. Yet this type of militancy did not pass uncritically. For example, the conservative *American Opinion*, published in May 1973 read, in part: "A.I.M.'s leaders love to strike warrior poses, though most of them . . . are convicted felons who . . . may not legally carry firearms." The article went on to denounce "the trigger-happy throng of criminals at Wounded Knee" and the patronization of their "radical chic" by liberals.[117]

It seems as if the Black Panther Party profoundly influenced AIM's turn to armed self-defense. Indicative is Wes Studi's (Cherokee) statement that "we followed in the steps of the Black Panthers. We said, well if the Black Panthers can take up arms, we can take up arms even better. So that's what we did." He went on to state that in late 1972 some Trail of Broken Treaties participants brought firearms. The taking up of guns was apparently discussed within AIM. Debates stressed "the right to sovereignty" and that "the fucking white man" has taken them "the point of a beaten down people. And we have had enough."[118] Between late 1971 and summer 1972, five Indigenous men died at the hands of white supremacists.[119] It was this gendered violence that provided a much-overlooked impetus for the ToBT demonstration.[120]

The racially motivated murder of Raymond Yellow Thunder (Lakota) and the Gordon, Nebraska, protests in early 1972 sparked internal debates over militancy and armed self-defense. Prior to the Gordon protests, the protesters had debated whether to bring some weapons into Gordon, with some advocating a militant approach and others favoring nonviolence. The latter approach won out.[121] Nonetheless, many Indigenous rank-and-file members carried concealed guns or had them tucked away in car trunks as they arrived in the border town.[122] The autobiographical account of Dennis Banks reveals that, from Gordon onward, AIM considered itself an advocate for Indigenous rights.[123] Henceforth, Indigenous men embraced a new militancy to ensure racial equality—if need be by taking up guns. Banks noted that "the attitude of white rednecks in South Dakota and northwest Nebraska is that they can kill an Indian just on a whim and get away with it." He went on to claim that "they should know now that if they point a gun at us and pull the trigger, somebody might . . . shoot back. AIM will take any step and all steps to ensure justice for our people. We are prepared to die for our cause."[124] Banks's combative rhetoric indicates that AIM would utilize defensive violence to protect themselves and their community.

During the trial of the murderers of Raymond Yellow Thunder in Alliance, Nebraska, AIM showed up in force and, when the guilty verdict was delivered, issued a public statement that read, in part: "The American Indian Movement will take any and all steps to ensure justice for our people. We are prepared to die for these beliefs and, as in any war, we are prepared to take the offensive to ensure the maximum protection."[125] While much of this martial rhetoric was consciously geared to attracting media attention, it also pointed to AIM's increasingly contentious stance.

The decision to openly take up arms occurred in yet another confrontation on the Cass Lake Reservation in Minnesota in May 1972. There, Natives and white authorities struggled over contested hunting and fishing rights. It was also the place where AIM held its second annual national convention (May 10–16, 1972). According to famed writer Gerald Vizenor (Ojibwe), the Cass Lake incident was "the first time the American Indian Movement had taken up the use of firearms."[126] Dennis Banks claimed that about three hundred armed AIM members arrived and, in a show of force, marched down to the lake, openly brandishing firearms.[127] A press conference was held on a rifle range. The assembled news reporter captured Dennis Banks's and Russell Means's warrior poses. While Means fired a pistol on the target range, Banks attempted to fire a shotgun, albeit unsuccessfully. Carrying a pistol and flanked by shotgun-carrying guards, Banks drew analogies between the war in Vietnam and the struggle of Indigenous peoples: "The war is in the churches and with the anti-Indian religious beliefs, in the slum housing, in the suicide rate of young Indian people," he said. "So we know we're hitting it on the head when we say the longest war is not Vietnam. The longest war has been against the American Indian."[128] AIM's open militancy put it in direct opposition to the Ojibwe tribe, which favored nonviolent tactics.[129] Debates about armed self-defense within AIM led to a deep schism, laying open the continual backstabbing, infighting, and bickering within the organization.[130]

Between the Gordon, Nebraska, protest and the Wounded Knee, South Dakota, takeover, Indigenous activists within AIM brought concealed weapons to virtually all major confrontations. There are indications that some guns were brought into the Gordon protests,[131] the BIA headquarters building,[132] the Custer courthouse riot,[133] as well as to numerous other protests that occurred in South Dakota and Nebraska.[134] For example, in mid-January 1973, AIM joined Chicanos in a series of protests confronting racial barriers in Scottsbluff, Nebraska, protesting police brutality. During the protests, a local high school was firebombed and a number of activists were arrested for possession of firearms, Molotov cocktails, and marijuana.[135] Cautious evidence suggests that the first instance of AIM warriors pointing their guns at police occurred during the Custer, South Dakota, riot in early February 1973 while trashing patrol cars and retrieving some rifles.[136] There, a small group of armed men eventually forced a larger group of policemen who sought to disperse the crowd to back down and retreat.[137]

This militarization of protest politics went hand in hand with a retraditionalization among Indigenous nationalists. The autobiographical accounts of Dennis Banks (Ojibwe) and Crow Dog (Lakota) point to a series of masculinized and masculinizing practices that are closely tied to Lakota warrior culture. For example, before setting out for Gordon, Nebraska, medicine man Leonard Crow Dog prepared Means, Banks,

---

*Opposite:* Leonard Crow Dog (Lakota) carrying a sawed-off shotgun during the BIA headquarters occupation in Washington, DC, in November 1972. Initially, AIM adhered to a concept of nonviolence. Following the racially motivated murder of Raymond Yellow Thunder (Lakota) in early 1972, AIM began to embrace the taking up of guns, both as a means of armed self-defense and as an affirmation of Indigenous manliness. (Richard Erdoes Papers, Yale Collection of Western Americana, Beinecke Rare Book and Manuscript Library)

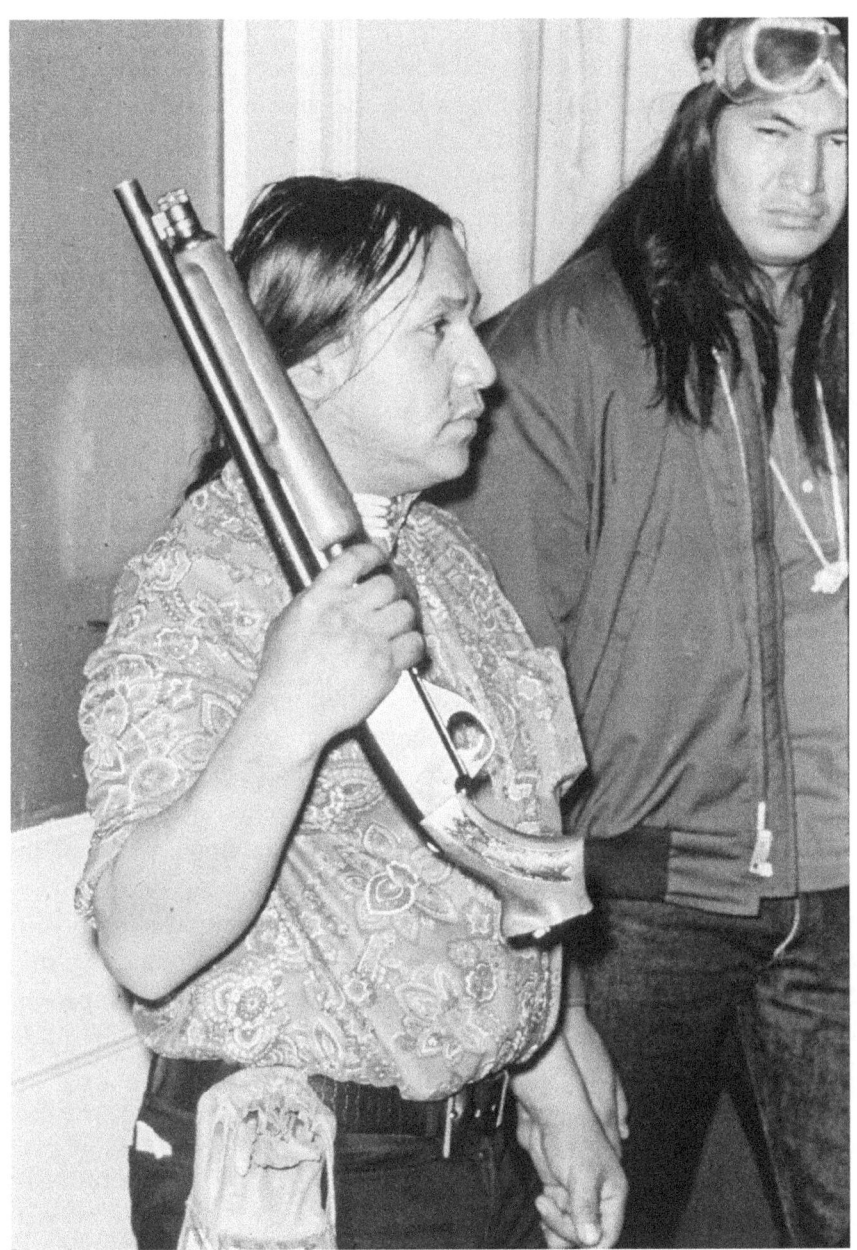

and the Bellecourt brothers for the upcoming confrontation and sprinkled them with gopher dust—"the kind that made Crazy Horse bulletproof"—cedared them, and smoked the pipe with them.[138] These cultural ceremonies carried particular significance that was not lost on movement participants: in old times, tribal warriors utilized these cultural practices and ceremonies to cleanse themselves and prepare for battle. The 1972 Cass Lake, Minnesota, meeting also revealed a deep schism about AIM's future spiritual and cultural guidance, with one faction favoring the medicine man Wallace and his son Godfrey Chips (Lakota) and another Leonard Crow Dog (Lakota), with the latter ultimately winning out.[139]

### Performing Warriorhood Between Media Bias, Cultural Reappropriation, and Warrior Identity

The male leaders of AIM quite consciously utilized the performance of Indigenous warriorhood to draw attention to Indigenous issues. Media coverage, while sympathetic, carried pervasive cultural images of the Native "other" and Indigenous warriorhood.[140] AIM's utilization of protest tactics—property seizure, marches, demonstrations, and more confrontational tactics—were a reflection of the protest group itself.[141] Indigenous organizations were small in size, marginalized, and lacked resources. As a result, they "aggressively sought media assistance to draw attention to their grievances," as sociologist Timothy Baylor has noted.[142] A case in point is Russell Means's approach to protest politics. According to an insider, "He revealed his bizarre knack for staging demonstrations that attracted the sort of press coverage Indians had been looking for: the capture of the Mayflower II on Thanksgiving of 1970, a brief occupation of Mount Rushmore in June 1971, and an abortive attempt to seize the BIA central office on 22 September of the same year."[143]

Dennis Banks would later admit that this confrontational style "was the only dramatic way that we could make our problems known throughout the community, throughout the world."[144] Sociologist Rachel Bonney claims that, from the outset, AIM was markedly "militant, involving the use of demonstration, confrontation, and occupation."[145] A key feature of AIM's protest activism included the occupation of federal property or unsettled land in order to draw attention to Indigenous issues in the news media.[146] AIM's tactics involved the creation of a "situation," followed by protests that were salient to the media, and, finally, the organization's departure once substantial or token results were obtained.

Three major factors contributed to the way the American Indian Movement was widely recognized as a militant organization and its members as warriors. First, AIM quite consciously sought to attract the media to the point of being media-savvy.[147] Russell Means privately confided: "I've had dealing with AP, UPI, and all three major TV networks, and the only thing they ever want to know is how many people went to the hospital and how many people went to jail."[148] AIM made a strategic choice to engage in militant protest activism in order to draw media attention but had little control over how the media broadcast the message.[149] Frequently, the media focused on the spectacle rather than the message.[150] During the takeover of the BIA headquarters in Washington, DC, in 1972, Mary Crow Dog (Lakota) realized the potential of militancy in order to gain media attention. "It was on this occasion," she reflected, "that I learned that as long as we 'behaved nicely' nobody gave a damn about us, but as soon as we became rowdy we got all the . . . media coverage we could wish for."[151] A similar statement came from Russell Means, who at the same event reportedly remarked to some reporters: "What do we have to do to get some attention? Scalp somebody?"[152]

The news media—Native and non-Native alike—frequently framed AIM protests as militant.[153] In his study on NBC news coverage of Indigenous protests between 1968 and 1979, Timothy Baylor claims that a total of 90 percent of the news segments drew on militant themes that overshadowed many of the real grievances and issues behind the protests.[154] This occurred to such an extent that media coverage had detrimental effects on the protesters' cause.[155] The media framed AIM as "militant" from the mid-1970s, prior to any of the major confrontations the organization would later become notorious for; this timing roughly corresponds with AIM's overall retraditionalization efforts and its road to radicalism.[156]

Second, Indigenous men within AIM quite consciously utilized stereotypical images of hypermasculine warriors as a tool of anti-colonial resistance. In so doing, AIM "intentionally manipulated stereotypes of the white man's Indian," as anthropologist Maureen Trudelle Schwarz claims.[157] Since the turn of the nineteenth century, white Americans, most often men, have utilized what historian Philip Deloria (Yankton Dakota) has called "playing Indian" themes to remake their gendered identities.[158] Indigenous people have continuously struggled to reclaim their cultural/racial capital within a larger society that continuously sought to appropriate their Indigeneity; in turn, they have invoked and revoked "the white man's Indian" to challenge white hegemonic manhood.[159] AIM activists engaged in "Indians playing Indian" themes during virtually all protest events. As "Indians playing Indian," Activists drew from colonial ambivalence and colonial mimicry. AIM's drawing on stereotypes such as noble/ignoble savagery fit into their effort to retake control over media images.[160]

Stereotypical images of Indigenous martial manliness—or what anthropologist Maureen Trudelle Schwarz calls the image of the "savage reactionary"—clearly dominated the news segments reporting on AIM's protests.[161] According to Timothy Baylor's findings, media images of Indigenous militancy highlighted "the breaking of laws, the use of weapons, gunfire, injury to individuals, and the destruction of property."[162] Stereotypical images were utilized by Natives and non-Natives alike because these cultural frameworks were the most easily recognized by their intended audiences, thus making the need to explain them obsolete.[163] In that sense, both the news media and Indigenous activists utilized cultural/racial capital as a resource: the news media focused on stereotypical imagery in order to sell the news story; Indigenous activists employed the performance of warrior masculinity to draw media attention. Indigenous activists' conscientious utilization of cultural/racial capital—in the absence of any economic or political resource, such as lobbying power—can be recognized as a valuable asset in the assertion of cultural distinctiveness and political sovereignty.[164] AIM activists quite consciously sought to put forth the image of martial manliness and barred from television cameras those activists who did not fit these images.[165]

Third, as much as Indigenous activists sought to play into media bias and exploit stereotypes of martial Indigeneity, they also considered themselves to be real warriors in the nationalist struggle against colonial domination.[166] It is a widely acknowledged fact that some AIM members came from reservations where cultural and warrior traditions were kept alive, yet that the majority of AIM's founders did not have that cultural immersion.[167] While AIM leaders publicly declared themselves warriors, they privately lacked substantial knowledge of cultural and warrior traditions.[168]

Various scholars have recognized AIM's protest tactics as street theater that helped to dramatize their cause.[169] As AIM members utilized "Indians playing Indian" tactics to gain media attention, news media reporting mirrored popular American imagery by portraying AIM as modern-day warriors. AIM members frequently played into the pervasive performance of warrior masculinity—through rhetoric, fashion, street theatrics, and confrontational protests. As Schwarz writes, AIM leaders "inhabited the stereotype of the war-mongering brave—braiding their hair, painting their faces with war paint, adorning themselves with beads and feathers—while reusing these stereotypes in striking and imaginative ways."[170]

However, viewing Indigenous nationalists solely within the context of media theatrics leaves a significant part of identity politics unexplored. A perspective that considers AIM activists exclusively as headline hunters and the media's warriors almost completely ignores the fact that AIM members frequently referenced themselves as warriors fighting for *their* homeland, *their* people, and *their* rights. In quite a genuine sense, they considered themselves warriors in a struggle against domestic colonialism, a significant aspect that is often overlooked when analyzing AIM's media theatrics.

Indeed, much of AIM's claim to warriorhood derived from numerous confrontations with various government officials and law enforcement officers throughout 1972 and 1973. The physical confrontations between Indigenous activists and police officers can also be read as symbolic battlefields where Indigenous and non-Indigenous men clashed over meanings of race, gender, and nation. These clashes provided Indigenous men some valid authority and legitimate grounding to their claim to warriorhood. Personal memories show that many Indigenous men drew considerable pride from these confrontations—as evidenced by Mary Crow Dog's account that they commemorated protest events as "battle honors."[171] Apparently, these various practices were considered manly and validated claims to warriorhood.[172]

Political scientist Jeremy Busacca has found that the invocation of warrior imagery served four interrelated and overlapping purposes: first, it associated AIM with Indigenous resistance, putting it in line with past warriors such as Crazy Horse and Sitting Bull; second, it gave its leaders "an aura of masculine authority"; third, warrior imagery highlighted AIM's militancy; and fourth, "the warrior image insinuated that AIM were deeply connected to the ancient ways," which was particularly important for the attempts of AIM to gain support across Indian Country.[173]

By early 1973, Indigenous men within AIM quite genuinely began to consider themselves warriors in the struggle for Indigenous rights and nationhood. However, news media reporting frequently featured a narrative of militancy with highly salient warrior imagery, rather than focusing on the underlying Indigenous struggle against colonial domination.[174] Paul Chaat Smith (Comanche) and Robert Allen Warrior (Osage) state that "in 1972 the organization was reaching out toward a traditional Indian past, becoming a warrior society of old combined with the attitude and language of third-world rebels of the 1970s."[175]

## Indigenous Civil Rights, Racial Conflict, and Contested Meanings of Manliness in Midwestern Border Towns, 1972–1973

Much of AIM's protest activism on the national stage—the Trail of Broken Treaties caravan, and the subsequent takeover of the BIA headquarters in Washington, DC, as well as the Wounded Knee takeover—was interspersed with civil rights activism that targeted border towns.[176] Historiography has not paid adequate attention to the gendered implications of racial conflict and the series of confrontations that took place in the early 1970s in Nebraska and South Dakota. The various clashes between Indigenous and Anglo-American men over the meaning of manliness and nation fueled AIM's militancy. By early 1972, the cultural alliance between urban neo-traditionalists and reservation traditionalists further drove AIM's political radicalism.[177]

Racial conflict between Anglo-Americans and Indigenous people in the Midwest was rooted in the ongoing legacy of US settler colonialism. Conflicting historical narratives were molded through more than a century of strained race relations. Race relations were characterized by historical denial and collective amnesia, on the one hand, and intergenerational historical memory and ongoing Indigenous struggles, on the other.[178] Whites based their claim to land and title on a legacy of settler-colonial dispossession and displacement of Indigenous people; subsequently they came to regard Indigenous people as part of a distant memory of the American consciousness.[179] Conversely, Indigenous people sought to keep the memory of the nation's troubled past alive; they based their ongoing struggle for political sovereignty on treaty rights.[180]

Simmering racial conflict exploded in a series of violent confrontations in South Dakota and Nebraska. The racially motivated murder of Raymond Yellow Thunder (Lakota) in Gordon, Nebraska, at the hands of white supremacists in mid-February 1972, and what appeared to be a double standard of justice prompted a series of protests in Gordon between March 6 and March 8, 1972.[181] The murder of another Indigenous man, Wesley Bad Heart Bull (Lakota), in Buffalo Gap, South Dakota, on January 21, 1973, at the hands of another white man led to a series of confrontations that climaxed at Custer, South Dakota, the county courthouse seat, on February 6, 1973.[182] These protests were interspersed with a series of tense confrontations between law enforcement officers and Indigenous activists. These confrontations took place in Scottsbluff, Nebraska, from January 14 to January 24, 1973; in Rapid City, South Dakota, from February 7 to February 9, 1973; in Sturgis, South Dakota, on February 9, 1973; and in Hot Springs, South Dakota, on February 15, 1973, and precipitated the Wounded Knee, South Dakota, takeover less than two weeks later.[183] Much of this protest was either related to the murder of Yellow Thunder or Bad Heart Bull or, alternatively, focused on challenging white privilege and racial discrimination in border towns.

Border towns, much like reservations, are part of the legacy of the US settler-colonialist order. Border towns represent the periphery of colonial rule and are miniature replicas of the colonial center; they are built on ancestral Indigenous homelands and located in close proximity to a tribal community and/or a reservation. Indigenous people are dependent upon border towns for employment, social and health services, and conducting business in general; white settler colonialists in turn depend upon Indigenous people and lands in the form of cheap labor and economic resources.[184] The social, political, and economic order within these border towns rested upon the authority of white male privilege. There was little space for racial equality when signs reading "No Dogs or Indians Allowed" upheld the supremacy of whiteness and manhood.[185] Border towns radiate a gender and racial hierarchy that is built on pervasive prejudice and anti-Indian sentiment, which in the past was perhaps less visible but just as insidious as Black segregation in the South.[186] Racial and gender bias against Indigenous people continues to be most rampant in border towns, as evidenced in severe socioeconomic disparities and a double standard of justice—selective law enforcement, abuse of police power, and disenfranchisement—that keeps Indigenous people in a subaltern position to the present day.[187] Racial and gender bias translates into disproportionate criminal conviction rates for Indigenous men and disparate violence committed against Indigenous women.[188]

The racist murder of Raymond Yellow Thunder (Lakota), the grandson of famed chief American Horse (Lakota), triggered AIM's intervention and established its reputation as a manly advocate of Indigenous people like no other previous political protest did. The extreme brutality that Yellow Thunder suffered at the hands of white supremacists triggered a massive political mobilization on Pine Ridge Reservation, South Dakota, a few miles to the north. On February 12, 1972, Raymond Yellow Thunder was kidnapped by a group of whites and beaten, stripped partially naked, driven around in the trunk of a car, thrown into the Gordon American Legion Club, beaten again, and then finally let go; his body was found more than a week later on February 20.[189] Adding to the volatility of the situation were unsubstantiated rumors: that he had been forced to dance "Indian style" in the American Legion hall; that he had been castrated; and that his murderers went free. The official authorities' refusal to allow relatives to view the body sparked further controversy.[190] However, a later, second autopsy confirmed the results of the first.[191] The subsequent trial resulted in a guilty verdict on May 26, 1972, for the main perpetrators, easing racial tensions considerably.[192] The tragic death of Raymond Yellow Thunder remains a source of scholarly controversy and has been sensationalized and grossly distorted to the present day.[193]

AIM quickly seized the media spotlight and pointed to the gendered and racial nature of the conflict. "We no longer are going to stand by and watch our women raped and our men beaten, run over and killed while the courts do nothing," Russell Means voiced his anger over the racist

A saloon with the sign "No Indians Allowed" in Scenic, South Dakota, adjacent to the Pine Ridge reservation, in 1975. The social, political, and economic order of border towns rested upon the supremacy of whiteness and manhood. AIM activists sought to dismantle the gender and racial hierarchy in South Dakota. The image is proof of the rampant anti-Indian racism of border towns close to reservations. (Richard Erdoes Papers, Yale Collection of Western Americana, Beinecke Rare Book and Manuscript Library)

murder and what appeared to be another miscarriage of justice. "With the help of the justice department we may be able to force the legal system of Nebraska to deal with these savage white men."[194] He also declared that they would "put the national spotlight" on Gordon and expose what he called "the racist state of Nebraska."[195]

The confrontation commenced on March 6, 1972, when AIM held a large rally at Billy Mills Hall on Pine Ridge, South Dakota, and then drove in a large caravan into the Nebraska town.[196] Fear of an armed invasion swept over white townspeople as Indigenous protesters made their way into Gordon.[197] The *Los Angeles Times* called the subsequent standoff "the largest confrontation between Indians and whites since . . . Wounded Knee [1890]."[198] The confrontation involved about thirty state troopers, policemen, and sheriffs (with the National Guard put on standby).[199]

They faced an angry crowd of about fourteen hundred Indigenous men, women, and children who descended upon Gordon, a town of two hundred.[200] For three days, Indigenous activists organized an economic boycott, participated in near-constant political rallies, and convened a people's grand jury—tools in a classic civil rights struggle.[201] In the town's auditorium, white men of authority found themselves in the midst of what had turned into a stage and court as angry Indigenous men gave white officials a piece of their mind before a crowd of onlookers, who packed the arena-style seats. For those watching, the whole scenario was like a world turned upside down.[202] However, the clash of masculinities amounted to little more than a symbolic victory.[203]

The Gordon incident constituted a major turning point in AIM's protest politics, sparking further processes of radicalization and retraditionalization within the organization. The new radicalism was visible in the way that both local reservation people and urban activists fought back against racial violence and oppression in an unprecedented, confrontational manner. After the Gordon confrontation, AIM's reputation as a militant advocacy group of Indigenous people soared.[204] *Shannon County News* called AIM "the shock troops of the Indian Nation."[205] The rising militancy was reflected in the adoption of nationalist symbolism, such as the AIM anthem and the inverted American flag.[206] For many reservation residents, the protest rally was an empowering experience.[207] For several days, local Lakota people who had long kept silent finally voiced their complaints and spoke out at "grand juries."[208] Bill Means (Lakota) pointed to the major implications of the event: "It was a turning point. We could not just carry signs and protest, but we would have to be willing to die to protect our people."[209] Leonard Crow Dog (Lakota) concurred, claiming "it was the beginning of a new Indian nation."[210]

The clashes between Indigenous civil rights activists and white supremacists were not only over racial inequalities; they can also be read as a struggle over power that was expressed in gendered terms.[211] Gendered rhetoric tapped into well-known historical narratives, resurrecting and reinterpreting imagery of the Indian Wars refought in the twentieth century. Both Indigenous activists and white supremacists utilized the rhetoric of manhood as a tool for political mobilization—either in defense of white manhood and womanhood or, alternatively, in pursuit of Indigenous rights and for protecting Indigenous women and men. Indigenous activists sought to dismantle the gender and racial hierarchy in South Dakota. White citizens demonized Indigenous men while espousing Western ideals of whiteness, racial superiority, and manhood in order to maintain social order and retain their authority.[212] The careful crafting and recrafting of images of white settlers doing battle with savage warriors gave white resistance to the Indigenous Rights Struggle a false sense of timelessness.[213]

The demasculinization of Indigenous activists by Westerners bore striking resemblances to white campaigns of "massive resistance" to the Black civil rights movement in the American South. There, White Citizen Councils were bent on resisting an overturning of the gender and racial hierarchy that rested on the twin pillars of segregation and disfranchisement. According to historian Steve Estes, white segregationists frequently espoused a "rhetoric of manhood that intersected with themes of Southern honor, social control, and racial violence."[214] White segregationists' gendered rhetoric sought to mobilize white men and women in defense of segregation but also pointed to deeper currents in 1960s and 1970s American society and a rising male insecurity as male bastions of power and control came under increasing attack.[215]

In turn, Indigenous men employed their cultural/racial capital to challenge and ultimately dismantle the gender and racial hierarchy in South Dakota. Russell Means described the reaction of Gordon residents to Indigenous protests as follows: "People left half-eaten breakfasts on kitchen tables, and abandoned their homes with doors wide open, as though their ancestors' worst nightmares had come true—a horde of bloodthirsty savages was invading their town. Rather than allow themselves to be scalped or raped, hundreds drove in panic into the wintry countryside."[216] This reaction of white residents testifies as much to the pervasiveness of stereotypical images of Indigenous manliness as to AIM's increasingly aggressive assertion of Indigenous rights and hypermasculine posturing.

By early 1973, South Dakota rose to become the center of simmering racial conflict. A report by the *South Dakota Advisory Committee to the U.S. Commission on Civil Rights*—conducted in 1975 and published two years later—confirmed abysmal socioeconomic disparities, police harassment and brutality, and widespread discriminatory practices among law enforcement as well as judicial and correctional systems toward Indigenous people.[217] As AIM set out to challenge the status quo in South Dakota, tensions erupted in a series of confrontations.[218] The white community reacted by prodding Rapid City mayor Don Barnett to take action. "I received dozens of letters and phone calls from angry white citizens who demanded that the police 'crack a few skulls' and drive AIM out of town and out of South Dakota," he recalled.[219] He also remembered that "townspeople came to me, and cowboys, saying if we don't get out there and kill 'em, they'd take the law into their own hands. Well, s—, I'm not going to kill anybody!"[220] White South Dakotans reacted to the Indigenous challenge by buffing up the number of law-enforcement officers, purchasing guns, and forming vigilante groups. Soon, white vigilantes began driving around in pickup trucks with loaded rifles and shotguns.[221]

The killing of yet another Indigenous man, Wesley Bad Heart Bull (Lakota), ignited a series of violent clashes between white law enforcement officers and Indigenous protesters. On January 21, 1973, Wesley Bad Heart was stabbed to death outside a bar in Buffalo Gap, South Dakota. On the surface, it looked as if just another Indigenous man had fallen victim to a white man and the double standards of the justice system in South Dakota. The disparity between the cases, however, was remarkable.[222] Unlike the Raymond Yellow Thunder case, where there was little doubt that the racial violence had been committed by white supremacists, the Bad Heart Bull killing was less clear-cut. This was in part because Bad Heart Bull had accumulated a massive criminal record and had caused the bar fight himself.[223] AIM quickly claimed that the assailant was only charged with second-degree manslaughter instead of first-degree murder.[224] Paul Chaat Smith (Comanche) and Robert Allen Warrior (Osage) argue that the rage over the killing of yet another Indigenous man had less to do with the details of his death and more to do with what was business as usual in that state.[225]

AIM prepared for a massive confrontation at Custer, South Dakota, the county seat of Buffalo Gap, to protest the pattern of racial discrimination against Indigenous people. In designating Custer as "the focal point of a National Day of Indian Rights,"[226] Indigenous protesters quite consciously sought to draw attention to present racial injustices by connecting them to those in the past, as historian Justin Hammer has pointed out.[227] There are few historical figures as ambivalent as Lieutenant-General George Armstrong Custer, who is either mythologized as an American hero or vilified as the personification of ruthless conquest of the American West.[228] "We hated that city already for its name," Leonard Crow Dog (Lakota) reflected in his memoirs.[229] AIM's leaders maximized the historical significance of the location named after the notorious Indian fighter.[230] Their threats of violence and the mounting pressure caused serious concern among Custer residents. "So the entire town became eager to get ready," a local resident remembered. "People practiced up on target practice, got their guns oiled, ammunition was bought."[231]

On the morning of February 6, 1973, Leonard Crow Dog, Russell Means, Dennis Banks, and Ted Means (Lakota), with news cameras rolling, fired up a crowd of roughly two hundred protesters inside the Mother Butler Center in Rapid City, South Dakota, readying for violent confrontation.[232] Leonard Crow Dog stressed that the only way to halt the racist violence perpetrated against Indigenous people was "to let the white man know we are not afraid"—if need be by picking up a gun. Then, brandishing a rifle, he stated, "We will be in Custer to sacrifice our lives. If the white man makes a move we're gonna get it on there."[233] Then, Dennis Banks directly addressed the possibility of using violence against their white oppressors:

> For those people who have killed Indian citizens . . . let them be in Custer today and prepare to die for what they believe in. Let all of those bastards, let all of those murderers be in Custer on February 6, and let each and every one of us have that same kind of gut-feeling that has hurt us every day. Let us take that gut-feeling to Custer today. And show America . . . that we will not tolerate any more abuse. That we will not tolerate any more killing. They have killed their last Indian.[234]

Making full use of the symbolic ambivalence of Custer and connecting it to the killing of Indigenous men at the hands of whites, Dennis Banks openly condoned using violence, even if it took a few lives: "If there are to be any more killings, we will be the killers. . . . From now on, they have killed their last Indian."[235]

The speeches were punctuated with reference to Lakota warrior themes. Speakers frequently evoked Crazy Horse, the epitome of the Lakota warrior and leader of the thousands of warriors who annihilated Custer and his outfit at the Battle of the Little Bighorn. The martial rhetoric resonated with the crowd, because it harked back to a shared history of resistance. In traditional Lakota culture, "hoka hey" or "it's a good day to die!" was meant to instill bravery in warriors before going to battle. The continual resurrection and reiteration of warrior themes fired up those who would descend upon the town of Custer—men, women, and children—for the anticipated confrontation. The last one to speak, Ted Means (Lakota), once again pointed to the symbolic significance of the border town: "There are Custer, South Dakotas all over the country," he stated. "They are going to remember! Custer is gonna feel that gut feeling that is inside of us, each and every day! That same gut feeling that Dennis talked about should be with us again. We are going to make them listen—with our bodies!" During the gathering, David Hill (Choctaw) stood on the podium with sunglasses and rifle in hand, embodying a martial pose that reflected the combative tone of the speeches. The assembled crowd then made its way from Rapid City to Custer in two separate car caravans. On the way, one car caravan stopped at City Hill, South Dakota, to overturn and burn a station wagon, the symbol of settler pioneers; racial tensions were ready to explode.[236]

The Custer courthouse incident would go down as the first race riot in modern South Dakota history.[237] The *Custer Chronicle* stated that by 1:40 p.m., a caravan of twenty-nine cars with one to two hundred men, women, and children arrived in the snowy streets of Custer, South Dakota; there, they joined another twenty to thirty activists who had arrived previously and were waiting in front of the courthouse.[238] Some carried or wore huge upside-down flags; others were wrapped in blankets against the cold and concealed weapons underneath them.[239] Outside the courthouse, a row of highway patrol officers blocked the entrance to the crowd of protestors while inside the courthouse an AIM delegation met with South Dakota state attorney Hobart Gates and some Custer officials. The discussion became increasingly heated as Dennis Banks and Russell Means verbally confronted white officials about the manslaughter charges and the supposedly low bail set for the accused murderer.[240]

Meanwhile, protesters outside the courthouse grew restless; a scuffle at the doorsteps of the courthouse turned into a fistfight.[241] The *Custer Weekly* reported as follows: "The militants stormed out of the office and apparently gave a signal for attack as it was this time the mob on the porch and front steps of the courthouse smashed through the doors and burst inside."[242] In an interview decades after the incident, Thelma Rios (Lakota) admitted that David Hill (Choctaw) instigated the Custer courthouse riot. "I was there. I saw him start it, punching a cop," she said. "At the time everybody thought it was great. He was a warrior."[243] The *Rapid City Journal* reported that in the ensuing courthouse brawl, policemen armed with riot batons battled Indigenous protesters carrying clubs, metal pipes, and other objects.[244] Jim Roubideau (Spirit Lake Nation) experienced the fighting firsthand. "We were fighting and they come maybe with a nightstick, so I blocked it and took it away and used it on them."[245] Law enforcement officers were able to push the protesters outside where "hand-to-hand combat" continued.[246] Outside the courthouse, police tossed tear gas canisters at the protesters, who threw them back.[247]

The scuffle at the Custer courthouse eventually became a full-scale riot that lasted for nearly three hours. Edgar Bear Runner (Lakota) pushed his way into the courthouse after the fighting started.[248] He described the events as follows: "We bloodied the guy, we took [his] helmet away [and] we bloodied him up. Then I ran across to help get gas at the filling station. [We] were filling up Molotov cocktails and busting the bottles on the building."[249] Then Bear Runner and others broke into the nearby gas station across the street, prepared firebombs, and tossed gasoline onto the courthouse. Soon, they turned their attention to the Chamber of Commerce building opposite the courthouse.[250] When the race riot finally ended, the Custer courthouse was partially burnt; the Chamber of Commerce, a log cabin-like building, had burned to the ground; a Texaco service station was vandalized; the office of the Standard Oil Co. bulk gasoline plant was damaged; two police vehicles were destroyed; several Indigenous and eight law enforcement officers were injured severely enough to require medical attention; and a total of twenty-seven activists had been arrested.[251]

Meanwhile, the town of Custer was struggling to come to terms with

Racial conflict led to a series of confrontations between Indigenous activists and law enforcement officers in Nebraska and South Dakota that climaxed in the town of Custer, South Dakota, on February 6, 1973. Following a scuffle at the courthouse, the protest turned into a riot. Here, state troopers are dragging a Lakota woman through the snow, ripping her blouse off in the process. (Richard Erdoes Papers, Yale Collection of Western Americana, Beinecke Rare Book and Manuscript Library)

the racially motivated violence.[252] For about a week, Custer turned into what the *Rapid City Journal* called an "armed camp."[253] A white resident remembered that "the tension was so high, the feelings were so much on edge . . . if a caravan of Indians had peacefully tried to drive down Main Street and one of the cars had backfired they would have just been wiped out totally. Without any questions asked." Armed men manned the roof of buildings and fire trucks and police cars barricaded the roads leading into and out of Custer.[254] Panic was so widespread that Custer mayor Gene Reese feared "overreaction that could lead to bloodshed."[255]

AIM members held a victory celebration in Rapid City. For Carter Camp (Ponca), the confrontation at Custer was an empowering experience, because it was the first time that Indigenous people had fought back: "We have to make sure that this war is fought in the white communities.

Demonstrators setting ablaze the Chamber of Commerce building at the Custer, South Dakota, demonstration on February 6, 1973. (Richard Erdoes Papers, Yale Collection of Western Americana, Beinecke Rare Book and Manuscript Library)

Not around where the Indian people live. We want to take it to their home and their businesses. Now, make sure that every white person in this area don't [sic] feel safe when he goes asleep at night. We want them to see mad red people in their dreams!"[256] On February 9, three days after the demonstration at Custer, racial violence erupted once again, this time in Rapid City, where four bars were severely damaged, sixteen people hurt, and forty arrested.[257] Further confrontations in Sturgis and Hot Springs, South Dakota, were narrowly avoided—in large part due to a massive show of force and martial posture from law enforcement officers.[258]

## Performing Warriorhood at the Takeover of the BIA in 1972

By the early 1970s, Indigenous nationalists increasingly targeted the BIA to contest their position of subalternity and limited agency. In 1970, AIM coordinated sit-ins in seven BIA offices across the nation.[259] On

September 22, 1971, more than a dozen Indigenous activists burst into the BIA headquarters office in Washington, DC, to place a citizen's arrest on BIA officials but were repulsed and arrested by police.[260] During the takeover of the BIA headquarters in Washington, DC, in early November 1972, AIM shut down eight BIA offices across the nation through demonstrations and occupations.[261]

The original idea of the Trail of Broken Treaties (ToBT), a cross-continental caravan, was to converge on Washington, DC, before the presidential election in order to focus media attention on the Indigenous protest agenda. Robert Burnette (Lakota), a World War II veteran and former Rosebud tribal chairman, developed the idea during a Sun Dance in August 1972.[262] It was endorsed by a coalition of eight Indigenous organizations.[263] Hank Adams (Sioux-Assiniboine), a US Army veteran, fishing rights activist from the Pacific Northwest and supporter of the Alcatraz Island occupation, drew up a Twenty-Point position paper.[264]

The Twenty Points sought to fundamentally restructure Indigenous-white relations. The proposal emphasized the restoration of bilateral treaty relations, the restoration of Indigenous lands, the repeal of termination, the protection of religious and cultural freedoms, increased funding to alleviate pressing socioeconomic conditions, full tribal control of reservations, and the abolition of the BIA.[265] In essence, as Vine Deloria (Yankton Dakota) put it, the Twenty-Point proposal sought to end the "quasi-protectorate status" of Indigenous people and restore tribal nations as independent nations.[266] The ToBT marked a major shift in AIM's protest agenda away from urban issues and civil rights toward reservation issues and treaty rights, thus providing a stronger link to the more traditional segments of Indigenous society.[267]

The circumstances surrounding the struggle for control over the BIA building in Washington, DC, are well established. The confluence of a number of interrelated developments and events—the political situation (with political campaigning taking place everywhere but the capital), a major logistics meltdown among ToBT organizers (with a failure to provide for food and accommodation), government antagonism (in anticipation of a violent showdown), as well as miscommunication and ensuing conflict between government officials and ToBT members led to the takeover of the BIA.[268] Indigenous activists considered the National

Park Service's refusal to hold religious ceremonies at Arlington National Cemetery and the Iwo Jima Memorial to honor two Indigenous war heroes—World War II veteran Ira Hayes and Korean War veteran John Rice—a major insult. However, they secretly found a way to do it anyway.[269] The weeklong occupation saw numerous clashes between police officers—General Service Administration (GSA) officers, US Marshals, Metropolitan police, Park Service police, and others—and Indigenous activists-turned-warriors barricaded themselves inside the BIA building, utilizing office furniture—desks, chairs, file cabinets—and armed themselves with makeshift weapons made from office equipment.

The occupation ended with a negotiated settlement: the government promised to study complaints and formally respond to the Trail's Twenty-Point proposal, to provide travel money, and to recommend amnesty for the occupiers.[270]

The confrontations usually followed the same pattern. Tensions rose whenever riot police made preparations to storm the building. Outside the building, Indigenous activists armed with makeshift weapons made of furniture and office equipment stood off against riot police. In anticipation of the ensuing violence, Indigenous men and women turned chair or table legs into clubs, transformed rebars into spears, prepared tomahawks by fastening knives, letter openers, and scissors to chair legs, or utilized chair seats as shields.[271] Indigenous Vietnam veterans prepared Molotov cocktails.[272] Some AIM warriors had brought concealed guns into the building.[273] Interspersed throughout the picket line of warriors in front of the building were also some warrior women. Together, they faced the line of law enforcement officers in riot gear with helmets, flak vests, sticks, and shields. According to Woody Kipp (Blackfoot), "there was always . . . a gaggle of warriors stationed near the doors, ready to secure them, if need arose."[274]

For the duration of the weeklong siege, every federal court order or ultimatum and threatened police action or attack prompted a new round of frenzied defense of the building. Tensions intensified as occupiers fortified the building even more—with everything they could lay their hands on—while warriors and police lined up to face each other in front of the building. Meanwhile, inside, women, children, and the elderly would retreat to the upper floors where they stacked dozens of typewriters and

Participants of the Trail of Broken Treaties caravan took over the BIA headquarters building in Washington, DC, in November 1972. The image shows a crowd of Indigenous men and women at the steps of the BIA building. Many are armed with clubs and have applied war paint on their faces in anticipation of a confrontation with law enforcement officers. In the front row to the lower right stands Vernon Bellecourt draped in a blanket. (Richard Erdoes Papers, Yale Collection of Western Americana, Beinecke Rare Book and Manuscript Library)

trashcans filled with hot water, ready to hurl them down on attacking police from staircases or windows.[275] Others prepared Molotov cocktails,[276] piled loose roof tiles upstairs,[277] or carried tipi poles to the roof to throw as spears at attackers when they attempted to break through the front entrance.[278] The continual threat of an impending attack kept the occupiers in crisis mode throughout the takeover. "The occupation proved similar to my Vietnam experience," Woody Kipp (Blackfoot), an ex-Marine remembered," long stretches of boredom punctuated by periods of frantic activity as deadlines for evacuation neared and evaporated."[279]

At times, amid the ever-present threat of violence, the takeover resembled an "Indian Woodstock" and a show of Indigenous pride.[280] During the occupation, Trail participants unfolded a banner across the BIA building reading "Native American Embassy," a visible assertion of

Three Indigenous men guard the entrance of the occupied BIA building in Washington, DC, 1972. Floyd Young Horse (*right*) drew considerable media attention due to his characteristic Indigenous looks, braids, and neck choker. Nationalist symbolism and ideology—such as the upside-down American flag and movement fashion—reflected cultural pride and militancy. Dual processes of radicalization and retraditionalization led to a renewal, revitalization, and remasculinization in Indigenous men. By late 1972, many Indigenous men in AIM had come to regard themselves as modern-day warriors in a struggle against domestic colonialism. (Richard Erdoes Papers, Yale Collection of Western Americana, Beinecke Rare Book and Manuscript Library)

their claim to political sovereignty and display of ethnic pride. They set up a twenty-foot-tall tipi on the front lawn, near the flagpole where the American flag flew upside-down at half-mast.[281] Media reporters, hippies, and celebrities—Black activists Stokely Carmichael, Marion Berry and Jim Williams; noted author Dr. Benjamin Spock; and Wavy Gravy from the Merry Pranksters—paid a visit to the liberated place.[282] Inside, Indigenous people in "a mixture of regalia and army fatigues" were in the middle of the festive atmosphere, whereas, outside, police forces had cordoned off the entire building, "with just enough threat of violence to keep everyone's nerves tingling," as Robert Burnette recalled.[283] In front of the BIA building, supporters formed a human chain between police and occupiers in an attempt to discourage violent confrontation.[284]

During the BIA takeover, the performance of warrior masculinity took place in a hybrid space in which media theatre, cultural practices, and political protest were closely intermingled, making it difficult to distinguish between what was staged and what was not. At times, the gendered rhetoric and performance of "Indians playing Indian" themes constituted a conscious effort by activists to attract media attention. At other times, Indigenous protesters took on a warrior persona to defend those inside the building. There were differences between the way Indigenous men performed their manliness inside the BIA building (away from the media limelight) and outside the BIA building (in the media spotlight). The aggressive display of warriorhood resulted in widespread media attention and favorable government negotiations. According to Dennis Banks, government officials reacted with "fear" once confronted with AIM warriors with their makeshift weapons.[285]

The news media picked up on the militancy of Indigenous activism, the performance of warriorhood, and the revolutionary posturing.[286] News reporting focused on violence and militancy, framing the protest event around stereotypical images as well as the gendered confrontations between law enforcement officers and AIM members. The choice of news reporting reflected a distinct media bias and AIM's choice of confrontation and militancy as an agenda-setting tool but submerged the issues underlying the protest.[287] In their revolutionary posturing, AIM's leaders once again referenced nineteenth-century Indian Wars refought in the present.[288] Indigenous nationalists frequently referred to the many Black law enforcement officers outside the BIA building as "buffalo soldiers"—a nickname that referenced Black cavalrymen who fought tribal warriors during the Indian Wars.[289]

Dennis Banks recalled how male AIM leaders and rank-and-file members sought to make an impact on the news media and utilized nationalist symbolism and rhetoric in what amounted to the performing of street theatrics. As he recalled:

> We appealed to the press to let the country know the reasons for the takeover and what our demands were. . . . And we dressed up for the occasion.

Indigenous activists at the entrance of the BIA building with makeshift weapons made of furniture and office equipment standing off against riot police. Some men have applied war paint on their faces. Carter Camp (Ponca) is on the far left of the group in the center; in the background are Bill Means (Lakota) and Clyde Bellecourt (Ojibwe). (Steve Northup Photographic Archive, The Dolph Briscoe Center for American History, University of Texas at Austin)

Russ wore a red shirt with a beaded medallion over his chest. An eagle feather dangled from the side of braids. Clyde wore a black, wide-brimmed Uncle Joe hat and a bone choker around his neck; I draped a colorful Pendleton blanket over my shoulders. The one in our group most interviewed by the press was Floyd Young Horse, a Minneconjou from Eagle Butte, South Dakota, because of his classic, full-blood face, his red-wrapped braids, and his fine sense of humor.[290]

The BIA takeover was another defining moment for Russell Means. Photographers shot a picture of him armed with a club, carrying a gas mask, and using a framed portray of Richard Nixon as a shield.[291] In his memoirs, Means cast himself in the starring role of a modern-day warrior who would go down fighting like his ancestors did, yet, conveniently, he played out his role in the media spotlight:

> We figured the police would come then. I thought of the traditional song our ancestors had sung on similar occasions, "It's a good day to die." I decided that our cause was everything. If it came down to it, that was a good way to die. While our elders and pregnant women huddled in the basement and tensions rose steadily, we told ourselves that although we had no weapons but Molotov cocktails and homemade clubs, we would make those pigs pay dearly for our lives.[292]

The AIM leader had virtually made a career as an activist by staging confrontations for the media and engaging in self-aggrandizing political rants. At this pivotal moment, he saw himself as standing up for "the cause" and his people as much in line with reinvented notions of Indigenous warriorhood. He and others would whip up everybody's emotions to the breaking point with continual "it's a good day to die" war cries. When a final attack to oust the occupiers at the height of the confrontation seemed imminent, he declared: "If we go, there's going to be a helluva smoke signal! This building is not going to be here anymore."[293] There was ample evidence that the occupiers had prepared to go down fighting and torch the entire building if police sought to evict them.[294]

During the BIA takeover, Indigenous men performed their warrior masculinities in culturally specific ways. Ritual performances mean different things to different people in accordance with their sense of belonging.[295] Certain rituals of performance are constitutive of protest or resistance masculinities.[296] Throughout the BIA takeover, Indigenous activists-turned-warriors recognized the significance of cultural ceremonies and practices. In his autobiographical account, Dennis Banks recalled that Crow Dog (Lakota) utilized cultural and warrior ceremonies, prayer, and sage to prepare Indigenous men for the imminent confrontation with police shortly after they had taken over the building:

> Crow Dog blessed the warriors with sage and then he fanned them off, using an eagle feather to fan smoke from the burning sage toward the men to bless them. A number of our men had painted their faces for war, with

Two unidentified Indigenous activists at the BIA with makeshift weapons. Activist to the left wears a red beret with "Indian Patrol" patch and an "AIM" badge on his leather jacket. Activist to the right has "Red Power" patch sewn on his jacket and the letters "AIM" sewn underneath his front pocket; on the other side of his jacket is the upside-down American flag with yet another sticker, "Fry Bread Power," and a ribbon. This revolutionary movement culture contained numerous elements that were genuine to Lakota culture and iconic to the general public, such as the Panther-inspired beret and jacket, and it conveyed cultural pride and political radicalism. The AIM uniform became the symbol of militant Indigenous manliness and the expression of defiant nationalism in the face of rampant racism. (Steve Northup Photographic Archive, The Dolph Briscoe Center for American History, University of Texas at Austin)

lipstick if they could find nothing else. I knew that the police outside—with their helmets and flak vests—realized they were not facing a bunch of flower children or student anti-war protesters. We were dead serious.[297]

Robert Burnette (Lakota) observed the scene and recalled that those who took part in the ceremony and got their faces painted expected "a fight to the death."[298] Floyd Young Horse (Lakota) was the first to put on war paint.[299] Most of the Indigenous men present were young students and

Vietnam veterans.[300] Many of these cultural ceremonies stood in line with an older cultural tradition of manhood/warriorhood. Throughout the seizure and as the occupiers awaited police attacks, Leonard Crow Dog held daily sacred pipe ceremonies. Woody Kipp saw himself as a warrior/veteran/activist, despite his own cross-cultural upbringing.

> As a former marine, I considered myself a warrior and didn't readily make a connection between warfare and spirit. I carried a big oak table leg with a dangerous nail sticking out its end. I was warfare. Those who prayed, who held traditional Indian ceremonies, impressed me, but I hadn't been raised around the Sacred Pipe; I had eaten the flesh and had drunk the blood of the Holy Christ through the ceremonies of the Catholic Church.[301]

Some Indigenous activists draped themselves in upside-down American flags, beat a drum, and sang the AIM song.[302] Soon, "It's a good day to die!" shouts and vows were heard from a number of men.[303] The assertion of warriorhood corresponded with displays of martial physicality. *Akwesasne Notes* described the initial encounter between Indigenous activists and police as follows: "Young men, stripped to the waist, painted their chests and wore their armbands and necklaces. Most prepared their weapons. . . . Tribal drums reverberated through the long halls of the building, and the Indians once again prepared to do battle with the white man."[304]

Indigenous men displayed their physicality—bare-chested, muscles flexed, with long, warrior-like hair held by red bandanas, brandishing weapons—in an additional effort to remasculinize in confrontations with police. Nationalist movements are deeply masculinist projects and frequently emphasize the need to remake the male physical body in attempts to reform the colonized society and to (re)invigorate the

---

*Opposite:* Russell Means (Lakota) holding a framed photo of President Nixon as a shield and carrying a club (*partially covered*) during the occupation of BIA building in Washington, DC. Here and elsewhere, Means revealed his bizarre approach to protest politics that attracted considerable media attention. Frequently, the media focused on the spectacle rather than the message. (Steve Northup Photographic Archive, The Dolph Briscoe Center for American History, University of Texas at Austin)

nationalist endeavor.³⁰⁵ Dominant society closely associates Indigenous male physicality with a primitive hypermasculinity.³⁰⁶ In displaying their physicality, Indigenous men tapped into well-known martial stereotypes while countering public perceptions of emasculation.³⁰⁷

The cultural practices and ceremonies that took place inside the BIA building sought to prepare Indigenous protesters-turned-warriors for an imminent confrontation with police (which never actually occurred). Some cultural practices and ceremonies (e.g., prayers, blessings, drumming, songs) were those that had been utilized to ceremonially prepare warriors or veterans for battle. The phrase "Hoka Hey, today is a good day to die!" frequently uttered by the Indigenous occupiers was traditionally used by tribal warriors to express a willingness and eagerness to die a honorable and brave death; it also referred to a belief in living without regrets.³⁰⁸ In the BIA takeover, the occupiers utilized what was at hand to serve their purposes, much in line with cultural strategies of reinvention: office furniture and equipment were transformed into weapons and lipstick was used as war paint.

The height of the escalation occurred on November 6, 1972, the day before the presidential election, in what look like an impending attack and attempt to evict the occupiers. At this point, according to Dennis Banks, "it looked as though we would have to fight for our lives."³⁰⁹ Trail leaders seriously discussed the option of burning down the BIA as a last act of defiance to ensure that the government's inevitable victory would be a costly one. The occupiers piled up records, soaked them with gasoline, and were ready to light them up at any moment. Meanwhile, across the BIA building, police took up a heavy martial posture, waiting for an order for the final attack that never came.³¹⁰ The police faced two rows of warriors, who stood in front of the building to protect those inside.³¹¹ The volatile situation was defused at the last moment; the order to clear the building was never given.³¹²

The sustained BIA takeover illustrated the extent of Indigenous resistance to settler-colonial rule. According to sociologist Michael Messner, "marginalized and subordinated men . . . tend to overtly display exaggerated embodiments and verbalizations of masculinity that can be read as a desire to express power over others within a context of relative

"We Became Warriors Again"  153

Russell Means (*left*) and Clyde Bellecourt (*right*) stand on a podium and give a press conference inside the occupied BIA building 1972. AIM's male leaders frequently sought the media limelight during protest events, pushing Indigenous women and their concerns into the background. (Richard Erdoes Papers, Yale Collection of Western Americana, Beinecke Rare Book and Manuscript Library)

powerlessness."[313] In their autobiographies, Clyde Bellecourt and Dennis Banks found the takeover of the BIA headquarters an empowering experience.[314] By taking over the BIA building, the occupiers took on a position of power they had previously been denied, becoming for a brief moment "masters of the building," as Banks put it.[315] The BIA takeover was symbolic of how Indigenous men articulated their quest for masculine power and authority and merged it with calls for sovereignty and self-determination. The Indigenous men's aggressive posturing against impeding attacks of law enforcement officers reflected their gendered role as warriors in the nationalist Red Power struggle as a whole. The 1972 BIA takeover was the first major protest event in which Indigenous men linked their militant masculinities with calls for political independence and self-determination. With the BIA takeover, they struck at the very heart of US settler colonialism. John Trudell (Santee Dakota) proudly explained: "We have destroyed it [the BIA]; they can no longer use it. Now it's only a memorial to the white man's shame."[316]

With the sustained seizure of the BIA, AIM had turned into "the most violence-prone Indian organization in the country," as Paul Chaat Smith (Comanche) and Robert Allen Warrior (Osage) put it.[317] For a week, ToBT participants effectively assumed control over the abhorred colonial agency. At its end, AIM's leadership proudly declared the BIA's destruction.[318] The destruction of the BIA was the most significant act of Indigenous resistance since the Battle of the Little Bighorn and "a bold strike against colonialism," according to Smith and Warrior.[319] Congressional hearings arrived at a damage of $250,000.[320] The GSA called it "the most destructive attack by citizens on federal property in the nation's history."[321] This also included the massive theft of tons of BIA documents, spirited away in two truckloads;[322] these were partially recovered a few months later in Robeson County, North Carolina, a center of Black and Indigenous militancy.[323] The GSA's public display of makeshift weapons was yet another effort to highlight the destructiveness of the occupiers.[324] According to Robert Burnette (Lakota), "the display proved that the rank and file people in the caravans didn't come to Washington expecting a fight, for better weapons could be found in a locker of any urban high school."[325] Following the ToBT, AIM cofounder George Mitchell quit in disgust over the way AIM leaders' ego trips had marred the course of the national protest event and the way they had split up the travel money.[326] AIM shifted its focus toward tribal politics and reservation affairs. As Wes Studi put it, "We moved from the Bureau of Indian Affairs back into our own communities and began to build resistance."[327]

In early December 1972, a congressional hearing stressed the use of government restraint to defuse an extremely volatile situation. "I am absolutely sure, in my mind, that they were prepared, some of them, to martyr themselves," declared Secretary of the Interior Rogers Morton. "They were looking for a fight; in other words, they were looking for violence as a means of furthering their cause."[328] Government officials agreed that the confrontation and repeated threats of sacrificing themselves were genuine.[329]

## Struggling to Restore Balance: Gender Relations and Sexual Politics Within AIM

Indigenous women frequently rationalized their "invisibility" in the Red Power movement by referencing their "behind the scenes work" on behalf of their tribal communities and nations.[330] Within their tribal structures, they were less concerned with Western perspectives on women's liberation, which categorized women in terms of mother and housewife, and sought to break away from this.[331] Rather, Indigenous women perceived their place and position from a cultural perspective in which womanhood and motherhood were traditionally respected and seen as an integral part of tribal society. Indigenous womanhood is thus frequently regarded as the source of cultural persistence against the relentless assimilationist onslaught of various settler-colonial policies.[332] As such, Indigenous women activists also eschewed Western feminism in favor of an Indigenous reproductive activism and asserted their obligation to bear children in order to revive the Indigenous population.[333] It should be noted that Indigenous women's perspectives were, and still are, far from uniform.[334] While there was certainly a group of Indigenous women who prioritized tribal survival and mothering, there were also those who questioned the centrality of motherhood and the supposed stark division between Indigenous and "white" feminisms and complicated some of the patterns.[335]

Indigenous women were involved in virtually every protest event in the 1960s and 1970s and did much of the grassroots organizing: they cofounded AIM, organized survival schools, seized the BIA, occupied Wounded Knee, marched to Washington, DC, and kept things going. Activist journalist Laura Waterman Wittstock (Seneca) observed that some women in AIM, such as Madonna Thunder Hawk (Lakota), Lorelei Means (Lakota), and Pat Bellanger (Ojibwe), were clearly leaders. She went on to state,

> Just having your picture on the news did not, in my estimation, mean that that's the only leadership AIM had. I think AIM did acknowledge that women's leadership was essential to what they were doing, because the women opened clinics, they manned the schools, said they were essential in health and education and other areas that were important to what AIM was saying it meant to do for the future of Indian people.[336]

Many Indigenous women who joined AIM aspired to build their communities by fighting for affordable housing, setting up alternative educational facilities and cultural programs, providing legal aid, and improving the conditions of the urban poor. That work began well before Wounded Knee and has carried on since. Media images of hypermasculine warriors kept Indigenous women out of the spotlight and, ultimately, discounted their pivotal role in grassroots organizing and in advancing Indigenous agendas. Historian Elizabeth Castle explains this simply: "Women were the backbone and men were the jawbone."[337] Indigenous women in AIM were deeply committed to the struggle for Indigenous rights. They, too, sought to remake their Indigenous and gendered identities. Feminist scholars have stressed Indigenous women's traditional leadership positions in tribal societies, which embraced matrilineality and egalitarianism. They point out that that during pre-colonial times, Indigenous women occupied gender roles and responsibilities equal and complementary to those of their male counterparts.[338]

Historiography suggests that Indigenous women constituted the backbone of AIM, but when men entered the picture, "they were pushed out . . . and into the kitchen," in the words of AIM lawyer Kenneth Stern.[339] Within AIM, Indigenous men's and women's joint struggle against colonial oppression often overshadowed another, equally significant struggle, namely, that of gender equality. The intrinsic role of masculinity in social movements for change and resistance has been variously noted.[340] Social movements have a tendency to regard the struggle against class and race oppression as having more significance than the struggle against gender oppression. In racialized masculinity politics, the struggle for equal rights is thus reduced to a struggle against class and race oppression but not gender inequality.[341]

Indigenous women commonly state that they constitute the backbone of the nation in resisting settler-colonialist policies, as they devote their energies first and foremost to grassroots issues—struggles that focus on the very existence of Indigenous peoples. In consequence, they have paid considerably less attention to the struggle for gender equality than women in other social movements for change.[342] Lorelei DeCora Means (Lakota) expressed the sentiment of many Indigenous women as follows:

> We are *American Indian* women, in that order. We are oppressed, first and foremost, as American Indians, as peoples colonized by the United States of America, not as women. As Indians, we can never forget that. Our survival, the survival of every one of us—man, woman, and child—*as Indians* depends on it. Decolonization is the agenda, the whole agenda, and until it is accomplished, it is the only agenda that counts for American Indians. It will take every one of us—every single one of us—to get the job done.[343]

She also dismissed those "who come to us wanting to form alliances on the basis of 'new' and 'different' or 'broader' and 'more important' issues" as being "less than friends," particularly given the fact that Western society most directly benefits from their ongoing colonization.[344]

Like other revolutionary movements for change, AIM found itself incapable of simultaneously confronting racial oppression and addressing issues of gender equality, from the leadership to the rank and file. AIM's male leadership rhetorically embraced gender equality, yet, in practice, never followed up on it.[345] According to one unidentified observer, Indigenous women would do the paperwork and answer the phones in the Twin Cities offices, yet rarely received the credit they deserved: "I saw many instances where women made a decision, but when it went public, it would be Clyde or Dennis on the television explaining what had been decided."[346] Autobiographical accounts are filled with narratives of Indigenous men seeking to protect Indigenous women from rape, sexual harassment, physical violence, or racism from the hands of whites. Yet while men in AIM sought to protect Indigenous women from white men's violence, many had a reputation for verbally and physically abusing women.[347]

Dennis Banks and Russell Means had a reputation for drinking, fighting, partying, and womanizing. "Some of the AIM leaders attracted quite a number of 'wives.' We called them 'wives of the month,'" Mary Crow Dog (Lakota) recalled.[348] She remembered that one unidentified male leader, "one of our great macho warriors, a good-looking guy, a lady's man" was swarmed over by women, in particular "white groupies."[349] She also expressed dismay at the fact that women, Indigenous and non-Indigenous alike, were willing to serve the needs of AIM's male leaders—from catering in the kitchen, to washing clothes, doing household chores, braiding men's hair, and providing sex.[350] Activist scholar Paula Gunn Allen (Laguna Pueblo) voiced her criticism of the chauvinist, sexist, and misogynistic treatment of women in no uncertain terms. As she put it, "These guys [Dennis Banks, Russell Means] were rippin' off the folks. They were drinkin' all the time, they were fuckin' their way across the United States, they were leaving a lot of uncared for babies behind, not to mention young women. Dreadful things."[351] It seems as if Banks and Means had no qualms about exploiting women and had numerous affairs. For example, by the time of his death, Russell Means was married a fifth time and had fathered nine children.[352] When Dennis Banks passed away, he was married (and divorced) multiple times, fathered nineteen children, and routinely failed to pay child support.[353] Russell Means had a history of violence against his wife and elders, and Clyde Bellecourt was arrested for domestic abuse of his wife.[354]

AIM's male leadership rhetorically embraced gender equality, yet, in practice, never followed up on it.[355] Indigenous scholar Devon Abbott Mihesuah (Choctaw) writes, "AIM male leaders . . . attempted to revive the Plains 'warrior role' of the past by stepping forward as aggressive leaders, but failed to advocate for a struggle against the bonds of colonial oppression and to embrace gender equality."[356] The media and men in the organization fostered the image of an exclusively male leadership, as this image made sense with the context of 1970s radical groups that encouraged a militant masculinity.[357] While AIM espoused a rhetoric of equality, it was incapable of enacting its ideals in practice.

AIM's male leaders rationalized their sexist attitude in various ways. In his lengthy autobiography, Russell Means argued that the "female-male balance" did not entitle women in the American Indian Movement to public leadership roles and media attention. He went on to point out the difference between women's and men's roles and the need to respect that "natural balance," thus effectively contradicting himself.[358] Another example comes from author Gerald Vizenor (Ojibwe), who observed the opening statements of the 1974 Wounded Knee trial. There, Dennis Banks rather unconvincingly tried to present himself as someone in tune with tribal cosmologies and gender roles, revealing a somewhat sexist view of women. Vizenor observed, "Banks seems to represent the dominant male view in his references to women as 'objects' and 'things' while at the same time he presents himself as a tribal traditionalist and a man of peace and spiritual visions."[359] The male AIM leaders also asserted that feminism was irrelevant to Indigenous women, as tribal societies were historically matriarchal and thus already respected women.[360]

Indigenous men within AIM utilized what Mihesuah calls "the colonialism excuse" to partially justify and explain their inherent sexism toward Indigenous and non-Indigenous women.[361] Male AIM leaders personally knew very little about traditional women's place in tribal societies and, when told, showed little inclination to adjust their behavior accordingly.[362] Apparently, many Indigenous men linked their toxic masculinities to the loss of the old ways—cultural and religious practices, social structures, political organization, and relationships to their land. They argued that the arrival of settler colonialism, Christianity, patriarchy, capitalism, and modernization had fundamentally transformed, some said lost, tribal-based systems of power and knowledge. This had ultimately deprived them of their culture and accounted for their lost role and place in society.[363] Russel Means considered "the Eurocentric male society" responsible for the corruption of tribal societies, the manipulation of their gender systems, and, ultimately, the toxicity in Indigenous men.[364] Mary Crow Dog shares a somewhat similar viewpoint, stating that much of Indigenous men's toxic behavior toward women stemmed from the loss of their own place in society that left them marginalized, disempowered, and with a need to compensate.[365]

Many Indigenous men were inculcated with the concepts of male privilege and patriarchy by dominant society. Indigenous men abided by the very ideals they struggled against, even though this contributed to their own subordination as a group.[366] According to Indigenous scholars Robert Alexander Innes (Plains Cree) and Kim Anderson (Cree/Métis), many Indigenous men were/are caught in a cycle of dysfunction: "As non-whites, Indigenous men's privilege is ultimately subordinated by white male privilege, so they are then confined to achieve their privilege through the oppression of those who are perceived from a hegemonic male perspective as being weaker and more vulnerable than they are."[367] Indigenous men within AIM had firsthand experiences with boarding schoolings, the military, and the judicial system—gendered and engendering institutions that promoted conformity, adaptation, and assimilation into dominant society. They had also experienced the cultural loss, social alienation, and self-destructive behavior at the intersections of reservation and urban life.[368] Indigenous men's adherence to hegemonic ideals of masculinity thus placed them in a contradictory and ambiguous position, putting them in direct opposition to their own liberation and that of Indigenous women. Perhaps it is for these reasons that Mary Crow Dog (Lakota) said that "our men had to fight their own men's lib battles."[369] Mary Crow Dog also expressed how internalized notions of male privilege played out in dysfunctional ways:

> The AIM leaders are particularly sexist, never having learned our true Indian history where women voted and participated in all matters of tribal life. They have learned the white man's way of talking down to women and regarding their position as inferior. Some gave us the impression that we were there for their use and that we should be flattered to have their children.[370]

Indigenous women in AIM—akin to Black women in the BPP—were well aware of dysfunctional gender roles within their respective movements; yet they did not want to weaken the joint struggle for group rights by publicly discussing gender and individual rights.[371] While many Indigenous women were critical of their male counterparts, they also spoke of those who treated them with dignity and respect in the highest regard. They valued those Indigenous men who did not seek to approve toxic behavior by condemning colonialism.[372]

Sexual dynamics in the American Indian Movement were influenced by the cultural revolution of the 1960s and 1970s. The sexual revolution challenged traditional codes of behavior in relation to sexual dynamics and interpersonal relationships. Mary Brave Bird (Lakota, formerly Mary Crow Dog) recalled that sexual relationships between men and women in the American Indian Movement were intense but also brief and casual and often left women pregnant.[373] Casual affairs were not unique to the American Indian Movement; after all, the sexual revolution served as a social backdrop to the protest politics of an entire generation. Women began to question gendered power relationships, traditional roles, and gender behavior. They began to hold the autonomy over their own relationships and were empowered with sexual agency, which was facilitated by the invention of the pill.[374] Woody Kipp "lost" his girlfriend to Russell Means. He remembered that "she was dark and pretty, and the fact that Russell Means was a handsome dude in his younger days said something about her beauty, as he had his pick of women at the time. The Weltanschauung of the movement meant, among other things, that a woman might be with one man one day and a couple of days later be seen with someone else."[375]

Some male leaders attracted quite a number of Indigenous and white female admirers. These women felt attracted to them due to their exposed position, their striking appearance, and their boldness in confronting authority. They also saw in them romantic macho militants, figures to admire. At Wounded Knee, these "groupies" were willing to cook, wash, sew, and braid the men's hair in addition to providing sex.[376] Partying, drinking, and womanizing reportedly got out-of-hand numerous times. During the AIM national convention at Cass Lake, Minnesota (May 10–16, 1972), Dennis Banks told the assembled leaders from around the country that they should be more considerate about their behavior, as it impacted the larger struggle for Indigenous rights, "that it [the movement] had to cut down on all the drinking and drugs and partying, the groupies and the 'Saturday-night warriors.'"[377] At another national convention in White Oak, Oklahoma (July 25–August 5, 1974), Russell Means was unsuccessful in being elected to an official position. An unidentified observer pointed out that this was because "Russ had his groupies, and his little groupie chapters, but it was all Saturday-night warriors and raising hell."[378] The remarks suggest that for one thing AIM leaders had a reputation for partying, drinking, and womanizing.

In practice, masculinist protest politics played out in similar ways to other minority movements for change. "By equating liberation with manhood," historian Elizabeth Castle writes in her comparative study of Black and Indigenous women's activism in the BPP and AIM, "women found themselves not only struggling for the cause, but also competing with oppressive notions of masculinities."[379] Thus the status of Indigenous women affiliated with AIM was that of a "double colonization": first, through racial inequality and white colonial domination and, second, through male privilege and female subordination—itself part of the legacy of colonization and the imposition of white heteropatriarchal masculinity.[380]

Women of color active in the BPP and in AIM felt that women's liberation advanced the goals of white, middle-class feminism, rather than women's issues within their own racial communities.[381] Indigenous women in particular viewed cooperation with white feminism not only as a diversion from their primary concern (the struggle against racial oppression) but, worse, as being complicit with colonialism (which kept them oppressed in the first place, as feminist scholars have pointed out).[382] However, many Indigenous women considered feminism a greater problem than dysfunctional gender roles within AIM or their tribal societies during the 1970s and even today. Janet McCloud (Tulalip), a fishing rights activist in the Pacific Northwest, put it this this way: "Many Anglo women try, I expect in all sincerity, to tell us that our most pressing problem is male supremacy. To this I have to say, with all due respect, *bullshit*. Our problems are what they've been for the past several hundred years: white supremacism and colonialism. And that's a supremacism and a colonialism of which white feminists are still very much a part."[383] Women of color, activists and scholars alike, have asserted that mainstream feminism remains essentially a white, middle-class phenomenon that does not take into account US colonization and the imposition of white supremacist heteropatriarchy. Indigenous women's struggles for gender equality have often been falsely portrayed as struggles against traditional practices and social structures.[384]

For many Indigenous women, the white feminist movement, typified by the National Organization of Women (NOW), held little appeal. Women's liberation focused on single issues (such as women's social and political enfranchisement), whereas Indigenous women had to confront multiple issues such as the recognition of their civil and treaty rights, the preservation of their families, and the environmental protection of their tribal lands. This basic struggle for survival not only separated Indigenous women from Western feminists but also united them with Indigenous men. Madonna Gilbert (aka Madonna Thunder Hawk, Lakota) put it this way: "In your culture you have lots of problems with men, maybe we do, too, but we don't have time to worry about sexism. We worry about survival."[385] According to Gilbert/Thunder Hawk, white women could focus on male dominance, but Indigenous women sought to advance their political agendas and empower themselves that way; therefore, women's liberation offered little to Indigenous women.[386]

## Conclusion

By 1972, Indigenous movement politics had facilitated a growing retraditionalization and a rising radicalization within AIM. Nationalist symbolism and movement culture expressed a newfound pride in Indigeneity, a development that was significantly heralded by the cultural alliance with reservation traditionalists. The radicalization within AIM found expression in frequent clashes with law enforcement officers. Together, these intertwined and parallel currents heralded the transformation from an Indigenous "protest masculinity" to a belligerent masculinity, a new kind of "warrior masculinity." The performance of warrior masculinity took place in a hybridized cultural space in which the lines between media bias, the conscious reappropriation of stereotypes, and a newly invented warrior persona were constantly blurred.

Indigenous militancy and the emergence of a warrior masculinity is best illustrated through AIM's border town activism and the takeover of the BIA headquarters. In Midwestern border towns, white citizens were intent on upholding white prerogatives. As Indigenous activists challenged these racial and gender hierarchies, they were met with organized resistance. The Gordon protest was a precursor to more violent confrontations, such as the Custer courthouse riot. Many border town confrontations made only regional news; other protests drew considerably more media attention because they occurred on highly symbolic sites. The BIA, the embodiment of US settler colonial rule, naturally became a chief target in the Indigenous nationalist struggle. The seizure of the BIA headquarters revealed a deep-seated anger, hate, and frustration. The occupation catalyzed gender dynamics in which ToBT participants cast themselves as manly defenders of women, children, and the elderly. For those present, the fight over the BIA building was a unifying moment in resistance to US colonial power that gave some credence to activists' claims to warriorhood.

Masculinized protest activism frequently overshadowed women's grassroots activism. Indigenous women were involved in behind-the-scenes activities that made the anti-colonial struggle possible in the first place. Indigenous women found that the struggle against racial oppression frequently superseded the struggle against gender oppression, thus submerging "women's issues" in service of the larger "cause."[387] Just like other women of color within other social movements for change, Indigenous women frequently abandoned their own quest for gender equality in favor of the supposedly greater goal of racial equality and social justice.[388]

# Chapter 4

# Warriors for a Nation at Wounded Knee, 1973

Nearly four decades after the Wounded Knee takeover, Carter Camp (Ponca), an AIM leader from Oklahoma and US Army veteran, reflected on his own role in the occupation. February 27, 1973, held particular significance for him, because on this date he led "a special squad of warriors to liberate Wounded Knee in advance of the main AIM caravan."[1] Riding with a contingent of sixteen men dispersed in a few cars, the group left Calico Hall, the place where, at a community meeting, local Oglala Lakota and AIM members had just made the decision to occupy the tiny hamlet. Riding in the lead vehicle, Carter Camp led the caravan through Pine Ridge and past the fortified BIA building—which, in anticipation of violence, had been manned with US Marshals, sandbagged, and stocked with machine-guns—right into the tiny hamlet of Wounded Knee.[2] Carter Camp recalled, "We were lightly armed and dependent upon the weapons and ammo inside the Wounded Knee trading post."[3] Well aware of the symbolic significance of Wounded Knee and his own role "as a warrior leading warriors," he prayed that he would do things right.[4] Upon their arrival, the group set up a perimeter, took eleven hostages, and cut phone lines. Having accomplished these tasks without incident, they waited for the arrival of the main, fifty-four-car-strong caravan.⁵ The Oklahoma contingent would not only be the first to enter Wounded Knee but would also be among the last to give up their weapons on May 8, when the occupiers surrendered, a fact they took great pride in.⁶ Carter Camp saw the Wounded Knee takeover as "the best, the most free time of my life."⁷

The gendered nation-building attempt at Wounded Knee saw two interconnected developments that went hand in hand: the declaration of the ION and the formation of a self-proclaimed AIM warrior society. In a real sense, these warriors for a nation emerged during the course of the armed confrontation and sustained takeover. This new, reinvented form of nationalist warrior masculinity emerged through the complex interweaving of two distinct currents—one veteran and the other activist—creating new directions for warrior societies and meanings of warriorhood.⁸ Scholars have only recently begun to make sense of the high participation of veterans at Wounded Knee. Both Tom Holm (Cherokee/Muscogee) and Al Carroll (Apache) examined the siege, with Holm exploring the general involvement of Indigenous veterans and Carroll providing insights into AIM's warrior society.⁹ In exploring hitherto overlooked aspects—the cultural construction of AIM's nationalist warrior masculinity and how it intersected with the declaration of the ION; competing notions of warriorhood among veterans and non-veterans; body-reflexive practices and nation-building; female warriors; and the performance of warriorhood and how it related to the news media—I seek to make new sense of these warriors for a nation and the intricate nature of gender and nationalism in evidence at Wounded Knee.

## Tribal Governance, Reservation Masculinities, and Intertribal Conflict

The 1973 conflict at Wounded Knee was rooted in long-standing sociopolitical conflicts within the Pine Ridge Reservation, South Dakota.¹⁰ Tribal governance was a form of indirect colonial rule set up under the provisions of the 1935 Indian Reorganization Act (IRA) and, naturally, supported by the BIA.¹¹ The reservation system exacerbated frictions within the tribal community over competing notions of manliness, culture, and politics. Intertribal conflict was compounded by the growth of the multiracial Indigenous population, which exacerbated sociocultural divisions, and the IRA form of tribal governance, which deepened political rifts.[12] The new form of governance was a foreign imposition on Oglala culture. Assimilationists—many of whom were of mixed blood—dominated the new government over the full-blood population.[13] The boundaries between intratribal factions were not clear-cut but blurred and frequently a matter of attitude rather than genetics.[14] The imposition of the IRA system of governance is directly linked to the takeover and seizure of Wounded Knee.[15] According to historian Clara Sue Kidwell, tribal politics were characterized by three key factors that directly translated into tribal conflict: first, the close alignment of Indigenous identity with blood and politics; second, internal conflict over forms of tribal governance (the IRA form of tribal rule versus traditional concepts, which stressed kinship ties with mutual obligations and responsibilities); and third, BIA dependency and an oppressive colonial regime. These translated into fierce antagonism and in-fighting among the Lakota.[16]

The direct cause of conflict at Wounded Knee stemmed from the severe disenchantment of local Oglala Lakota with Tribal Chairman Richard Wilson and tribal politics on Pine Ridge.[17] Shortly after taking office in early 1972, political tensions heightened over Wilson's adversarial leadership and AIM's direct challenge to his political regime.[18] Critics charged Wilson with mismanagement, failure to call the tribal council into session, a tribal resolution granting him broad-sweeping powers, the prohibition of public gatherings and due process, and unreasonable searches and seizures.[19] The BIA granted a request to beef up the 13-strong police force with a 45-strong auxiliary force.[20] The auxiliaries, or Wilson's political enforcers, would become known as the "goons," a derisive name that the new force proudly adopted as its patriotic acronym: Guardians of the Oglala Nation (GOON). Together, these moves gave Wilson broad-sweeping political powers. The strongest intratribal opposition came from the Oglala Civil Rights Council (OSCRO), a grassroots organization.[21] After impeachment proceedings failed, OSCRO ultimately turned to AIM for help.[22] The request provided AIM with some legitimacy upon the reservation; it also showed how the cultural alliance between neo-traditionalists and traditionalists transitioned into a political alliance.[23]

The express purpose of the Wounded Knee takeover was to draw attention to the intratribal conflict on Pine Ridge, to jeopardize the existent form of tribal governance, and to reinstate the 1868 Fort Laramie Treaty as legally binding. The treaty had been made on an equal nation-to-nation basis between the Lakota people and the United States. From the beginning, the occupiers made it clear that the "imposed" IRA-style form of tribal governance violated the treaty and ought to be replaced by another form of tribal governance.[24]

## Fighting US Colonialism: Indigenous and Non-Indigenous Veterans at Wounded Knee

In late February 1973, America awoke to an unfolding conflict that seemed to have come right out of the nineteenth century. Opposing a powerful force of US law enforcement agents, equipped with the latest Vietnam-era military hardware, was a poorly armed and outnumbered group of roughly three hundred Indigenous occupiers—men, women, and children—elements that made for a highly politicized confrontation replete with symbolism.[25] The Wounded Knee takeover brought up gendered analogies of yet another "Indian War," refought in the twentieth century, this time between modern-day warriors and Vietnam-era US troops; at the same time, it evoked notions as the last protest event of the "Sixties."[26]

The government's response to the takeover came with a massive buildup of military hardware and personnel to suppress the Indigenous nationalist movement. Tribal police and federal law enforcement officers—BIA police, FBI agents, US Marshal Service (USMS), and others—quickly set up roadblocks. The USMS deployed their Special Operations Group (SOG), a unit that contained many ex-combat veterans and was trained in counterinsurgency.[27] The 6th US Army provided military advisors: Colonel Volney Warner, chief of staff of the 82nd Airborne Division, a counterinsurgency expert, and de facto commander on the scene; Colonel Jack Potter, deputy chief of logistics for the 6th US Army; and other officers.[28] The US military advised, armed, transported, and equipped federal agents at Wounded Knee.[29] The US Army drew up a "battle plan" in case negotiations failed.[30] Colonel Warner would later compare the role of the US military at Wounded Knee to that of the Military Assistance and Advisory Command (MAAC) in Vietnam.[31] Federal law enforcement agents carried out a range of military duties—patrolling, guard duty, manning bunkers and roadblocks, cutting off supplies, operating military hardware, enforcing a media blackout, and so on—rather than law enforcement duties. Among federal law enforcement agents, there were many Vietnam veterans: the Wounded Knee occupiers noted that law enforcement officers frequently referred to them as "gooks."[32] Tribal government-sponsored vigilantes (GOONs) were also involved in the siege, as well as members from the all-white Rancher's Association (RA)—groups who manned roadblocks and took part in shootouts alongside government forces. On the first day of the occupation, the US government deployed 250 government personnel, helmeted and armed with M16 machine guns; a further buildup of forces occurred throughout the siege.[33] The US government utilized the latest Vietnam-era technology such as Armored Personnel Carriers (APCs), helicopters, Phantom jets, automatic rifles, nighttime illumination flares, gas, night-vision scopes, flak vests, helmets, C-rations, and other Vietnam-era weapons and equipment to contain the takeover.[34]

What characterized the siege of Wounded Knee were bunkers, trenches, and roadblocks; a demilitarized zone (DMZ) or no-man's land between the occupiers, on the one side, and federal agents, white ranchers, and GOONs, on the other; a Ho Chi Minh Trail into the tiny hamlet through which the occupiers were resupplied with food, weapons, and ammunition; and heavy shootouts between both sides that punctuated the long stretches of boredom throughout the siege. The siege bore a striking resemblance to the Vietnam experience, as was widely observed. Black activist Angela Davis, who visited Wounded Knee but was not allowed into the hamlet, summed up her impression with: "It's just like a Vietnam battlefield out there!"[35] Bill Means (Lakota), a paratrooper who had fought at Khe Sangh, recalled: "Man, I survived Vietnam, and now I'm gonna get killed on my own land, my own reservation."[36] Jim Roubideau (Spirit Lake Nation) remembered: "They were shooting machine gun fire at us, tracers coming at us at nighttime just like a war zone. We had some Vietnam vets with us, and they said, 'Man, this is just like Vietnam.'"[37]

Indigenous activists erecting a tipi at the Wounded Knee, South Dakota, standoff. The hilltop church is in the background. To the left is the cemetery of the victims of the 1890 massacre. In front of the church are fortifications and bunkers. (Richard Erdoes Papers, Yale Collection of Western Americana, Beinecke Rare Book and Manuscript Library)

The Wounded Knee siege included the taking and the release of hostages (the local residents of the Wounded Knee Trading Post); visiting delegations and negotiations; the landing of a small plane within the village perimeter; a three-plane airdrop with supplies from anti-war protesters; an aborted walk in support of the besieged; and wide national and international media coverage.[38] Despite its overwhelming military stance, the US government exercised a policy of restraint. A total of four government negotiators sought to bring the seizure to a halt with a negotiated settlement. When the opening of the roadblocks did not dissolve the occupation but instead led to an influx of activists, the government finally settled on a containment strategy and media blackout. This, combined with the fatal shooting of two Indigenous occupiers and the severe wounding of one US Marshal, finally brought the seventy-one-day occupation to an end.[39]

Fortification with rifle barrels pointing out of loopholes at Wounded Knee. Many Vietnam veterans-turned-activists joined the takeover. They utilized their military experience to fortify the tiny hamlet by establishing roadblocks, building bunkers, and digging trenches. AIM utilized the upside-down American flag (internationally known as a distress signal) as an expression of its defiant nationalism, attracting considerable attention. (Richard Erdoes Papers, Yale Collection of Western Americana, Beinecke Rare Book and Manuscript Library)

A roadblock at the Bigfoot Trail, the road leading into Wounded Knee, by US Marshals. During the Wounded Knee standoff, both sides—law enforcement officers, BIA police, and GOONs, on the one hand, and the Indigenous occupiers, on the other—established roadblocks to control entry to the Wounded Knee hamlet. (Courtesy of the Denver Public Library)

Indigenous and non-Indigenous veterans played a crucial part in the siege, as Tom Holm and Al Carroll have noted.[40] There are no exact numbers, but rough estimates range between 75 and 150 male veterans, which represented between one-third and half of the fluctuating village population. Vietnam veterans featured prominently in the defense of the tiny hamlet; yet there were also some World War I, World War II, and Korean War veterans.[41] According to Ken Tiger (Seminole), a Marine and Vietnam veteran: "There was a lot of people there that had been in Vietnam. And a lot of people had just been in the military. Some older people had come in and they had actually been in Korea. They knew how to give orders. They knew how to take orders. And they knew how to do things that they didn't have to be told twice."[42]

Al Cooper, a white civil rights activist of Mississippi Freedom Summer and member of the Black Panthers, found a new calling in the Indigenous cause. He observed: "There was a lot of veterans there. You could see it in their faces. The horror was still there from the war and the debilitated faces from alcoholism and drugs and whatnot. They were self-medicating because they went to Vietnam and they did and saw things that they'd never done or seen [before]."[43]

The veterans defending Wounded Knee were highly militarily skilled; some had combat experience in Southeast Asia, and several had received Special Forces training.[44] George Lamont (Lakota), a paratrooper from Pine Ridge, South Dakota, recalled: "Well, there was quite a few [Indigenous veterans] I know. Because last I heard they had the 82nd [Airborne Division] standing by in Omaha, Nebraska, when this Colonel [Volney Warner] came and observed. And he was saying, 'Okay I trained most of those guys there in there,' which were mostly all the airborne guys, you know."[45]

Two veterans—Carter Camp (Ponca), a US Army veteran with a

---

*Opposite:* Panoramic view of Wounded Knee, a small and isolated piece of marginal land in the middle of sweeping plains on the Pine Ridge reservation. In the foreground is an armored personnel carrier (APC) that was utilized by federal agents during the prolonged siege to maintain a watch on the occupiers; in the background is the Wounded Knee church. (Richard Erdoes Papers, Yale Collection of Western Americana, Beinecke Rare Book and Manuscript Library)

two-year tour in Germany, and Stan Holder (Wichita), a Green Beret and combat veteran with two tours in Vietnam—organized the defense of Wounded Knee and the military forces of the occupiers. The defenders established a foot patrol to secure the hamlet, to aide backpackers, and to keep government infiltrators out. The men serving in the defense of the ION were divided into four squads, each led by an experienced veteran, often someone with combat experience.[46] At times, the defenders organized their fighting forces like mobile guerilla squads, while the government's forces remained in their static positions.[47]

Wounded Knee, sitting in the middle of a valley surrounded by ridges and gently sloping hills, was barely militarily defensible. Veterans utilized their experience as well as readily available material to turn it into a well-fortified position. They established a series of bunkers and roadblocks that guarded the perimeter and entrance into the tiny hamlet. Construction material and tools from an unfinished housing project were utilized to build bunkers, construct trenches, and dig holes. The defenses were built chest-deep and were made up of earthwork, wooden boards, and sand-filled cement bags and pillowcases; cinder blocks, turned sideways, allowed for gun ports. Wooden boards, put overhead, provided both concealment and protection against inclement weather. Car wrecks were utilized to seal off the roads into and out of Wounded Knee. A command post was established inside the Sacred Heart Church.[48] Inside Wounded Knee, veterans fortified their positions and flew the upside-down American flag, a symbol of AIM's defiant nationalism. The bunkers even drew the admiration of government officials.[49] The defenses of Wounded Knee—bunkers, roadblocks, trenches, and holes—guarded the roads into the tiny hamlet and provided for overlapping fire.[50] Woody Kipp (Blackfeet) recalled: "Our bunker [at Wounded Knee] was well constructed, with a dirt wall in front and topped with sandbags. We lay flat on the ground, the bullets streaking over us at a distance of about four feet, the red tracers sparking the night air into a deadly brilliance. These were the same machine guns I had been trained to use to kill Viet Cong."[51]

The defenders were armed with small-caliber hunting rifles and shotguns, some of which they had "liberated" from the Wounded Knee Trading Post.[52] One veteran, Bobby Onco (Kiowa), carried an AK-47 from his tour in Vietnam, the only automatic rifle the occupiers possessed. The presence of an AK-47, the standard weapon of communist troops, was of great symbolic, yet little direct, military value. The weapon allowed absurd media assertions that Wounded Knee was a communist-inspired plot, at a time when thousands of returning veterans brought home hundreds or thousands of AK-47s as souvenirs and ammunition was hard to come by.[53]

For seasoned Vietnam veterans such as Woody Kipp (Blackfeet), the standoff at Wounded Knee compared to their war experience in that long periods of boredom were interrupted by short intervals of excitement.[54] However, when there were firefights, "it was heavier than the firefights that most of us saw in Vietnam," Bob Anderson, a white veteran, remembered. "At night time the firing from the government positions was so intense it looked like 'Puff' [the Magic Dragon] gunships used in Vietnam were encircling the area. Streams of tracers would lash out from all directions raking the village and bunkers."[55] He related how the disparate war was fought:

> A typical short exchange might find the government guns pouring in 5,000 to 10,000 rounds while we returned less than 50. The principle guiding our warriors in the battle was to conserve ammunition and equipment, to practice guerilla tactics of firing only when we had a target, not to indiscriminately and voluminously waste resources like the government forces. Our warriors carried their whole supply of ammunition on their bodies while the government positions would call for ammo resupply during firefights; the government relying upon an abundant technology for defense while our men used the terrain.[56]

Paradoxically, the shots fired came from the very same government these veterans had defended in the jungles and rice paddies of Vietnam. Pat Kelly, a non-Indigenous veteran who served as a combat medic in Vietnam, stated: "I'm a Vietnam veteran, and the things I've seen here—the tracers, the flares, the government burning off all the cover down to the last shrub, the APCs—it's what I experienced in Vietnam. It's like a flashback to Da Nang."[57]

More than any protest event before or since, the Wounded Knee occupation marked the confluence of two main currents in the formation of the nationalist warrior masculinity. The first current stemmed from protest and identity politics in the American Indian Movement. Since 1972, Indigenous men in AIM had engaged in a series of increasingly violent confrontations with police officers, government officials, and border town supremacists. As such, they came to consider themselves the vanguard of the Indigenous anti-colonial struggle. The second current stemmed from Indigenous military veterans, many of whom considered their military service as in line with much older tribal warrior traditions. They had been fundamentally shaped by military service—frequently with a combat tour in Vietnam—that evoked severe doubts about the nature of the war. As they took up arms, they became the second current of warrior masculinity. The Wounded Knee takeover saw the meeting of these two distinct, yet also partially overlapping, currents of nationalist warrior masculinity.

Indigenous Vietnam veterans joined the occupation for a wide range of reasons. Some did so out of feelings of severe alienation, cognitive dissonance, and a "dual sense of betrayal" at the hands of the US government.[58] For example ex-Marine Woody Kipp (Blackfeet) directly attributed his service tour in Vietnam to his involvement at Wounded Knee: "I was employed by the US government to fight what it called 'communist aggression,' but the aggressive racial hatred of the Americans toward the pastoral Vietnamese would have much to do with why I went to Wounded Knee a few years later."[59] Many saw no contradiction in fighting the very government they had previously served. In part, they rejected the form of tribal governance and indirect colonial rule they had been raised under. Some also sought to emulate their warrior ancestors of the past.[60] An unnamed Navajo Vietnam veteran joined the occupiers, saying, "I knew my place to go to defend my land and treaties . . . to defend my own people."[61]

Ken Tiger (Seminole), a Marine veteran who spent nearly a year in Vietnam, was asked by an alternative newspaper reporter what it was like "as an Indian fighting white man's war against non-white people." Tiger responded by explaining his dual sense of allegiance to "his" people and "his" land first and the American nation second: "People used to ask about it when I was over there. I figured the communists might come and try and take our land here. I was fighting for the land—I wasn't fighting for the Government. I knew this [Indigenous] land was ours and always will be. I never thought it was a personal war against the Vietnamese. To me it always seemed like it was against the communists."[62] Tiger could see clear parallels between the Indigenous struggle against domestic colonialism and the Vietnamese struggle for national liberation. He realized what the Vietnamese fought for: "I could tell they like their land, too. . . . It was theirs and they wanted to keep it."[63] This time, he also defended "his" land; as he stated: "I'm still here at Wounded Knee fighting whoever is out there trying to take it away from me. And right now it is the American forces trying to take it away from me. That's who I am fighting."[64] Above all, he realized that the Wounded Knee experience was an event that constituted part of a long line of Indigenous resistance against settler-colonial encroachment: "Wounded Knee shows Indian people what kind of a government they were fighting for in Viet Nam. Maybe how their parents and grandparents were treated and mistreated. I think a lot of them will change once they realize why we're here."[65]

To many Indigenous veterans, the Vietnam experience evoked serious doubt about the nature of the conflict itself and evoked striking analogies between US imperialist and colonialist endeavors abroad and the treatment of Indigenous people(s) at home. Bobby Onco (Kiowa), an Air Force veteran and member of a Special Operations unit, served through 1970 and 1971 and was briefly a prisoner of war: "I was out in the boonies and it was 'kill or be killed.' I realized then that I was killing my same color of people, same kind of skin and color of hair, but yet they are smaller. I found they were fighting for something they believed in, too," he recalled.[66] An expert in guerilla warfare, he also recalled an incident at Wounded Knee when he would have been able to ambush a small team of the SOG but was told to let them go via radio.[67] Indigenous veterans like him had literally brought the Vietnam War back with them, putting their guerilla warfare skills to use in the armed anti-colonial struggle at home.[68]

Woody Kipp (Blackfeet) instantly recognized the popping sound of gunfire when he was shot at in his bunker at Wounded Knee—the last time he had heard that sound was in the defense of Da Nang Air Base against attacks by the North Vietnamese Army (NVA):

> In that moment . . . , I realized the United States military was looking for me with those flares. I was the gook now. . . . Right here in America, the land of the democratic tradition, the home of the free, the brave, yes, in my own homeland, the one I had eagerly sallied forth to defend . . . that country . . . was now sending up a flare in the night . . . that was looking for me. . . . I realized this country was not what I thought it was.[69]

Moments of realization like this cast away any remaining doubt about political allegiance.

In a strange coincidence, the conflict also saw two generations of Indigenous veterans—Enos Poor Bear (Lakota), a WWII vet and former tribal chairman, and his son, Webster Poor Bear (Lakota), a Vietnam vet—joining side by side in the defense of Wounded Knee. Following a firefight in which his son was wounded, Enos Poor Bear came out and spoke to activists and the news media: "My son went through Vietnam without getting a scratch, and now he gets shot by the same government that sent him there. I think he should get a medal for what he did at Wounded Knee."[70] An increasing number of veterans saw striking parallels to the war in Vietnam and to the 1890 Wounded Knee massacre.[71]

Many non-Indigenous Vietnam War veterans who joined the Wounded Knee occupation came from the anti-war movement. Madonna Thunder Hawk (Lakota) recalled that veterans—no matter their ethnic/racial background—were a welcome sight: "When they came in, I mean they were treated like real leaders. And they were because they had combat experience. We probably wouldn't have survived, and things probably wouldn't have went the way they did, if it wasn't for those guys. Everybody treated them with respect."[72] A contingent from a New Mexico chapter of Vietnam Veterans Against the War (VVAW) was probably the single largest group of non-Indigenous veterans at Wounded Knee.[73] The national VVAW organization brought in medical supplies.[74]

Similar to their Indigenous counterparts, non-Indigenous veterans shared a feeling of betrayal by the country they had served. Many vets returned from military service with heightened political awareness and became active in social movements for change, such as the students' rights, civil rights, and anti-war movements, or joined the Red Power movement. These veterans carried nicknames such as "White Bob," "Honkey

Killer," and "Hillbilly."[75] Bob Anderson, a white air force veteran who had trained Indigenous tribesmen in counterinsurgency in Southeast Asia, joined the anti-war movement and then the Wounded Knee occupants with other VVAW veterans from New Mexico. The Vietnam War experience had left him deeply disillusioned, just like his Indigenous counterparts:

> Here we had a lot of us people like myself who had been fighting for our government against the Vietnamese, trying to suppress them and here we realized that we were on the wrong side in that war. And here was a chance to stand up for people like myself and to try to correct some of that. And then the Native Americans, they realized they had gone off and fought against the Vietnamese and the Vietnamese weren't their enemies, but the problem was right here at home. So it was like Martin Luther King talking to the black soldiers, you know, your struggle is not over there, it is over here.[76]

Owen Luck, another white veteran with two tours as a medic in Vietnam, went to Wounded Knee as a photojournalist. Together with Ron Rosen, another medic, he joined the defenders, putting his medical skills into practice treating the gunshot wounds of Vietnam veterans Milo Goings (Lakota) and Rocky Madrid, a Chicano activist.[77] Substantial support for the stance at Wounded Knee came from anti-Vietnam protesters, most notably an airlift of much-needed supplies for the besieged.[78]

While Indigenous veterans' claims to warriorhood rested on military service and combat experience, many Indigenous men within AIM based their assertion of warrior status upon the anti-colonialist struggle for self-determination, sovereignty, and nationhood. They considered their manifold clashes with law enforcement officers and government officials as rites of passage or "war honors" and proudly displayed the names of these events on their Levi's jackets.[79] Quite fittingly, Al Carroll (Apache) describes AIM as an outlet for Indigenous people to tap into a warrior tradition without having to take the traditional route through military service—a compelling argument given the organization's early role model, the Black Panthers.[80] However, these claims to warrior masculinity did not stand up against the scrutiny of veterans.

Veterans—regardless of their ethnic background—shared a mutual bond due to their military and combat experience; yet they related quite differently to those who did not have that sort of profound experience that defined their masculine identity. For example, Tony Bush (Lakota), a paratrooper, trusted Stan Holder (Wichita), a Green Beret, because "we both were in a country where we spilled blood."[81] These veterans related to each other through a mutual bond of trust because of their shared experience. However, things were quite different when it came to male non-veteran activists in AIM. Veterans observed that once firefights started, many reacted in an unmanly way, not as trained professionals would, and, panic-stricken, did not know what to do. "I saw them as wannabe warriors," Tony Bush remembered, "because not anyone had any combat experience at all under their belt."[82] At times this unmanly behavior was too much to bear for a seasoned combat veteran like him:

> When the shit hit the fan, the bullets came close, they learned how to keep their mouth shut and move. . . . They watched the vets. . . . If they found out he was a vet, he'd have about 10, 15 devout followers. Pretty soon, he'll say: "goddamn you, you're getting too close to me, too close to my ass, man. . . . You make me think you want to try to get friendly with me."[83]

What also separated veterans from nonveterans was their willingness to put their lives on the line for the cause. For example, during one stage of the occupation, Woody Kipp (Blackfeet), like many other veterans, lined up in front of Crow Dog's tipi. Inside the tipi, a buffalo skull altar had been set up. Once inside, Crow Dog painted his face and prayed for him in his Lakota tongue. The sacred red war paint, Crow Dog had explained, was a symbolic warrior practice.[84] The cultural practice and ceremony, as Kipp recalled, prepared him for the possibility of death in a firefight:

> When my face was painted for war, I accepted the possibility that we would die that afternoon when the federal forces moved in at five o'clock. I thought of the refrain voiced by the natives, the refrain supposedly uttered by the mystic and warrior Crazy Horse: "It's a good day to die." I tried to work my mind as it sounded when we were drunk or stoned, but it didn't come. Instead, I kept thinking of my tiny daughter just a few weeks old.[85]

While many Indigenous men at Wounded Knee sought to portray themselves as modern-day warriors fighting for the cause, their people, their homeland, and their rights, few nonveterans actually lived up to their own ideals. Local resident and US Army veteran Walter Littlemoon (Lakota) shared the following observation: "What disappointed me at the time was to hear the members of AIM holler, 'This is a good day to die!' However, when the shooting started they'd run and hide, even pushing women out of the way. They did not attempt to protect even their own members."[86] As these observations indicate, claims to warriorhood and the reality of combat diverged considerably, and many self-proclaimed AIM warriors did not live up to their own manly ideals.

## Wounded Knee: Symbolic Site of Wounded Nationhood and Colonial Oppression

Speaking of the gendered nature of nationalism, gender studies scholar Cynthia Enloe has observed that nationalist movements spring from men's experiences, which are rooted in masculine memory, humiliation, and hope.[87] The locality of Wounded Knee, site of the 1890 massacre, contains a powerful, multilayered symbolism that directly related to the gendered nation-building attempt in 1973.[88] To the Lakota, Wounded Knee is a deeply ingrained event in their cultural history that related to gendered notions of victimhood, cultural memory, and hope.

The massacre site epitomizes the victimization of the Lakota people through military conquest, political oppression, and cultural exploitation. On December 29, 1890, nearly three hundred Lakota men, women, and children were massacred by members of the Seventh Cavalry Regiment on the Pine Ridge Reservation, South Dakota. The chain of events leading up the tragedy are closely tied to the Ghost Dance, the killing of Chief Sitting Bull on December 15, 1890, and the violent suppression of the spiritual revitalization movement. In what can be read as an ongoing injustice to the Lakota people to the present day, various legal proceedings brought by Wounded Knee survivors' associations or US Senators (Francis Case, R-SD in 1939 and James Abourezk, D-SD in 1975)—to obtain a government apology, a Wounded Knee memorial, compensation to the heirs and descendants of the massacre victims, and revocation of the twenty Medals of Honor for the US soldiers committing that atrocity—all have been met with continual refusal to consider the Wounded Knee incident a massacre.⁸⁹ The Wounded Knee massacre was well known to the American public through Dee Brown's recent *Bury My Heart at Wounded Knee* (1970), a history of conquest of the American West that evoked strange parallels to the Vietnam War.⁹⁰ By the 1970s, some survivors of the massacre were still around, passing on the cultural memory in oral histories.⁹¹

The Wounded Knee massacre site directly related to cultural memory also. The Wounded Knee Trading Post added another, no less humiliating and victimizing layer of symbolism. A business monopoly in the otherwise marginalized and impoverished reservation community, it was closely tied to the exploitation of Lakota culture and history. The business enterprise capitalized on the cultural memory of the dead and lived off the economic exploitation of reservation residents, causing deep resentment and anger in an atmosphere of increased political sensitivity and cultural awareness.⁹²

Wounded Knee tapped into gendered hopes as well. In 1973, Indigenous activists had quite consciously selected the historic site in order to establish a continuum between past and present injustices, suffering, and hardship.⁹³ Wounded Knee represented a place where "a dream of revitalization had been anchored," as anthropologist Maureen Trudelle Schwarz puts it.⁹⁴ The very place that represented the destruction of a people's way of life was also a site where political sovereignty and cultural identity could be restored and reaffirmed and where the US government could be compelled to reexamine the 1868 Fort Laramie Treaty—or so nationalists believed.

All in all, the Wounded Knee massacre site entailed a multilayered symbolism that related to notions of wounded nationhood/peoplehood; it referred to notions of ongoing colonial oppression, domination, and exploitation; and it was closely related to claims for national reclamation, cultural revitalization, and moral regeneration. These calls resonated with Indigenous men and their intertwined quest for a renewed warriorhood and nationhood. This gendered enterprise was part of a larger project that tied Indigenous men to the recuperation of traditional male roles and practices as well as to the reclamation of tribal nationhood, with parallels to Indigenous experiences elsewhere.⁹⁵

## The AIM Warrior Society for the Independent Oglala Nation (ION)

On March 11, 1973, the siege of Wounded Knee saw two closely interrelated events: the declaration of the ION and the setting up of a warrior society by the defenders of the village. Nationalist projects, whether colonial or anti-colonial, reconfigure gender orders and assign men and women gendered places. Within the nationalist project, women are cast in the role of biological, cultural, and symbolic reproducers of nation; militarized men, in turn, frequently take on a role as defenders of freedom and honor or as protectors of their homeland, people, and women.[96] The ION was a nation forged under siege. It was no coincidence that the declaration of the ION went hand in hand with the setup of a self-proclaimed "warrior society."[97] The overwhelming forces of US colonial dominance led to the grounding of a tribal nation that was coded as highly masculine, as evidenced by the highly salient images of warrior-veterans. Soon, the defenders of Wounded Knee began to regard themselves as a warrior society for the ION. It is no coincidence that when setting up the ION warrior society, AIM looked into Lakota society and culture for orientation.

Within nineteenth-century Lakota culture and society, there was a wide range of male and female sodalities. However, most sodalities were all-male rather than female.[98] The Lakotas had two basic kinds of fraternal organizations: policing-military societies as well as civil societies, all of which played an integral part in their respective tribal communities. Policing or warrior societies carried out a wide range of overlapping social, legal, civil, religious, economic, political, and military functions. Lakota civil societies were composed of accomplished elder tribal leaders and made political decisions. Just as there were men's sodalities, there were women's sodalities within Lakota culture also. Their actions ranged from artisan interests (such as quilling and tanning) to the performing of rituals to celebrate hunting, and religion, and war.[99] Women frequently joined men's warrior societies as singers and dancers, indicating that these organizations were indeed part of a normal family responsibility in the honoring of a male warrior relative.[100]

Two Indigenous men standing guard at the Wounded Knee hilltop church. Both are watching their surroundings with binoculars from behind fortifications; one is armed with a rifle. In the background is the Wounded Knee church tower with a flag, an expression of AIM's nationalism. The photo captures a pivotal point during the occupation. On March 11, 1973, the occupiers declared the Independent Oglala Nation and set up a modern-day warrior society. The signpost to the left relates to the 1890 massacre and indicates the spot where the Battery Hotchkiss Guns were placed. (Richard Erdoes Papers, Yale Collection of Western Americana, Beinecke Rare Book and Manuscript Library)

Historically, warrior societies played a pivotal role within nineteenth-century Plains Indian social and cultural life. Policing or military societies were tasked with preserving the order on the move, regulating the communal buffalo hunts, policing the camp, preparing ceremonies, and sponsoring feats. Military solidarities also maintained individual and public welfare by distributing property, providing charity for the needy, and sponsoring feasts to the larger community. Warrior societies created a significant bond between society members, which, in turn, promoted social stability and tribal solidarity. Warrior societies also helped foster a martial ideology and ethos by sponsoring social gatherings with songs, dances, and feats that involved the recounting of coups and military achievements and the public validation of accomplishments, together with the redistribution or giving away of property to the larger community. In that sense, military societies cultivated among their members and others a military spirit that apparently aimed to assure the longevity of the tribe.[101] Warriors in "no-flight" societies (commonly referred to as "Dog Soldiers") carried the martial ethos to the extreme and often took a vow before battle not to retreat.[102] Anthropologist William Meadows writes that, most importantly, "Plains men's military societies visibly promote[d] the common central theme of a warrior tradition."[103] He contends that a "shared martial ideology (and at times ethos) . . . has remained an important part of ethnic identity."[104] Despite change over time, "the traditional roles, symbols, and warrior ethos of these [pre-reservation] military society systems continue via [contemporary] military societies."[105]

Given the centrality of warrior societies in pre-reservation Lakota societies, it is perhaps no coincidence that AIM's leaders and members were heavily influenced by real and imagined warrior ideals. However, as historian Al Carroll (Apache) points out, men in AIM understood the warrior ethos somewhat differently from traditional views and concepts regarding warriors and were ironically influenced by other social movements of their time—Black radicalism, student protest, and the counterculture. As he puts it, "the most accurate way to describe AIM in the 1970s is that it was an outlet for Natives who wanted to be a part of the warrior tradition but could not in the newly 'conventional' way of becoming a veteran."[106] AIM's leader frequently claimed that they modelled AIM after the Black Panther Party and they utilized small-scale violence to draw attention to their cause.

In a radio interview, AIM leader Carter Camp (Ponca) described the deeper meaning of the AIM warrior society.[107]

> A warrior society . . . means the men and women—both really—of the nation who have dedicated themselves to give everything that they have to their people. They think that a warrior should be the last one to eat. He should be the first one to give away his moccasins and the last one to buy new ones. That type of feeling amongst Indian people is what a warrior

society is all about. He of course is also ready to defend his family in time of war. He is ready to hold off any enemy and probably willing to sacrifice himself for the good of his tribe and his people. That's what a warrior society is to Indian people, and that's how we tried to envision ourselves.[108]

According to Carter Camp, the newly established warrior society, just like warrior societies of old, was, first and foremost, about protecting and defending the tribal nation. Camp imagined the warrior society as a selfless guardian and protector of the ION. In his understanding, warriorhood was closely tied to notions of selflessness to the point of self-sacrifice in order to ensure the survival of the community. To him, the ION was "a community of warriors empowered by stories held in the land since 1890, warriors of many nations united in their selfless actions of their comrades-in-arms fighting by their side."[109] Altogether, the AIM warrior society drew from various cross-cultural understandings of warriorhood that pointed to a new direction for warrior societies and the right way to be a warrior.[110]

Carter Camp, himself a veteran and Indigenous rights activist, apparently sought to emulate warrior traditions and the spirit behind them through his own actions. He was among the first to seize the Trading Post, worked as a primary organizer in the Wounded Knee defenses, and acted as a spokesperson throughout the siege. He was also among those who signed the final agreement and remained inside the hamlet when the other defenders were gone. Camp's sister, Casey Hornik-Camp (Ponca) claimed that "he was the only person in [a] leadership position in Wounded Knee who never left Wounded Knee, not to go out and do press junkets, not to go and sit in a hotel for a while, none of that. He was a war leader there. He stayed inside with his warriors."[111]

Stan Holder (Wichita) added yet another dimension to the notion of AIM warrior society. He claimed that the warrior society was indeed "more of a brotherhood, than an army with a chain of command."[112] He voiced an Indigenous understanding of warriorhood as a reciprocal relation between individual warrior and tribal community, rather than a Western understanding of soldiering as a role.[113] What banded the AIM warrior society together was "to defend the . . . women and children" of the newly declared tribal nation and "to defend the sacred land."[114]

Unlike Western armies with a military chain of command and discipline, the warrior society was built upon informal structures, mutual trust, and leadership based on experience and ongoing success.[115] This approach to things military was partially confirmed by participant-observer Carol Talbert who wrote that "the Indian military was loosely organized yet efficient, cooperative yet individualistic."[116]

However, at times ideals and realities were far apart. Indeed, it seems that the idealized warrior society was more of a ragtag army made up of those with extensive military experience alongside those who had none. The occupiers had to ensure that its armed members possessed sufficient discipline to maintain a state of order and obedience in order not to cause any involuntary harm to those within the community and those besieging them. At some point during the occupation, Stan Holder left to retrieve supplies for the besieged but was captured by law enforcement officers; this led to a breakdown of discipline in Wounded Knee and prolonged firefights.[117] On strength of his pledge that he would restore order and discipline and then turn himself in, Holder was picked up from a Rapid City, South Dakota, jail by helicopter and returned to the village.[118] According to Stan Pottinger, assistant attorney general of the Civil Rights Division of the Justice Department and government negotiator,

> Holder went in, cease fire immediately, no more fighting, no more shooting. . . . He appeared at RB1 [Road Block 1] with his hands on his head, exactly as requested and Colburn and all of us were so pleased with what was going on that we said: "Would you go back and stay there? Back into the village?" He said: "Terrific." So, we sent him back. It was on the condition that at the end we would say: "Would you resubmit to arrest?" And he said: "Yes I will."

Pottinger described Stan Holder as "probably . . . the coolest head at Wounded Knee . . . during the time I was there."[119] Bill Hall, Director of the US Marshal Service, reflected on how his predecessor Wayne Colburn related to Holder:

> The AIM people had this position which they designated as Chief of Security. I know that Wayne [Colburn, Director of the USMS, 1970–1976]

really established an admiration, certainly a sense of respect for one of the people that had that position, Stan Holder. Wayne trusted him very much and got to the point where when he wanted to do anything, he would say well, "Do you give me Stan Holder's word on it, I will do it." . . . I suspect it was somewhat reciprocal.[120]

This example illustrates that for one, Stan Holder sought to live up to the proclaimed ideals of the ION warrior society. Apparently, Holder enjoyed a great level of credibility on both sides.[121] This went so far that after the Wounded Knee occupation, when Holder faced federal charges, Assistant Attorney Stan Pottinger testified for Holder in court against Harvey Heard, another assistant attorney general.[122] Other AIM leaders such as Russell Means and Dennis Banks also commanded the respect of the US Marshals. Bill Hall reflected, "Well, I guess I was looking at them as a professional opponent. I thought they were brave people. I admired their courage, I did not agree with what they were doing or the way they were doing it."[123]

The warrior society's main purpose was to serve the newly established Independent Oglala Nation. It comes as little surprise that members publicly pledged to defend the nation, even to death.[124] "It is different when you are on the frontlines fighting someone who you think is your enemy out somewhere else," as white Air Force veteran Bob Anderson reflected, "and then when you come home then you realize these struggles against your own government. And the struggle is of such a nature that you might have to give your life."[125] An unnamed Navajo Vietnam veteran claimed: "People stay here, because they believe; they have a cause. That's why we lost in Viet Nam, cause there was no cause. We were fighting a rich man's war . . . being used as cannon fodder. . . . At Wounded Knee, we're doing pretty damn good, morale-wise."[126] A Chicano Vietnam veteran stated: "I just came here because I'm against the thing . . . and the only way I can fight is to come out here and put my ass on the line. I ain't got a lot of money. The only thing I got to give whatever I can do—help 'em out physically."[127] The statement suggests that the self-proclaimed, modern-day warrior society saw itself as in line with an older tradition of martial manhood embodied by Indigenous warriors of the last century

and claimed that its foremost concern was to take care of the people and ensure their well-being throughout the siege.

The siege fostered a comradery among those who defended the newly declared nation. Russell Means' brother Bill Means (Lakota), a Vietnam veteran, recalled how the siege influenced the daily activities of the ION,

> It almost is taking me back a year or two to Vietnam, because you're around people that you put your life on the line every day. And just like Vietnam, the daytime was kind of like the resting time, and you stay awake all night, because if there's any action, it usually happens at night, including people coming in that were bringing supplies that we were sending patrols out to escort them in the best we could.[128]

Some occupiers developed lasting friendships while pulling duty in the bunkers and experiencing intense gunfights. According to Lenny Foster (Navajo), the son of a Navajo code talker who had participated in numerous protests, "We were all in that bunker. . . . So we developed some rapport and we became real comrades in the struggle."[129]

The warriors at Wounded Knee utilized what historian Al Carroll calls "traditional protective spiritual medicine" to reinvent their warrior masculinities.[130] At various times during the siege, medicine men Leonard Crow Dog (Lakota) and Wallace Black Elk (Lakota) conducted cultural practices that included prayers, blessings, chants, and war paint or held ceremonies such as the sweat lodge.[131] Indigenous veterans carried special medicine pouches that they credited with protective powers.[132] Upon the conclusion of the siege, FBI agents noted that although Indigenous veterans calmly gave themselves up into custody, they got very angry if federal agents mishandled or damaged their medicine pouches, as this represented the desecration of a sacred item for them.[133] Some veterans also wore Ghost Dance or ribbon shirts, which they believed would make them bulletproof.[134] The two medicine men utilized traditional herbs to doctor flesh wounds of injured warriors.[135]

Vietnam veteran Milo Goings (Lakota), the first to be wounded in a firefight, was honored in a ceremony for his bravery.[136] According to Stan Holder, the AIM warrior society assigned magpie feathers for "counting coup."[137] During pre-reservation times, the martial practice of counting coup—that is, touching an enemy warrior, woman, or child with a hand, by stick, or something else and then making a safe escape—had been the ultimate test of manhood. Coups were also recognized for other brave acts such as stealing horses. The coup constituted the basis of a graded war honors system that distinguished between four different kinds of coups. Those who counted coup were allowed to wear an eagle feather notched and decorated in a certain way that reflected a warrior's degree of bravery and social status. Intertribal warfare often resembled more of a rough game rather than a bloody battle, because honor was bestowed upon individual warriors not for killing someone but for demonstrating one's physical and spiritual superiority over an enemy.[138] At Wounded Knee, participant-observer Carol Talbert recounted acts of individual bravery done "primarily for the sake of having outwitted the 'feds.'" In one such incident, someone "crept up to an APC during a cease-fire, jumped on top of it, slammed the lid shut, and did a war dance in the moonlight, atop the tank. He said the troopers stayed inside, as they probably thought he would shoot them if they opened the lid."[139] Acts of bravery like this were replete with symbolism of the Plains Indian tradition of counting coup. In counting coup, these warriors likewise sought to demonstrate their bravery and daring, establishing a link that connected past and present.

The newly established warrior society was not just a reinvented replica of the past but instead constituted a remasculinizing tool in the struggle for sovereignty and nationhood. In a 1973 interview, Carter Camp elaborated on the function of the AIM warrior society: "Indian warriors aren't paid and fed, clothed and housed. Indian warriors know they have to be husband, father, and a man of their tribe—a warrior. In fact, being a warrior has to be secondary," he stated in alluding to the inextricably close link between individual warrior and tribal community.[140] In addition, "[the warriors] will begin to teach revolutionary people who come to them that this a big part of the total revolution."[141] Apparently, the AIM warrior society did not only fight in defense of the people within the ION and a return to the days of nation-to-nation treaty-making. Rather, the self-proclaimed warriors for a nation considered themselves part of the larger revolutionary struggle underway in American society.

The setting up of the AIM warrior society and the declaration of the

ION were two closely intertwined events. The gendered analogy of a remasculinized Indigenous manhood and a hyper-virile nation occurred in direct opposition to the overwhelming forces of US colonialism. The ION was a nation forged under siege and emerged in the midst of firefights between AIM warriors and US law enforcement officers. From the occupiers' perspective, at virtually any point in time, political negotiations could give way to the execution of a military battle plan that would end the occupation. For the time being, the presence of news media reporters ruled out the military option. In a sense, the new nation had to be built on warriors in order to face off with the US agents—an element pointing to the inextricable link between nationalism, militarism, and masculinity.[142]

## Between Indigenous and Western Concepts of Nation-Building and the Gendering of the ION

In nation-building processes such as the one at the occupation of Wounded Knee, dimensions of masculinized nationalism and nationalized masculinities were closely intertwined.[143] Cultural associations with the gender of a nation—that is, the way the nation defines itself in relation to the racial and ethnic constructs that it also puts forward—are dependent upon a series of factors. My focus here is on the way gendered nation-building is linked to cultural associations between masculinity and the nation—the leaders of the nation, the military, citizenship, and male bodies. The nation's leadership can influence how the nation is perceived and how it perceives itself. The nation's military, usually an all-male institution, occupies a metonymical function, because war, peace, conquest, and defeat can render the nation either "vulnerable and feminine" or, alternatively, "strong and masculine." Whereas imperialist and colonialist endeavors or an attack on a nation may lead to a masculinization of the nation, military defeat and subjugation may lead to the nation being imaged as feminized or emasculated. In addition, patriotism is closely associated with inherently manly traits such as courage and honor that can be embraced by men or women.[144]

From the outset, the ION was coded as a highly masculine nationalist project forged in militarized conflict. From an outside perspective, it was gendered through the performance and emulation of modern-day warrior masculinity. Historically, the 1890 massacre at Wounded Knee stood as a symbol for a nation defeated, a nation victimized, a nation suffering, and collective trauma. To the occupants, the historic site equally symbolized a place that entailed the potential for cultural and spiritual renewal.[145] Wounded Knee thus marked a symbolic site where past and present notions of nationhood and manhood could be reinvented. The AIM warrior society served as a military force to defend and protect the community. In so doing, it evoked gendered meanings of the renewal, revitalization, and remasculinization of a nation. Russell Means and Dennis Banks featured prominently as the faces of the ION, providing a point of identification for both the occupiers and the media.

When the Indigenous occupiers constructed the Independent Oglala Nation, they actively tapped into numerous nationalist elements. Sociologist Joane Nagel claims that nation-building "involves 'imagining' a national past and present, inventing traditions, and symbolically constructing community"—elements that also tend to foster nationalist ethnocentrism through an "us" versus "them" dichotomy.[146] Scholars of nationalism state that key elements of a nation are existent while other significant elements are imagined. For example, the military can function as an embodiment of the nation, or certain physical aspects or qualities (bravery, courage, military prowess) can take on representational functions to signify the nation at large. Gender-coded images like these influence the public perception of a nation.[147] Indigenous nationalists at Wounded Knee quite skillfully sought to establish a national identity and set up cultural boundaries. The builders of the ION called for a political goal (statehood), believed in a collective commonality (nationhood), and utilized armed conflict (that is, the convergence of nationalism and militarism) to further their aims.[148]

On March 11, the occupiers declared the Independent Oglala Nation (ION).[149] The setup of the ION constituted an effort to return to negotiate with the US government on a nation-to-nation basis, as prior to 1871.[150] The idea for declaring the independent nation came from reservation traditionalists, as AIM cofounder Eddie Benton-Banai (Ojibwe) claims.[151] Plans for the newly declared nation called for a return to a reinvented form of the traditional *tiospaye* (extended family unit).[152] The ION was to consist of a three-layered form of government. Built from the bottom to the top, this included communities (*tiospaye cikala*), district councils (*tiospaye*) and a people's council (*oyate omniciye*). According to *Akwesasne Notes*,

> each community would decide on its own governmental structure. The seven districts within the nation would select their own chairman or headman. These seven headmen would form the governing body for the nation, and the leadership of the council might rotate among the seven members. The executive departments (such as housing, social services, etc.) would function under the people's council. The present judicial system would be abandoned, and a new code of offenses would be adopted. Headquarters would be moved from Pine Ridge to some central location, and Pine Ridge might be left to its own municipal government.[153]

The plans for a new tribal government called for local self-government under traditional chiefs, headmen, and spiritual leaders, selected, instead of elected, by local people. The envisioned form of tribal governance— supposedly in tune with an "Indian way"—constituted an attempt to abolish the IRA-style form of government and replace it with an Indigenized version. According to historian Akim Reinhardt, Indigenous activists advocated "a decentralized, community-based system in line with Oglala values and political culture," a system that stressed grassroots empowerment through self-governance.[154] The Department of the Interior speedily rejected the petition on legal grounds, thus effectively dodging the question of tribal sovereignty.[155] An attempt to circumvent the US government and gain recognition from the United Nations failed.[156]

From its inception, the ION set up a makeshift bureaucracy to deal with everyday pressing concerns. This bureaucracy worked toward the goal of statehood, yet stood in striking contrast to cultural understandings of the traditional *tiospaye*.[157] A number of committees dealt with pressing day-to-day concerns such as housing, medical care, food supply, security, the influx of new arrivals, information, and defense.[158] The Wounded Knee Trading Post became a meeting hall to house the daily evening assemblies of the newly established nation. Just like a modern nation, the ION issued citizenship cards to its members. On March 16, the ION granted citizenship rights to 182 Oglalas, 160 other Indigenous people, and 7 white people.[159] According to some accounts, new residents of the ION received a medicine bundle upon arrival.[160] To traditional Indigenous people, medicine bags are closely connected to their identity. They carry special religious and spiritual significance, as they are believed to wield some protective power over their owner.[161]

The inclusive character for the "imagined nation" showed in its diverse membership that incorporated Lakotas, other Indigenous people, Chicanos (offering them dual citizenship), and non-Indigenous people.[162] Apparently, the membership was not based on racial or inherited attributes. What qualified activists—Indigenous and non-Indigenous—to join the "imagined nation" was their willingness to embrace "the cause" and to put their bodies on the line. It can only be speculated about whether ION's willingness to incorporate non-Lakotas was representative of its "imagined character" as a nation. It is equally uncertain whether the ION represented older Lakota values that based Lakota-ness and membership not on racial and inherited attributes but on a willingness to be Lakota. Among AIM's most prominent leaders, only Russell Means was Lakota.[163]

Support for the new nation came from the Six Nations Iroquois Confederacy delegation from upstate New York, whose Chief Oren Lyons (Iroquois) stated, "We support the Oglala Sioux Nation or any Indian nation that will fight for its sovereignty . . . [and] their right to conduct their own affairs."[164] The very makeup of the new nation testified to its imagined character. Essentially, everyone could join if accepted by the Wounded Knee community, regardless of race or religious faith. Eddie Benton-Benai (Ojibwe) characterized the ION as "a community of brotherhood." As he put it, "it's people whom we generally call the Third World Movement, the long-hairs, anti-war people, peace people, these kinds of people whom we really welcome."[165]

Many aspects of the ION were imagined and centered on community-building efforts. According to activist Lorelei DeCora (Winnebago), "we were surrounded by the military might of the United States, but we were a community that had no police, no monetary system, no laws other than what we wanted to make. We were a community that was given a taste of freedom."[166] Many occupiers shared feelings of empowerment and a sense of exhilaration.[167] John Adams, a clergyman who

At negotiations in a tipi on April 5, 1973 (*left to right*): unidentified man, Carter Camp (*partially covered*), Leonard Crow Dog, Dennis Banks, Russell Means, Wallace Black Elk, Ramon Roubideaux, and Assistant US Attorney General Kent Frizzell. (Stanley Lyman Photographic Collection, Marriott Library, University of Utah)

negotiated on behalf of the National Council of Churches (NCC) was "deeply impressed" by the "community spirit" of the ION. He shared the following observation: "I noticed a closeness among the people, a kind of freedom. I think you knew they really felt that 'this was [is] our territory, that we were [are] there; we have established the fact that we are a nation here.'... That is the reason [that] when they gave me a passport I took it seriously."[168]

The formation of the Independent Oglala Nation occurred in an inherently hybrid space in which Indigenous understandings of tribal sovereignty and Western nationalism were complexly intertwined and layered. On the one hand, the setup of the ION highlighted the concept of *tiospaye* (or, for that matter, a form of tribal sovereignty) and stressed a sense of peoplehood (or, for that matter, a sense of Lakota-ness). What made this attempted return to tribal sovereignty so contested and ambiguous was its layering with colonial concepts. Indigenous nationalists continually stressed Western concepts of nationalism (e.g., national sovereignty, decolonization, and nationhood/statehood through rhetoric, symbolism, and governance). Throughout the siege, AIM nationalists repeatedly claimed they sought to establish a nation separate from the United States.[169] The setup of the Independent Oglala Nation points to the complexities and ambiguities of Indigenous nation-building endeavors in the larger encompassing society and the layering of tribal concepts of self-governance and being with Western nation-building.

## National Reclamation, Cultural Revitalization, and Moral Regeneration

Indigenous activists frequently drew connections between the 1890 Ghost Dance and their presence, evoking cultural revitalization, national reclamation, and political reempowerment, as in Indigenous movements elsewhere.[170] *Akwesasne Notes* quotes Russell Means: "The white man says that the 1890 massacre was the end of the wars with the Indian, that it was the end of the Indian, the end of the Ghost Dance. Yet here we are at war, we're still Indians, and we're Ghost Dancing again."[171] Among the occupiers were some Ghost Dancers who wore ribbon and ghost shirts. Robert Anderson, a Vietnam veteran and white participant, observed several of these Ghost Dances. "I didn't think that the Ghost Dance shirts would stop bullets, but a lot of people did," he reflected. "And a lot of people thought they'd see visions and ghosts, people from the past, people from the massacre there." For Indigenous participants, the Ghost Dances carried significant meaning and connected them to both their cultural heritage and their ancestors; as Anderson put it, they were "people defending their nation and their people like they had done in the past."[172] Historian John William Sayer considers the Ghost Dances of 1890 and 1973 as major challenges to the nation's dominant values and institutions.[173] In that sense, Wounded Knee can be interpreted as a bodily enactment of religious freedom, cultural revitalization, and political sovereignty, and of embodied experiences, especially emotions. For the local Oglala, there was a genuine spiritual connection and meaning to the massacre site.

Indigenous people from across the country attached a symbolic meaning to Wounded Knee, in which US colonialism and oppression intersected with notions of cultural revitalization, national reclamation, mental decolonization, and the regeneration of positive Indigenous identities. The takeover at Wounded Knee symbolically linked and united tribal nations across the country in resistance to colonial oppression, in Indigenous sovereignty, and in ethnic pride. In taking over Wounded Knee, Indigenous nationalists linked past and present injustices with morality and sought to renew, revitalize, and rebuild self and society. Autobiographical accounts of Wounded Knee frequently exhibit feelings of empowerment and liberation in resistance to US colonial domination. They frequently relate how the siege of Wounded Knee forged a Pan-Indian community. According to Carter Camp, the Wounded Knee siege instigated a pride in Indigeneity and touched off the cultural renewal of songs, dances, cultural practices, ceremonies, and rituals.

> We were fighting every day and in danger every day. But it was a lot of fun. During the lulls in the fighting, or during the time when there was not actual danger, it was just a wonderful time being together. People would bring out the drum every night and we'd sing together, and different tribes would sing their songs. We had Indian ceremonies that are very special to us, but we don't bring 'em out in public. But now we could have 'em right there where everybody could participate. We don't have to hide them around anymore. We had the elders, medicine men, women and children—all in Wounded Knee with us. We were a strong community. We all had work to do and fighting to do. But at the same time, we could live together and do the things that we wanted to do, say the things that we wanted to say and understand this world the way that Indian people understand it. So it made us feel good. We just really were able to come together in a unity that you don't hardly find in Indian Country.[174]

## *Male Bodies, Bodily Practices, Cultural Renewal, and the Independent Oglala Nation*

Gender scholar Raewyn Connell has theorized that male bodies are "both objects and agents of practice, the practice itself forming the structures within which bodies are appropriated and defined," a pattern

Connell calls body-reflexive practice.[175] The male body is not only a physical but also a cultural construct. The body is thus an inscriptive surface for masculinity and cultural meaning where ideas about nation are inscribed and reinscribed.[176] Cultural discourse constructs ideas of the male body, and cultural practices transform the male body and its physical aspects. In turn, cultural inscriptions create subjectivities. Similarly, bodily practices can reinscribe power, and, depending on the context, can be viewed as normative or resistant to hegemonic cultural constructs. As a cultural construct, the male body is perception-based and at certain moments can be alternatively viewed as demasculinized, masculinized, or remasculinized.[177]

Throughout the occupation, the occupiers sought to generate media coverage through the staged/bodily performance of warrior masculinity.[178] Yet at the same time, they also sought to remake their male subjectivities through body-reflexive practices—ritual and bodily processes that are inscribed in the body and enacted through embodied movements and engagements.[179] For the unsuspecting onlooker, these performative and transformative efforts became inherently hybridized and undistinguishable from one another. Historiography has viewed the gendered performance of Indigenous men solely within the context of creating media attention. Rather than following this approach, I intend to illustrate how cultural practices are related to the male body and serve as a locus where ideas of the nation are constructed.[180]

A few days into the armed standoff, *Time Magazine* reported on the display of traditional Lakota culture, male bodies, and warrior masculinity as follows:

> Seven Indian leaders stripped, some naked, others to their shorts, and entered an Indian sweat lodge—a wooden framework covered by an orange carpet and a purple blanket—to receive clarity of mind and body. The warriors, perhaps 150 of them, seemed perfectly willing to die. With the sun setting behind their backs and the chill wind whipping up puffs of dust, they formed a semicircle and watched as the tribal fathers emerged from the steaming lodge.
> 
> A Sioux spiritual leader named Leonard Crow Dog struck up a chant in the Lakota language. As each warrior passed by, he blessed him and painted a

Medicine man Leonard Crow Dog (Lakota) painting faces for war. The members of the AIM warrior society wear red bandanas. By early 1973, Indigenous men in the American Indian Movement viewed themselves as warriors fighting for *their* people, *their* homeland, and *their* rights. In quite a genuine sense, they considered themselves in a modern-day struggle against domestic colonialism, a significant aspect that is often overlooked in analysis of AIM's media theatrics. (Richard Erdoes Papers, Yale Collection of Western Americana, Beinecke Rare Book and Manuscript Library)

slash or a circle of red powder under the left eye. Each warrior then stepped into a white tepee, making a holy sign over the bleached skull of a buffalo.[181]

The cultural practices employed by the warriors at Wounded Knee involved songs, war paint, sweats, and ceremony—embodied actions and bodily experiences—that can be understood as attempts to renew, revitalize, and remasculinize and give new cultural meaning to their masculinities and bodies. Significantly, these cultural and warrior practices corresponded with the declaration of the ION later that same day.

The warriors at Wounded Knee employed a wide range of ceremonial (or ritualistic) and bodily practices, most of which were conducted by traditional medicine men Leonard Crow Dog (Lakota) and Wallace Black

Elk (Lakota). Ceremony—here used as an umbrella term for cultural practices, ceremonies, and rituals—is a larger reflection of Indigenous worldviews, reality, and ways of thinking and doing. Ceremony is (tribal) culture specific and community based and involves song, dance, and tribal language.[182] Body-reflexive practices included the sweat lodge (*inípi*), the Ghost Dance, the *yuwipi* ceremony, and peyote meetings, as well as fasts and vision quests.[183] The *inípi*—a sweat bath in a small circular wooden framework covered with blankets, with boiling hot stones in the center of the hut—was intended to purify body and spirit. The *yuwipi* ceremony, a high ritual in Lakota culture, is a healing ceremony in which the healer makes contact with spirits.[184] Further cultural and embodied practices included singing, dancing, drumming, the smoking of the pipe, and the donning of paint.

The occupiers' use of cultural and warrior practices can be read as both an act of cultural renewal and as an effort to remasculinize the warriors for a nation.

First, the use of cultural and warrior practices and male physicality can be read as an act of cultural renewal and a defiant display of nationalist ethnocentrism that directly relates to the suppression of cultural and religious practices by the US government. By the late nineteenth century, following the forced subjugation of the Lakota people, a number of government policies—reservation confinement, assimilation, boarding school education, allotment—were intent on suppressing their traditional way of living. For example, the Indian Office banned cultural practices, rituals, and ceremonies that seemed repugnant to assimilation, such as "giveaways," and songs and dances, among others, the Sun Dance and Ghost Dance. The ban, however, did not mean a complete eradication of Lakota cultural and religious beliefs and expressions. Prior to the 1973 takeover, some traditional Lakotas continued to keep their cultural ways alive, yet they could only do so in hiding.[185] In actively engaging in their own cultural traditions through song, dance, and ceremony, Indigenous nationalists exhibited their cultural pride and reaffirmed their ethnic identity.[186]

Second, the occupiers' utilization of body and bodily-reflexive practices can be understood as an effort on the part of the occupiers to remake their warrior and male subjectivities as well as become more masculine than the colonizer. Quite literally, this retraditionalization went hand in hand with a remasculinization within Indigenous men and masculinities. The occupiers' use of these practices was equally an attempt to reconnect to a tribal heritage of warriorhood; these specific cultural and warrior practices traditionally were to purify, protect, and prepare warriors for combat. Traditionally, religious and spiritual ceremonies were intended only for specific purposes and were therefore utilized exclusively on meaningful occasions, quite consciously and sparingly. The Ghost Dance, for example, included prolonged dancing until a vision occurred. In striking contrast, the warriors at Wounded Knee excessively took sweats or participated in the Ghost Dance.[187] The overindulgence in sacred ceremonies was an apparent attempt of Indigenous nationalists to reinvent their male subjectivities, to prove themselves, and to measure up to and be more masculine than the colonizer. In that sense, cultural and warrior practices can be understood as an effort to remasculinize in an effort to shed domestic colonialism by declaring an independent nation and by opposing US hegemony.

### Warrior Women at Wounded Knee

From its inception, the staunchest support for the Wounded Knee takeover came from Indigenous women who stood at the center of grassroots activism.[188] According to Bob Anderson, a white Vietnam veteran, "women were actually the backbone of the way things ran and were organized. The women were the great organizers of the community . . . [and] they had a strong role in the community."[189] Local Oglala grassroots women formed the Oglala Sioux Civil Rights Organization (OSCRO) in opposition to current reservation politics.[190] Feeling threatened by the heavy posture of federal agents on Pine Ridge, these Indigenous women advocated a military confrontation. According to Ellen Moves Camp (Lakota), a local resident and OSCRO member, "our men were scared, they hung to the back."[191] By directly appealing to their manhood, Moves Camp shamed men into taking action and occupying Wounded Knee. Moves Camp is frequently quoted as saying: "You AIM people, what are you going to do? You are supposed to be warriors. What are you going to do? If you men can't do it, then we women will."[192] During the Wounded Knee siege, local reservation residents Gladys Bissonette (Lakota) and Moves Camp were among the primary negotiators with the government.

Within the masculinist nation-building project of the ION, women took on highly significant, yet largely overlooked roles that shifted between domesticated motherhood and female warriors who were standing side-by-side with their male comrades in arms as near equals.[193] While Indigenous women's pivotal role in the occupation was frequently overshadowed by that of their male, attention-seeking counterparts, the male defenders of Wounded Knee were utterly dependent upon women's efforts in maintaining the occupation. Yet they preferred women to stay in the background, a stance partially due to their own internalized notions of patriarchy, which superseded knowledge of women's traditionally strong roles in tribal communities.[194] Media coverage almost completely ignored Indigenous women, partly due to widespread gender and racial bias, and partly due to the hyper-visibility of Indigenous warriors.[195]

Throughout the siege, women frequently took on domestic chores—housekeeping, laundry, cooking—or cared for the sick and injured; yet they also played a key part as participants in planning, maintaining, and resupplying the Wounded Knee community. Inside the Wounded Knee hamlet, "we did the shit work, scrubbing dishes or making sleeping bags out of old jackets," Mary Crow Dog (Lakota) stated.[196] White women grew aware of what they perceived as inferior tasks and subservient duties of their Indigenous counterparts. Mary Crow Dog recalled:

> At one time a white volunteer nurse berated us for doing the slave work while the men got all the glory. We were betraying the cause of womankind, was the way she put it. We told her that her kind of women's lib was a white, middle-class thing and that at this critical stage we had other priorities. Once our men had gotten their balls back, we might start arguing with them about who should do the dishes. But not before.[197]

Indigenous women recognized the necessity of this work at the time, as it contributed to the overall goals of liberation. Yet at the same time, they realized that their relegation to supposedly minor roles also reflected the masculinist culture within AIM. Crow Dog's statement of "our men getting their balls back" directly related to her previous statement that Indigenous men—just like Indigenous women—were fighting their own liberation battles. Indigenous women maintained that their "behind-the-scenes-work" was essential, and they showed a capacity to be flexible in their activism, switching from cooking, washing clothes, tending to the sick and injured to speaking in public if the opportunity arose.[198] Apparently, Indigenous women and Black women shared similar attitudes toward racist oppression and the gendered sexism in their respective movements. Feminist author and activist bell hooks has noted that throughout US history and despite the reality of Black sexism, Black women have endorsed the struggle in the name of political solidarity. As she put it, "there is a special tie binding people together who struggle collectively for liberation. Black women and men have been united by such ties."[199]

AIM's male leaders sported images and conveyed attitudes that left few doubts about their blatant chauvinism. Robert Burnette (Lakota) observed, "Young female reporters tend to think of themselves as the advance guard of the feminine [sic] liberation movement, and Means' unabashed male chauvinism is blatantly obvious to anyone who has spent ten minutes in his company. Banks's good-luck beret with its Playboy-bunny patch spelled things out even more clearly."[200] The display of a "cool pose"—language, mannerism, gestures, and movements that exaggerate masculinity—certainly alienated women, particularly feminists. The "cool pose" performances and chauvinist and misogynistic behavior of Banks and Means, while empowering to them, merely bolstered sexual imagery.[201] In his lengthy autobiography, Means rationalized the gendered disparities in the division in labor with the particular circumstances of the occupation. "Inside the Knee, nobody had time to worry about gender roles," he said.[202] "Following the lead of strong, traditional women who knew what nature expected of them, everyone came to respect the balance between the sexes."[203]

Indigenous women at Wounded Knee realized that the federal government and the media would rather listen to men than to women. While these women acknowledged that men took the media spotlight during the occupation, they did not approve of the sexist language, practices, and behavior of their male counterparts. Neither did they accept the underlying notion of male dominance that relegated women to subservience. While Indigenous women acknowledged the necessity of letting men speak on behalf of the occupiers, they were primarily concerned with advancing their political agenda.[204]

Gender studies scholar Anne McClintock argues that there is no nation that offers men and women an equitable access to rights and resources in the nation-state,[205] while gender scholar Nira Yuval-Davis states that, within nationalist struggles, women occupy a number of interrelated functions as biological, cultural, and normative reproducers of the nation as well as active participants.[206] At Wounded Knee women embodied all these iconic roles—from giving birth, getting married, and organizing the communal kitchen, housing, medical care, and supplies to participating in defense and in government negotiations.[207] Indigenous women utilized the "weapons of the weak" to support the armed nationalist struggle.[208] As one woman recalled: "Most of our underground work was handled by local reservation women, hiding people, feeding them, hiding rifles, hiding and packing supplies."[209]

As stated, nationalist struggles tend to replicate the very patriarchy they struggle against, with women of color suffering the most.[210] Indigenous women thus struggled with "a double oppression" through racial domination and gender inequality. While Indigenous women prioritized the struggle against US colonialism over the struggle for gender equality, they also took on the roles of warriors. Gender scholar Cynthia Enloe describes the nation as a highly masculinized space, but women can overcome their marginalized status and gain entry into masculinist politics, according to Enloe, if they "convincingly cloak themselves in a

---

*Opposite:* Indigenous women at the Wounded Knee Trading Post during the 1973 takeover. Indigenous women organized and maintained the prolonged occupation, running the day-to-day affairs while also taking up arms to defend the village. Indigenous women within AIM frequently complained about unequal gender roles and the sexist behavior of some Indigenous men. At Wounded Knee, Indigenous women skillfully renegotiated their gendered position of power within the masculinist organization. In taking on a female warrior subjectivity, they reconnected to a tradition that had been in existence prior to the reservation period—or so they claimed. (Courtesy of the Denver Public Library)

particular masculinized style of speech and action."[211] At Wounded Knee, some Indigenous women successfully renegotiated their way into this masculine landscape as warrior women and female comrades in arms. By joining their male counterparts in the armed revolutionary struggle, they established a link to cultural and warrior traditions that had lain dormant for decades. In an interview, Regina Brave (Lakota), a Navy veteran and one of the female defenders, put it this way: "Wounded Knee showed the general public that there were Indian women who were warriors. Throughout history we had Indian women who were warriors. But since it was non-Indian people who wrote the history, the idea of women taking up guns and taking up arms to fight beside their men was unheard of by the general public, especially . . . non-Indian women."[212]

Just like their male counterparts, Indigenous women occupied bunkers, took part in roving patrols, exposed themselves to lethal gunfire, and were wounded.[213] *Akwesasne Notes* reprinted the experiences of another Indigenous woman, named Kathy:

> Being in Wounded Knee taught us a new kind of bravery: being shot at as you sit in a bunker—bullets and tracers whizzing and zinging by—or dodging from foxhole to foxhole or running out with a stretcher to bring back the wounded, or manning—womanning—a bunker all day or night.[214]

Kathy attributed her ability to handle fear of firefights to her experiences as an Indigenous woman.[215] Throughout the siege, women played a pivotal part in hitchhiking in and out of Wounded Knee, bringing in much-needed food supplies, ammunition, and manpower; providing the besieged with crucial information; and occasionally taking up a gun.[216]

At Wounded Knee, Indigenous women who took up arms referenced their decision to do so with cultural traditions, real or imagined. For example, Regina Brave pointed out that during the pre-reservation period, it was not uncommon for Indigenous women to assume a warrior identity to protect their communities. She also pointed to the Brave Hearted Women, a women's society whose members participated in war parties as both medics and warriors and who took part in the Battle of the Little Bighorn (June 25–26, 1876).[217] Indeed, there are several indications among Plains Indian societies during pre-reservation times that Indigenous women took on the roles and responsibilities of warriors.

For example, during the Battle of the Rosebud (June 17, 1876), a Northern Cheyenne woman named Buffalo Calf Road Woman (aka Brave Woman) saved her wounded warrior brother and her rescue helped rally the Cheyenne warriors—allies of the Lakotas—to win the battle.[218] Apparently, Regina Brave took pride in defending her community, and she saw it as her right and duty not to leave this role and responsibility solely to men.[219]

Feminist scholars M. Annette Jaimes and Theresa Halsey rightfully claim that "military activity—including being a literal warrior—was never an exclusively male sphere of endeavor [prior to reservation confinement]."[220] There are indications of warrior women among Plains Indian societies, among the Piegan (Blackfeet) in Alberta and Montana, as well as among the Crow, Cheyenne, and the Dakotas in the United States. What remains unclear, though, is the actual extent of women's participation in military activities among Plains Indian societies.[221] There is also some controversy about female sodalities among the Lakotas. For example, anthropologist Raymond DeMallie has found that "that there was no developed tradition of warrior women in Lakota society."[222] A case in point is the Brave Hearted Women's Society that might have been more concerned with retrieving the wounded and fallen from a battlefield and helping the families than with engaging in war and warfare. However, Indigenous women—activists and military veterans alike—affirm the existence of female warrior societies among the Lakotas and point to the differences within the various *tiospayes*. Apparently, a woman could assume her male relative's/husband's place in a warrior society.[223] The oral voices of Indigenous women also give credence to the existence of pre-reservation warrior women. While there was no institutionalized tradition of warrior women sodalities among the Lakotas, there were warrior women among the Dakotas who shared the same language. With the Dakotas, women who had achieved war honors were called *winoxtca* (the female equivalent to the male *akíčita*).[224]

However, I have found no historical evidence or names of individual Lakota women who assumed a warrior persona during pre-reservation times (while there are names of women with other tribal affiliations). Contemporary negotiations of cultural systems and gender identities are often conditioned by the variety of Indigenous and non-Indigenous discourses.

Scholars of the Red Power movement should thus be cautioned against attempts to romanticize and homogenize the pre-reservation period and instead should recognize the multiplicity of Indigenous tribal-specific gender systems and the intertwined roles and responsibilities.[225]

At Wounded Knee, the taking up of manly functions by Indigenous women—for example, work in bunkers and on security detail—did not pass unopposed by their male comrades in arms.[226] Carter Camp admitted that the occupiers had a "training class in weaponry for some women who wanted to do that."[227] As he reflected, "for one thing, our Indian leaders frown on women taking that sort of a role. We believe that women have a role and they play that role and the men play their role as warriors."[228] Carter's statement reveals just how much the occupiers were influenced by dominant norms and beliefs. The male defenders felt threatened by the female occupiers taking up arms, because it put the functions of male protector and female protected in jeopardy and directly challenged male superordination and female subordination. "I think men were threatened more than anything," Regina Brave put it. "Instead of looking at these women as partners, they looked at them as rugs or playthings or something [akin] to a little trophy to put on the shelves."[229] Bob Anderson remembered that

> some of the guys thought that that was not a cool thing. They weren't crazy about it. But there wasn't much resistance to it [either]. Everybody just sort of said: "come on out and join" and so . . . one of the bunkers . . . was predominantly staffed by women and . . . they started taking positions and roles in the leadership of the security and they were always in the negotiations that were held up in what we called the DMZ zone.[230]

Indigenous women had to renegotiate their positions within the masculinist movement culture through their commitment and their displays of competency. Regina Brave (Lakota), realized that many of AIM's rank and file were young, inexperienced, and could not handle their weapons properly: "They didn't have the experience of fighting for their people. . . . None of them had ever been in the military. . . . In fact, they were from urban areas. . . . And so, I thought these young men could cause the death of a lot of people, because they could easily panic which happened; and these guys were stingy with their guns."[231]

Soon, Indigenous women realized the threat these untrained militants posed for the entire community. Although Indigenous women helped the new arrivals to break down their weapons, clean them, and handle them properly, two shooting accidents occurred. It was only through an appeal to reason that these men finally started to take the women seriously. As Regina Brave recalled,

> so, then I went in to argue. And they were trying to deny me, because I was a woman. Yet my argument was: "Hey, I didn't hear of any women has shoot a hole through their foot. I again never hear of any women shoot a hole through their hand." Plus, I had the experience I had already been in a military service—I'm a Navy veteran and plus I grew out in the country out here. And we hunted for a living.[232]

Indigenous women figured that the military inexperience and unmanly behavior of the male weapon-carriers put everybody at risk. During a firefight, the inexperienced men would panic and run away for cover, rather than protect the hamlet and the people inside. Realizing the implications of this, Regina Brave made the decision to carry a gun and actively defend the hamlet: "And I figured: 'Okay, I'm gonna carry a gun. I'm going to join a squad. I'm going to be a part of this . . . because this is serious business. Those people are firing you real life bullets. I used to stand on the hill and watch the tracers come in. Thousands of bullets coming into Wounded Knee.'"[233]

A group of four Indigenous women carried guns while engaging in the day-to-day tasks within the small community. Warrior women carried their guns and coffee pots to the different bunkers to supply the defenders, stood trench duty, did the cooking and cleaning, did the laundry, chopped wood, and hauled water. For Regina Brave, that commitment included a willingness to put her life on the line: "I thought to carry a gun. And I thought if I'm gonna go down, I'm gonna take someone with me."[234] Other than Indigenous men who regarded armed women as a threat to their masculine position of power, Indigenous women considered their function as complimentary. "It was almost like the women have always had not just one role, like we had several. And we were good at every one of them," Regina Brave said. "And we took care of our men. At Wounded Knee we stood with them. We took care of each other."[235]

Some women became so accustomed to the siege that they slept through firefights due to exhaustion.[236]

Female nationalists were not afraid to confront the male leaders when things were not in the general interest of the ION community. Toward the final stage of the occupation, as fewer supplies and ammunition came in, an AIM leader started hoarding supplies while the community starved. During an ensuing confrontation, Dennis Banks pointed his gun at Madonna Thunder Hawk (Lakota) and Lorelei DeCora (Winnebago) but gave up his supplies when a number of veterans cocked their rifles and pointed their barrels at him. Madonna Thunder Hawk recalled that "it shocked me to think that one of our leaders would be hoarding food." She also recalled, "I'll never forget that he pulled a gun on Lorelei DeCora."[237] She attributed much of the stress to the unfolding of that situation.

In general, warrior women found it considerably harder than their male counterparts to take up arms in the defense of the hamlet, in particular given the chauvinistic attitude of AIM leaders. Prior to the seizure of Wounded Knee, Indigenous women had participated in the takeover of the BIA and defended the building against impending attacks by policemen. Their adoption of warrior functions at the BIA and Wounded Knee can partly be attributed to the fluidity of these situations, in which necessity and circumstances greatly contributed to Indigenous women's roles as warriors.

The historiography of the Red Power movement suggests that, in many contexts, Indigenous women regarded themselves as warriors, just like their male counterparts.[238] However, the media's fascination with what Madonna Thunder Hawk (Lakota) called "warrior type" imagery meant that women's militancy was frequently ignored.[239] Among the very few images of armed women taken at Wounded Knee that made the front pages across the country was a picture of Regina Brave guarding a bunker and holding a rifle. It seems that the Wounded Knee takeover only briefly upset gender roles within AIM. Regina Brave recalled, "Our men—they were proud of their women. They stood back in and said: 'Hey, the women woke up.' But we never went to sleep. We were always there. We were just not recognized in that manner, because our men have bought into this other society's idea of what women should be. So we took our places back."[240]

In the wake of the takeover, however, Indigenous women once again found themselves subordinated within the nationalist and masculinized movement. "We were doing what Indian women did for thousands of years, which was to stand behind the men and prop them up," recalled Margo Thunderbird (Lakota). Together with Anna Mae Aquash (Micmaq), she worked on behalf of AIM in Minnesota and California.[241] As she stated, "We wanted to present an image, and the angry Indian man was better than angry Indian women.... The men were show time."[242]

## The Media's Warriors or Freedom Fighters: Between Guerilla Theater and Guerilla Warfare

The Wounded Knee takeover was probably the most media-reported event of the entire Red Power era. In the news coverage of Wounded Knee, the image of the modern warrior—carrying guns, fortifying perimeters, and manning roadblocks—was highly salient.[243] These hypermasculine images dominated the news media and were accompanied by headlines such as "Raid at Wounded Knee," "The Siege of Wounded Knee," "Guerilla Theater at Wounded Knee," "Renegades: The Second Battle of Wounded Knee," "Showdown at Wounded Knee," and "Wounded Knee: The New Indian War."[244] With few exceptions, the media's warriors were portrayed as monolithic, one-dimensional Indigenous militants prone to violence, most commonly embodied through AIM leaders Dennis Banks and Russell Means.[245] This was epitomized in media imagery of armed, modern-day warriors facing today's surrogates of the US Cavalry: law enforcement officers, BIA police, USMS, and others.[246] Media studies scholar Gail Guthrie Valaskakis has noted that "at Wounded Knee . . . the media mapped modern warriors onto the contours of Native resistance in representations of armed conflict and expressions of Indian radicalism that resonated across the deeply rooted borders separating Native and other North Americans."[247]

The news media reported imagery of modern-day warriors seemingly relegated to the past, thus portraying Indigenous people within the confines of news templates. In so doing, it deliberately utilized the stereotypical attribution of warrior imagery in order to capitalize on the Indigenous occupiers. In her article "Bamboozle me not at Wounded

Knee" for *Harper's Magazine,* Terri Schultz stated, "We wrote good cowboy-and-Indian stories because we thought that was what the public wanted."[248] Robert Burnette (Lakota) observed that "the TV crews who provided visual coverage thrived on photogenic scenes of Indians in war paint, with guns, and the grotesque APCs tearing through the tall grass."[249] Early meetings between government officials and AIM representatives included a tipi and the smoking of the peace pipe for the benefit of cameramen. Alternative news reporter Kevin Barry McKiernan noted that television crews commonly reported on "Indians regaled in feathers, armed with rifles and riding bareback on ponies."[250] Media newscasts frequently focused on Wild West–like gunfights between AIM warriors and white law enforcement officers, or, to a lesser extent, on the tribal factionalism that caused the takeover in the first place, largely ignoring the underlying grievances and abysmal living conditions of reservation residents and with little firsthand knowledge of what went on inside the tiny hamlet.[251]

News reporting frequently made for a rather one-sided, heroic tale of noble AIM warriors struggling against their colonial oppressors (the US government and a despotic tribal chairman).[252] The gross imbalance of weaponry—old shotguns and ludicrously inept squirrel rifles pitted against high-tech machine guns and modern tanks—seemed to confirm this view and was continually reiterated by the occupiers.[253] The tale of a downtrodden underdog fighting for national liberation and self-determination seemed to be further substantiated by analogies to the Vietnam War.[254] What also worked in the occupiers' favor was the fact that many news reporters were Vietnam veterans themselves and sympathetic to the cause.[255] The extent to which public sympathy was behind the occupiers was revealed in a Lou Harris poll that showed that 51 percent of those questioned supported the ION, 21 percent opposed it, and 18 percent were uncertain where they stood.[256] The *New York Times* reported, "Perhaps for the first time since . . . 1776, the American people gave their support to an armed insurrection against the government of the land."[257] Of those surveyed, 93 percent answered that they had followed the Wounded Knee incident through the media and 76 percent were convinced of the historical mistreatment of Indigenous people.[258] Newspaper coverage of the incident increased in complexity over time.[259]

Armed Indigenous activists at a Wounded Knee roadblock. Indigenous men in AIM considered themselves members of a warrior society for the newly established Independent Oglala Nation. The AIM warrior society drew from various cross-cultural understandings of warriorhood that pointed to new pathways for warrior societies and the right way to be a warrior. Indigenous veterans' claims to warriorhood rested on military service and combat experience; many therefore looked suspiciously upon those Indigenous men in AIM who based their assertion of warrior status upon their confrontations with law enforcement officers. (Richard Erdoes Papers, Yale Collection of Western Americana, Beinecke Rare Book and Manuscript Library)

The occupiers' continual performance of warriorhood was directed toward media publicity, not conflict resolution, in what amounted to an attempt to keep the takeover in the media spotlight.[260] The unfolding Watergate scandal and the conclusion of the Vietnam War with the Paris Peace Accords frequently overshadowed the Wounded Knee takeover; the remote location of the takeover, along with a media ban and news blackout, further hindered coverage. Throughout the occupation, AIM made a conscious effort to draw media attention through various means—for example, through the arrival of Angela Davis and Ralph Abernathy, as well as through Marlon Brando's refusal to accept an Oscar for his performance in *The Godfather*.

However, recurring elements of "Indians playing Indian" in the form of warrior masculinity helped to command media attention.²⁶¹ Carter Camp (Ponca) recalled: "As long as we are good Boy Scouts behaving ourselves, nobody gives as shit. But as soon as we're waving guns, the media come running. If it takes waving guns to get our grievances before the public, then that's what we have to do."²⁶² An early attempt to entice media coverage came in the form of hostage-taking—something that the media wouldn't miss.²⁶³ Russell Means recounted in his autobiography how he restarted a firefight in order to keep the confrontation and media attention alive: "Without a confrontation to focus public attention on Wounded Knee, the government could ignore us. The war would be over and we would lose. I decided to start a fire fight so the marshals would put the roadblocks back up and we could continue the battle."²⁶⁴

In a very real sense, the gendered performance of warriorhood—by men and women—tricked law enforcement into believing that the occupiers had more military hardware than anticipated, thus keeping media coverage on the takeover. Activist accounts reveal that the occupiers quite successfully evoked the presence of mines (that were in fact empty film containers); a grenade launcher (through a transformed stove pipe); and a heavy machine gun (by utilizing shell casings and ammo cans)²⁶⁵—fictitious weapons that were nowhere to be found once the occupation ended.²⁶⁶ In so doing, they created the impression of a strong martial posture that correlated with their warrior performance. In one staged incident, activists stumbled into a press conference with fake shell casings, with the media subsequently reporting that they had heavy machine guns.²⁶⁷ According to Russell Means,

> that worked so well that we tried it again, dummying up a length of stovepipe and assorted hardware to look like a bazooka or an RPG, the Soviet-made

---

*Opposite:* AIM warriors at Wounded Knee. The occupiers' performance of warriorhood was geared toward media publicity, not conflict resolution. The occupiers drew on their "cultural/racial capital move." Here, two activists have boarded a lawnmower and one holds a rifle. In the background are three more activists: one on horseback and two others on foot—one draped in an upside-down American flag. (Courtesy of the Denver Public Library)

equivalent. We laid it in a corner of the security building, partly covered with a blanket, and sent a man to invite a reporter to see me up there. When he came in, I jumped up, made a show of sending a couple of guys to screen off the suspicious-looking gear in the corner and told the newsie to leave. Then I loudly chewed the defender's butt for bringing him inside. Within hours the feds "knew" that we had acquired antitank guns.[268]

The occupiers also realized by listening in on two-way radio conversations that law enforcement officers interpreted traditional powwow music as death songs and feared an imminent suicide attack when it was played.[269] In the words of Dennis Banks, "We used every trick in the book to create an impression of strength."[270]

However, the occupiers' attempts to play into the media's sensitivity to conflict and battle and to manipulate the media for their own purposes ultimately backfired.[271] The choice of armed conflict reinforced impressions of AIM as militant, aggressive, and radical, thus overshadowing the larger issues surrounding the occupation.[272] As the occupation dragged on, reporters grew weary of the occupiers who staged warrior drama for the sake of the media, with some reporters admitting they had fallen for these martial performances of "Indians playing Indian."[273] Desmond Smith, writing for the liberal *Nation,* considered the Wounded Knee takeover "from start to finish a staged event."[274] The article read: "As AIM warriors moved into Wounded Knee, the local NBC affiliate, KUTV, was right alongside; the trading post was wrecked by armed activists and filmed exclusively by KUTV's camera."[275] It went on to state that "AIM greatly increased its coverage with its quasi-military preparations: cleaning weapons, digging trenches, preparing roadblocks, holding powwows, etc."[276] An embarrassing incident where a TV cameraman helped activists slaughter some rustled steer for food—after the activists had shot it multiple times but not killed it—shed doubt about some occupiers' ability to handle guns properly and defend themselves.[277] *Time* reported an incident that was symbolic of the way the occupiers unabashedly manipulated the news media:

> Cameras, over here, [Means] called out one afternoon, directing photographers to where the bunkers were being enlarged. Then AIM forces

"arrested" four men attempting to enter their compound. Released a few minutes later, the men were paraded at gunpoint with their hands up past whirring cameras, [and] then let go. Learning that one photographer had missed a shot of the men leaving, AIM guards forced the "prisoners" to re-enact their release.[278]

The same article quoted ABC producer Bill Brown, who recalled: "I put the question to them: 'Are you setting up a provisional government?' Shortly afterward AIM leaders declared Wounded Knee the Oglala Nation," in what seemed yet another attempt to keep the media focus on the confrontation.[279] In a letter to *Time*, Brown also added what he found was missing from the article: "The AIM leadership had refined the craft of confrontation to a remarkable degree, making it pictorial as well as picturesque. They know that a mounted and armed Indian patrol is a rare and newsworthy sight in this century."[280] At some point, the press became so cynical that they started calling AIM's leading spokesperson at Wounded Knee "Chief Sitting Bullshit."[281]

AIM leaders' continual vying for media attention through martial rhetoric and performance also led to frictions inside the Wounded Knee community. Bob Free, an Indigenous fishing rights activist from the Pacific Northwest, charged AIM leaders with being media-savvy and concerned with self-aggrandizement rather than the occupation itself:

> Things have gone to your head. Your noses are stuck up in the air. You only want to talk to the media. You guys better get your act together. Spend some hours a day with the people doing bunker duty. Spend an hour, now and then, digging slit trenches. Collect garbage. We're all Indians here. There's nothing here like a higher-class Indian for the media and a lower-class Indian doing the work.[282]

In a fitting analysis of the staged performance of warriorhood and the media coverage surrounding it, *Newsweek* stated: "If the showdown at Wounded Knee resembled guerilla theatre more than guerilla warfare, the bitter grievances behind it were real enough."[283] In their autobiographical accounts, activists justify the media theater and staged performance of warriorhood as a means to highlight grievances; they likewise point to the seriousness of the entire situation involving the wounding of several activists and a USMS, along with the death by shooting of two Indigenous activists.[284] Indian Country itself was divided over AIM's militant tactics.[285] Noted writer Gerald Vizenor (Ojibwe), who closely followed AIM activism from its inception in Minneapolis to the present, called AIM "a symbolic confrontation group."[286] Doubting their performance of warrior masculinity, Vizenor characterized AIM as follows: "To some, the radicals are the heroes of dominant histories, but to others the leaders of the movement are the freebooters of racism."[287] He also went on to call them "the warriors of the headlines," due to their guerilla theatrics, and "militants" who "decorate themselves in pastiche pan-tribal vestments, and pose, at times, as traditionalists, and speak a language of confrontation and urban politics."[288]

As the above accounts show, the performance of warrior masculinity by the occupiers, on the one hand, and the application of martial-race thinking by the news media, on the other, produced highly ambiguous results. Both the occupiers and the news media drew on the "cultural/racial capital" of Indigenous warrior imagery.[289] The news media attributed culturally and racially inherent warrior skills and traits to the occupiers in order to sell news stories. In turn, the occupiers consciously and strategically employed warrior imagery and "Indians playing Indian" tactics to keep the takeover in the news cycle. More importantly, the occupiers utilized their "cultural/racial capital" in order to (re)assert their cultural and political sovereignty and proclaim the ION.[290] Initially, these complexly intertwined strategies of cultural stereotyping and exploitation as well as cultural perseverance and continuity seemed to work for the benefit of each side; yet, in the long run, they backfired, obscuring the central issues.[291]

### Wounded Knee 1973: Confronting US Hegemony, Reclaiming Indigeneity and (Re)Asserting Political Sovereignty

On May 8, 1973, the seventy-one-day standoff—the longest domestic disturbance in the nation's history—ended with a negotiated settlement. The remaining occupiers laid down their arms and were arrested, thus ending the siege of Wounded Knee. US Marshals replaced the upside-down

AIM flag with the Stars and Stripes, thus symbolically restituting US hegemony, and, to add insult to injury, gave a gun salute.[292] The siege resulted in two activist deaths—Frank Clearwater and Lawrence "Buddy" Lamont—and a severely injured US Marshal, Lloyd Grimm.[293] Clearwater (an activist of disputed heritage) was shot a day after his arrival at Wounded Knee, on April 17, and died a week later.[294] Lamont (Lakota), a recently returned Marine from Vietnam, was shot and killed on April 27, 1973.[295] During the takeover, 500,000 rounds of ammunition were fired into the hamlet, and the Wounded Knee Trading Post was seriously damaged.[296] The US government promised to investigate charges made against the Wilson administration and complete a review into the 1868 Fort Laramie Treaty.[297] The Wounded Knee takeover was inconclusive in terms of upsetting the balance of power in the tribal council, and it did not create a sovereign nation.[298]

The Wounded Knee siege left the local reservation community and Indian Country divided over AIM. During the siege, Wounded Knee residents who ran out of supplies started leaving, while others were prevented from returning to their homes by roadblocks. As a local Wounded Knee resident recalled, "We Lakota felt we were being held captive. Roads were blocked. People were scared of being hit by a stray bullet or hurt by the disrespectful behavior of AIM members."[299] After the siege, returning residents found the Trading Post and Post Office gone, wrecked churches, and homes ransacked and looted.[300] The reservation subsequently turned into a battleground between AIM and Wilson sympathizers.[301] Between 1973 and the mid-1970s, there were a number of Wounded Knee–like occupations on reservations between competing tribal factions.[302]

The takeover at Wounded Knee added yet another layer of deeply symbolic meaning to existent notions of culture, place, gender, and nation. In occupying Wounded Knee, Indigenous activists sought to replace gendered notions of powerlessness, defeat, and subalternity with those of cultural and political empowerment. To many, the declaration of the ION represented the most visible sign of Indigenous resistance in a centuries-old struggle against US hegemony. Wounded Knee is considered a key protest event with far-reaching consequences for reforged Indigenous-settler colonial relations and tribal sovereignty as well as ethnic identity and cultural pride.[303] The takeover overshadowed a prolonged struggle of the Lakotas to gain compensation for the Black Hills and an apology for the massacre.[304]

By taking over Wounded Knee, Indigenous nationalists linked their challenge to the present form of tribal governance to larger questions of self-determination, sovereignty, and nationhood. When AIM took over Wounded Knee, it made three demands: first, a congressional investigation into treaty rights violations; second, an investigation into BIA affairs; and, finally, a plea for a Senate subcommittee to explore conditions on all Sioux reservations in South Dakota. The three points were a condensed version of the Twenty-Point proposal put forth at the Trail of Broken Treaties.[305] Throughout the takeover, negotiation strategies frequently shifted in order to keep the occupation alive and create media exposure. However, a key demand remained the reinstatement of the treaty-making days. During a May 17, 1973, meeting between government representatives and traditionalist elders, Matthew King (Lakota) pressed government officials to acknowledge the substance of the demands: "We are not asking for the negotiation of new treaties," he stated. "We are merely asking that the treaties that already exist be enforced. Unilateral actions by the Congress and the States cannot destroy the natural elements of sovereignty."[306] However, government representatives maintained that Congress had eliminated the president's right to negotiate treaties with tribal nations as sovereign bodies. By maintaining that the self-governing status of tribal nations could not be reinstated, the US government effectively dashed any hopes of sovereign nationhood.[307]

The issue of tribal sovereignty and its intricate relationship to Indigenous manhood was raised once again at a Senate hearing into the causes and aftermath of Wounded Knee, held on June 16 and 17, 1973, in Pine Ridge and Kyle, South Dakota, by South Dakota senator James Abourezk. In his statement at the US Senate hearing, Means effectively linked a lack of tribal self-determination to a loss of Indigenous manhood. "Every time a person on the reservation tries to assert his manhood in any way, shape or form, he is struck down and taught a lesson right quick, because the Bureau can't afford that," he claimed.[308] AIM attorney Ramon Roubideaux (Lakota), a World War II vet, eloquently explained that when US Congress unilaterally ended treaty-making processes between the federal government and tribal nations in 1871, it also severely impacted

Indigenous manhood and tribal sovereignty. Over time, he stated, "the U.S. government in its so-called paternalism and with the connivance of puppet tribal government have destroyed the manhood that we have always had or [it] attempted to destroy it."[309] The Wounded Knee takeover, then, was a complete rejection of the handling of Indigenous affairs under US colonial rule and an effort to cast off government dependency and paternalism. In his mind, tribal governments did not represent the majority of Indigenous people on reservations.[310] Robert Burnette (Lakota), former tribal chairman of the Rosebud reservation and himself a WWII veteran and activist, echoed the plea for self-determination and equal treatment: "We are men who . . . have a capability of controlling our own lives and our destiny."[311]

The Senate hearing once again shed light on the envisioned, three-layer form of tribal governance. The setup of the ION constituted a conscious effort to return to the concept of tribal sovereignty that existed prior to 1871 and deal with the United States on a nation-to-nation basis.[312] In the words of Russell Means, they envisaged "the establishment of separate states under a protective status for all Indian nations" similar to the status of San Marino in Italy.[313] Legal scholar Edward Lazarus has pointed to the ambiguity of this proposal, as it "was poorly grounded in tribal self-rule." As he put it, "the Wounded Knee occupiers . . . , many (if not most) of whom were not Sioux, were in essence asking for an outside power (the US) to intervene in Sioux internal affairs and install a government of 'traditional chiefs.'" A return to the treaty-making era and the Second Treaty of Fort Laramie (1868) would entail a bureau superintendent who controlled reservation affairs and the tribal council. This was nothing short of a form of direct colonial rule, rather than tribal self-governance and sovereignty. The new form of governance also meant that the "chiefs" would come to their titles through heredity or self-selection. From an opposite perspective, this effectively meant the disenfranchisement of all those Lakotas who did not recognize a hereditary descendant of Red Cloud as a leader; it equally entailed "the right of mainly Chippewa [sic] agitators to occupy a part of their reservation and impose change through force."[314]

The nation-building project of the Independent Oglala Nation highlighted distinct concepts of governance—Indigenous and Western—and combined them in complex and contested ways. Indigenous nationalists stressed the inherent right to tribal sovereignty (through the concept of *tiospaye* that emphasized notions of kinship and tribal affiliation) and peoplehood (or, for that matter, a sense of Lakota-ness as established through a communal connection to sacred history, land, ceremony, and language). Whatever their exact plans, it seems as if Indigenous nationalists sought to end indirect colonial rule under the existent IRA-style form of tribal governance, cast off government dependency and paternalism, and seek a return to tribal sovereignty. Yet they failed to articulate their vision properly. At the same time, Indigenous nationalists continually stressed Western concepts of nationalism. Throughout the siege, AIM nationalists repeatedly claimed they sought to establish a nation separate from the United States.[315] The setup of the Independent Oglala Nation points to the complexities and ambiguities of Indigenous nation-building endeavors in larger encompassing society. The ION was born from frustration and political dissent with one tribal leader (Dick Wilson), then turned into an indictment of an entire tribal council system (the IRA) and the BIA, and ultimately ended in the calls for an independent nation.[316]

## Conclusion

The takeover of Wounded Knee symbolized the summit of nationalist warrior performance and Indigenous nation-building efforts. As Indigenous men began to confront their own subaltern status—first in the Twin Cities, then in border towns, and ultimately on the national stage—they continually reinvented their cultural and masculine subjectivities. AIM's masculinized protest politics arose from feelings of powerlessness and emasculation and led to exaggerated claims to masculinity and power. As Indigenous men confronted an oppressive bureaucracy and long-standing grievances, they also began to search for meaning in their cultural roots. The combining of protest politics and identity politics functioned as a self-generating force of cultural pride and political radicalism, leading to a renewal, revitalization, and remasculinization of Indigenous men—perhaps most visible in the form of hypermasculine warriors at Wounded Knee. The historic massacre site of Wounded Knee contains a deep-layered symbolism that allowed Indigenous men and women to reinvent self and society vis-à-vis dominant society.

The siege of Wounded Knee indicated the confluence of two hitherto separate currents of warriorhood: These were Indigenous men who considered themselves the modern vanguard of anti-colonial resistance and Indigenous veterans who saw themselves as in line with an older tradition of warriorhood. Disenchanted Indigenous veterans pushed the US government to its limits, yet without the dire consequences of the past. In the words of Al Carroll, "they saw no contradiction in fighting first for the military and then against the government."[317]

Wounded Knee was a highly gendered nation-building attempt that emerged in direct resistance to US colonial forces intent on suppressing militant Indigenous nationalism. The ION was a highly masculinized nation, in large part due to the high number of veterans fighting on either side. This raised the analogy of yet another Indian War of the nineteenth century refought in the Vietnam War era. Both Indigenous veterans and activists-turned-warriors joined forces in opposing US colonial rule and a complicit, colonized Indigenous elite. Indigenous men remasculinized through both the founding of the AIM warrior society and the declaration of the ION. This remasculinization went in hand with a return of Indigenous people to their cultural traditions—that is, a retraditionalization. In the face of adversity, the warriors for a nation practiced cultural traditions in what must be understood as both an expression of their defiant cultural resistance and ethnic pride. The gendered performance of nationalist warriorhood was not undisputed among the occupiers: first, because veterans did not regard nonveterans as warriors and, second, because Indigenous women took up arms also, challenging inculcated male norms and ideals. However, the performance of warriorhood was not only an expression of defiant nationalism and cultural resistance; it also sought to keep the occupation in the media spotlight. For all these reasons, the ION was coded as a highly masculinized nation.

Indigenous women played a key part at Wounded Knee, running the day-to-day affairs of the occupation. They occupied ambiguous and complex positions, simultaneously reaffirming male privilege (through the taking up of roles of domesticated motherhood) and challenging it (through the picking up of the gun). At times, women joined their male counterparts as comrades-in-arms in the firefights, thus successfully renegotiating themselves into AIM's masculine microculture and nationalist ideology. In taking on a female warrior subjectivity, Indigenous women reconnected to a less well-established tradition of warrior women that had been in existence prior to the reservation period—or so they claimed. Moreover, in taking up arms, they directly challenged male privilege and the patriarchal nature of the American Indian Movement. Indigenous men felt somewhat threatened by the participation of women in the armed confrontation, yet for their part they accepted it out of pure necessity. In the Wounded Knee aftermath, Indigenous women embarked on a female quest for empowerment, self-determination, and decolonization.

Indigenous nationalists remained ambiguous whether they attempted to set up a separate nation or sought to (re)assert tribal sovereignty within the American nation. Throughout, their nationalist endeavor remained outright fuzzy and ambiguous in combining Indigenous and Western concepts. For one thing, the newly imagined ION constituted part of a larger, yet unsuccessful attempt to return to the nation-to-nation era and restore tribal sovereignty as outlined under the 1868 Fort Laramie Treaty; it also constituted an effort, albeit unsuccessful, to shed imposed indirect colonial rule. Whatever their intent, the takeover served Indigenous people(s) as a means of regaining a sense of empowerment and regenerating positive identities. Al Carroll points out that the sustained Wounded Knee occupation created new ways to be a warrior and new directions for warrior societies.[318] From the 1970s through the present day, Indigenous nationalists renewed and revitalized cultural and warrior traditions in contemporary struggles in Canada where tribal communities continue to uphold their land ownership, their treaty rights, and their sovereignty in resistance to continual settler-colonial encroachment.[319] In that sense, Indigenous nationalists heralded new pathways in what it means to be warrior—with major implications for Indian Country.

# Chapter 5

# Reinventing Warriorhood and Nationalist Struggle after 1973

In the wake of the Wounded Knee takeover, the US government brought heavy charges against AIM. Dennis Banks and Russell Means were tried together at the Wounded Knee leadership trials in St. Paul, Minnesota. In his opening statement at the 1974 Wounded Knee leadership trials, Russell Means offered insight into the intricate nature of the Indigenous Rights Struggle and how it intertwined with notions of culture, history, and masculinity. In essence, the AIM leader saw five pathways for Indigenous men on the Pine Ridge reservation to construct and express a sense of manliness:

> There are only five options open to the Indian male on the reservation to express his manhood. . . . One is through athletics.
> Another way is to join the service, put on the uniform and say, "Look, I'm a man."
> Of course, there is another way. That is to grab the bottle, drink it, go down to the other bar and fight your brothers and sisters . . . or . . . go home and mistreat your wife and tell her, "Look, I'm a man."
> And there is another way. . . . That is . . . to cut your hair, put on the tie and become a facsimile of the white man.

> There has been . . . lately a new way to express your manhood, and that's been [through] the American Indian Movement, to express Indianness in the Lakota way.[1]

The pathways for Indigenous men to express their masculinity—according to Means—were sports, military service, drinking and violence, adhering to white ideals of manliness and abandoning Indigeneity, or joining AIM and embracing a culturally immersed form of manhood. According to the way Means framed his argument, most versions of Indigenous masculinity were complicit with, submissive to, or adopted dominant ideals: both sports and military service allowed Indigenous men to compete with whites on an equal basis and gain privilege, yet, at the same time, worked in ways that perpetuated colonial domination and the subordination of Indigenous men.[2] Drinking and gendered violence offered short-term feelings of virility, yet acted in support of white, hegemonic patriarchy.[3] The internalization of dominant ideals of manliness means the perpetuation of the colonial legacy of subordination.[4] Only the last option was presented as viable: the adoption of a decidedly Lakota-inspired cultural expression of manhood as an assertion of cultural pride and identity.

In the aftermath of the Wounded Knee takeover and amidst intense governmental repression, AIM embraced new directions, transforming the struggle for Indigenous rights. AIM's venture into protest politics had a lasting impact across Indian Country and transformed Indigenous–settler colonial relations. While the anti-colonial struggle has been widely heroized across Indian Country, there has been much controversy about AIM's leaders and whether they were revolutionary icons or charlatans. For example, Indigenous Vietnam veterans—participants or observers in the armed struggle at Wounded Knee—have remained divided over competing claims of warriorhood, nation-building, martial virtues, and leadership. While AIM leaders have remained conspicuously silent when it comes to the question of whether they lived up to their own warrior ideals, veterans claimed that AIM leaders' personal flaws and lack of manly virtues severely hampered the organization.

## Political Warriors: Transforming Warrior Masculinity and Nationalist Struggle After 1973

Following the BIA takeover in November 1972, the US government embarked on a relentless domestic counterintelligence campaign to repress Indigenous nationalist militancy; this was paralleled by a strategy to alternatively coopt or incorporate Indigenous dissent. The FBI classified AIM as "extremist," "violent," and "violence-prone" and as a viable threat to political hegemony.[5] The FBI's war against AIM lasted from 1972 through 1978 and has its own historiography.[6] The Wounded Knee Legal Defense/Offense Committee (WKLD/OC) defended the warriors for a nation in a massive series of legal proceedings brought by the US government. After the takeover, there were 562 arrests and 185 indictments, yet there were only fifteen convictions, an extremely low number given the massive charges laid.[7] By late 1973, many of AIM's warriors had been forced into exile or underground, imprisoned, or killed. In the Wounded Knee leadership trials of 1974, Dennis Banks and Russell Means were tried together. They effectively turned the courtroom into a political arena and walked free after a year of courtroom hearings in a trial that was dismissed on the grounds of severe government misconduct.[8] Historian and lawyer John William Sayer notes that during the trials,

> the media portraits of the well-known male defendants and their equally famous male attorneys, William Kunstler and Mark Lane, drew on already fixed images of the white male militants of the Sixties and the stereotypical Indian warriors of Hollywood. These same images of masculinity were cultivated by the participants themselves and then accentuated in the media, reinforcing old stereotypes and at times overshadowing more important issues.[9]

The Wounded Knee leadership trial diverted some attention from the underlying all-out US government attempt to quash the Indigenous nationalist movement.

From mid-1973 through late 1976, a campaign of political repression and physical violence rocked the Pine Ridge reservation as the US government sought to incapacitate the Indigenous nationalist movement. The US Commission on Civil Rights characterized this low-level civil war fought between AIM adherents and GOONs as a "reign of terror."[10] According to activists, this low-level civil war ultimately cost the lives of up to sixty-nine AIM members and supporters; among those killed were twenty-one women and two children.[11] The FBI arrived at a total of fifty-seven killed.[12] A considerably lower figure comes from journalist Tim Giago (Lakota), himself from Pine Ridge.[13]

Whatever the total number of violent deaths, the most prominent female victim of the "reign of terror" was Anna Mae Pictou-Aquash (Mi'kmaq), whose body was found on February 24, 1976, about two months after her execution-style murder.[14] Aquash fell victim to paranoia induced within AIM and "bad-jacketing." AIM members initially claimed Aquash had been murdered by the FBI;[15] yet her killing was in fact an inside job conducted by AIM members who believed she was an FBI informant.[16] Two AIM members—Arlo Looking Cloud (Lakota) and John Graham (Southern Tutchone Champagne and Aishihik First Nations)—ultimately confessed to the murder; yet it appears that they acted on the behest of someone else, probably Vernon Bellecourt.[17]

At the peak of government-sponsored violence, the FBI claimed it had only investigative powers and insufficient manpower to handle the cases.[18] The extreme violence indicated that the US government considered Indigenous nationalists a direct threat to its model of indirect colonial rule. Annette M. Jaimes and Theresa Halsey have pointed to the great gender disparity in targeted killings in what they consider a repetition of a "historical pattern," reminiscent of nineteenth-century killings of famous Indigenous warriors and leaders such as Crazy Horse or Sitting Bull.[19] The structure of the violent repression of the Indigenous nationalist movement bore striking parallels to Latin America.[20]

Both FBI agents and AIM warriors regarded themselves in antagonistic terms. There is ample evidence that FBI law enforcement in Indian Country understood itself as a colonial police force with BIA or tribal police officers as government surrogates.[21] A 1976 statement by FBI agent Norman Zigrossi, in charge of the Rapid City office, offers a glimpse into gendered and racialized perspectives of the FBI: "They [the Indians] are a conquered nation, and when you are conquered, the people you are conquered by dictate your future. This is a basic philosophy of mine. If I'm part of a conquered nation, I've got to yield to authority. . . . [The FBI must function as] a colonial police force."[22] In masculinized analogy, AIM considered the FBI as the resurrection of the US Cavalry bent to uphold colonial rule. In a revealing statement, AIM leader John Trudell claimed that

> we see the FBI as an extension of Custer's Seventh Cavalry of the 19th century. The justification they use to go after us is, that we're revolutionaries. But . . . we are not a revolutionary group. We are part of a race of people who have been struggling against invaders for 400 years. We . . . have a right to our land and our own value system within their system which is all around us.[23]

On June 26, 1975, amid escalating violence and paranoia, a firefight erupted on the Jumping Bull compound Pine Ridge Reservation that left two FBI agents (Ronald Coler and Jack Williams) and one AIM activist (Joe Stuntz Killsright) dead. In the ensuing manhunt, the FBI swept the reservation in a massive search for the suspected killers.[24] Ultimately, Leonard Peltier (Ojibwe/Lakota/Dakota) was found guilty of murder and sentenced to life imprisonment, despite evidence of overwhelming government misconduct.[25] Activist and writer Jim Vander Wall characterized Leonard Peltier as a "warrior caged" who represents "a symbol . . . to indigenous people everywhere who are struggling against illegal expropriation of their lands and destruction of their cultures."[26] Government repression effectively crushed the Indigenous nationalist movement.[27]

## AIM as an International Warrior Society, 1974 to the Present

After the seizure of Wounded Knee, Indigenous activists continued to struggle for self-determination, tribal sovereignty, treaty rights, and nationhood, yet they moved away from armed confrontation toward political protest and legal battles. Indigenous men reinvented themselves once again, becoming political warriors in turn. In 1974, AIM helped to set up the International Indian Treaty Council (IITC), an organization of tribal nations and Indigenous people from across the globe to work for self-determination and sovereignty.[28]

From its inception, the IITC played a central role in internationalizing Indigenous struggles and placing them before the world community. In 1974, the IITC published its "Declaration of Continuing Independence of the Sovereign Native American Indian Nations," which demanded the recognition of treaties (and, as such, also the recognition of the ION), rejected the imposition of colonial policies, and stated its support for sovereignty and tribal nationhood. By channeling energy from an deteriorating AIM to the IITC, Indigenous activists sought to bypass the US government, putting its politics under international scrutiny.[29] In 1977, the IITC gained recognition from the United Nations as a nongovernmental organization (NGO) with special consultative status.[30] This went hand in hand with a refashioning of the concept of Indigenous sovereignty—away from a notion encompassing national sovereignty toward Indigenous human rights.[31] In 2007, Indigenous peoples drafted the "U.N. Declaration on the Rights of Indigenous People," demanding the recognition of tribal nations, treaty rights, tribal lands, cultural integrity, and environmental protection.[32] It might come as a surprise to note that as AIM moved away from confrontation politics, it still inspired other nationalist movements around the world.[33] From 1973 onward, a number of AIM leaders traveled Europe on several occasions and built transatlantic sovereignty alliances and solidarity networks on both sides of the Iron Curtain that provided AIM with financial donations that helped support WKLD/OC and maintain the Indigenous struggle for sovereignty.[34] The transition from warriors to diplomats did not pass without criticism—a number of Indigenous organizations derided the IITC as "AIMsters playing diplomat."[35]

By late 1973, AIM was publicly calling itself an international warrior society but left open what that meant precisely. A leaflet, put out by a support group after the conclusion of the siege of Wounded Knee, contained a reprint of the 1868 Fort Laramie Treaty, several bulletins with the workings of the ION, negotiation proposals, and the agreement that brought the siege of Wounded Knee to an end.[36] However, the cover image of the leaflet, titled "Red Man's International Warrior Society," was the most illustrative component, bearing striking resemblance to another Louis Hall (Mohawk) painting.[37] The title "International Warrior Society" articulated yet another claim to warriorhood, yet the name was

Image of the photo exhibition "I'm Not Your Indian Anymore—A Photographic History of the American Indian Movement" at the All My Relations Arts gallery in Minneapolis, June 2013. The wall features images of AIM activists taken during protests, demonstrations, and takeovers, along with pictures of hearings, conferences, and meetings. (Photo by author)

more indicative of a spirit of resistance than of any substantiated claims to warriorhood.

### Indigenous Women and the Struggle for Self-Determination, Sovereignty, and Decolonization after 1973

In the aftermath of Wounded Knee and writing from his prison cell to await trial, Carter Camp called upon women to step forward and carry on the struggle. Indigenous women, he demanded, should "shun the honkies" and instead chose a "warrior." As he explained, "the most beautiful thing in the world, and the most frightening for the conqueror, is to see an Indian woman standing proudly beside her man, facing the fight together with him, confident of victory."[38] In the aftermath of Wounded Knee, much of the ongoing grassroots struggle for Indigenous rights can indeed be attributed to the commitment of Indigenous women who filled the vacancies of men.[39]

In 1974, Indigenous women established their own organization, called Women of All Red Nations (WARN). Their primary concern remained the struggle for cultural and political empowerment. Yet they also began, increasingly, to contest male privilege, thus battling their state of "double oppression" on multiple fronts.[40] Paula Gunn Allen (Laguna Pueblo) related that many Indigenous women found the sexism and chauvinism of their male counterparts off-putting. As she recalled,

> finally these women had enough. . . . Finally three women called them [Dennis Banks and Russell Means] in and they said in no uncertain terms, "We'll show you who the real warriors are here. We are! You think you're so big. You haven't done nothing and you can't do nothing without us." Every Indian knows that. You want something done, call a woman. They all know that. The men know it, the women know it. But the situation is such, that the white world wants things Indian . . . you know who they call. They call the men.[41]

According to Lorelei DeCora Means, Indigenous women developed "an awareness of the distinctive gendered experience of Indian men and women at the hands of the U.S. government."[42] WARN became active in the areas of education, healthcare, treaty rights, and putting an end to domestic violence, forced sterilization, and uranium mining.[43] "Indian women have had to be strong because of what this colonialist system has done to our men. . . . After Wounded Knee, while all the persecution was going on, the women had to keep things going," said DeCora of the overall female sentiment. WARN activists also sought to educate children to carry on the Indigenous struggle into the next generation.[44]

During the 1970s, two concerns of major importance to WARN were coerced sterilization and the removal of Indigenous children to non-Indigenous adoptive and foster homes. WARN advocated for Indigenous women's reproductive rights and advanced a scathing rebuke of the federal government's funding of sterilizations through the Indian Health Service (IHS).[45] Indigenous women regarded forced or coerced sterilization as a direct affront to their personal reproductive rights as members of a sovereign nation and as a challenge to the tribal sovereignty of that tribal nation. Every instance where an Indigenous women lost her reproductive capacities weakened tribal sovereignty, as the tribe's political power resided in its population size.[46] Ultimately, Indigenous women and feminist activism effected a change in federal regulations and a halt to sterilization abuse.[47] Indigenous women also instigated passage of the Indian Child Welfare Act (1978) to counter adopting and fostering out Indigenous children to non-Indigenous families and communities.

However, throughout the struggle against forced or coerced sterilization, AIM's leaders failed to offer much tangible support. In February 1978, when Dennis Banks and Lehman Brightman organized the "Longest Walk," the issue was adopted as a major concern only at the request of Indigenous women.[48] Russell Means made appearances on ABC's *Good Morning America*, NBC's *Today*, and CBS *Morning News* and used the airtime to highlight some of the sterilization abuse.[49] Clyde Bellecourt's autobiography also touches upon the issue but fails to mention that Indigenous women were the primary driving force against sterilization procedures.[50] While AIM's male leaders recognized forced sterilization as a problem, they did not offer much concrete assistance.[51] It might not come as a surprise that the field of Indigenous feminism has arisen from Indigenous women activism of the 1960s and 1970s.[52] Within this larger context, further female-organized grassroots movements formed, signifying a stirring empowerment of Indigenous women.[53]

### The Decline of Red Power Militancy, 1973–1978

The Wounded Knee takeover only briefly sparked conflict on various reservations across the nation.[54] These confrontations were less symbolic but more violent than previous ones. But despite the aggressive posturing of Indigenous warriors in their demand for self-determination and sovereignty, Red Power militancy was in decline.[55]

The "Longest Walk," a peaceful, transcontinental protest march that commenced on Alcatraz Island and reached Washington, DC, in July 1978, is commonly regarded as the last major Red Power protest event.[56] The protest demonstration formed in opposition to a rising anti-Indigenous backlash, which aimed to end tribal sovereignty (through the withdrawal of treaty-guaranteed services and the curtailing of tribal rights), in what amounted to a just another era of termination.[57] During the marches, Indigenous veterans and activists carrying eagle staffs took the lead, in a

The Longest Walk from San Francisco to Washington, DC, was intended to draw attention to Indigenous issues dealing with tribal sovereignty and anti-Indian legislation, 1978. The longshot image is a back view of Indigenous protesters—men, women, and children—marching on a highway with several tribal flags indicating the protesters' affiliation to their respective tribal nation. (Richard Erdoes Papers, Yale Collection of Western Americana, Beinecke Rare Book and Manuscript Library)

position of honor; they also worked as security during the entire protest event.[58] The roughly two thousand participants in the "Longest Walk" came from a cross-section of Indian Country.[59] The "Longest Walk" manifesto, a reaffirmation of tribal sovereignty, recounted the parallel trajectories of settler colonialism and the ongoing transnational struggle of Indigenous peoples across the Americas.[60] Red Power protest activism had moved in a cycle from festive activism (at Alcatraz), to armed confrontation (at Wounded Knee), to nonviolent protest for Indigenous unity (the "Longest Walk").[61]

By the mid-1970s, the self-proclaimed AIM warrior society had fallen into disarray, disintegrating under persistent assault from the US government and the society's own internal contradictions.[62] The 1973 shooting (and severe wounding) of Clyde Bellecourt by Carter Camp,[63] the 1975 shooting at the Jumping Bull compound on Pine Ridge (that implicated Leonard Peltier),[64] the late-1975, execution-style killing of Anna Mae Aquash (Mi'kmaq), the highest-ranking woman within the male-dominated organization,[65] and FBI COINTELPRO tactics severely destabilized the organization.[66] AIM's implication in Aquash's murder severely tarnished its public image as a self-righteous warrior society fighting on behalf of Indigenous people.[67] The fate of Perry Ray Robinson, a Black civil rights activist who joined the siege at Wounded Knee, remains a matter of controversy.[68] By the mid-1970s, AIM had disintegrated into several competing factions.[69]

## AIM Leaders after 1973

While the leaders of AIM left the armed anti-colonial struggle behind, they remained cultural and political nationalists. Following the siege at Wounded Knee, they reinvented themselves yet again, becoming active in the cultural nationalist movement.

Following AIM's demise, Russell Means embarked on an illustrious career in political activism and acting. Means ran for tribal chairman at Pine Ridge twice—once in 1974, and again thirty years later—each time to be defeated. However, his work for community empowerment made an impact through the establishment of KILI radio station and a hospital at Pine Ridge. In addition, he channeled his energy into the International Indian Treaty Conference, the international arm of the AIM warrior society. In 1981, he and his brother Bill established the Yellow Thunder Camp in the Black Hills—and maintained it for five and a half years—to initiate the reacquisition of sacred lands. In the mid-1980s, Means became increasingly involved with Nicaragua's Miskito peoples' armed fight against the Sandinistas in South America. In the 1990s, he embarked on a career as an actor, once again performing as a warrior, this time in Hollywood blockbusters, starring in *Last of the Mohicans* (1992), *Natural Born Killers* (1994), *Pocahontas* (1998) and *Pathfinder* (2007). Certainly, a case can be made that his role in AIM was one that prepared him for a career in genuine acting. Means's flair for dramatizing Indigenous issues during AIM's heyday suggests that this benefitted his "actorvism."[70] According to historian James Stripes, the term "actorvism" implies "a method employed by members of AIM in the early 1970s that often appeared at least as concerned with garnering media attention as with promoting a specific program for political change"—a method similar to but different from the "Indians playing Indian" theme.[71] Indeed, voices from Indian Country have accused Russell Means of impersonating Indigenous characters, in part because Means spent relatively little time on reservations while growing up. Throughout his life, Means believed in Indigenous national separatism.[72]

Dennis Banks's subsequent life reflected his ongoing commitment to Indigenous issues. During the 1970s, Banks was a lecturer at and director of D-Q University at Davis, California. Since 1978, he has organized several transcontinental walks and runs that started at the meaningful site of Alcatraz and concluded in Washington, DC—among them the "Longest Walk II" (in 2008) and the "Longest Walk III" (in 2011). In 1994, he led the four-month "Walk for Justice," retracing the route from San Francisco to Washington, DC. In a 2012 interview, Banks claimed that he had crossed the country in seven events.[73]

Other AIM leaders, such as John Trudell and Carter Camp, have found their calling as cultural warriors. Trudell abandoned confrontational politics altogether after he lost his entire family in a suspicious fire that occurred briefly after he had led a demonstration in Washington, DC, and burnt the American flag on the steps of the FBI building. Instead, he embarked on a career as a musician, writer, and actor. His filmography includes *Thunderheart* (1992), where he played a character resembling Leonard Peltier; *On Deadly Ground* (1995); and *Smoke Signals* (1998). Trudell served as a special advisor to the documentary *Incident at Oglala* (1992) about the 1975 shootout and the ensuing violence on Pine Ridge. He also released a series of CDs and poems, which provided Indian Country with liberating and empowering messages of decolonization. Like others, Camp remained a nationalist warrior throughout his life yet channeled his energy into the parallel cultural nationalist movement, organizing an annual Sun Dance at Rosebud Reservation and protesting against the Keystone Pipeline.[74] The Bellecourt brothers continued to work on community organization in the Twin Cities. However, Clyde Bellecourt occasionally relapsed into criminal activity, never entirely able to leave his "toxic masculinity" behind.[75] Russell Means (d. 2012), Carter Camp (d. 2014), John Trudell (d. 2015), Dennis Banks (d. 2017), Leonard Crow Dog

(d. 2021) and the Bellecourt brothers (Vernon, d. 2007; Clyde, d. 2022) have since passed away. However, these and other activists were keen to protect their movement's legacy through a number of autobiographies, documentaries, and movement histories.[76] Clyde Bellecourt was instrumental in the founding of the AIM Interpretative Center in Minneapolis, Minnesota, which hosts a growing collection of photos, documents, and movement memorabilia.[77]

Following their involvement with AIM, many Indigenous men and women remained active, pursuing new pathways to fight for cultural and political empowerment and sovereignty. They picked up their lives where they had left off, yet the effects of their activist years shaped their lives for years to come. For example, Vietnam veteran-turned-nationalist Woody Kipp became involved in ceremony and tried to learn more about his own people, the Blackfeet, and their culture, history, language, and mythology.[78] Wes Studi embarked on a career in acting, playing various warrior roles in *Dances with Wolves* (1990), *The Last of the Mohicans* (1992), *Geronimo: An American Legend* (1993), *The New World* (2005), and *Hostiles* (2017), among others. For him, acting became a way to deal with war-related stress. As he recalled, "I substituted the adrenaline rush of battle with what was chemically the same experience, except that it was derived from acting.... I found the same intensity of experience, but in a productive fashion." This, he says, helped him heal his wounded masculinity.[79]

## Cultural Warriors: Indigenous Renewal and Transformed Indigenous-Settler Colonial Relations

Red Power activism resulted in a massive cultural, political, and economic renaissance across Indian Country.[80] Indigenous activism was led by a high sense of moral uprightness, inspiring a massive cultural renewal that led to a renewed sense of culture, tradition, and history.[81] The renaissance's impact is evident in the proliferation in literature, the arts and crafts, music, and film, the emergence of Native Studies programs and establishment of tribal colleges, a fundamental restructuring of Indigenous-white relations, far-reaching legislation, and economic transformation.[82] Red Power movement activism inspired a renewed sense of Indigeneity.[83] The

Indigenous cultural and nationalist movement replaced feelings of alienation, inferiority, powerlessness, and emasculation with those of pride, worth, agency, and significance—paralleling Indigenous experiences elsewhere.[84] The renewed sense of Indigeneity was visible in the learning of tribal languages, the adoption of Indigenous names, hairstyles, and dress, teachings in culture and history, and a renewal of cultural and religious traditions, practices, ceremonies, rituals, and beliefs that had formerly been out-ruled by the US government.[85] An increasing awareness of Indigeneity shows in a rising ethnic identification in the US census and population growth among Native Americans—a strong indication of an end to invisibility and a debunking of the myth of the "vanishing race."[86]

Indigenous peoples in the United States and elsewhere have utilized various decolonization strategies to recuperate traditional forms of Indigeneity.[87] For example, tribal communities have initiated a revitalization of traditional practices, languages, and religious beliefs. Tribal museums are instrumental in the recovery, repatriation, and preservation of material culture and artifacts, the revitalization of crafts, and the reclamation of artifacts and human remains.[88] At the same time, Indigenous people have begun to seek pathways to balanced, complimentary, and empowered gender relations within their communities.[89] Rather than reviving traditions that have been lost through colonization (and are therefore contentious), Indigenous communities have begun to revitalize tribal values as well as tribal culture-specific practices, epistemologies, and gender ideologies.[90]

The Indigenous renaissance ultimately prompted a fundamental restructuring of Indigenous-settler colonial relations; most notably through the turning away from termination policies and the initiation of an era of tribal self-determination since the Nixon administration. Federal Indian policies reaffirmed treaty rights and tribal sovereignty and increased Indigenous control over the BIA.[91] A wide range of legislation affecting all areas of Indigenous life—land restoration, education, health, economy, financing, child care, and religious freedom—has improved the life of tribal communities in virtually every sphere.[92] Among the most significant are the Indian Self-Determination and Education Assistance Act of 1975, which encouraged tribal communities to take over supervision of most public services, and the American Indian Religious Freedom Act of 1978, which upheld the protection of Indigenous cultural and religious practices. This new relationship has allowed Native Americans to regain a measure of self-control over their own lives.[93] Since the Reagan administration, the US government has begun to deal with tribes on a "government-to-government" basis.[94] As of today, the US government sees its main responsibility toward tribal nations as fulfilling trust responsibilities and implementing self-determination and self-governance. The paradigm shift in federal Indian policy, however, does not translate into a reality of tribal sovereignty, as the US government continues to regard Indigenous-settler colonial relations in terms of guardianship and wardship.[95] The Indigenous Rights Movement continues the struggle against settler-colonial power.[96]

These broad-sweeping changes in Indian Country and dominant society aside, AIM's long-time impact in its primary zone of confrontational protest politics, South Dakota and Minnesota, remains disputed. In his longitudinal study on AIM's audience, the "bystanders," sociologist Davis W. Everson provides evidence that settler-colonial society has discursively reconfigured the American Indian Movement over a time span of more than four decades (i.e., between 1973 and 2015). According to his findings, an unintended consequence of AIM activism was "the emergence of a novel 'privilege narrative' legitimating the unequal white-Native racial order."[97] The study's results might come as a surprise, as a national Lou Harris poll of 1973 found the general audience sympathetic to the Indigenous cause with, as we have seen, 51 percent supporting the Independent Oglala Nation at Wounded Knee.[98] In comparison, the Black Panther Party never gained more than 10 percent of white support, as indicated by Gallup polls from the 1970s.[99] Within South Dakota, a historical conquest narrative emerged that interweaved opposition to Indigenous militancy and the need for "law and order" with negative stereotypes. This privilege narrative effectively delegitimizes the Indigenous Rights Struggle in what is an attempt to perpetuate the existent racial order of white dominance.[100] Conversely, in Minnesota, AIM succeeded in garnering a sympathetic general public that was partially driven by historical guilt and positive stereotypes.[101]

To an outside observer, it might come as a surprise that, at the height of Indigenous militancy, AIM considered itself not only a warrior society but also a cultural or spiritual movement. Parallel to and intertwined with Red Power political activism was a cultural national movement that engaged in decolonization efforts and sought to revitalize Indigenous cultural identities. Indeed, Indigenous political nationalism (which sought to reconcile US national sovereignty with Indigenous claims to self-determination, sovereignty, and nationhood) was closely linked to cultural nationalism (which sought, according to political scientist John Hutchinson, "the moral regeneration of the historic community" through reference to its unique culture, history, and geography).[102]

Indigenous men and women sought to reinvent their gendered and cultural subjectivities by reconnecting to their cultural heritage. Indigenous nationalists claimed that first and foremost they were part of a cultural and spiritual movement that was concerned with the revival of traditional culture(s). Dorothy Ninham (Oneida), a participant at the Wounded Knee siege, put it this way:

> What we set out to do and that was to bring back our culture, bring back our traditional ways, and to revive them. We've always been a spiritual movement. A lot of people talk about the American Indian Movement like it was a renegade bunch of people. But what they don't know is that we always took the direction from medicine people, from spiritual leaders. And we always followed their direction. We never did anything unless we were invited to come into an area. Wounded Knee was one area where we were invited to come in and help the people out at that time.[103]

Indian Country has widely associated the Wounded Knee takeover with a cultural renewal of songs, dances, traditional practices, ceremonies, rituals, and the revitalization of tribal languages. Indigenous nationalists frequently claimed that this turning toward cultural traditions was more significant than actually protest activism. While Indigenous activists sought to gain the media limelight to draw attention to their cause—often by media-savvy tactics and rhetoric—they also actively sought to reclaim their Indigeneity after decades of colonial abuse and whitewashing. Many Indigenous activists realized that even "Indians playing Indian" tactics and militant rhetoric could not hide the fact that a sense of

Sun Dance on Pine Ridge, South Dakota, 1972. The image shows several Sun Dancers. The men are bare-chested, carry sage wreaths around their head and wrists, blow eagle-bone whistles, and dance around a Sun Dance tree (not visible in the image). Traditionally, Lakota men prepare for the Sun Dance through fasting, sweats, vision quests, prayer, song, and dance. The ceremony involves the piercing of skin and the dancing around a pole. Typically, the Sun Dance is a physical and spiritual test for the dancers and a sacrifice to their people.

As Indigenous men and women engaged in the struggle for their political rights, they also reached out in their cultural heritage to remake their Indigenous identities. Processes of political radicalization and cultural retraditionalization are closely connected. AIM therefore claims major credit for sparking a cultural renewal of songs, dances, traditional practices, ceremonies, rituals, and the revitalization of tribal languages. (Richard Erdoes Papers, Yale Collection of Western Americana, Beinecke Rare Book and Manuscript Library)

genuineness remained missing as long as they did not bridge that cultural chasm that separated them from their own Indigeneity. In the words of Dennis Banks, "you can yell and scream at the top of your lungs on the pulpit, but if you have no real spiritual purpose then all the rhetoric is just rhetoric. It has no meaning."[104] Wounded Knee was significant in that it instigated this turn toward cultural renewal. Dennis Banks put it this way:

"I began to realize that the strength of this movement was not just about protesting. We have to have something inside of us that would direct us in a spiritual manner. And we started going into the ceremonies. And then our purpose was driven, I think stronger and harder, because now we had the roots of some spiritual strength."[105]

AIM consistently portrayed itself as both a political and a cultural movement. It is for this reason that Russell Means characterizes himself as "a cultural nationalist."[106] Medicine man Charles Kills Enemy (Lakota) characterized the AIM warriors as the "shock troops for sovereignty," implying that tribal/political sovereignty also involved cultural sovereignty.[107] A widely distributed mimeographed text titled "What is the American Indian Movement" provides insight into the various elements defining Indigenous martial and cultural manliness within the self-proclaimed warrior society:

> They [the AIM warriors] are the catalyst for Indian Sovereignty. . . . AIM is first, a spiritual movement, a rebirth of our people, and then a rebirth of dignity and pride in a people. . . . The American Indian Movement is attempting to connect the realities of the past with the promise of tomorrow. . . . They know that the Indian way is not tolerated in White America, because it is not acknowledged as a decent way to be. Sovereignty, Land, and Culture cannot endure if a people is not left in peace. The American Indian Movement is then, the Warrior Class of this century, who are bound to the bond of the Drum, who vote with their bodies instead of their mouths. THEIR BUSINESS IS HOPE.[108]

According to the above statement, Indigenous activists linked their warrior masculinities to intertwined notions of nationalism, culture, and history. In so doing, they relied heavily on memory work and adaptation to contemporary realities. The linkage of masculinized nation-building efforts and cultural traditions amounted to a political, cultural, and spiritual re-empowerment (often through the overindulgence in cultural practices, ceremonies, and rituals) in what constituted an overall effort to reinvent their gendered subjectivities.[109]

Carter Camp explained the underlying causes attributed to the nation-building attempt and cultural renewal at Wounded Knee as follows:

> In Wounded Knee a Traditional Society of the Nations [*sic*] was born and lived. Guided by those ones who had been taught and kept the old ways of our people, and most especially the powerful ways of the Lakota Nation, we put ourselves in defiance of those who would crush our people. We decided to fight for survival and that fight is still joined to this day. In the minds of the world we were a "vanishing race[,]" an entire race of people consigned to the annals of history. But at Wounded Knee we stood to tell the world they were wrong and we intended to survive as a people for another five hundred years. We chose to make our stand at Wounded Knee where *wasicu* [white] historians had said our red world had ended in 1890.[110]

According to Camp, it was the intergenerational alliance between reservation traditionalists and urban activists that instigated a cultural transformation and escalated the political struggle against the settler-colonial nation. Camp also alluded to mutually reinforcing dynamics of cultural renewal and political activism that brought about both a fundamental redefining of Indigeneity and self-determination. Quite skillfully, Camp put the Wounded Knee takeover in line with a long tradition of Indigenous resistance to settler-colonial encroachment.

From the outset, the warriors for a nation combined their resistance to US colonialism with a reinvention of cultural and religious practices. The rising Indigenous militancy against US colonial domination thus went hand in hand with a growing interest in their cultural practices and traditions. As Indigenous men and women within the American Indian Movement reinvented their subjectivities, they moved away from civil rights and integration toward separatism and nationalism. This shift was in large part paralleled by the reformulation of their gendered subjectivities.[111]

Across Indian Country, the takeover of Wounded Knee was an expression of cultural pride and dignity.[112] According to Oscar Bear Runner (Lakota), a WWII veteran and Lakota code talker who served in Europe:

> People sacrificed their jobs and families and personal livelihoods to make a concerted change ... so that our ... kids ... will understand and be proud of who we are, be able to say I'm Lakota, or be able to say I'm culturally distinct ad culturally different, and I have a right to be as such. These are the things that we were shooting for.[113]

Wounded Knee showed that a subaltern people could speak truth to power and confront past and present injustices. As Vietnam veteran Bill Means (Lakota) put it, "the idea that grassroots people could stand up against the most powerful military force in the world—and do it with dignity and pride—that still stands out because of all the things that came out of Wounded Knee. I think the revival of our culture, identity, of our pride was probably the most interesting thing."[114]

Webster Poor Bear (Lakota), himself a veteran of the Vietnam War and the occupation, treasured his venture into protest and identity politics: "I would do it again. I would get shot at again, die, if necessary. When you live like that, it's an honorable way to live. [I'm] very proud of the people who have stayed with us at Wounded Knee and [I'm] very honored and privileged to have stood with them."[115]

Participation in the cultural nationalist movement constituted a larger effort of Indigenous men to regenerate positive masculinities through decolonization efforts.[116] Lenny Foster (Navajo) joined Denver AIM as a student, hitchhiked to Alcatraz Island, and participated in the Cass Lake demonstration, the Raymond Yellow Thunder protests, the Trail of Broken Treaties caravan and subsequent takeover of the BIA building, and the occupation at Wounded Knee. To him, Wounded Knee stood out, because it significantly altered his Indigenous male subjectivity. As he put it: "Wounded Knee was such a beautiful experience for me because it matured me as an Indian person, developed my spirituality, because I had opportunities to use a sweat lodge every morning and use the prayers and learned about the pipe and the songs and what the Oglalas have with the sweat lodge ceremonies. I learned a lot about all of that."[117] To him, the standoff was both liberating and empowering in that it made him more aware of his Indigeneity: "It's liberation, liberation of our soul, our spirit to be proud and dignified. I think it's very empowering, if you feel good for yourself."[118]

Gary Rowland (Lakota) witnessed the occupation as a child. He considered Wounded Knee a watershed moment due to the revival of Lakota culture: "After Wounded Knee, there was a resurgence of our spirituality. Sun Dances spread out in different communities. And today churches are empty and the majority of our people are back into the traditional way of worship like Sun Dance and *inipi* (sweat lodge). And so in that sense spirituality woke us up and we're strong again."[119]

Above all, the Red Power movement and AIM were fueled by a moral righteousness and driven by the commitment of young people to stand up for what they believed in. More than anything, the struggle against colonial domination was powered by a high idealism to make a change in the world and to better the lives of Indigenous people. In that sense, many Indigenous nationalists regarded themselves as warriors for *their* people, *their* homeland, and *their* rights. According to Lenny Foster,

> we were fighting for our treaty rights. We were fighting for our religious rights. We were fighting for our human rights. . . . Indian people were being beaten all the time. It was up to the young people . . . to stop those attacks on their people. . . . We were willing to stand up to the injustices. . . . [Wounded Knee] was a beautiful experience. . . . I was 24 years old. We were young. We are idealistic, adventurous, willing to take on federal Marshals, the FBI. We believed in the power of our medicine.[120]

In reflecting on the legacy of AIM, veteran-turned-activist Wes Studi (Cherokee) pointed to a number of interrelated issues: the righteousness of the entire Indigenous Rights Struggle, a changed Indigenous–federal relationship with a curtailed power of the BIA, as well as a reawakening of Indigenous pride:

> What do you remember most about taking part is that kind of energy. . . . You feel like you are doing something that is bigger than yourself. And you're a part of something that is bigger than yourself. And you have a just cause. It's a good thing to feel like you are doing the right thing, that you're on the right side of history and that what you're saying is true.
>
> Many people sacrificed time, life throughout that struggle and . . . many people went to jail over incidents. And there were many incidents other than just the takeover in [Washington] D.C., you know: There was Scottsbluff. There was Custer. And then out down in Oklahoma actually there were takeovers of small towns.
>
> And like I say it was a heavy situation, but you also have to think ahead.

When you begin to attack an institution. . . . What actually happened then was American Indians began to attack the institution that had been used to oppress them for centuries.[121]

Just like their male counterparts, Indigenous women considered anti-colonial resistance as not only a political battle for Indigenous rights but also a cultural struggle for maintaining their Indigeneity. Dorothy Ninham (Oneida), one of the warrior women at the siege of Wounded Knee, remembered that she "felt really good," because "we weren't ashamed to say we're Native anymore." Traveling from Wisconsin to South Dakota during February/March in the back of a pickup truck in order to help in the defense and bring in supplies, she reflected that "this is the first time we really felt pride. Our people are back there and they're fighting. . . . It affected people all over the country."[122] Indigenous women continually stressed the intergenerational significance of the survival of their culture, language, and heritage for their children, families, and tribal communities.

In an interview on her activist years with AIM, Phyllis Young (Lakota) described Indigenous women as follows: "We are patriots to our own people. . . . I am a Lakota patriot first. . . . I am a spoiled American [second]. I drink coca cola and I like the elevators and other things."[123] Her personal view on Indigenous women's cultural/political identity closely parallels that of Indigenous men. However, for Indigenous women, identity politics seemed to have different implications, as women frequently tied anti-colonial resistance to grassroots activism in their families and communities, whereas men had a tendency to get more involved in political protests. Perhaps the greatest accomplishment of Lakota women was the preservation of a land base, a distinct culture, their spirituality, and their language. Indigenous women's participation in the struggle was fueled by a desire to preserve their culture for their children and future generations.[124] As Young put it, "We had to create lives that were acceptable for our children. We fought so we could have choices. We didn't have those choices. . . . Our choice was taking back our culture and keeping it for ourselves, keeping it for our children. Because they need an identity. They need a language. They need a culture to survive."[125]

Regina Brave (Lakota) voiced a similar view. She considered militancy necessary for drawing attention to Indigenous issues. As she recalled: "We were standing up. We were militant. We were radial. . . . We knew that the only language this country would understand was violence because that's the only language they knew." Female nationalists like her struggled for the recognition of Indigenous rights, not personal validation. As she put it, "none of us ever were looking for recognition. We weren't looking for fame. We were just a part of a group of people that were standing up for our rights." At the same time, they were also trying to make a good future for their children, grandchildren, and later generations: "And that's what we're fighting for. All our lives we've fought for survival. Not only survival of who we are, but survival of our language, our culture and our very heritage." What made women become warriors in the anti-colonial struggle was their willingness to stand by their men and children. "Hey, we are part of this, too. We could not have survived for over 500 years if the men and women did not stand together," as Brave put it.[126]

After the occupation at Wounded Knee, Indigenous women sustained the anti-colonial struggle through legal efforts, the establishment of alternative schools, the growth of the international Indigenous movement, the fight against illegal sterilization and natural resource pollution by corporate interests, and the preparation of healthy food in Indigenous communities, playing an integral part in the ongoing struggle for Indigenous identity, rights, and lands.[127]

### "Don't Forget the Warriors": Remembering and Commemorating Warriors and Nationalist Struggle

In summer 2013, Clyde Bellecourt and Dennis Banks gave speeches in the All My Relations arts gallery on E. Franklin Ave., Minneapolis, to showcase the photo exhibition *I'm Not Your Indian Anymore* by Dick Bancroft. The photography exhibition—suitably named after Floyd Westerman's famous lyrics of the song "B.I.A."—featured photos from more than four decades of AIM's endeavor into protest and identity politics. The photo collection chronicled numerous demonstrations, protests, and conferences and contained displays with memorabilia such as buttons, patches, bumper stickers, posters, paintings, and art. Since 1971, Dick

Bancroft and his camera had followed AIM. The book *We Are Still Here: A Photographic History of the American Indian Movement*, published in early 2013 with photos by Bancroft and informative texts by Laura Waterman Wittstock (Seneca), was an impressive record of the group's struggle for change.

The visual display of AIM's history indicated that the organization was concerned with its legacy and how its struggle was commemorated and remembered. Additionally, Bellecourt was eager to set up the "AIM Interpretative Center" on Franklin Avenue to collect, preserve, and exhibit a growing collection of photos, documents and movement memorabilia of AIM's history. Since 2011, this formerly downtrodden district of Minneapolis's "red ghetto" had transformed into a "cultural corridor" lined with Indigenous-owned businesses, agencies, shops, and offices. Rather than a museum, Bellecourt envisioned a "live" interpretative center "to tell the truth about our people who resided here for thousands of years."[128] Within this larger project, the commemoration and remembrance of AIM was to occupy no small part—or so the plan went—as Bancroft's photos were meant to be transferred into a permanent exhibition.[129] Bellecourt was probably also concerned with ensuring that his own legacy lived on, as other AIM leaders and members had already published their as-told-to autobiographies (Russell Means, 1995; Leonard Crow Dog, 1995; Dennis Banks, 2004). Bellecourt followed with his autobiography in 2016.

Indigenous struggles for self-determination, sovereignty, nationhood/statehood, and decolonization—such as AIM's struggle—involve a critical remembering and commemorating of the past.[130] Decolonization projects frequently include a reimagining of Native America in which dominant narratives are denaturalized and marginalized memories are regenerated in order to re-create the past and present.[131] Similarly, decolonization processes involve a gendered transformation of Indigenous people.[132] According to literary scholar Astrid Erll, cultural memory involves three dimensions: material, mental, and social. The material dimension involves mnemonic artifacts, symbols, and landscapes; the social dimension includes mnemonic practices such as ceremonies, rituals, and epistemologies, as well as carriers of memory; and, finally, the mental dimension involves a community's shared schemata, concepts, and codes (such as cultural values, norms, and beliefs).¹³³ Yet each act of remembering or commemorating is also linked to a process of forgetting.¹³⁴ Indeed, forgetting is constitutive of the formation of a new identity; this mnemonic practice becomes particularly relevant in Red Power cultural nationalism when Indigenous people discard unwanted identities and adopt new ones.¹³⁵

The written and oral histories of AIM's leaders all remember the Indigenous Rights Struggle as a culturally and politically empowering experience. However, they are bitterly divided over their own manly roles within the Indigenous nationalist movement and their individual legacy. They were irreconcilably split over what it meant to be a modern-day warrior and what warrior virtues consisted of, in what was yet another expression of the internal contradiction, deep division, and profound factionalism of AIM. Carter Camp wrote a number of short articles on his experiences, insights, and perceptions of the Independent Oglala Nation and the AIM warrior society. These reflections are the most thorough on the subject matter, perhaps due to Camp's status as a veteran/warrior and his self-identification with warriorhood. His articles are also the most critical, owing to his disenchantment and split with AIM's leaders.¹³⁶

Carter Camp offered his own reflections on the significance of Wounded Knee and intertwined notions of warrior and nation in his article "War Stories and Wounded Knee 1973," published in *News from Indian Country*, the largest newspaper by and for Indigenous people in America. The publication coincided with the thirtieth anniversary of the declaration of the ION.¹³⁷ The 1890 and 1973 Wounded Knee incidents were connected, Camp stated:

> It has been generations since our warriors rose to fight an enemy while standing on the dust of our ancestors. That last happened at Wounded Knee, in 1890. . . . In 1973 another battle happened . . . along the Wounded Knee Creek. Once again warriors were forced to rise up in defense of their people and stand on hallowed ground and fight. Once again warrior's blood was sacrificed and lives were freely given to revive the heartbeat of a Nation, brave deeds and selfless actions became the measure of a society called the "Independent Oglala Nation."¹³⁸

Having established the link between the Wounded Knee incidents, he turned his attention to the form and expression of warriorhood in Indian Country. Camp distinguished between three different generations of Indigenous warriors. The first generation of warriors were those who lived on the Great Plains. They defined their manliness by demonstrating martial virtues of honor, truth, courage, fortitude, strength, and selflessness—tribal virtues that defined the concept of honorable intertribal warfare. According to Camp, "the warrior [was carefully] chosen to stand up in front of all the Nation and recite the actions he had taken on behalf of his people," a public act that validated his deeds and gave him social prestige. The second generation of warriors were veterans who served in wars fought in foreign lands. Carrying on an older tradition, not in buckskin but in uniform, they also told war stories. The third generation of warriors emerged in 1973 at Wounded Knee, when "once again warriors were forced to rise up in defense of their people and stand on hallowed ground and fight."[139] However, despite their heroic struggle, "honorable and truthful warriors have put away their brave heart stories and the songs of their deeds are silent," because "the leaders of the battle ran away and left their community while under attack."[140] Camp attributed the end of the occupation to AIM's leaders' desertion of their own warriors, a thing unheard of in earlier times.[141] According to him, "they lacked the virtues of a warrior, their honor was locked in the *wasicu* [white] cities and jails they came from and they could not rise above it."[142] He considered the other leaders corrupted by their exposure to the assimilationist influences of white America and their own personal flaws.

Camp's article points to the deep internal divisions with AIM over the meaning of warriorhood and the manly virtues that go with it. This is perhaps best encapsulated by Camp's outright hostile assessment of fellow AIM leaders and his deep disillusionment and severe resentment of their allegedly unmanly behavior. The article went on to criticize Russell Means for his self-indulgence in celebrity status; Clyde Bellecourt for his unmanly behavior (he would not carry a gun and sat in a warm trailer for most of the Wounded Knee siege) and being media-savvy (as he had a cameraman in tow); and Vernon Bellecourt for his cowardice in never even paying a visit to Wounded Knee—in short, framing them as betrayers of the cause out of petty self-interest.[143]

Camp took serious offense at the fact that at the thirtieth anniversary celebration of the Wounded Knee takeover, "the chickens of the knee" were honored.[144] As he explained, "we never imagined that even our traditional 'war stories' would be stolen and dishonored by old, greed-driven AIM leaders, we never thought they would do the unimaginable and claim a warrior's honors when they earned none."[145] The real tragedy lay in the fact that "men without honor" accepted "false honors," which in fact belonged to the warriors of the ION who had been silent for the past three decades.[146] These leaders had further dishonored the memory of AIM by turning it into a mere "fundraising tool" for serving their own needs.[147]

The charges were not unsubstantiated. Russell Means and Clyde Bellecourt left the siege mid-way for publicity tours to raise funds and awareness;[148] other leaders such as Dennis Banks slipped through the defenses prior to the armistice.[149] During the last four days of the siege, a handful of veterans spent their time deceiving the surrounding government forces in order to buy more time for those on the run. Carter Camp and his contingent of warriors from Oklahoma had spearheaded the occupation and held out to the very end; in light of this fact, Camp's disillusionment with fellow AIM leaders is understandable. The only veterans who ultimately surrendered were the ones from Oklahoma.[150] The deep antagonism between competing factions of AIM and the sense of betrayal was perhaps best illustrated by Camp's shooting and severe wounding of Bellecourt shortly after the siege.[151]

Camp gave particular homage to those warriors who were "doing the work of the nation, fighting the battles, supplying the needs to the people and protecting our elders and children."[152] To him, the ION was built on Lakota virtues of honor, courage, and fortitude.[153] Inside the Wounded Knee hamlet, the article went on, "cooks were shot by the *wasicu* [whites] as were veterans in the bunkers, medics were sniped while bandaging wounded and even our mailman was attacked while delivering mail."[154] What made the takeover at Wounded Knee unique was this particular experience: "Wounded Knee was a community of warriors empowered by war stories held in the land since 1890, warriors of many Nations [sic] united by the selfless actions of their comrades-in-arms fighting by their side."[155] These genuine warriors made great sacrifices "to revive the heartbeat of the nation," and, like generations before them, were honored with eagle feathers to commemorate their courage and fortitude. The leaders of this generation of warriors were Vietnam veterans such as Stan Holder, Craig Camp, Russ Redner, Buddy Lamont, Luke Tenfingers, Ken Tiger, and other "warriors between sixteen and sixty years old" who "formed an encircling wall of protection around our lands and dared any invader to enter."[156]

In a 2004 obituary, Carter Camp credited medicine man Wallace Black Elk (Lakota) with providing spiritual guidance for the particular needs of the ION warrior society at Wounded Knee.[157] Wallace Black Elk was a traditional Lakota and descendent of the legendary Nicolas Black Elk, well-known for his cultural and spiritual insights through *Black Elk Speaks* (1932). Lakota elders and traditionalists such as Wallace Black Elk, Frank Fools Crow, Charlie Red Cloud, Leonard Crow Dog, Pete Catches, Matthew King, along with Phillip Deere (Muskogee Creek), and Horace Dauki (Kiowa) from Oklahoma were credited with immersing the warriors for a nation into cultural and warrior practices.[158] The article went on to pay respect to Wallace Black Elk and the other spiritual leaders who had kept the traditional ways alive, supported the male and female warriors, and lent "their sacred strength and blessing to the warrior society in their fight for the People." The article described the AIM warrior society as a ragtag army led by veterans and composed of men and women from a cross-section of lives. What made these warriors for a nation special was their dedication to the cause, willingness to put their lives on the line, and desire to emulate the cultural ways and ideals of their warrior ancestors and seek out spiritual guidance from medicine men: "We could fight and we were willing to die without exception, but to be a warrior society in the old way we needed to be more than that, we needed the guidance of a wise man to differentiate us from the hired *wasicu* [white] killers [soldiers]. So, we turned to Wallace Black Elk to be that guiding teacher."[159]

According to Camp, the warriors of the ION managed to culturally immerse themselves and emulate the ways of their ancestors: "It was a rule among us for each patrol or squad to be cleansed in a[n] *inipi* [sweat lodge] and for each to pray for bravery and success in the old way. Uncle Wallace was called on to do this scared thing for us, to make us worthy to fight and perhaps to die for our little nation."[160]

Both Camp (Ponca) and Stan Holder (Wichita) shared similar views in *Akwesasne Notes* of their activist days in the armed struggle against colonial oppression. Camp stated he "found freedom" in the various confrontations at the BIA headquarters, Scottsbluff, Custer, and Wounded Knee. In linking the Indigenous anti-colonial struggle with decolonization struggles across the world, he found a deeper meaning for himself and coming generations. "I found I was a warrior," Camp went on. "I can feel the freedom of my Grandfathers coming back, and I know my Grandchildren will live without the yoke we are fighting to throw off."[161] Holder saw himself as part of a long line of warriors who had defended Native America since the arrival of white settler colonialists in 1492. Like others, he saw a deep meaning in reconnecting to his Indigeneity, reclaiming his warrior identity, and resisting the oppressive forces of US settler colonialism. He also noted the fact that many of the warriors who fought in the struggle for self-determination, sovereignty, and nation were behind bars, leaving Indigenous women and children without defense against colonial oppression.[162]

### Indigenous Vietnam Veterans' Perspectives on AIM, Warriorhood, and Nationalism

Indigenous Vietnam veterans hold a wide spectrum of views on male AIM members and their exaggerated claims to warriorhood and nation. These views encompass the entire spectrum, from full recognition as modern-day warriors to outright contempt as "wannabe warriors." Veterans' perspectives touch upon personalities, protest tactics, and symbolism along with interwoven understandings of Indigenous manliness/warriorhood and nationalism/patriotism, respectively. Interestingly, all veterans' perspectives place the reciprocal relationship between warrior and tribal community at the center of their considerations. Yet they arrive at disparate conclusions about AIM's notion of warriorhood and warrior society. All veteran statements indicate that they operate with a cultural understanding of warriorhood. While some Vietnam veterans looked upon AIM men as warriors in the traditional sense of the word, only a few considered them genuine warriors, predominantly because they lacked military training and combat experience—cultural elements closely associated with martial manliness and warriorhood.[163]

Those Vietnam veterans who consider AIM activists' claims to warriorhood valid do so from a culturally based perspective. For example, Nick Leading Fighter (Lakota), a Marine combat veteran who saw action during the Tet Offensive, considered himself a warrior in the tribal sense. As he stated: "We veterans are [fighting] for *our* country and *our* people" (emphasis mine). According to his understanding, Vietnam veterans and AIM activists alike operated in the broader context of an Indigenous struggle that was directed toward the defense of *their* people and *their* homeland, both at home and abroad. While some served in the US military to defend their tribal community and homeland against communism abroad, others joined the Indigenous nationalist movement in an attempt to maintain their own cultural identity and political sovereignty vis-à-vis colonial domination. Nick Leading Fighter's understanding of what it means to be a warrior harks back to traditional concepts of tribal community, peoplehood, and the role of warrior societies. He found that "the AIM people were against the government. . . . [They fought] for their rights, yes, they were warriors. The government did wrong to the Indian people and they were fighting against that. It's kind of defending themselves."[164] The above statement relates to a traditional understanding of the responsibility of warriors to defend their people and land against outside threats.

A similar view comes from Alfred Theodore Boneshirt Whiting (Lakota), who was a US Navy radio operator stationed in Waukegan, Illinois, during the Wounded Knee occupation. Whiting followed the takeover closely over the radio and decided to leave the military:

> I could hear the gunfire. I could hear the chatter, the Armed Forces and the racial discrimination—that they were talking bad about Lakota people. After that, I made a decision, I was just going to leave. . . . They offered me a good discharge. . . . It was in my record: I was a member of the American Indian Movement. I guess they didn't want me in there any longer, so they let me go.[165]

While Whiting did not participate in the Wounded Knee takeover itself, he struggled against racial discrimination in South Dakota, such as the withholding of voting rights and biased law enforcement. He found that many Lakotas went into the military with "a colonized point of view" and served as "mercenaries" for the US government. He also regarded AIM nationalists as warriors and credited the organization for combating racism and for bringing back ceremonies and spirituality to the Lakota people.[166]

Within AIM, Vietnam veterans were highly respected because of their proven warrior/veteran status and combat experience. AIM needed veterans, because, in the words of Vietnam veteran Fritz Wallace Eagle Shield (Lakota),

> they thought that we could handle the weapons if they needed them. . . . I think what they thought we were going to do was, yeah, we were going to bring weapons and we were going to help them that way. [To join AIM was also to show support through action:] you voted with your body. You showed up and you said: "Here I am. I'm here to support you." And: "What do you need me to do? I'm here to help out."[167]

Veterans were less afraid to actively participate in confrontational protest events. Their military and combat experience made them valuable assets in the masculinized struggle for nationhood, while also providing AIM with legitimacy for their claims to warriorhood and nation.

Another view recognizes AIM's legacy in sparking a cultural and political renaissance across Indian Country but essentially denies them any claim to warriorhood. Errol Brown Eyes (Lakota), a Vietnam veteran and AIM supporter, recalled: "I supported what they were doing over here, but I never involved it with what I was doing in the military." With his brother getting married during the Wounded Knee siege, he felt that those inside the hamlet looked "as if it was just fighting for a change of government, fighting to expose what was going on here." Although sympathetic to the cause and exposure of tribal government mismanagement and corruption, he stated, "I didn't really look at them as warriors." He did not take offense at the utilization of the upside-down flag as a sign of distress, because "it did not really bother me . . . if that was how they wanted the people to know what they were doing, it's fine, you know." As a veteran, he did not see a contradiction between his service in the white man's army and his peripheral involvement in AIM. As he expressed his

Robert Charles Onco (aka Bobby Onco), Kiowa from Oklahoma, holding up an AK-47 rifle that he took from his service tour in Vietnam and broadly smiling. The photograph was taken after a ceasefire agreement between AIM forces and federal marshals at Wounded Knee on March 9, 1973. With the caption "We Remember Wounded Knee," the photo became an iconic poster. (Richard Erdoes Papers, Yale Collection of Western Americana, Beinecke Rare Book and Manuscript Library)

own (hybrid or complicit) patriotism: "I did not go there [Vietnam] to fight for the American flag. I did not fight for the United States."[168]

Journalist Laura Waterman Wittstock (Seneca) knew many Indigenous veterans from Minnesota and South Dakota who joined AIM upon their return from Vietnam. Wittstock's observations corroborate views that many Indigenous veterans regarded neither AIM's leaders nor its rank-and-file members as warriors. As she recalled,

> Many of them had an attitude that Russell Means and Dennis Banks were disingenuous, because . . . —unless you've been in the war, you don't know what it's like. If you don't know what it's like, you're not going to be able to relate to . . . what's happening to your people. That seemed to be a general view.[169]

She also had the impression that many Indigenous Vietnam veterans did not consider Russell Means and Dennis Banks as leaders and thought they were "phony." These veterans joined the occupation of Wounded Knee regardless: "You had veterans coming from everywhere to support Wounded Knee for that very reason that you went to war and you showed your bravery. And then you go to Wounded Knee and you do the same thing. You're willing to die."[170] These veterans were different from AIM nationalists because "they knew how to be warriors in the sense of those who conduct war. In the old sense of warrior, it is an anointing. You don't just pop—you are a warrior."[171]

The overwhelming majority of veterans thus did not look upon men in AIM as warriors. Richard Kirkie's view (Crow Creek Sioux) may be representative of many veterans' views. Kirkie served five and a half years in the US Army, with tours in Korea, Germany, and Vietnam. During his tour in Vietnam—in an APC unit escorting convoys—he saw heavy combat, was wounded several times, and received a number of medals. Upon his return home, he spent three years in hospital, then used the GI Bill to go to college and subsequently worked as a prison and youth counselor in South Dakota. An honored member of the respected Red Feather Society, he found,

> They're not warriors. . . . I look at them as troublemakers. You know, their goal might be the right goal, but they go about it the wrong way. And what is a warrior? A warrior is the one that goes to war and fights for his country, his community, his reservation, his people. And come back, you know, wounded and all and then makes something of himself here. Get an education, working with the young youth, setting a good example and that, you know? Sure, we can't change all these things and that. But we do it in a way we don't hurt other people or yourself. Whereas Russell and Dennis Banks and those guys, they want to be the warrior by hurting people, you know? The Wounded Knee thing: Well, being destructive, what did it do for them? How did it help them? Did it serve their goals?[172]

Kirkie's statement captures a common criticism. Indeed, many Pine Ridge reservation residents found that AIM could highlight a problem in front of media cameras but did not empower local people to build lasting community structures.

Many veterans took offense at the organization's confrontational tactics, media-related performance of warriorhood, and outright anti-patriotism. To many, the aggressive posturing as warriors in front of the news media did not sit well, nor did the provocative nationalist symbolism. George Lamont (Lakota) took offense at the latest generation of AIM warriors engaging in protest at Whiteclay, Nebraska. Clad in military fatigues and flying the American flag upside-down, he noted,

> They're dishonoring the uniform I wore. I wore it and I fought with it in Vietnam. The same fatigues I wore, you know. The woodland fatigues. . . . And that's to me . . . I don't even look at them like they're warriors. To me, they're just trying to make a name for themselves. And they're doing it the wrong way. And then that [upside-down American] flag. . . . To me that's dishonoring me, as a warrior, because I fought in a war, you see.[173]

George Lamont not only regarded the wearing of woodland fatigues as a mark of respect that nonveterans did not deserve, he also considered the inverted use of the US flag as unpatriotic. Part of this reasoning reached back to the 1876 Battle of the Little Bighorn when Lakota, Cheyenne, and Arapahoe warriors captured the regimental flag of Custer's outfit.

> That American flag, well back in Custer's Last Stand, you see we captured that. The warriors captured that flag. It still doesn't belong to United States, it belongs to the Native Americans. You see? And that's still our flag, no matter what. That's why you should treat it with respect, you know? For all the warriors that fought out there at Custer's Last Stand, you know? Don't fly it upside down, fly it proudly and cherish it because a lot of warriors gave their life up there, you know? Just to kick ass.[174]

Custer's captured flag, a symbol of the Lakota's greatest victory over the US military, had come to symbolize Indigenous resistance against US colonialism as a whole. Custer's regimental flag is occasionally displayed at powwows, thus epitomizing the complexities, contradictions, and ambiguities of Indigenous patriotism and nationalism. This contradiction between divided loyalties becomes evident in the annual celebration of the Little Bighorn at the Indian Memorial—on the slopes of Custer's Last Stand Hill—where Indigenous veterans engage in a patriotic display of service uniforms and flags, celebrating both the victory over US troops in defense of their nationhood as well as their allegiance to the very same nation their warrior ancestors fought in 1876.[175] Among multiple meanings, the captured object is a symbol of both past resistance against settler encroachment as well as Indigenous people's allegiance to the American nation in the present. George Lamont expressed this sentiment as follows:

> Well we fought for the country, let's put it that way. This is our land, right? So in other words, the white people always say, "It's our land, you know? It's the United States." Actually, it's ours, you know? It's not theirs. And so this way we go to war. So the war won't be over here, you see? And what if any one of these days it might be here, you know?[176]

Others like Tyrone Apple (Lakota), a Vietnam combat veteran from Pine Ridge, returned from abroad with a severe sense of betrayal and alienation. Initially, he recalled:

> I wanted to join those [AIM] guys. . . . And when I came back [from Vietnam] my father was on the tribal council and AIM came and divided the whole nation. . . . The AIM guys thought they were the bosses. . . . They never belonged to nothing. They were all prison members, they were gang members from prison. . . . They never went to Army or anything. They were all in prison. And that's where they learned how to push people around.

Following a series of confrontations with activists, Apple decided that AIM was not for him: "When I see them doing that, and I didn't want to be none of them."[177] Instead of joining AIM, he became part of Wilson's GOON squad.

Despite these widely disparate views on what AIM did and what it stood for, veterans respected certain individuals in the activist organization. Terry Quilt (Lakota), a Marine Vietnam veteran, said:

> I was living here [Crow Creek] at that time. And I wasn't too hip on that AIM at the time. Because, you know, I said they were kind of going against

what I believed in and what I fought for and all that. So they were fighting for their, for the land and all that. So, you know, fighting for the Indian rights and all that. And so I had a few of the AIM buddies I served with over in Vietnam and all that. And they come back, you know, and they joined AIM.[178]

Gary Rowland (Lakota), a local Wounded Knee resident who witnessed the occupation as a child and later became a paratrooper wholeheartedly supported AIM. During the Wounded Knee occupation, he made a vow to never honor the US flag: "My forefathers Crazy Horse, Sitting Bull, Chief Big Foot—they were the enemies of the United States flag. And so I consider the flag today as my enemy. And I denounced my citizenship with the United States government also." In large part, this discontent comes from the dishonoring of the treaties by the US government. Roland went further in that he considers Indigenous veterans sellouts. As he put it: "They betrayed our people. And this United States government colonized our people. So like today on this reservation, you know. People are brainwashed and they have false pride, you know."[179] Roland took offense that Indigenous veterans believed they had fought for their freedom when in fact Indigenous people on reservations are treated as third-class citizens.

In explaining why he had joined the military in the first place and became an enemy of the very government he had served with, he elaborated,

> When you join the military, you take an oath of office to protect the United States constitution against all enemies foreign or domestic. And I was too young to know better. . . . I was a professional soldier. . . . But during Wounded Knee, the government had machine guns, M16s, M50 caliber machine guns. And two jet came down real close on each side of the steep of the church there. And they could have bombed us. . . . They could have knocked us out in just a few seconds. So from then on I made a vow to myself that I'll never honor this United States flag.[180]

Rowland holds strong views of his fellow veterans. During the Wounded Knee takeover, Rowland, highly familiar with the terrain, backpacked to Porcupine, South Dakota, to bring in supplies. To the present day, he recalls a situation when he saw a number of Indigenous veterans with gear and guns near the local American Legion in Gordon, Nebraska, who supported the Wilson regime.

> If it comes down to the nitty and the gritty, all these Native American veterans will protect the United States flag and the government. . . . They paid their allegiance to the United States flag. And they'll kill their own people like at Wounded Knee, 1890. . . . They've become traitors. I consider them traitors of our people. Sell-outs.[181]

For Rowland, there was no real distinction between nationalists' and veterans' claims to warriorhood: "As long as we have our spirituality, you know, those [AIM] people are the real warriors of today. And AIM is the only organization that is willing to defend our people and in time of trouble anywhere. And AIM is known as an international Indian warrior society. And I fully believe in their cause and the founding principle of AIM. . . . And that's why I joined AIM."[182] As he put it, "I was so proud to be with the American Indian Movement fighting for treaty rights and the corrupt tribal chairman at that time."[183]

The veteran considers the American Indian Movement part of an ongoing resistance to US colonization: "Well, I consider Crazy Horse as part of the American Indian Movement. It's an ongoing movement. and up to this day and in the future, you know, that warrior society will never cease to exist. You know, we're a natural warrior's defense to our people: men, women, children. So that's the original real warrior society."[184]

He further added that his children have grown into AIM and that "they're the AIM warriors of today [in the fight against alcoholism]. So I am proud of my family, my kids. They're actively engaged in our struggle and defense of our people. And they're the real warriors."[185] To the present day, Rowland considers himself a member of the Independent Oglala Nation and has remained active: protesting the Custer Memorial in 1976 (the centennial of the Battle of the Little Bighorn); participating in the Chief Big Foot Memorial Ride in 1986—a pilgrimage on horseback from Standing Rock to Wounded Knee, retracing the historic journey in 1890 of the Lakota chief and his followers that ended in the Wounded Knee massacre; and establishing the local Wounded Knee Museum.[186]

## The American Indian Movement's Legacy Across Indian Country

Native Americans commonly place the Wounded Knee takeover within the larger context of Indigenous resistance to US settler colonialism as well as the legacy of Indigenous religious and cultural revitalization movements, thus establishing a viable link between the two incidents at Wounded Knee, in 1890 and 1973. Frequently, rhetorical discourse touches upon larger issues of cultural survival as an Indigenous people. For example, Carter Camp (Ponca) considered the Wounded Knee occupation a defining event for himself and Indian Country as a whole:

> Because the struggle is one of survival, there are also times when a warrior must stand even at the risk of one's life. I believed that when I was 30 and I believe it today at 70. But to me Wounded Knee '73 was really not about the fight, it was about the strong statement that our traditional way of living in this world is not about to disappear and our people are not a vanishing race. . . . I know our fight was worth it and those we lost for our movement died worthy deaths.[187]

Clyde Bellecourt (Ojibwa) echoes a similar sentiment, although he actually never wielded a gun at Wounded Knee, fearing parole violation.[188] In his autobiography he claimed: "Although we were prepared to give our lives for our people, AIM wasn't just a bunch of militants walking around with rifles. We founded AIM in order to upgrade the conditions of Indian people, their health, education, and welfare. Opening schools and clinics, for instance, were natural extensions of the American Indian Movement's core values."[189] In his opinion, AIM was instrumental in bringing about a tremendous cultural renewal across Indian Country and empowering a downtrodden people: "The movement has created that atmosphere you know made people feel that they can stand up for themselves. They can be warriors. We kind of empowered people."[190]

Eddie Benton-Banai (Ojibwe) concurred, attributing much of the cultural renewal in Indian Country to AIM: "I think in time with young people and warriors—going to ceremony, being involved in ceremony—slowly the spirit came to take its place in people's minds and in their hearts.[191]

The autobiographical accounts of Russell Means, Bellecourt, and Dennis Banks are conspicuously silent on the meaning of warriorhood. Instead, they frequently link the takeover at Wounded Knee to larger projects of national reclamation and cultural revitalization. Bellecourt considered the Wounded Knee occupation a unifying event that was possible only through the AIM warrior society and its warriors: "AIM united the . . . people from many . . . Indigenous nations, bringing us together as warriors who were cooperating in our fight against the government that had waged a war of genocide against all of us. If the government wanted to wipe out this new generation of Indians, this generation wasn't going to take it anymore, Wounded Knee in February 1973 was the chance."[192] However, Bellecourt did not play an active part in the ION warrior society, as he admits in his as-told-to autobiography.[193]

A much bolder self-assessment comes from Russell Means who claims that "just every admirable quality that remains in today's Indian people" resulted from AIM's protest and identity politics. He stated that

> in the 1960s and 1970s we lit a fire across Indian Country. We fought for changes in school curricula to eliminate racist lies. . . . We fought for community control of police. . . . We fought to instill pride in our songs and in our language, in our cultural wisdom. . . . We fought for our dignity. . . . Thanks to AIM, for the first time in this century, Indian people stand at the threshold of freedom and responsibility.[194]

Means saw AIM's achievements as belonging primarily to the fight against police brutality and racist stereotypes and in instigating a cultural renewal across Indian Country. AIM's fight against was not just against colonial oppression and Indigenous rights; it was also about pride and dignity.

Banks recounted Wounded Knee as "the greatest event in Native America in the twentieth century" and "our shining hour."[195] In an interview more than four decades after the Wounded Knee takeover, he recalled a particular moment that filled him with pride in being Native:

the moment when news reached the besieged that Sacheen Littlefeather, a twenty-six-year-old-activist and aspiring actress who introduced herself as Apache, refused the Academy Award on behalf of Marlon Brando because of the negative portrayal of Native Americans in Hollywood.[196] Dennis Banks recalled:

> I remember seeing [the Academy Award ceremony] on television here when Wounded Knee was taking place and when they're shooting at us at that evening in March. And they said: the winner is Marlon Brando. And Brando wasn't there to go up and accept it. There was this Indian girl Sacheen Littlefeather who walked up there and said that Marlon Brando declines to accept because of the terrible treatment that Native people are getting. And she says more particularly the ones at Wounded Knee at this very hour.
>
> And oh man all the guys out there, the young warriors went running outside and they're shooting up in the air. . . . There was pride. Pride was floating amongst us. It was drifting amongst us. We were bathing in pride. We were showering with pride.[197]

AIM's spectacular protest politics and performance of warriorhood bestowed celebrity status on leading movement figures while submerging the accomplishments of rank-and-file members. The siege at Wounded Knee made Means and Banks the most famous Native Americans of the twentieth century.[198]

Militant actions and rhetoric along with the media's fascination with Third World warriors and Vietnam anti-war radicals cast AIM leaders in the limelight, but this publicity increasingly separated them from their constituencies. "We got lost in our manhood," John Trudell later reflected in an interview, "we became men who became leaders and then we started protecting our political leader image, our political leader identity, which became more important than the overall needs of the community."[199] Russell Means claimed that AIM deteriorated "in direct proportion to the amount of fame that began to surface for leadership."[200] An elderly Pine Ridge resident offered the following observation about Means: "He just never got over all that fuss, everybody treating him like a hero. It went to his head. Sometimes I think Russell's biggest problem is that he didn't get shot or at least injured at Wounded Knee."[201]

The above assessments have a similar implication, namely that the celebrity status of AIM's leadership overshadowed the larger contribution of the rank-and-file warriors for a nation. Much of the criticism leveled at AIM had to do with either militancy or the human weaknesses of individual members, often overlooking their larger contributions across Indian Country. The statement of one unidentified Indigenous woman may serve as a conclusion for the conflicting meanings of warrior masculinity and nation:

> Few acknowledge that real change began to take place only after the tremendous sacrifices of the young warriors of the American Indian Movement. The beneficiaries of the Movement [accept the gains] while the real warriors lie unrecognized in their graves or in prison cells . . . we need our warriors, and where are they? In prisons, in hiding, pursued relentlessly by the FBI. . . . How many [of us] will take the time to send a card or a letter to the warriors rotting in prisons? It is time Indian people, those who have received most from the American Indian Movement, took some time to count their blessings, to give credit where credit is due. Don't forget the warriors, we may never see their like again.[202]

AIM's venture into protest politics instigated tremendous changes of self and society across Indian Country, yet few could agree what the impact really was.[203] In their autobiographies, AIM leaders Russell Means, Dennis Banks, and Clyde Bellecourt credit their activist years with achieving far-reaching change across Indian Country: cultural and political empowerment through transformed Indigenous–settler colonial relations and an increased degree of self-determination, cultural revitalization, and cultural pride.[204] Critics stated that AIM highlighted a problem yet did not follow through by making a compelling case for its own vision of change.[205] Scholars have found it difficult to pinpoint the organization's legacy due to its anti-intellectualism, shifting demands, internal divisions, and lack of public discourse. AIM assumed credit for legislative change and a more positive media image; and the claim that the organization brought about an altered self-perception among Native Americans and an ethnic resurgence in Indian Country cannot be ignored, either.[206] A balanced analysis comes from Donald Fixico, who considers Indigenous nationalists to be twentieth-century warriors fighting on behalf of their communities: "In essence, members of the Red Power movement were the warriors of the community. In a pan-Indian militaristic manner, they sought to fight for their people like warriors of the 1800s. They were, indeed, warriors of the twentieth century. They were warriors who did not fit into mainstream America. . . . The Red Power movement offered an alternative and hope."[207]

Whether the highly masculinized anticolonial struggle has made participants in the American Indian Movement "heroes of contemporary history" or "freebooters of racism" is highly subjective, as historian Rolland Dewing states. It seems as if the long-term effects outweigh some of the movement's major flaws.[208]

### Heroizing Warriors and Anti-Colonial Struggle Through Paintings and Songs

From early on, Indian Country began to remember and commemorate AIM warriors and the Indigenous Rights Struggle through paintings and songs.[209] In December 1973, Clyde Bellecourt received a warrior painting from artist Louis Hall (Mohawk) that subsequently took a prominent place on AIM and WKLD/OC promotional brochures and leaflets. Hall was a traditionalist and activist and participated in the 1974 Mohawk occupation of Ganienkeh in upstate New York to repossess Indigenous lands. An artist and prolific author, he wrote a *Warrior's Handbook* as well as *Warrior Society Newsletters* (from 1983 to 1989).[210] Hall's painting titled "Red Man's International Warrior Society" is replete with symbolism and is indicative of AIM's legacy as a warrior society. The painting depicts two warriors: a bare-chested, muscular Mohawk warrior with folded arms and a Wounded Knee veteran with a modern M16 rifle. Both warriors look toward an Indigenous woman with a torch similar to that of the Statue of Liberty. Further elements of the painting are the upside-down American and Canadian national flags, US Congress and the Canadian House of Commons, and a Christian church. The painting makes a bold connection between past and present Indigenous struggles. It prominently features Indigenous warriors who contest the agents of settler colonialism (as evidenced in their stances and direction of view). In addition, it gives inspiration to Indigenous nation-building efforts through an eagle, the embodiment of strength, wisdom, and spirituality. The inscription below references AIM as a modern warrior society carrying out this nation-building effort. The text reads:

> American Indian Movement
> Pledged to fight White man's injustice
> to Indians, his oppression, persecution,
> discrimination and malfeasance in the
> handling of Indian Affairs. No area in
> North America is too far or too remote—
> when trouble impends for Indians,
> A.I.M. shall be there—to help the native
> people regain human rights and
> achieve restitutions and restorations
> Painting and words by Louis Hall Dec. 1973[211]

The painting illustrates the state of dependency of Native America (through the upside-down flags), colonial oppression (through the government, the church), the agents of change (warriors), the parallels between Indigenous struggles in Canada and the United States (which are directed against quasi-colonial governments and the church), and the goal of the anti-colonial struggle: political sovereignty (or freedom), personified by the iconic Indigenous woman and her symbolic flame. In an analogy to the Statue of Liberty, the Indigenous woman holds a torch in her right hand (to illustrate freedom). In her left hand, instead of the Declaration of Independence she carries a wampum belt—a Mohawk way of communicating and remembering treaties between the US government and the Mohawk nation—as a reminder of the broken treaties.[212] The painting is illustrative of the spirit of its times and was influenced by two related Indigenous armed struggles that occurred in 1973: one fought at Wounded Knee, South Dakota, and the other in Kahnawake, Quebec, where the Mohawk Warrior Society battled Canadian police.[213] The painting ultimately gained prominence among Indigenous people in Canada and America when the Mohawk Warrior Society occupied Ganienkeh in upstate New York in 1975.[214]

Hall wrote extensively on the meaning of warriorhood and warrior

Painting by Louis Hall (Mohawk) from 1973 that he gifted to Clyde Bellecourt (Ojibwa). The original image was on display at the "BIA—I'm Not Your Indian Anymore" exhibit at the All My Relations Arts gallery in Minneapolis in 2013. This image was also painted on the wall of the privately owned Wounded Knee Holocaust Museum at Wounded Knee, South Dakota. (Photo by Doug Kiel. Used with permission.)

societies among the Iroquois. In his writings, he connected tribally specific meanings of warrior masculinity with those of Indigenous struggles against settler-colonial encroachment, thus making an impact on Indian Country as a whole. In his "warrior manifesto," published in 1983, he claimed that:

> In the Iroquois way, every man is a warrior—lately [1983], the girls and even older women have demanded instructions in the arts of the warriors. . . . As a youth, every Iroquois male is taught the arts of war, so that he'll be ready to defend his country and his people. . . . It is the function and duty of the Mohawk Warrior Society to defend and protect the people of the Mohawk Nation.[215]

In his painting, Hall drew a connection between the seemingly disparate Indigenous struggles fought in different parts in the United States and Canada. He also drew connections between the different kinds of warriors and warrior societies: the urban, Pan-Indian AIM warrior society, on the one hand, and the largely tribal and/or land-based Mohawk warrior society, on the other.[216]

AIM activists and sympathizers followed different discursive practices in remembering the nationalist struggle at Wounded Knee. A series of twelve woodcuts by Bruce Carter, a Korean War veteran, carved in outrage over the massacre at My Lai in 1969, depicted Wounded Knee in highly gendered terms. The woodcut "We Remember Wounded Knee 1890–1973" (originally titled "American Enculturation, 1970") depicts an unarmed Indigenous woman and child surrounded by US soldiers with fixed bayonets, referencing the first incident at Wounded Knee as one of female victimization and white male domination.[217] The woodcut became one of the most popular images commemorating the Wounded Knee battles of 1890 and 1973 and was widely distributed in poster form and reprinted in various activist brochures, pamphlets, and alternative newspapers. By contrast, the most renowned poster of the takeover at Wounded Knee featured Bobby Onco (Kiowa), a Vietnam veteran, with a bandana and his AK-47 assault rifle, thus commemorating the 1973 event as a masculine struggle for a nation.[218] A series of other posters, published in *Akwesasne Notes* and elsewhere, established further connections between both Wounded Knee 1890 and Wounded Knee 1973. As literary scholar Elizabeth Rich has pointed out, AIM consciously utilized the "Remember Wounded Knee" metonymy, conflating 1890 and 1973 into a transcendent event. Accordingly, the multiple and complex layers of the Wounded Knee metonymy refer to ongoing government abuses, a repetition of events, and continuing Indigenous resistance.[219]

In their iconography and design strategies, AIM drew from the Black Panther example. The Black Panthers developed a distinct liberation aesthetics that stressed intersectional oppression and resistance. Art history scholar Louise Siddons has pointed out that "AIM unabashedly borrowed visual strategies and political support from Black Power and liberation aesthetics enhancing the intersectional value of Red Power visual politics for the Panthers." Yet AIM also created "a distinct iconography for their movement" that drew from Plains Indian regalia and historic imagery.[220]

Indigenous folk and rock music has commemorated and remembered the Wounded Knee massacre and siege, frequently recontextualizing the 1890s and 1973 events to stand for all past and contemporary injustices committed against Native Americans. With the siege of Wounded Knee underway, Redbone recorded what is arguably its most compelling song, "We Were All Wounded at Wounded Knee" (1973). At the time, the song was considered so controversial that Redbone's music label CBS/Epic Records refused to press it. When it was recorded in various European countries, American radio stations refused to play the single. The song conveyed messages of survival and resistance and called for social, political, and moral regeneration.[221] Another song, "Bury My Heart at Wounded Knee," (1992) by Buffy Sainte-Marie (exposed of falsely claiming Indigenous ancestry in 2023), carries the same name as Dee Brown's book. The song traced the Indigenous Rights Struggle from the 1970s onward against government repression, corporate interests in reservation resources, and church missionizing. The song itself highlighted ongoing systemic colonial practices and policies perpetrated against Indigenous people.[222]

## Heroizing Warriors and Anti-Colonial Struggle at Key Protest Sites

At key protest sites, Indigenous nationalists remembered their political struggle through commemorative performances and mnemonic material. In a 1981 interview, Dennis Banks reflected on the significance of remembering and commemorating the Indigenous Rights Struggle. As he noted, the events at Alcatraz and Wounded Knee each represent "a memorial to the land struggle that we have in this country. . . . It's a reminder of a struggle, whether it's a memorial for a fallen hero or a memorial to an event. It's important that we gather in a continuing effort, to provide a connecting point for our young generations."[223] Dennis Banks also recalled that prior to the emergence of AIM there were few memorial events across Indian Country, but now there were regular memorial services for deceased activists and protest events. To him, this demonstrates a heightened awareness of the ongoing struggle for Indigenous rights.[224]

For several years, Gary Rowland's privately owned museum (est. 2000) on the slopes of the Wounded Knee hill cemetery reiterated themes of colonial oppression and a history of Indigenous anti-colonial struggle. The museum's exhibits linked Lakota culture, leadership figures, and events to the 1973 occupation. The oversize portrayals of Russell Means and Leonard Crow Dog were literally put in line with those of famed historical warriors, chiefs, and medicine men such as Crazy Horse, Sitting Bull, Red Cloud, and others. The exhibition commemorated pivotal events in Lakota history such as the Wounded Knee massacre and the Little Bighorn battle. Part of the exhibition featured photos of the first incident at Wounded Knee (e.g., the massacre, the mass grave, the Wounded Knee monument) alongside those of the second incident at Wounded Knee (e.g., AIM warriors) under the inscription "The Indian Wars are not Over." In connecting the disempowering memory of the 1890 massacre with the empowering takeover of 1973, the exhibit presented a discourse of ongoing Indigenous cultural survival, political sovereignty, and resistance to settler colonialism. In putting Wounded Knee 1890 and 1973 in line with one another, the exhibit not only commemorated gendered notions of victimhood, humiliation, and wounded nationhood but also connected them to issues of moral regeneration, spiritual healing, and cultural revitalization, as well as the larger projects of national reclamation and remasculinization. An inscription commemorated the Wounded Knee takeover and the fallen warriors Buddy Lamont, Frank Clearwater, and Pedro Bissonette, who were killed during "the reign of terror." The inscribed text credited AIM as ostensibly instrumental "in a lot of the positive changes that affect us today. Indian Pride was revived and the resurgence of our Spirituality began." At the same time, the museum exhibit commemorates cultural nationalists' efforts to center Indigenous warriors within the commemorative landscape of the Little Bighorn (by featuring the plaque placed at the Custer memorial in 1988).

The museum exhibit reiterated themes of warriorhood and nationalism through a variety of iconic images and texts. Above the door, a black and white flag modeled after the POW-MIA flag symbolically portrayed an imprisoned Lakota brave (with a watchtower and barbed wire) while echoing hopes for a decolonized Lakota nation (through the inscription "We Shall Be Free"). The theme of colonial domination was underscored by the words POW (Prisoner of War) and BIA (Bureau of Indian Affairs). Themes of colonial oppression and anti-colonial struggle were further reinforced through Hall's painting, a replica of the one given to Bellecourt. An inscription denouncing the violation of the 1868 Fort Laramie Treaty by the US government was juxtaposed with the iconic image of Crazy Horse and a saying attributed to him: "A man does not sell the land he walks upon."[225] Since my last visit to Wounded Knee in 2019, the museum had ceased to exist: the building was desolate with broken windows and a shattered door and was stripped of its exhibits and displays. With only the walls and the roof of the building standing and barely withstanding the natural elements, the mnemonic site contained only some dilapidated and fading iconography of the movement's struggle.

The final resting places of warriors Buddy Lamont (in the same cemetery of the 1890 Wounded Knee massacre and at the site of the 1973 takeover) and Frank Clearwater (on the private property of Leonard Crow Dog) establish further connections between past and present Indigenous struggles. It is also for this reason that Buddy Lamont is commemorated at KILI radio station, 3.5 miles from Wounded Knee, with a special plaque.

The privately owned Holocaust Museum at Wounded Knee, summer 2013. The museum is situated in a circular shaped, silo-like building with painted walls at the slope of the Wounded Knee Massacre cemetery, which holds the remains of those Lakotas who were massacred in 1890. Since my last visit in 2019, the museum has fallen into disarray. (Photo by author)

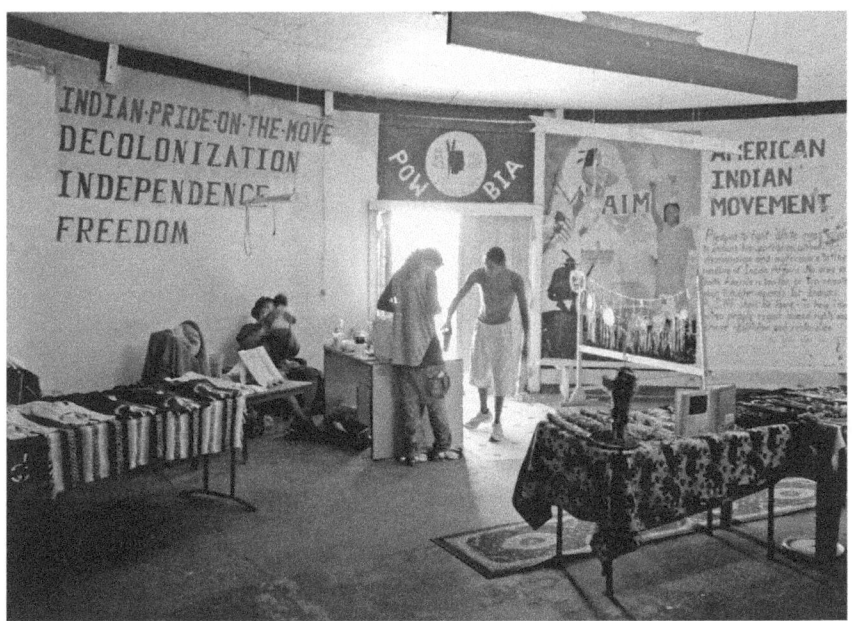

View of museum entrance from inside. (Photo by author)

Flag over museum door entrance. In the center of the image is an imprisoned warrior, a watchtower, barbed wire, and the inscription "We Shall Be Free." Acronyms underneath read POW (Prisoner of War) and BIA (Bureau of Indian Affairs). (Photo by author)

Museum wall to the left of the door entrance. The text to the left reads:
Tasunke Witko
<Crazy Horse>
Support Native Resistance
A Man Does Not Sell the Land He Walks Upon
Shall Return in the Last Days
(Photo by author)

Museum wall to the right of door entrance from viewer's perspective. To the far left is an image of Louis Hall titled "American Indian Movement" from 1973 (for closeup see page 268). The text to the right reads: "During the 1970s terror once again filled the Pine Ridge Indian Reservation. The traditional LAKOTA People were being terrorized and murdered. The Corrupt Tribal Chairman and his GOONs along with the F.B.I. carried out the reign of terror. The Chiefs and Headsmen had meetings and called A.I.M. to come and assist. On February 27, 1973 the siege began here and the War was on for seventy-one days. Two LAKOTAS were killed in action, Buddy Lamont and Frank Clearwater who gave the Ultimate Sacrifice. LAKOTA War leader Pedro Bissonette was gunned down by the B.I.A. Police six months after the Takeover. The American Indian Movement was instrumental in a lot of the positive changes that affect us today. Indian Pride was revived and the resurgence of our Spirituality Began." (Photo by author)

Museum wall opposite to door entrance. To the left, an inscription on the wall reads "The Indian Wars Are Not Over." Underneath are photos of the 1890 massacre—the battlefield, mass grave, and obelisk memorializing the Lakota dead—side-to-side with the 1973 Wounded Knee Occupation. To the center and right there are images of Leonard Crow Dog, Russell Means, Sitting Bull, and Red Cloud (*not visible in photo*), a flag of the Chief Bigfoot Memorial Ride, and photos of the 1890 and 1973 events.

In the center are two plaques. The wooden plaque (*left*) reads: "On June 25th 1988 Under the Leadership of Russel [*sic*] Means of the American Indian Movement and Garry Rowland of the Bigfoot Riders arrives at Custer Battlefield, Montana. A metal plaque was placed at the foot of Custers marker In Honor of the Warriors who defeated Custer, captured the U.S. Flag. General Custer was a mass murderer of our people. A demand was made to change the Name of the memorial. The U.S. Congress Enacted a Bill to change the Name of the memorial. The U.S. Congress Enacted a Bill in 1991 to change the name to Little Bighorn Memorial."

The steel plaque (*right*) reads: "In honor of our Indian Patriots who fought and defeated the U.S. calvary. In order to save our women and children from mass-murder. In doing so, preserving rights to our Homelands, Treaties and Sovereignty. 6/25/1988 G. Magpie, Cheyenne."

The steel plaque was installed June 25, 1988, the 112th anniversary of the Battle of the Little Bighorn on Last Stand Hill next to the granite pillar inscribed with the names of 220 of the cavalrymen buried there. The plaque was placed there by about forty Indigenous activists led by Russell Means despite objections from National Park Service rangers. (Photo by author)

Stories of cultural traditions/spirituality, Indigenous resistance to settler colonialism, and warriorhood are kept alive not only through visual art, song, and commemorative performances at key protest sites but also in feature films and documentaries. Hollywood has portrayed AIM in a series of fictional films such as *Powwow Highway* (1989), *Thunderheart* (1992), and *Lakota Woman: Siege at Wounded Knee* (1994).[226] More recently, a number of documentaries have shed light on AIM's struggle. *A Tattoo on My Heart* (2004) and *We Shall Remain: Wounded Knee* (2009) focus on the Wounded Knee siege. Other documentaries, such as *A Good Day to Die, Dennis Banks and the American Indian Movement* (2010) and *Trudell* (2005) focus on the lives of known AIM leaders. Another documentary by Kevin McKiernan, *From Wounded Knee to Standing Rock: A Reporter's Journey* (2019), critically examines the 1970s activism in Indian Country, launching its own investigation into the murder of Anna Mae Aquash. Shorter documentaries such as *Taking AIM, The Story of the American Indian Movement* (2010) and *Hanta Po, All of My Relations, An Historical Photographic Essay on the American Indian Movement, 1968–2006* (undated) depict the history of AIM.[227] *Warrior Women* (2019) concentrates on Indigenous women, focusing largely on post–Wounded Knee activism of the 1970s.[228] The commemoration and heroization of Anna Mae Aquash and Leonard Peltier—in death or, alternatively, in prison—have instigated its own corpus of film and literature.[229]

## Conclusion

In the aftermath of the Wounded Knee takeover, AIM warriors reinvented themselves once again. The abandonment of the armed struggle for nationhood went hand in hand with the transformation of nationalist and warrior subjectivities. Faced with severe government repression, AIM warriors wound up either dead or in jail or went into hiding, leading to the organization's ultimate collapse. However, AIM warriors left behind new pathways to warriorhood and notions of warrior society. The setup of the International Indian Treaty Council allowed Indigenous activists to bypass their quasi-colonial government by seeking redress through the United Nations. Public discourse labeled the AIM warriors as an "International Warrior Society," a name suggesting a martial spirit in the struggle for Indigenous lands, treaty rights, and sovereignty, yet bearing no genuine resemblance to any previous warrior societies.

After 1973, AIM's former leaders remained cultural and political nationalists, working in manifold ways on behalf of Indigenous issues. Frequently, their personalities continued to obscure the ongoing struggle of those who bore the brunt of government repression. The Wounded Knee takeover left AIM's leaders bitterly divided. The heaviest criticism came from veterans-turned-activists who sought to emulate the warrior ideals of their ancestors, most notably Carter Camp. Throughout, AIM's claims to warriorhood, warrior society, and interwoven notions of nationalism (and for that matter, patriotism) came under heavy criticism from Vietnam veterans. Many Indigenous veterans saw AIM activists as "wannabe warriors" and criticized their unpatriotic flying of the upside-down American flag. The autobiographical accounts of AIM's most notable leaders—Russell Means, Dennis Banks, and Clyde Bellecourt—show an absence of a major discourse on what it meant to be a warrior, suggesting that this critique was at least partially justified.

The warriors for a nation left behind a far-reaching legacy across Indian Country as evidenced through the Indigenous renaissance. The armed struggle at Wounded Knee, the declaration of the ION, and the AIM warriors continue to be commemorated throughout Indian Country. Frequently, this has led to processes of heroization featuring AIM leadership figures side by side with famed (Lakota) warriors, the conscious connection of Wounded Knee 1890 with Wounded Knee 1973, the heroization of warriors fallen (e.g., Frank Clearwater, Buddy Lamont, Pedro Bissonette), caged (e.g., Leonard Peltier), or otherwise deprived of their lives (e.g., Anna Mae Aquash), or the heroization of the Indigenous warrior and Indigenous nationalist struggle against US settler colonialism as a whole (as encapsulated in the paintings of Louis Hall).

# Conclusion

The controversial construction of the Dakota Access Pipeline (DAPL) on the Standing Rock Indian Reservation in 2016 drew a massive movement of Indigenous men and women fighting as warriors in defense for *their* rights, *their* lands, and *their* resources. Calling themselves water protectors and land defenders, they created the largest gathering of Indigenous people for the past hundred years. They were joined by thousands of non-Indigenous supporters–environmentalists, Indigenous rights activists, veterans, and celebrities. The NoDAPL protests originated from within the tribal community of Standing Rock and evolved into an unprecedented transcultural and transnational alliance to stop the blatant enforcement of corporate interests backed by the US government. The US Army Corps of Engineers projected the pipeline would run through four states—North Dakota, South Dakota, Iowa, and Illinois—covering 1,200 miles. In legal challenges and protest demonstrations, the Standing Rock Sioux Tribe and its supporters argued that they were not adequately consulted about the pipeline's route and that the pipeline had been rerouted in order to avoid predominantly white residential neighborhoods. Running underneath Lake Oahe, a Missouri River reservoir, they also expressed fears that an oil spill would contaminate their water and land resources. Construction would further damage sites of great historic, cultural, and religious significance near the lake, violating treaty rights.¹

In the fall of 2016, Selma-like protests unfolded with law enforcement officers brutalizing nonviolent protesters with police batons, attack dogs, rubber bullets, pepper spray, and water cannons in subzero temperatures in order to disperse them. The American Civil Liberties Union (ACLU) reported that the pouring in of personnel and equipment from over seventy-five law enforcement agencies from across the nation and the National Guard "created a battlefield-like atmosphere at Standing Rock. Escalated police militarization was used to intimidate and silence water protectors' free speech and their right to protest a pipeline which passes near sovereign territory."² By December, thousands of people had made it to the protest camp, among them many veterans who arrived to act as shields for protesters who for months had clashed with law enforcement officers.³ "Men and women who fought for our nation are now standing up for the first occupants of this land," said David Archambault II, tribal chairman of the Standing Rock Sioux Tribe in a *Reuters* interview. "They're saying enough is enough. It's symbolic to us."⁴ The NoDAPL movement on the Standing Rock reservation constituted a pivotal moment in twentieth- and twenty-first-century Indigenous history that sparked a national controversy and a massive outpouring of public support. The presence of Indigenous and non-Indigenous veterans provided both an aura of authority and legitimacy. Following months of negotiations, the Obama administration stopped the project, but the Trump administration enforced the building of the pipeline, which became operational in summer 2017.

A series of factors—national and international media attention, massive solidarity, and concerns over the environment and tribal sovereignty—facilitated NoDAPL mobilization. The blatant violation of Indigenous people's rights and the nonviolent nature of the NoDAPL protests left little room for ambiguity and reaffirmed the righteousness of the cause. This protest activism stood in stark contrast to the excessive force of law enforcement officers and complete disregard for tribal sovereignty and Indigenous people. Adding further ambiguity, TigerSwan, a private security firm that had conducted counterinsurgency campaigns as a contractor during the "War on Terror" in the Middle East, protected DAPL and provided information to the law enforcement agency policing the NoDAPL protests. As the protests propelled from a local episode into a global event, they widely eclipsed the Wounded Knee takeover more than four decades earlier.[5]

The similarities and differences between the NoDAPL movement at Standing Rock and the siege at Wounded Knee were striking. Both protests evolved around the issues of tribal sovereignty, treaty rights, and nationhood and in conflict with US hegemony; and both saw the performance of warriorhood, albeit in strikingly different forms. In 1973, Indigenous nationalists occupied the national spotlight through the display of warrior masculinity and nationalism, engaging in gunfights with law enforcement officers. In an interview, Dennis Banks pointed out that the NoDAPL protests were different in the way Indigenous people carried the fight against settler-colonial encroachment into the twenty-first century: "They are bringing their tribal flags. During the first two or three weeks, I saw one flag go up and I sensed a much stronger nation, a much stronger nationhood forming. And this what I felt was beautiful. I have not seen this kind of gathering and bringing in of support. I have never seen it in my entire life."[6] Every time he came to visit Standing Rock, he saw more support and tribal flags going up and witnessed the building of community and solidarity.[7] When Clyde Bellecourt was asked to draw comparisons between Wounded Knee and Standing Rock, he pointed to the enormous size of the NoDAPL protest site (with thousands of supporters) and its length (from April 2016 to February 2017). He considered these activists a new cohort "ready to take up the fight for our people."[8]

The Standing Rock protests drew on a convergence of issues—tribal sovereignty, corporate encroachment upon Indigenous lands and resources, environmental activism—and a complex array of seemingly disparate movements, organizations, and coalitions, such as environmentalists, veterans, and social justice advocates, as well as intertribal and Pan-Indian alliances. Similar to the IdleNoMore movement that commenced in Canada in December 2012 and connected First Nations' sovereignty rights and environmental protection, NoDAPL also emerged as a women-led, grassroots movement that was decidedly different from AIM's masculinist movement culture. Indigenous women—organizers, activists, and veterans—led the anti-colonial struggle. The NoDAPL showed new pathways for how tribal communities could highlight their cause in ways that their own warrior societies or grassroots movements alone could not. The NoDAPL protests pointed to new directions in the defense and protection of Indigenous people, lands, and rights, with the media, transnational and transcultural alliances, and legislative efforts as the most potent weapons. Indigenous women took the lead as yet another kind of warrior in what was a deeply intergenerational struggle.[9]

Many Indigenous women veterans of the 1973 Wounded Knee takeover were present during the 2016/17 Dakota Access Pipeline protests on Standing Rock. In recognition of her leadership at these protests, Regina Brave received the ACLU's highest honor, the Roger N. Baldwin Medal of Liberty. She was among the last protesters to be arrested when police cleared the camp in early 2017.[10]

## The American Indian Movement: New Warriors, New Warrior Society

*Reinventing the Warrior* describes and analyzes certain cultural constructions and performative expressions of warrior masculinity in the 1960s and 1970s, most commonly embodied by the self-proclaimed warriors of AIM and by Indigenous Vietnam veterans. More specifically, this book examines *particular* conceptualizations of warrior masculinity (that principally relate to Lakota culture) within *certain* cultural, temporal, and geographical settings (e.g., South Dakota, Nebraska, the Twin Cities). This study is guided by an understanding that Red Power activism cannot solely be understood as a struggle for self-determination, tribal sovereignty, nationhood, and decolonization but must also be seen as a way for Native Americans to remake their gendered identities. Participation in Red Power activism provided an avenue for Indigenous men to overcome feelings of disempowerment, emasculation, and cultural disconnect in the increasingly confrontational struggle for Indigenous rights and to remake self and society.

Within a larger context of colonial domination, Indigenous men continually reinvented their masculine and Indigenous identities. Colonial imaginings of the racialized "other" portrayed Indigenous men as either unmanly or hypermasculine—ambiguous perceptions that found their expression in martial race ideology and government paternalism. Institutionalized containment, institutional settings, and colonial policies left Indigenous men with few avenues for maintaining their Indigeneity and reconnecting to traditional notions of what it means to be a man.

Traditionally, the most common pathway to be recognized as a warrior has been participation in the US military. From World War I through World War II, Korea, and Vietnam, military service has allowed Indigenous men to reinvent self and society in complex processes of cultural and political nation-building. In a seeming paradox, generations of Indigenous men have joined the very same military their warrior ancestors fought decades earlier, thus entering into a highly complex and ambiguous relationship with the American nation-state. In utilizing a foreign institution for their own purposes and not necessarily those intended, they have transplanted existent traditional notions of warriorhood into the US military, syncretizing both Indigenous and Western cultural and martial traditions and systems. US military service has allowed Indigenous men to exhibit a hybrid patriotism that has enabled them to reconnect to manly occupations—as protectors of *their* people and *their* homeland and as providers for *their* families, kin, and communities. Most commonly, veterans take on multiple responsibilities within their tribal nations, serving as role models for future generations of Native Americans.

During the 1960s and 1970s, a new pathway to being a warrior opened up for Indigenous men through protest activism. The emergence of this nationalist warrior masculinity itself was the result of complex gendered and gendering processes. In the Twin Cities, Indigenous men and women confronted the conditions that kept them marginalized and oppressed. The formation of an Indigenous protest masculinity marked a new way of thinking about being Indigenous in the face of the massive political and cultural turmoil underway in American society. By the early 1970s, AIM had become increasingly committed to the struggle for Indigenous rights. Protest politics evolved from demonstrations, picketing, and marches into more confrontational tactics that involved takeovers, violent clashes, and finally gunfights. Deeply embedded in the anti-colonial struggle were Indigenous men's attempts to empower, renew, and remasculinize themselves through dual efforts of retraditionalization (i.e., through reaching out into their culture) and radicalization (i.e., through engaging in masculinized protest politics). These modern-day warriors embodied a warrior masculinity that was militant, nationalist, and inherently hybridized in nature.

This new and innovative warrior construct entailed new and old understandings of warrior and warrior society and combined traditional and modern military ways with protest culture. Perhaps most significantly, AIM nationalists pioneered new ways to be a warrior and new understandings of warrior society, yet without the common pathway through military service. Most notably, they sought to emulate the cultural traditions of their warrior ancestors and veteran-comrades in new and innovative ways that best fit their own contexts and needs. Since the 1970s, the AIM warrior model has inspired new warrior traditions and societies that have come to exist side-by-side with established warrior/veteran traditions.[11]

Between 1968 and 1973 lay significant years of change that bore witness to a profound transformation of Indigenous men and masculinities and their nationalist endeavors. During this period, AIM transformed from a nonviolent civil rights organization into an armed anti-colonial resistance group that ultimately promoted the founding of a separate nation. The new warrior prototype emerged from the confluence of multiple developments: a desire to reconnect to cultural heritage, a radicalization in protest politics, and efforts to attract media attention through the performance of warrior masculinity. In 1973, AIM gained widespread notoriety for uttering calls for warriorhood and nationhood at Wounded Knee. The modern-day AIM warriors were indeed the result of years of protest and numerous confrontations in urban areas, border towns, and reservations. These gendered and (en)gendering processes involved the three stages of emasculation; followed by remasculinization, renewal, and revitalization; and, finally, hypermasculinity.

First, the colonial policies of termination and relocation had an unanticipated outcome, namely, the emergence of an Indigenous protest masculinity that developed between 1968 and 1971. The founding members of AIM shared historical experiences of colonialism and cultural loss as a motivation to regenerate positive and culturally grounded Indigenous identities. They built upon a shared sense of Indigeneity, or

Pan-Indianism, that laid the basis for mobilization and ethnic cultural resurgence. Within the urban context of the Twin Cities, Indigenous men experienced socioeconomic disparities and rampant racism on a daily basis. These experiences led to exaggerated claims to the gendered position of masculine power. It is no coincidence that much of AIM's protest politics were directed against those institutions that Indigenous people most commonly associated with their own oppression: the white bureaucracy of the Twin Cities and the Bureau of Indian Affairs. As AIM began to challenge power inequalities and racial bias, Indigenous men transformed their male subjectivities into protest masculinities.

Second, processes of renewal, revitalization, and remasculinization transformed these protest masculinities into warrior masculinities during much of 1972. This new warrior masculinity was most visible at the takeover of the BIA headquarters building in Washington, DC, and was already in place prior to the Wounded Knee takeover. Processes of political radicalization and cultural retraditionalization were closely intertwined and paralleled one another. From the inception of AIM, its members sought to reconnect to their ethnic heritage and bridge the cultural chasm that distanced them from their relatives on reservations. They did so by forming a cultural alliance with reservation traditionalists that soon turned political. Closely related to this cultural retraditionalization is the radicalization of protest activism, as epitomized by the "getting in your face" approach and media-savviness. Together, these dynamic processes account for the emergence of modern-day warriors for a nation.

AIM ideology stressed a generic sense of Indigeneity that became a vehicle of cultural awareness and ethnic pride. Nationalist symbolism and ideology—the upside-down American flag, the AIM song, and movement culture and fashion—reflected ethnic pride, awareness, and growing militancy. As Indigenous nationalists developed their own ideology, they borrowed from contemporary social movements—the counterculture, anti-war protest, and the Black civil rights movement, among others—and merged these elements with Indigenous culture. The Ojibwe founders also heavily drew from Lakota cultural elements—language, customs, and traditions—and resituated them in their own context. These trends in nationalist ideology and culture were paralleled by a shift in the political agenda—away from civil rights and integration toward treaty rights, sovereignty, and national separatism.

Finally, the Wounded Knee takeover significantly contributed to perceptions of Indigenous nationalists as modern-day warriors for a nation. A combination of factors—news media bias, Indigenous attempts to reappropriate racial and gender stereotypes, and Indigenous nationalists' genuine self-perception as warriors—added to common perceptions of AIM as a militant organization. For one, media reporting was geared toward the coverage of militancy and reiterating martial images of Indigeneity. For another, Indigenous activists quite consciously utilized stereotypes for their own purposes through strategies of colonial mimicry and colonial ambivalence. The idea of "Indians playing Indian" encapsulates efforts to reappropriate cultural notions of warriorhood, retake control over media images, and use them to their own advantage. In quite a real sense, AIM's leaders utilized their cultural/racial capital and the performance of warrior masculinity to attract media attention. Many Indigenous men genuinely considered themselves warriors in the anti-colonial struggle. Their claims to warriorhood derived from numerous clashes with law enforcement officers. AIM warriors took pride in the performance of warriorhood and commemorated protest events as "battle honors" on patches and ribbons attached to their clothing.

The performance of warrior masculinity brought together a complex set of social dynamics: renewing, revitalizing, and remasculinizing in the struggle for Indigenous rights; reconnecting to cultural heritage and expressing a newfound ethnic pride; unifying Indigenous people in the struggle against US settler colonialism; providing legitimacy and expressing a righteous cause; connecting past and present struggles and mobilizing Indigenous dissent; gaining media attention; and serving as a vehicle for cultural and political empowerment.

In numerous border town confrontations, Indigenous nationalists not only challenged racial and gender inequality but also contested dominant meanings of manhood and nation. In border towns, white Americans frequently compared the Indigenous Rights Struggle to yet another Indian War refought in the twentieth century. As in the Black civil rights struggle in the Deep South, white Americans demonized Indigenous masculinity through a gendered rhetoric espousing the ideals of whiteness, racial superiority, and manhood. The killings of Raymond Yellow Thunder and Wesley Bad Heart Bull set off a series of border town confrontations. While the Gordon, Nebraska, protest resembled a classic civil rights struggle with economic boycotts and political demonstrations, the Custer courthouse riot would go down in history as the first race riot in modern South Dakota history.

The takeover of the BIA headquarters in Washington, DC, the quasi-colonial government overseeing agency, was a forceful display of Indigenous militancy and nationalism. The takeover led to violent clashes between AIM activists-turned-warriors and law enforcement officers. The burning down of the building and the martyrdom of AIM warriors was only narrowly averted. The takeover demonstrated how far AIM warriors were willing to push the government in pursuit of their nationalist agenda. During the takeover, Indigenous nationalists took recourse to cultural and warrior traditions (e.g., through songs, prayers, and blessings) to prepare for impending clashes with police officers. The aggressive display of Indigenous hypermasculinity can be read as a desire to express power within a larger context of relative powerlessness. The Twenty Points put forth at the Trail of Broken Treaties envisioned a fundamental restructuring of Indigenous–settler colonial relations. They were later condensed into three demands at Wounded Knee. The BIA takeover indicates that both the hypermasculine expression of warriorhood and a nationalist agenda were firmly in place prior to the Wounded Knee takeover.

Wounded Knee constituted a powerful attempt to culturally and politically build a nation separate from the United States. The closely interwoven and parallel setup of the Independent Oglala Nation and the ION warrior society occurred while being in struggle against surrounding government forces. In combination, these actions constituted a powerful tool in the pursuit of national separatism. The Wounded Knee occupation instigated a renewal of Lakota traditions that spoke of the interwoven cultural and political nature of the nation-building attempt. For many occupiers, the revitalization of Lakota cultural practices, ceremonies, and rituals was an empowering experience. Bodily and body-reflexive practices not only allowed the occupiers to remake their gendered subjectivities but were equally a display of nationalist ethnocentrism that closely tied claims of religious freedom and cultural distinctiveness with those of political sovereignty. The Indigenous nation-building effort was a deeply masculine project that went hand in hand with remasculinizing and retraditionalizing efforts through cultural and warrior practices.

The takeover of Wounded Knee was perhaps the most significant nation-building attempt of the Red Power era. The Wounded Knee massacre site contains a powerful, multilayered symbolism that relates to colonial oppression and economic and cultural exploitation. It is equally a place where notions of cultural revitalization, national reclamation, and moral regeneration are anchored. The ION represented a community of resistance where some nationalist elements were imagined and others existent. Many Indigenous activists linked the Wounded Knee occupation with the revival of the 1890 Ghost Dance. They connected the takeover with larger projects of cultural renewal, mental decolonization, moral and political recuperation, and the regeneration of culturally grounded Indigenous identities. The gendered transformation that occurred in Indigenous men and women combined claims to a culturally grounded Indigeneity with calls for a nationalist liberation ideology.

The Wounded Knee occupation bore witness to the confluence of two distinct currents of warrior masculinity—one activist and the other veteran. The different claims to warriorhood rested either on military service or on protest activism. AIM warriors drew from a similar code of the warrior as Indigenous veterans did, yet that code translated into a different display of warrior masculinity, both in appearance and in behavior. At Wounded Knee, AIM began to understand itself as a warrior society for all Indigenous people, a claim that found expression in the founding of the International Indian Treaty Council (IITC).

## Indigenous Vietnam Veterans in the American Indian Movement

Indigenous Vietnam veterans played a significant part in AIM. Returning veterans were disillusioned about the very nature of the war and their own complicity in what they considered a colonial and imperialist enterprise. While they fought a foreign war abroad, they were faced with colonialism at home. Termination policies were intended to denationalize, detribalize, and de-Indigenize Native Americans as Native Americans. Indigenous Vietnam veterans' sense of betrayal was further augmented by a sense of double discrimination: first, as Vietnam veterans and participants in a highly unpopular war and, second, as members of a marginalized minority within American society. Indigenous Vietnam veterans participated in virtually every Red Power protest event, playing key functions in both reaffirming and challenging AIM's construct of warrior masculinity.

The Wounded Knee takeover involved the highest number of Indigenous Vietnam veterans of any protest event of the Red Power era. Vietnam veterans spearheaded the takeover, organized the defenses, maintained the siege, and were among the last to surrender to government agents. More than has hitherto been acknowledged, Indigenous veterans played a significant role in constructing, reconstructing, perpetuating, and questioning (and thus, undermining) the AIM warrior construct; they were also fundamental in reinforcing cultural and political nationalist sentiment. Wounded Knee would not have been possible without the numbers of veterans and their active involvement. Both the declaration of the Independent Oglala Nation and the setup of the AIM warrior society were viable only because of veteran participation. As veterans joined the takeover of Wounded Knee, they provided AIM activists-turned-warriors with a sense of righteousness, legitimacy, and militancy. Indigenous veterans quite literally brought the war home, putting their military expertise to use for the occupiers; to many, the Wounded Knee experience involved flashbacks to Vietnam. The veterans' roles in Wounded Knee provided some validity to AIM's claims to warriorhood and nationhood. Vietnam veterans brought yet another sense of righteousness to the cause of anti-colonial struggle. Bearing witness to how "other" peoples' aspirations to national independence were crushed by American intervention and how they themselves had been used as political pawns in a highly ambiguous national endeavor pushed these veterans to defend Indigenous people, lands, and rights against settler-colonial encroachment at home.

At Wounded Knee, Indigenous Vietnam veterans were instrumental in resurrecting the warrior ideal of the past. Several cultural and warrior practices—such as medicine bags, war paint, songs, dances, and ceremony—established a deliberate link between past and present, allowing

Indigenous men to reconnect to their cultural heritage, exhibit ethnic pride, and remasculinize in the struggle against government agents. Indigenous Vietnam veterans' claims to warriorhood were based on military service that often involved combat. As veterans, they bonded through that shared experience. The high level of credibility that Vietnam-era veterans enjoyed among activists as well as government representatives is perhaps best encapsulated in the episode when Stan Holder was captured by federal agents, then returned to the Wounded Knee hamlet on government request, and, after restoring order, turned himself in again. However, in the aftermath of the siege, many veterans shared the feeling that they had been let down by AIM's leaders, the very people for whom they had put their lives on the line. Carter Camp harshly criticized AIM leaders for their lack of martial virtues and for not living up to the self-proclaimed ideals of the warrior society, thus pointing to the inherent contradiction and ambiguity of the newly invented warrior construct.

Unsurprisingly, Indigenous veterans held a wide range of views on the self-proclaimed AIM warriors, from full recognition to outright contempt. Many veterans regarded AIM members as "wannabe warriors" due to their lack of military training and combat experience—cultural elements commonly associated with warriorhood. They considered AIM's confrontation politics and performance of warriorhood a means of attracting the news media. They took offense at AIM's provocative flying of the upside-down American flag—an indication of the complexities, ambiguities, and contradictions of Indigenous patriotism. By contrast, some veterans considered AIM's claims to warriorhood legitimate. They viewed AIM's anti-colonial struggle within a broader context of protecting Indigenous people, ancestral homelands, and tribal rights against settler colonial encroachment, much like the tribal warriors of pre-reservation times.

### Indigenous Women in the American Indian Movement

Indigenous women played a pivotal part in the grassroots activism and behind-the-scenes activities within AIM. For example, they were instrumental in the running of survival schools. These schools sought to provide an educational alternative and were part of an overall attempt to remake children's Indigenous and gendered identities and understand themselves in terms of a more general sense of Indigeneity. Indigenous women claimed they were in a state of double oppression, first, through colonial domination and, second, through gender inequality. AIM's male founders were severely inculcated with and adhered to hegemonic cultural ideals. This is perhaps best summed up by the notion that Indigenous women constituted the backbone of AIM, but once men entered the scene, they were pushed into subservient roles and out of the picture. Until the mid-1970s, when Indigenous women founded their own organization, they privileged the struggle against racial inequality over the struggle for gender equality.

In the gendered processes of nation-building as they occurred during the 1960s and 1970s, Indigenous women played a key part in constructing, perpetuating, and ultimately in challenging Indigenous men as masculine and as warriors. Indigenous women participated in all major protest events. Keenly aware of the dynamic interplay between the performance of warrior masculinity and media attention, AIM warriors consciously sought to have the media's focus on themselves, rather than on female activists. In complying with these demands, Indigenous women helped to reinforce warrior masculinity.

During the Wounded Knee takeover, Indigenous women occupied ambiguous and complex positions, simultaneously reaffirming male privilege (through the taking up of roles of domesticated motherhood) and challenging it (through the picking up of the gun). Throughout the siege, the male defenders were utterly dependent upon women for the day-to-day running of the occupation, a significant role frequently overshadowed by their male counterparts. At times, women activists joined their male counterparts as comrades-in-arms, thus successfully renegotiating themselves into AIM's masculine microculture and nationalist ideology. In taking on a female warrior persona, Indigenous women reconnected to a less well-established tradition of warrior women that had been in existence prior to the reservation period—or so they claimed. Moreover, in taking up arms, Indigenous women directly challenged male privilege and the patriarchal nature of the American Indian Movement. Male nationalists felt somewhat threatened by women wearing and using guns in the armed confrontation, yet for their part mostly accepted this out of pure necessity.

In the Wounded Knee aftermath, Indigenous women began to address their own issues. Their struggle for gender equality increasingly put them increasingly at odds with Indigenous men who abided to ideals of male privilege and patriarchal social structures that constitute an integral part of colonization. As Indigenous women in AIM began to embark on a female quest for empowerment, self-determination, and decolonization, they established their own organization, WARN. In their major struggles against coerced or forced sterilization and the adopting out of Indigenous children to non-Indigenous parents and foster homes, women in WARN rarely received more than lukewarm support from men in AIM.

## The Cultural Memory and Legacy of the American Indian Movement

The legacy of the Red Power movement came with a far-reaching cultural and political renaissance across Indian Country. The Red Power movement empowered Indigenous men and women to remake their cultural identity and redefine power relations with the federal government. Within the larger context of the Red Power movement, Indigenous people sought to revitalize their cultural traditions, arts, music, belief systems, and tribal languages to show their newfound ethnic pride in their own cultural heritage and express their Indigeneity. The renewal of traditional epistemologies also served as a tool to decolonize Indigenous minds, bodies, and spirits in what constituted a larger effort to remake self and society. Indigenous Vietnam veterans utilized cultural and warrior ceremonies for bodily and spiritual healing.[12] Indigenous nationalists inspired a Pan-Indian solidarity in resistance to US colonial society with far-reaching implications for their relative position of power and their relationship with the American nation. Indigenous activism instigated a gendered transformation in Indigenous men and women. Indigenous men and women challenged racial stereotypes of Indigenous people as powerless, vanishing, savage, and primitive. Instead, they redefined Indigeneity as a valuable status imbued with cultural, spiritual, and political significance, attaching new meanings and value to what it meant to be Indigenous.[13]

From its emergence as a community's response to pressing urban issues in the late 1960s, to its radicalization in the early 1970s, to its peak of militancy in 1973 through its final demise toward the mid/end of the 1970s, AIM fundamentally challenged the hegemonic nature of settler colonialism and white male power structure that kept Indigenous lands, minds, and bodies colonized. After Wounded Knee, the AIM warrior society disbanded under both its own internal contradictions and government suppression. Wounded Knee left AIM bitterly divided over competing claims to warriorhood. Decades after the takeover, some AIM leaders took credit for the actions of those who made the occupation possible in the first place. After Wounded Knee, the AIM warriors became both political warriors (by utilizing conventional means to seek reform) and cultural warriors (by becoming active in the cultural nationalist movement). At their core, AIM leaders remained cultural and political nationalists. Indigenous activists have mythologized the anti-colonial struggle and AIM personalities to heroic proportions, thus providing recognition and legitimacy to their struggle.

## New Directions of Indigenous Warriors and Warrior Societies: Tribal Warriors, Street Gangs, and Military Veterans

From the post-Vietnam, post–Red Power era onward, Indigenous men and women have followed new pathways and directions of warriorhood. Since the 1970s, Indian Country bore witness to the broadening and proliferation of notions of Indigenous warriorhood. The most common avenue for Indigenous men to be considered as warriors in their tribal communities continues to be military service. In recent times, Indigenous women have begun to join the military in increasing numbers. Just as their male counterparts, they serve to protect their people and their homeland, to provide for their families, to better themselves, and to continue cultural and warrior traditions, carrying on family and veteran traditions, as the rising number of Indigenous female veterans indicate.[14] Indigenous veterans have served in every conflict in the post-Vietnam era, such as Grenada, Panama, Somalia, the Gulf War, and the War on Terror in Afghanistan and Iraq and elsewhere around the globe.[15] Law enforcement jobs also offer Indigenous men and women some martial-related social status within their tribal communities.[16]

While Indigenous warriorhood continues to be most often associated with military service, Indigenous people have reinvented the warrior concept within other contexts, too. Al Carroll has observed that "Wounded Knee II marked a change in the meanings many Natives attach to warrior societies and how to be a warrior."[17] In drawing from the Vietnam War experience and resituating it into their respective contexts, AIM syncretized protest activism with military traditions, thus setting an example for future activism.

Since the late 1960s, Canada has seen what political scientists Taiaiake Alfred (Mohawk) and Lana Lowe call "the modern warrior society movement," which emerged within the larger struggle of the Indigenous rights movement against settler-colonial encroachment.[18] These modern-day warrior societies include the Mohawk Warrior Society, which took over Moss Lake in upstate New York in 1974 and defended Indigenous land rights in a number of clashes with American and Canadian state law enforcement officers well into the 1990s, perhaps most prominently in the 1990 Oka crisis; the Ojibway Warrior Society, which occupied Anicinabe Park in Kenora, Ontario, in 1974; and the Mi'kmaq Warrior Society, which took over a residential school and demanded the return of lands in 1994. Various warrior societies—the West Coast Okiijida, Mohawk Warrior Societies, the Esgenoopetitj Rangers, Listiguj Rangers, and Mi'kmaq Warriors—joined ranks in defense of fishing and hunting rights at the Burnt First Nation in New Brunswick, Canada, in 2000.[19] Together, these incidents provide a chain of militant episodes that has seen the emergence of tribal warrior societies in defense of *their* tribal people, lands, and rights. These warrior societies organize largely along tribal lines and around land issues while drawing from a culturally infused understanding of warrior and nation similar to that of the AIM warrior society.[20]

These reinvented and resituated notions of tribal warriorhood aside, the warrior concept has also been transplanted into other contexts. For example, Indigenous gangs both on and off reservations frequently draw on warrior imagery to establish a link to their cultural roots, yet they represent an aberration in the traditional warrior ideal.[21] American culture has appropriated Indigenous warriorhood in an effort to reinforce hegemonic notions of race, gender, and nation. During each war, American culture has drawn from warrior imagery along the binaries of noble and ignoble savagery.[22] The appropriation of Indigenous names and symbolism testifies to the pervasiveness of this warrior imagery, inspiring critical discourse over stereotyping in the military, sports, and popular culture generally.[23] In a shift from the past, Indigenous people voice criticism of recent twenty-first-century wars, raising critical questions about America's role in overseas wars, patriotism, and their own participation in these nationalist endeavors.[24]

The cultural ideal of warriorhood continues to exert tremendous influence across Indian Country and the American nation. The various cultural constructions and expressions of warriorhood indicate that the meanings many Indigenous people attach to warrior society and what it means to be a warrior have widened—encompassing warriors/veterans (in a newer tradition of military service); another kind of tribal warriors and warrior societies (most commonly influenced by the AIM example); and claims to warriorhood voiced by street gang members. The cultural, temporal, and geographical context across which Indigenous people have reinvented themselves as warriors points to the changing nature of Indigeneity itself.

# Notes

### A Note on Terminology

1. Reeser, *Masculinities in Theory*, 13.
2. Gibbon, *The Sioux*, 2–9.
3. Bruyneel, *The Third Space of Sovereignty*, ix–x.

### Introduction

1. Akwesasne Notes, *Voices*, 55–58, 65–90, 153–174, 194–201, 246–248.
2. Anonymous, "Protest: Raid at Wounded Knee," *Time Magazine* 101, no. 11, March 12, 1973.
3. Johnson, Nagel, and Champagne, "American Indian Activism and Transformation," 305–310.
4. Johnson, Nagel, Champagne, "American Indian Activism and Transformation," 291–292.
5. Tully, "The Struggles of Indigenous People for and of Freedom," 50.
6. Johnson, Nagel, Champagne, "American Indian Activism and Transformation," 305–310.
7. Several studies into AIM have been conducted yet remain unpublished. Segal, "The American Indian Movement"; Couture, "The American Indian Movement"; Baylor, "Modern Warriors"; Akard, "Wocante Tinza." For a (somewhat outdated) historiography on the American Indian Movement, see Baringer, "Indian Activism and the American Indian Movement."

8. Davis, *Survival Schools*, 7.

9. See Smith and Warrior, *Like A Hurricane*.

10. Kýrová and Tóth, "Red Power at 50: Re-Evaluations and Memory" (Special Issue), 107–237.

11. Johnson, Nagel, and Champagne, "American Indian Activism and Transformation," 283–314; Johnson, Nagel, and Champagne, eds., *American Indian Activism*.

12. Johnson, Nagel, and Champagne, "American Indian Activism and Transformation," 284–292.

13. Nagel, *American Indian Ethnic Renewal*; Johnson, Nagel, and Champagne, *American Indian Activism*; Johnson, Nagel, Champagne, "American Indian Activism and Transformation," 283–314.

14. Johnson, Nagel, and Champagne, "American Indian Activism and Transformation," 283–284.

15. Kýrová and Tóth, "Red Power at 50," 107–116, 108.

16. Shreve, *Red Power Rising*; McKenzie-Jones, *Clyde Warrior*.

17. See Cobb, Berger, and Skopp, "A Sickness That Has Grown to Epidemic Proportions." Daniel Cobb and Loretta Fowler have begun to broadly contextualize twentieth-century Indigenous activism. Cobb, *Native Activism in Cold War America*; Cobb and Fowler, *Beyond Red Power*.

18. Rennard, "We're Still Here," 167–182; Kýrová and Tóth, "Red Power at 50," 109; Hitchmough, "Performative Protest and the Lost Contours of Red Power Activism," 225.

19. Deloria, *Behind the Trail of Broken Treaties*.

20. Cornell, *The Return of the Native*.

21. Nagel, *American Indian Ethnic Renewal*.

22. Jaimes and Halsey, "American Indian Women."

23. Langston, "American Indian Women's Activism."

24. Mihesuah, *Indigenous American Women*, 115–171.

25. Mihesuah, *Indigenous American Women*, 119.

26. Mihesuah, *Indigenous American Women*; Castle, "Keeping One Foot in the Community"; Castle, "The Original Gangster."

27. Castle, "Black and Native American Women's Activism."

28. Voigt, "Warrior Women."

29. Davis, *Survival Schools*, 6.

30. Davis, *Survival Schools*, 6, 118–119; Krouse, "What Came Out of the Takeovers," 533–547.

31. O'Sullivan, "We Worry About Survival"; O'Sullivan, "Informing Red Power and Transforming the Second Wave."

32. Troy R. Johnson, *Red Power: The Native American Civil Rights Movement* (New York: Chelsea House, 2007), 69–75.

33. Baylor, "Modern Warriors," 168–206; Castile, *To Show Heart*, 117–146; Schwarz, *Fighting Colonialism*, 15–43.

34. Mihesuah, *Indigenous American Women*, 108, 122, 163ff; Jaimes and Halsey, "American Indian Women," 329f; Castle, "Black and Native American Women's Activism," 86.

35. Kimmel, *Manhood in America*, 189–210.

36. Mihesuah, *Indigenous American Women*, 163ff.

37. Innes and Anderson, *Indigenous Men and Masculinities*, 11, 15.

38. Voigt, "Between Powerlessness and Protest."

39. Davis, *Survival Schools*, 42–51.

40. Messner, *Politics of Masculinities*, 70–80; Nagel, "Masculinity and Nationalism"; Nagel, "Nationalism."

41. Mihesuah, *Indigenous American Women*, 163ff.

42. Mihesuah, *Indigenous American Women*, 163ff.

43. Voigt, "Warriors for a Nation"; Voigt, "Between Powerlessness and Protest." These articles contain some of the findings of this book from chapters 2 and 4.

44. See Holm, *Strong Hearts*; Carroll, *Medicine Bags and Dog Tags*. Historian John Little (Dakota) also explores Indigenous Vietnam veterans but does not cover veterans' postwar activism. Little, "Vietnam Akíčita"; Little, "Sioux Warriors and the Vietnam War."

45. Carroll, *Medicine Bags*, 162.

46. For analyses of veteran involvement at Wounded Knee, see Holm, *Strong Hearts*, 171–179; Carroll, *Medicine Bags*, 163–172.

47. Baylor, "Modern Warriors," 179–182.

48. Schwarz, *Fighting Colonialism with Hegemonic Culture*, 15–43.

49. For exemptions, see Voigt, "Warriors for a Nation"; Voigt, "'Fighting for Their Freedom at Home'"; Robinson, "Hey Uncle, Uncle Sam!"

50. Nagel, *American Indian Ethnic Renewal*; Nagel, "American Indian Ethnic Renewal."

51. Jackson and Balaji, *Global Masculinities*, 17–30 (see esp. 21).

52. Wendt and Andersen, *Masculinities and the Nation*.

53. Innes and Anderson, "Introduction," 3.

54. Tengan, "(En)Gendering Colonialism," 239.

55. Quoted in McKegney, *Maculindians*, 5.

56. For a discussion, see: McKegney, *Maculindians*, 1–11.

57. McKegney, *Maculindians*, 1–11; Innes and Anderson, "Introduction,"

3–17; Hokowhitu, "Tackling Māori Masculinity"; Tengan, "(En)Gendering Colonialism."

58. Innes and Anderson, *Indigenous Men and Masculinities*.

59. McKegney, *Maculindians*, 1f; McKegney, *Carrything the Burden of Peace*, ix.

60. Cannon, *Men, Masculinity, and the Indian Act*.

61. Diné historian Lloyd Lee sheds light on Navajo masculinities from a culturally centered perspective yet offers little insight into the cultural, social, and historical formation of Indigenous masculinities within the United States as a whole. Lee, *Diné Masculinities*.

62. Nagel, "Nation," 397–413; Clark and Nagel, "White Men, Red Masks," 109–130; Klopotek, "'I Guess Your Warrior Look Doesn't Work Every Time,'" 251–271.

63. Morgensen, *Spaces Between Us*; Driskill, *Queer Indigenous Studies*; Rifkin, *Settler Common Sense*; Rifkin, *When Did Indians Become Straight?*; Rifkin, *The Erotics of Sovereignty*; Brown, *Two Spirit People*. This may not obscure the fact that a lack of sources has left much of that history—and, for that matter, the Indigenous Rights Movement—unexplored. See Morgensen, *Spaces Between Us*, 93–104.

64. Nickel and Fehr, *In Good Relation*; Barker, ed., *Critically Sovereign*; Green, *Making Space for Indigenous Feminism*; Huhndorf, Suzack, Perreal, and Barman, eds., *Indigenous Women and Feminism*; Smith, *Conquest*; Maracle, *I Am Woman*; Shoemaker, *Negotiators of Change*; Allen, *The Sacred Hoop*.

65. Arvin, Tuck, and Morrill, "Decolonizing Feminism," 8–34; Ramirez, "Race, Tribal Nation, and Gender"; Smith, "Native American Feminism"; Guerrero, "'Patriarchal Colonialism' and Indigenism," 58–69; Guerrero, "Civil Rights versus Sovereignty," 101–122.

66. The concept of intersectionality derived from Kimberlé Crenshaw and was subsequently taken up by Patricia Hill Collins and Sirma Bilge. Crenshaw, *Critical Race Theory*; Collins and Bilge, *Intersectionality*.

67. Morrell and Swart. "Men in the Third World," 95.

68. Bruyneel, *Third Space of Sovereignty*, xviii.

69. For example, see Nagel, *American Indian Ethnic Renewal*, 130–141, 158–178, 190–197, 204–205, 246–248; Blansett, *A Journey to Freedom*, 273n5, 275n10.

70. Blansett, *A Journey to Freedom*, 4.

71. Blansett, *A Journey to Freedom*, 4.

72. Shreve, *Red Power Rising*, 6–15.

73. Shreve, *Red Power Rising*, 6–8, 13.

74. Blansett, *A Journey to Freedom*, 4, 272n4.
75. Holm, Pearson, and Chavis, "Peoplehood," 11–15.
76. Fixico, *Call for Change*.
77. Instead of the term "peoplehood," historian Catherine Price uses the notion of the "sacred hoop." Price, *The Oglala People*, 1ff.
78. Anderson, *Imagined Communities*, 5–6.
79. Enloe, *Bananas*, 94–95; Nagel, "Nation," 400f; Nagel, "Masculinity and Nationalism," 247f.
80. Calhoun, *Nations Matter*, 9; Billig, *Banal Nationalism*; Yuval-Davis, *Gender and Nation*, 21; Breuilly, *Nationalism and the State*, 1–18.
81. Balibar, "The Nation Form: History and Ideology," 331.
82. Nagel, "Nation," 400.
83. Nagel, "Nation," 400f; Nagel, "Masculinity and Nationalism," 247f.
84. Nagel, "Masculinity and Nationalism," 246–247; Anderson, *Imagined Communities*; Hobsbawm and Ranger, *The Invention of Tradition*.
85. Nagel, "Masculinity and Nationalism," 248.
86. Brown, "Are There Good and Bad Nationalisms?"; Brown, "The Ethnic Majority: Benign or Malign?"
87. Blansett, *A Journey to Freedom*, 3–4, 272n4.
88. Blansett, *A Journey to Freedom*, 3–4, 272n3.
89. Waetjen, "The Limits of Gender Rhetoric," 121–122; Waetjen, *Workers and Warriors*, 2.
90. Enloe, *Bananas*, 87ff.
91. Waetjen, "The Limits of Gender Rhetoric," 122; Waetjen, *Workers and Warriors*, 2–6.
92. Nagel, "Masculinity and Nationalism," 244, 249.
93. Nagel, "Masculinity and Nationalism," 252–254; Nagel, "Nation," 402–404.
94. Waetjen, "The Limits of Gender Rhetoric," 123–124.
95. Wendt and Andersen, *Masculinities and the Nation*, 1–18.
96. Kimmel, *Manhood in America*, 5.
97. Connell, *Masculinities*, 76–81.
98. Connell, *The Men and the Boys*, 29–32.
99. Demetriou, "Connell's Concept of Hegemonic Masculinity"; Whitehead, *Men and Masculinities*, 88–94; Wendt and Andersen, *Masculinities and the Nation*, 3–4.
100. Demetriou, "Connell's Concept of Hegemonic Masculinity," 343–355.
101. Demetriou, "Connell's Concept of Hegemonic Masculinity," 355.

102. Demetriou, "Connell's Concept of Hegemonic Masculinity"; Summers, *Manliness and Its Discontents*, 11–13; Jackson and Balaji, *Global Masculinities and Manhood*, 17–24; Wendt and Andersen, *Masculinities and the Nation*, 7–8.

103. Connell and Messerschmidt, "Hegemonic Masculinity, Rethinking the Concept," 848.

104. Omi and Winant, *Racial Formation in the United States*; Ferrante and Browne Jr., *The Social Construction of Race and Ethnicity in the United States*; Cornell and Hartmann, *Ethnicity and Race*.

105. See Nagel, *American Indian Ethnic Renewal*.

106. Scott, "Gender"; West and Zimmerman, "Doing Gender"; Conway, Bourque, and Scott, "Introduction: The Concept of Gender"; Scott, "Unanswered Questions."

107. Butler, *Gender Trouble*, 185f, 191.

108. Graham and Penny, *Performing Indigeneity*, 1–31.

109. Tengan, *Native Men*; Hokowhitu, "Haka," 273–304.

110. Hobsbawm, "Introduction: Inventing Traditions," in *The Invention of Traditons*, 9.

111. Nagel, *American Indian Ethnic Renewal*, 46.

112. Usbeck, "Selling the Natural-Born Warrior," 175–193.

113. Usbeck, "Selling the Natural-Born Warrior," 175–178.

114. Deloria, *Playing Indian*. See also Nagel and Clark, "White Men, Red Masks"; King, *Unsettling America*, 27–42.

115. Schwarz, *Fighting Colonialism*, 25–33.

116. Tengan, "The Return of Kū?"

117. Rosenthal, "Beyond the New Indian History"; Iverson, "American Indian History"; Richter, "Whose Indian History"; Iverson, "American Indians in the Twentieth Century."

118. Fixico, *Call for Change*.

119. Fixico, "Ethics and Responsibilities in Writing American Indian History," 29–39.

120. Thompson and Bornat, *The Voice of the Past*, 3–8; Thompson, "The Voice of the Past," 33–39.

121. For a brief overview, see Liamputtong and Ezzy, *Qualitative Research Methods*, 129–130 (narratively oriented interviews), 56–58 (semi-structured interviews).

122. Wengraf, *Qualitative Research Interviewing*; Holstein and Gubrium, eds., *Inside Interviewing*.

123. Rosenthal, "Biographical Research," 50.

124. For example, see Chilisa, *Indigenous Research Methodologies*; Smith, *Decolonizing Methodologies*; Strega and Brown, *Research as Resistance*; Wilson, *Research Is Ceremony*.

125. Fixico, *Call for Change*.

126. Fixico, *Call for Change*.

127. Reinhardt, *Ruling Pine Ridge*, 159–163.

128. Higate, ed., *Military Masculinities*.

129. Walker, *Lakota Society*, 28–34, 38–39, and 58–60; Price, *The Oglala People*, 13–18.

130. Medicine, "Warrior Women," 274. For meanings of the Ojibwe terms *ogicidaa* (for men) and *ogicidaakwe* (for women), see Vukelich, "Ojibwe Word of the Day"; LaDuke and Cruz, *The Militarization of Indian Country*, 3ff.

131. Gibbon, *The Sioux*, 1.

## Chapter 1. Indigenous Men and Peoplehood under US Colonial Domination

1. Josephy, Nagel, and Johnson, *Red Power*, 39–43.

2. Johnson, *The American Indian Occupation of Alcatraz Island*.

3. Johnson and Garvey, "The Government and the Indians," 153–185; Johnson, *American Indian Occupation of Alcatraz*, 50, 75, 172–195. See also Kotlowski, "Alcatraz, Wounded Knee, and Beyond."

4. Johnson, *American Indian Occupation of Alcatraz*, 196–216.

5. Gary Leach (Colville/Sioux), interviewed by Irene Silentman and Anna Boyd, February 5, 1970, Doris Duke Oral History Project, American Indian Historical Research Project, transcript tape 453, 9, in Center for Southwest Research, Special Collections, University of New Mexico, Albuquerque, NM. 15.

6. Johnson, *American Indian Occupation of Alcatraz Island*, 217–221; Johnson, *We Hold the Rock*; Smith and Warrior, *Like a Hurricane*, 1–83.

7. Nagel, *American Indian Ethnic Renewal*, 131–212; Nagel, "American Indian Ethnic Renewal," 958–961; Johnson, Champagne, and Nagel, "American Indian Activism and Transformation," 303–310.

8. Meadows, *Military Societies*; Carroll, *Medicine Bags*; Holm, *Strong Hearts*, 15–25.

9. Nagel, *American Indian Ethnic Renewal*, 113ff.

10. Wolfe, "Elimination of the Native," 388.

11. Wolfe, "Elimination of the Native," 393; Wolfe, "Structure and Event," 82–101.

12. Gender studies scholar Tiffany Lethabo King argues that settler colonialism was a genocide-centered, rather than a land-centered, project. She finds that the growth of white settler colonial studies ultimately works to undermine Indigenous studies in the form of a "discursive genocide" in which Indigenous theories and methodologies disappear. See King, "New World Grammars," 80–83, 88–90; King, *The Black Shoals*, 63–73; Barker, *Critically Sovereign*, 22ff.

13. Kauanui, "A Structure, Not an Event."

14. See, for example, Yuval-Davis, *Gender and Nation*, 1; Enloe, *Bananas*, 87ff; Yuval-Davis and Anthias, *Woman-Nation-State*; Mayer, *Gender Ironies of Nationalism*.

15. Rizzo and Gerontakis, *Intimate Empires*; Reeser, *Masculinities in Theory*, 171–199; Connell, "Globalization, Imperialism, and Masculinities," 74–77; Nagel, "Nation," 397–413; McClintock, *Imperial Leather*, 352–389; Stoler, "Making Empire Respectable," 373–399.

16. Enloe, *Bananas*, 83ff; Nagel, "Masculinity and Nationalism," 244ff.

17. Reeser, *Masculinities in Theory*, 178–179.

18. Nagel, "Masculinity and Nationalism"; Nagel, "Nation"; Enloe, *Bananas*, 83–124.

19. Enloe, *Bananas*, 91f.

20. Nagel, "Nation," 398–399.

21. Jackson and Balaji, *Global Masculinities*, 17–30.

22. Tengan, "(En)gendering Colonialism"; Morgensen, "Cutting to the Roots"; Rizzo and Gerontakis, *Intimate Empires*, 12–110, 205–256.

23. Stoler, "Carnal Knowledge and Imperial Power," 51–101; Stoler, "Making Empire Respectable," 373–399; Lamphere, Ragon, and Zavella, *Situated Lives*, 1–22.

24. Tengan, *Native Men Remade*, 34; Tengan, "(En)gendering Colonialism," 239f.

25. Nagel, "Masculinity and Nationalism," 249; Clark and Nagel, "White Men," 112–113.

26. Kimmel, *Manhood in America*.

27. Balaji and Jackson, *Global Masculinities*, 18. See also Reeser, *Masculinities in Theory*, 144–170.

28. Reeser, *Masculinities in Theory*, 147–158.

29. According to Sinha's findings, "colonial masculinity" was a politics that informed both the manly colonizer and the unmanly colonized through a hierarchy of masculinities, with an elite white masculinity at the top; followed by the martial races (that were cast as loyal but simple, yet,

at the same time, martial manliness commanded respect); and lastly, the unmanly or feminized clever-but-treacherous colonized Indian men at the bottom (Sinha, *Colonial Masculinity*, 1–32). In response to these cultural strategies of oppression, Indian men constructed an oppositional masculinity. According to women's studies scholar Sikata Banerjee, Indian men took up certain elements of hegemonic masculinity that challenged their subaltern status and influenced their anti-colonial movement against British colonial rule. For example, Indian men took up bodybuilding to remake their physicality, and they incorporated Western elements of intellectual thought to create an independence movement against British colonial rule (Banerjee, *Make Me a Man*; Banerjee, *Muscular Nationalism*).

30. Enloe, *Bananas*, 99–103; Stoler, "Carnal Knowledge," 56.

31. Bell, *Relating Indigenous and Settler Identities*, 5–6.

32. Hokowhitu, "Indigenous Men and First Nations Masculinities," 331.

33. Reeser, *Masculinities in Theory*, 144–170; Jackson and Balaji, *Global Masculinities*, 17–30.

34. In Hawaii and New Zealand, Indigenous responses to settler colonialism differed and instigated divergent popular discourses that oscillated between denigrations and celebrations of Indigenous masculinity. Whereas Native Hawaiians were seen as emasculated men in an essentially feminized place, Māori masculinities were privileged as hypermasculine warriors. In the Hawaiian context, where Native men fiercely resisted US colonialism, the ignoble savagery discourse validated subjugation, colonization, and land encroachment in a paternalistic guise. In the New Zealand context, the Māori initially violently opposed British settlers, yet during WWI and WWII they demonstrated complicity with the British Empire (akin to Native Americans in the United States during the same period), thus shifting dominant discourse from ignoble savagery to noble savagery. The latter discourse of noble savagery has validated the assimilation and integration of Māori into white society. However, in both the Hawaiian and the New Zealand contexts, Indigenous boys underwent a harsh physical regime through government-run schools and manual labor. Both hegemonic discourses coexist side by side, contributing to a noble/ignoble ambivalence about Indigenous masculinities' violence in popular culture today. Hokowhitu, "Haka"; Hokowhitu, "The Death of Koro Paka," 118ff.

35. Shoemaker, *Negotiators of Change*, 9.

36. Hixon, *American Settler Colonialism*, 9–11; Berkhofer, *The White Man's Indian*, 84; Rizzo and Gerontakis, *Intimate Empires*, 59.

37. The authority of the bureau pervaded all legal and practical matters

of an Indigenous person's life. Without BIA consent, an Indigenous person could not withdraw money from their own bank account or make decisions about their personal property (which was under supervision) or their own land (which was held in trust). The situation was worsened by the sheer volume, complexity, and peculiarity of Indigenous laws that confounded BIA administration. Cahn, *Our Brother's Keeper*, 5ff.

38. Nagel, *American Indian Ethnic Renewal*, 237–248.
39. Reeser, *Masculinities in Theory*, 186.
40. Holm, *Strong Hearts*, 88–90, 137–138.
41. For example, in British colonial India of the second half of the nineteenth century, this belief translated into recruitment practices that shifted away from Bengal and lower India toward populations thought to produce martial races such as the Sikhs and Gurkhas in the North. Streets, *Martial Races*, 1–17.
42. Holm, "Patriots and Pawns," 350–354; Holm, "The Militarization of Native America," 462–464, 470–473.
43. Morgensen, "Cutting to the Roots," 39.
44. Morgensen, "Theorising Gender," 3; Nagel, "Masculinity and Nationalism," 249.
45. In analogy to this concept, white settler colonialists have imagined the relationship between the American nation and tribal nations as one between a white, patriarchal father and that of his incompetent Indigenous children. This model found manifold expression in the Indigenous–settler-colonial relationship. Cahill, *Federal Fathers And Mothers*, 39–40.
46. McKegney, *Maculindians*, 3.
47. Rifkin, *When Did Indians Become Straight?* 5–6.
48. McKegney, *MascuIIndians*, 2.
49. Morgensen, "Cutting to the Roots," 39, 42.
50. Bruyneel, *Third Space of Sovereignty*, xiff.
51. Bruyneel, *Third Space of Sovereignty*, 3–6.
52. Bruyneel, *Third Space of Sovereignty*, 65.
53. This guardian-warden relationship, however, suffered from an inherent conflict of interest: The Office of Indian Affairs/Bureau of Indian Affairs acted under the supervision of the Department of the Interior. As such, it not only acted as the trustee of Native interests but also represented economic interests in Native land, water, and minerals—the most powerful anti-Native interests in the country. Indigenous people and the bureau were in a love-hate relationship. While the bureau provided much-needed

services, it also exercised tremendous control over Indigenous people's lives. The bureau has the dubious distinction of being the oldest and the most deeply entrenched federal agency. Its massive size and monolithic structure inhibited progress and slowed action. Throughout its existence, the BIA was charged with gross mismanagement, corruption, and opportunism. Wilkens and Stark, *American Indian Politics*, 90, 104, 108–111, 129, 154–156.

54. Bruyneel, *Third Space of Sovereignty*, 1–25.
55. Braun, "Building on Native Sovereignty," 15–17.
56. Braun, "Building on Native Sovereignty," 38–39.
57. Wolfe, "Elimination of the Native," 388.
58. Braun, "Building on Native Sovereignty," 31.
59. Thomas, "Colonialism, Classic And Internal."
60. For a case study see Reinhardt, *Ruling Pine Ridge*.
61. Omi and Winant, *Racial Formation*, 37.
62. Adams, *Education For Extinction*.
63. *Official Report of the Nineteenth Annual Conference of Charities and Correction* (1892), 46–59.
64. Adams, *Education for Extinction*, 21–24, 51–55.
65. Adams, *Education for Extinction*, 173–181.
66. Prucha, *The Great Father*, 204–205, 224–228.
67. Reinhardt, *Ruling Pine Ridge*, 10.
68. Braun, "Building on Native Sovereignty," 37–42; Nagel, *American Indian Ethnic Renewal*, 113–157. For federal Indian policies see Fixico, *Termination and Relocation*; Fixico, *Urban Indian Experience*; Burt, *Tribalism in Crisis*; Castile, *To Show Heart*; Castile, *Taking Charge*; Clarkin, *Federal Indian Policy*.
69. Fixico, *Termination and Relocation*, 21–44.
70. Fixico, *Termination and Relocation*, 91–133, 183–197.
71. Braun, "Building on Native Sovereignty," 38.
72. Nagel, *American Indian Ethnic Renewal*, 118–119.
73. Fixico, *Termination and Relocation*, 183.
74. Sorkin, *Urban American Indian*, 10.
75. Sorkin, *Urban American Indian*, 25.
76. Fixico, *Urban Indian Experience*, 13.
77. Fixico, *Urban Indian Experience*.
78. Davis, *Survival Schools*, 57.
79. Davis, *Survival Schools*, 20, 57.
80. Miller, *Indians on the Move*, 9, 69, 160–186.

81. Fixico, *The Urban Indian Experience*, 43–60.
82. Fixico, *Urban Indian Experience*, 6, 30; Fixico, *Indian Resilience*, 113, 124–150.
83. Fixico, *Urban Indian Experience*, 5; Fixico, *Indian Resilience*, 104ff.
84. Fixico, *Urban Indian Experience*, 2–7; Fixico, *Indian Resilience*, 108ff.
85. Fixico, *The Urban Indian Experience*, 26–42.
86. Trush, *Native Seattle*, 7–9. For further studies of urban Natives, see LaPier and Beck, *City Indian*; Peters and Andersen, eds., *Indigenous in the City*; Carpio, *Indigenous Albuquerque*; Rosenthal, *Reimagining Indian Country*; Ramirez, *Native Hubs*; LaGrand, *Indian Metropolis*; Strauss and Arndt, eds., *Native Chicago*; and Danziger, *Survival and Regeneration*.
87. Miller, *Indians on the Move*, 4.
88. Grounding his analysis in the long history of Indigenous mobility—an Indigenous survival strategy—Miller shows that Indigenous movement to cities predates many relocation programs. Apparently, the relocation program fit larger patterns of Indigenous mobility and an ongoing tradition of two-way mobility between cities and reservations. Indigenous people utilized relocation on their own terms, rebuilding their communities in ways the BIA did not anticipate. Previous studies of Indigenous urbanization have focused on the maladjustment paradigm. Miller, *Indians on the Move*, 184.
89. Miller, *Indians on the Move*, 8.
90. Miller, *Indians on the Move*, 184ff, quote p. 185.
91. Miller, *Indians on the Move*, 13.
92. Antone, "Reconstructing Indigenous Masculine Thought," 27.
93. Morgensen, "Colonial Masculinity," 48.
94. Innes and Anderson, *Indigenous Men and Masculinities*, 10.
95. See Cornwall and Lindisfarne, *Dislocating Masculinity*.
96. Whitehead, *Men and Masculinities*; Beynon, *Masculinities and Culture*.
97. McKegney, *Maculindians*; Innes and Anderson, *Indigenous Men and Masculinities*; Tengan, *Native Men Remade*; Tengan, "(En)gendering Colonialism"; Hokowhitu, "Producing Elite Indigenous Masculinities"; Hokowhitu, "Death of Koro Paka"; Hokowhitu, "Indigenous and First Nations Masculinities."
98. Nagel, *American Indian Ethnic Renewal*, 113–157.
99. Sociologist Joane Nagel maintains that Indigenous people did not reinvent self and society *in spite of* but rather *because of* assimilation processes. She claims "the American Indian ethnic renewal of recent decades arose in reaction to, and thus in many ways was dependent on, trends in

Indian affairs that were mainly assimilationist in character and intent." Nagel, *American Indian Ethnic Renewal*, 114.

100. Fixico, *Indian Resilience*, 113; Nagel, *American Indian Ethnic Renewal*, 113–121.

101. Nagel, *American Indian Ethnic Renewal*, 113–157.

102. Fixico, *Urban Indian Experience*, 4ff; Fixico, *Indian Resilience*, 96–118; Nagel, *American Indian Ethnic Renewal*, 113–157.

103. Fixico, *Indian Resilience*, 107ff; Nagel, *American Indian Ethnic Renewal*, 120–121.

104. Lucero, "'Being Indian in the City,'" 196.

105. Rosenthal, *Reimagining Indian Country*, 117–119.

106. Davis, *Survival Schools*, 37–51, 55–67.

107. Weibel-Orlando, *Indian Country, L.A.*, 60.

108. Holm, Pearson, and Chavis, "Peoplehood."

109. Anthropologist Renya Ramirez claims that Indigenous people maintain a sense of connection to both their tribal homelands and urban spaces through participation in cultural circuits, the maintenance of social networks, and shared activities. They also develop a diasporic consciousness and maintain their sense of collectivity through transnationalism. See Ramirez, *Native Hubs*.

110. Nagel, *American Indian Ethnic Renewal*, 113–141.

111. Van Deburg, *New Day in Babylon*, 11–28; Ogbar, *Black Power*, 3–4.

112. Shipway, *Decolonization and Its Impact*.

113. Dudziak, *Cold War Civil Rights*.

114. Rosier, "'They Are Ancestral Homelands,'" 1300–1326.

115. Cobb, "Talking the Language of the Larger World," 161–177.

116. Nagel, *American Indian Ethnic Renewal*, 158–212.

117. Johnson, Nagel, and Champagne, *American Indian Activism*, 9–44; Johnson, Champagne, and Nagel, "American Indian Activism and Transformation," 283–314; Cornell, *The Return of the Native*, 128–148.

118. Department of Veterans Affairs (ed.), "American Indian and Alaska Native Service Members and Veterans," September 2012. Henceforth: AIAN report 2012, 4–5.

119. Holm, *Strong Hearts*, 10f, 123.

120. AIAN report 2012, 4–5.

121. Meadows, *Military Societies*, 395.

122. Meadows, *Comanche Code Talkers*, 91–93.

123. Shigematsu and Camacho, *Militarized Currents*, xv–xlviii.

124. Enloe, *Ethnic Soldiers*, 11–22.

125. Camacho and Monnig, "Uncomfortable Fatigues," 147–179.

126. Camacho and Monnig, "Uncomfortable Fatigues," 159–163.

127. Camacho and Monnig, "Uncomfortable Fatigues," 163–168.

128. Proponents of dependency theory are Alison Bernstein and Donald Parman. See Bernstein, *American Indians and World War II*, 22–42; Parman, *Indians and the American West*, 107–111. For discussions of dependency theory, see Meadows, *Comanche Code Talkers*, 9–11, 83–84.

129. Holm, *Strong Hearts*, 18–25, 117–123; Meadows, *Comanche Code Talkers*, 9–14, 83ff; Carroll, *Medicine* Bags, 1–13.

130. Rosier, *Serving Their Country*, 9–10.

131. Rosier, *Serving Their Country*, 9–10.

132. Personal interview, Ed Charging Elk.

133. Holm, *Strong Hearts*, 117–123; Meadows, *Comanche Code Talkers*, 11–14.

134. Carroll, *Medicine Bags*, 8f.

135. Thomas L. Roubideaux, *South Dakota Vietnam Veterans Oral History Project*, South Dakota Historical Society, Pierre, South Dakota, 2.

136. Holm, *Strong Hearts*, 118.

137. For the concept of syncretism, see Meadows, *Military Societies*, 20ff; Meadows, *Comanche Code Talkers*, 84ff; Holm, *Strong Hearts*, 69, 101, 117, 191.

138. Holm, *Strong Hearts*, 120.

139. These findings are closely related to my own findings in that cultural notions (whether they are related to protecting or providing) motivate Indigenous enlistment; however, I find that the complex reasons for Indigenous participation in the military cannot be reduced to a monocausal motive. John, "From Warrior to Soldier."

140. Holm, "Militarization of Native America."

141. Studi, "Conversations with Wes Studi."

142. Studi, "Conversations with Wes Studi."

143. Fixico, *Call for Change*, 17–40; Holm, Pearson, Chavis, "Peoplehood," 13–15.

144. Holm, "Culture, Ceremonialism, and Stress," 237–251; Holm, "PTSD in Native American Vietnam Veterans," 83–86. See also Meadows, *Military Societies*; Carroll, *Medicine Bags*; Holm, *Strong Hearts*.

145. Meadows, *Military Societies*; Carroll, *Medicine Bags*.

146. Carroll, *Medicine Bags*, 1–13; Holm, *Strong Hearts*, 18–25; Meadows, *Comanche Code Talkers*, XIV, 9–14; Meadows, *Military Societies*.

147. Wendt, *Warring over Valor*.

148. Barsh, "American Indians in the Great War," 278, 298n7; Bernstein, *American Indians and World War II*, 40–43; Holm, *Strong Hearts, Wounded Souls*, 158–164.

149. For World War I, see Britten, *American Indians in World War I*; Krouse, *North American Indians in the Great War*. For World War II, see Townsend, *World War II and the American Indian*; Franco, *Crossing the Pond*; Bernstein, *American Indians and World War II*. For overview studies, see Harris and Hirsch, eds., *Why We Serve*; Viola, *Warriors in Uniform*. The Indigenous code talkers of World War I and World War II have inspired their own corpus of literature.

150. Rosier, *Serving Their Country*, 46.

151. Britten, *American Indians in World War I*, 28–50; Tate, "From Scout to Doughboy"; White, "The American Indian as Soldier"; White, "The American Army and the Indian," 78ff.

152. Townsend, *World War II*, 69–72; Bernstein, *American Indians and World War II*, 22–24; Rosier, *Serving Their Country*, 91–93.

153. For a discussion of Indigenous draft resistance during World War I, see Britten, *American Indians in World War I*, 67–72; Zissu, "Conscription, Sovereignty, and Land," 537–566; Barsh, "American Indians in the Great War," 281. For World War II, see Bernstein, *American Indians and World War II*, 22–39; Franco, *Crossing the Pond*, 41–79; Townsend, *World War II*, 81–124. See also Rosier, *Serving Their Country*, 49–52 (for World War I); 93–96 (for World War II).

154. Townsend, *World War II and the American Indian*, 123; Franco, *Crossing the Pond*, 49–50; Bernstein, *American Indians and World War II*, 31–33; Rosier, *Serving Their Country*, 95–96.

155. Carroll, *Medicine Bags*, 150.

156. Krouse, *Indians in The Great War*, 36; Britten, *American Indians in World War I*, 101–102; Bernstein, *American Indians and World War II*, 60–63; Holm, *Strong Hearts*, 137–139.

157. Holm, *Strong Hearts*, 88–90, 137–138; Usbeck, "Fighting Like Indians"; Usbeck, "Selling the Natural-Born Warrior"; Franco, *Crossing the Pond*, 120–153.

158. Meadows, "Honoring Native American Code Talkers," 6–10.

159. Barsh, "American Indians in the Great War," 289–292; Bernstein, *American Indians and World War II*, 40–63; Townsend, *World War II and the American Indian*, 125–169.

160. Holm, *Strong Hearts*, 89.

161. Ickes, "Indians Have a Name for Hitler."

162. Holm, *Strong Hearts*, 122.
163. Holm, *Strong Hearts*, 11.
164. Personal interviews.
165. Holm, *Strong Hearts*, 100.
166. Anonymous, "Indian Complains of Lack of Freedom," *Wichita Daily News*, December 14, 1948, 6.
167. Hewitt, "The Indian Who Never Got Home," 12–20. Personal interviews, with Indigenous Korean war veterans.
168. Viola, *Warriors*, 94.
169. Britten, *American Indians in World War I*, 84–85.
170. Britten, *American Indians in World War I*, 159–187.
171. Cowger, *National Congress of American Indians*.
172. Franco, *Crossing the Pond*, 190–204; Franco, "Empowering the WWII Native American Veteran," 32–37; Townsend, *World War II*, 215–228.
173. Holm, *Strong Hearts*, 137–141; personal interviews.
174. Espey, "America and Vietnam: The Indian Subtext."
175. Personal interview, Madonna Thunder Hawk.
176. Studi, "Oscar-winning Cherokee Actor."
177. Dunlay, *Wolves for the Blue Soldiers*, 200–201, 206–209.
178. Studi, "Oscar-winning Cherokee Actor."
Dunlay, *Wolves for the Blue Soldiers*, 200–201, 206–209.
179. Studi, "Conversations with Wes Studi."
180. Studi, "Conversations with Wes Studi."
181. Studi, "Oscar-winning Cherokee Actor."
Dunlay, *Wolves for the Blue Soldiers*, 200–201, 206–209.
182. Studi, "Conversations with Wes Studi."
183. Holm, *Strong Hearts*, 171–175.
184. Johnson, Champagne, and Nagel, "Roots of Contemporary Native American Activism," 134.
185. Holm, *Strong Hearts*, 174.
186. Holm, *Strong Hearts*, 169–183; Carroll, *Medicine Bags*, 163–172.
187. Josephy, Nagel, and Johnson, eds., *Red Power*, 22–26.
188. Quoted in Collier, "Salmon Fishing in America," 44.
189. Fixico, "Foreword," in *The American Indian Occupation of Alcatraz Island*, xi.
190. Nagel, *American Indian Ethnic Renewal*, 131–141, 163–175, and 187–233; Nagel, "American Indian Ethnic Renewal," 958–961; Smith and Warrior, *Like a Hurricane*, 88–93; Johnson, Champagne, Nagel, "American Indian Activism and Transformation," 301–310. For examples of cultural

renewal, see Johnson, *Alcatraz: Indian Land Forever*; Johnson, *You Are on Indian Land*; Rader, *Engaged Resistance*, 7–46; Johnson, Nagel, Champagne, *American Indian Activism*.

191. Johnson, Nagel, and Champagne, "American Indian Activism and Transformation," 292.

192. Cornell, *Return of the Native*, 180.

193. The federal government took no punitive action to bring the Alcatraz occupation to an end; it responded to the occupation of the BIA headquarters in Washington, DC, with a policy of appeasement; and ruled out the use of force to bring the occupation of Wounded Knee to a halt. Although the FBI had begun to target AIM by late 1972, the Nixon and Ford administrations stayed committed to sponsoring legislation to advance Indigenous rights. Kotlowski, "Alcatraz, Wounded Knee, and Beyond," 201–227; Castile, *To Show Heart*; Castile, *Taking Charge*.

194. Johnson, Nagel, and Champagne, "American Indian Activism and Transformation," 305ff.

195. Brave Bird, *Lakota Woman*, 75f; Crow Dog, *Crow Dog*, 159f.

196. Baylor, "Modern Warriors," iii–iv.

197. Nagel, *American Indian Ethnic Renewal*, 163–175.

198. Fixico, *Indian Resilience*, 124–125, quote p. 124.

199. Herzberg, *The Search for an American Indian Identity*.

200. Cowger, *The National Congress of American Indians*.

201. Shreve, *Red Power Rising*; Smith, *Hippies, Indians, and the Fight for Red Power*.

202. For the political dimensions of Red Power nationalism, see Shreve, *Red Power Rising*, 6–15.

For cultural nationalism, see Hutchinson, *The Dynamics of Cultural Nationalism*; Hutchinson, "Cultural Nationalism," 75–94.

203. Sneider, "Complementary Relationships," 64.

204. Sneider, "Complementary Relationships," 65.

205. Nagel, "Masculinity and Nationalism," 247–248.

206. Sneider, "Complementary Relationships," 65.

207. Sneider, "Complementary Relationships," 65.

208. Sneider, "Complementary Relationships," 65.

209. Hutchinson, *Dynamics of Cultural Nationalism*, 9, 12–21; Hutchinson, "Cultural Nationalism," 75, 83.

210. Hutchinson, *Dynamics of Cultural Nationalism*, 16; Hutchinson, "Cultural Nationalism," 83.

211. Hutchinson, *Dynamics of Cultural Nationalism*, 8–10, 12–21.

212. Hutchinson, "Cultural Nationalism," 75.
213. Hutchinson, *Dynamics of Cultural Nationalism*, 9, 14.
214. Hutchinson, *Dynamics of Cultural Nationalism*, 9–10, 12–21; Hutchinson, *Dynamics of Cultural Nationalism*, 91.
215. Hutchinson, "Cultural Nationalism," 87.
216. Kelly, *The Rhetoric of Red Power*, 16.
217. Bruyneel, *Third Space of Sovereignty*, 123–169.
218. Deloria, *Custer Died for Your Sins*, 180–181.
219. For an in-depth analysis, see Deloria, *Custer Died for Your Sins*, 169–195; Bruyneel, *Third Space of Sovereignty*, 134–169. See also Martinez, *Life of the Indigenenous Mind*.
220. Bruyneel, *Third Space of Sovereignty*, 149.
221. Bruyneel, *Third Space of Sovereignty*, 147–159.
222. Bruyneel, *Third Space of Sovereignty*, 150–153.
223. Kelly, *Rhetoric of Red Power*, 70–78.
224. Kelly, *Rhetoric of Red Power*, 76–78.
225. Scholars stress the fuzziness of the concept of Black Power yet highlight the Black Panthers' nationalist separatist agenda. See Van Deburg, *New Day in Babylon*, 11–28; Ogbar, *Black Power*, 3–4. For the argument and theory of Black Power politics, see Carmichael and Hamilton, *Black Power*.
226. Kelly, *Rhetoric of Red Power*, 77.
227. Nagel and Clark, "White Men," 111; Nagel, "Nation," 398–399.
228. Hixon, *American Settler Colonialism*, 10; Brunyeel, *Third Space of Sovereignty*, 8.

## Chapter 2. From Powerlessness to Protest: Reinventing Indigenous Men in AIM, 1968–1972

1. Means, "I Wanna Wear That Uniform."
2. Means, "I Wanna Wear That Uniform."
3. Means, "I Wanna Wear That Uniform."
4. Connell, *Masculinities*, 110.
5. Morgan, "Class and Masculinity," 169.
6. Beynon, *Masculinities and Culture*, 20, 19–23.
7. Pyke, "Class-Based Masculinities, 544–545.
8. Pyke, "Class-based Masculinities," 531–533.
9. Connell, *Masculinities*, 109–112, and 114–118.
10. Connell, *Masculinities*, 116–117.
11. Xaba, "Masculinity and Its Malcontents."

12. Connell, *Masculinities*, 111.
13. Pyke, "Class-based Masculinities," 542.
14. For the Brown Berets, see Chávez, "'Birth of a New Symbol,'" 205–222; Roesch, *Macho Men and Modern Women*. For the Black Panther Party, see Estes, *I Am a Man!*, 153–177. For the Puerto Rican Young Lords, see Nelson, *Women of Color*, 119–120. For an overview of Black manliness in the United States, see hooks, *We Real Cool*.
15. McKegney, *Maculindians*, 4–5, 26; Hokowhitu, "Death of Koro Paka," 115–141.
16. Bell, *Relating Indigenous and Settler Identities*, 28–32.
17. Hokowhitu, "Death of Koro Paka," 134.
18. Hokowhitu, "Death of Koro Paka," 133.
19. Hokowhitu, "Death of Koro Paka," 115.
20. McKegney, *Maculindians*, 1–11.
21. Innes and Anderson, "Introduction," 4, 11; McKegney, *Maculindians*, 4–5.
22. Davis, *Survival Schools*, 6.
23. Clyde Bellecourt quoted in Davis, *Survival Schools*, 35.
24. An unidentified Indigenous activist quoted in Couture, "American Indian Movement," 49–50.
25. Banks, *Ojibwa Warrior*, 62–63. For the names of AIM's founders see Davis, *Survival Schools*, 252n2.
26. Shoemaker, "Urban Indians and Ethnic Choices," 431–447; D'Arcus, "The Urban Geography of Red Power," 1241–1255. See also Brunette, "The Minneapolis Urban Indian Community," 4–15.
27. The given data are those that correspond best with Indigenous estimates. Davis, *Survival Schools*, 21–24.
28. League, *Indians in Minneapolis* (1968).
29. League, *Indians in Minneapolis* (1968), 15ff, 51.
30. Davis, *Survival Schools*, 31–37; Shoemaker, "Urban Indians and Ethnic Choices," 431–447.
31. Grassroots organizing conveyed an empowering message to the entire oppressed Native community, providing them with an ideology of liberation from within. Organizers took people to welfare agencies, employment centers, and courtrooms to advocate for their needs, interests, and rights. They confronted school administrators, teachers, and principals when they felt students and parents were unjustly treated. They provided assistance and counsel to inmates in correctional facilities. Among the initial initiatives of the Twin Cities Native community and AIM were the setup

of Native-controlled institutions such as the American Indian Center, the Legal Rights Center, the Indian Health Board, and the Little Earth Housing Project. These alternative institutions challenged racial discrimination from existent, white-dominated institutions that from the perspective of Native Americans were filled with ignorance and anti-Native sentiment. See Davis, *Survival Schools*, 31–37.

32. Davis, *Survival Schools*, 31–32.

33. Davis, *Survival Schools*, 93–96.

34. About fifty people were involved in AIM at the beginning. They were mostly Ojibwe (67.5%), Sioux (10%), or of another tribal affiliation (10%). This was fairly representative of the Indigenous population of Minneapolis as a whole; there were also a significant number of non-Indigenous persons (16%). The data considers both patrollers and non-patrollers. See Cohen, "Indian Patrol," 20–21, 133.

35. Cohen, "Indian Patrol," 46.

36. Anonymous, "Red Power: The American Indian Movement," *Warpath* 2, no. 2 (March 1969): 12.

37. Davis, *Survival Schools*.

38. AIM objectives sheet reprinted in Cohen, "Indian Patrol," 47.

39. Cohen, "Indian Patrol," 52.

40. Davis, *Survival Schools*, 1–9, 42–51.

41. Davis, *Survival Schools*, 42–51.

42. Banks, *Ojibwa Warrior*, 31.

43. Banks, *Ojibwa Warrior*, 12–57.

44. Bellecourt, *Thunder Before the Storm*, 10, 14–15.

45. Bellecourt, *Thunder Before the Storm*, 16–40.

46. Scott, "Gender," 1067–1075.

47. Nagel, *American Indian Ethnic Renewal*, 113–158.

48. Nagel, *American Indian Ethnic Renewal*, 114.

49. Morgensen, "Cutting to the Roots," 48–49.

50. Innes and Anderson, "Introduction"; Morgensen, "Cutting to the Roots."

51. Adams, *Education for Extinction*, 100–101.

52. Swain, "Masculinities in Education," 213–229.

53. Adams, *Education for Extinction*, 149–150.

54. Adams, *Education for Extinction*, 100–101, 222 (on total institutions); 121–124 (on discipline).

55. Banks *Ojibwa Warrior*, 26.

56. Child, *Boarding School Seasons*, 277.

57. Bellecourt, *Thunder Before the Storm*, 16–17.

58. Pyke, "What Is Internalized Racial Oppression and Why Don't We Study It?," 551–572.
59. Banks, *Ojibwa Warrior*, 28.
60. Pyke, "What Is Internalized Racial Oppression," 557.
61. Barrett, "The Organizational Construction of Hegemonic Masculinity."
62. Holm, "Patriots and Pawns," 346.
63. Personal interview, Dennis Banks.
64. Barrett, "Organizational Construction of Hegemonic Masculinity," 95–97.
65. Barrett, "Organizational Construction of Hegemonic Masculinity," 84–99.
66. Kipp, *Viet Cong*, 36.
67. Banks, *Ojibwa Warrior*, 54.
68. Banks, *Ojibwa Warrior*, 55.
69. Banks, *Ojibwa Warrior*, 54–55.
70. Kipp, *Viet Cong*, 28.
71. Kipp, *Viet Cong*, 35, 28.
72. Kipp, *Viet Cong*, 35, 36.
73. Kipp, *Viet Cong*, 44.
74. Kipp, "The Eagles I Fed Who Did Not Love Me," 211.
75. Holm, *Strong Hearts, Wounded Souls*, 169–183.
76. Westermeyer, "Indian Powerlessness," 46.
77. Westermeyer, "Indian Powerlessness," 46.
78. Kimmel, *Manhood in America*, 191–193.
79. Westermeyer, "Indian Powerlessness," 47f.
80. Davis, *Survival Schools*, 82–91.
81. Westermeyer, "Indian Powerlessness," 45.
82. Westermeyer, "Indian Powerlessness," 45, 46, 47, 50, 51, 52.
83. Westermeyer, "Indian Powerlessness," 51.
84. Westermeyer, "Indian Powerlessness," 51.
85. Westermeyer, "Indian Powerlessness," 45.
86. Westermeyer, "Indian Powerlessness," 51.
87. Fixico, *The Urban Indian Experience*, 97.
88. Bellecourt, *Thunder Before the Storm*, 47.
89. Bellecourt, *Thunder Before the Storm*, 47.
90. Compare Beynon, *Masculinities and Culture*, 19–23.
91. Fixico, *The Urban Indian Experience*, 97.
92. A statistical poll measured the Minneapolis agencies' impressions of

Indigenous adults and youth on a broader basis. A questionnaire employing "semantic differential" pairing of adjectives gave a more comprehensive and collective picture of bureaucracy attitudes toward Indigenous people. The poll was based on 696 respondents from the Departments of Employment, Health, Education, Welfare, Law and Corrections, and others. Woods and Harkins, *Attitudes*, 35–38. See also League, *Indians in Minneapolis* (1968), 45; Westermeyer, "Indian Powerlessness," 51.

93. Woods and Harkins, *Attitudes*, 16–17.

94. Fixico, *Urban Indian Experience*, 86–106.

95. Davis, *Survival Schools*, 31–32, 42–51.

96. For example, see: League, *Indians in Minneapolis* (1968), 28, 93.

97. Minnesota Advisory Committee, *Bridging the Gap*, 63.

98. Minnesota Advisory Committee, *Bridging the Gap*, 60.

99. Minnesota Advisory Committee, *Bridging the Gap*, 60. These numbers are somewhat akin to the findings of another study by the LVW, which stated that although Indigenous people only made up 1.6–2.0 percent of Minneapolis's total population, 11 percent of those sent to the Minneapolis Workhouse were Indigenous men. League, *Indians in Minneapolis* (1968), 2, 49–50.

100. Minnesota Advisory Committee, *Bridging the Gap*, 65–67 (quote on page 65).

101. League, *The Police and the Community*, 16–17 (1971); League, *The Police and the Community: A Second Look*, 14–25 (1976). See also Banks, *Ojibwa Warrior*, 59.

102. The report found that local law enforcement agencies lacked Indigenous personnel, that the system was not sensitive to Indigenous issues, that the white-oriented penal system failed to rehabilitate Indigenous offenders, that local law enforcement agencies differed in their treatment of Indigenous people, and that police had an inadequate complaints system. Minnesota Advisory Committee, *Bridging the Gap*, 60–75, 94–96.

103. Banks, *Ojibwa Warrior*, 59.

104. League, *Indians in Minneapolis* (1968), 49–50; Minnesota Advisory Committee, *Bridging the Gap*, 65–67.

105. Weyler, *Blood of the Land*, 35–36.

106. Piché, "Imprisonment and Indigenous Masculinity"; Tengan, *Native Men*, 11, 61.

107. Piché, "Imprisonment and Indigenous Masculinity"; Tengan, *Native Men*, 11, 61.

108. Morgensen, "Cutting to the Roots," 48–49.

109. Davis, *Survival Schools*, 3–6; Banks, *Ojibwa Warrior*, 60–62; Bellecourt, *Thunder Before the Storm*, 48.
110. Hayes, "Blood Brothers," 80.
111. Messerschmidt, *Masculinities and Crime*, 85.
112. Bonney, "The Role of AIM Leaders in Indian Nationalism," 213.
113. Quoted in Davis, *Survival Schools*, 45.
114. Quoted in Mencarelli and Severin, *Protest*, 146.
115. Quoted in Davis, *Survival Schools*, 46.
116. Davis, *Survival Schools*, 45–47, 50–51; Bellecourt, *Thunder Before the Storm*, 36–43.
117. Personal interview, Clyde Bellecourt.
118. Quoted in Mencarelli and Severin, *Protest*, 146.
119. See Bellecourt quote in Davis, *Survival Schools*, 47.
120. Zimmerman, *Airlift*, 117.
121. Zimmerman, *Airlift*, 118.
122. Banks, *Ojibwa Warrior*, 58–59.
123. Bonney, "The Role of AIM Leaders in Indian Nationalism," 213.
124. Sabo and Kupers, "Gender and the Politics of Punishment," 5ff.
125. Adams, *Education for Extinction*, 21–24; Barrett, "Organizational Construction of Hegemonic Masculinity," 80; Piché, "Imprisonment and Indigenous Masculinity," 198–202.
126. Fixico, *Termination and Relocation*, ix–xiv; Fixico, *Urban Indian Experience*, 2–7, 173–189.
127. Davis, *Survival Schools*, 42–51, Voigt, "Between Powerlessness and Protest," 221–241.
128. James G. Abourezk Papers, Dennis Banks, interviewed by James Abourezk, July 20, 1980, transcript, 26, Archives and Special Collections, University Libraries, University of South Dakota, Vermillion, SD.
129. Anderson and Innes, *Indigenous Men and Masculinities*, 11.
130. Mihesuah, *Indigenous American Women*, 163–171. See also Castle, "Black and Native American Women's Activism," 86, 96; Jaimes and Halsey, "American Indian Women," 332.
131. Innes and Anderson, "Introduction," 10–11.
132. Davis, *Survival Schools*, 37–51, quote on page 37.
133. Bonney, "Role of AIM Leaders," 213.
134. Bonney, "Role of AIM Leaders," 214.
135. McDowell, Rootham, and Hardgrove, "Precarious Work, Protest Masculinity, and Communal Regulation," 847–864; Peteet, "Male Gender and Rituals of Resistance," 31–49.

136. Innes and Anderson, *Indigenous Men and Masculinities*, 4–17.
137. Fixico, *Indian Resilience*, 6–7.
138. Personal interview, Dennis Banks.
139. Banks, *Ojibwa Warrior*, 60–61; Bellecourt, *Thunder Before the Storm*, 29–47.
140. Fixico, *Urban Indian Experience*, 3–7.
141. Fixico, *Indian Resilience*, 6.
142. Bonney, "Role of AIM Leaders," 213; Bellecourt, *Thunder Before the Storm*, 49; Banks, *Ojibwa Warrior*, 61.
143. Two reports by League of Women Voters (1968; 1971) observed that a high number of Indigenous people were charged with misdemeanors, drunkenness, vagrancy, simple assault, and traffic offenses. A follow-up report by the LVW (March 1976) indicted that Indigenous people were frequently charged with public profanity and breach of peace offenses when reacting to insults and abuse from police. The 1976 report also pointed out that police recognized cultural differences, by endorsed different standards of treatment. See League, *Indians in Minneapolis* (1968), 49–54; League, *Police and the Community* (March 1971), 12–13,16; League, *Police and the Community, A Second Look* (March 1976), 14–15. See also Minnesota Advisory Committee, *Bridging the Gap*, 63.
144. Minnesota Advisory Committee, *Bridging the Gap*, 65–67.
145. League, *Indians in Minneapolis* (1968), 49–54.
146. Banks, *Ojibwa Warrior*, 59.
147. Quoted from *A Good Day to Die*.
148. League, *Indians In Minneapolis* (1968), 49–54. League, *Police and the Community* (1971), 16.
149. For a discussion, see Davis, *Survival Schools*, 31–32, 256–257n35); Banks, *Ojibwa Warrior*, 59.
150. Personal interview, Pat Bellanger, June 20, 2013
151. League, *Indians in Minneapolis* (1968), 52; League, *Police and the Community* (1971), 16. See also Davis, *Survival Schools*, 31–32.
152. League, *Police and the Community*, 12–13 (quote page 13).
153. Dick Cunningham, "Student Patrol Fights for Indians in Court," *Minneapolis Tribune*, May 11, 1967.
154. Couture, *American Indian Movement*, 28–29; personal interview, Pat Bellanger, June 24, 2013.
155. Bellecourt, *Thunder Before the Storm*, 50.
156. Couture, *American Indian Movement*, 58.
157. Couture, *American Indian Movement*, 58.

158. Estes, *I Am a Man!*, 153–177; Wendt, "'They Finally Found Out that We Really Are Men,'" 553–559; Ogbar, *Black Power*, 86–87, 100, 107.

159. Estes, *I Am a Man!*, 156ff; Ogbar, *Black Power*, 86–87.

160. Wendt, "They Finally Found Out That We Really Are Men," 557.

161. Ogbar, *Black Power*, 100.

162. Wendt, "'They Finally Found Out that We Really Are Men,'" 557.

163. Van Deburg, *New Day in Babylon*, 158–159.

164. Brian Anderson, "Indian Patrol's First Night Quiet," *Minneapolis Tribune*, August 25, 1968; Cohen, "Indian Patrol," 780.

165. See Cohen, "Indian Patrol," 55–118; Cohen, "Indian Patrol in Minneapolis: Social Control and Change"; Cohen, "The American Indian Movement and the Anthropologist."

166. Cohen, "Indian Patrol," 49.

167. Banks, *Ojibwa Warrior*, 63; Means, *Where White Men Fear to Tread*, 163.

168. Banks, *Ojibwa Warrior*, 63; Means, *Where White Men Fear to Tread*, 163.

169. Davis, *Survival Schools*, 31–32.

170. AIM gained considerable news media coverage from the *Minneapolis Tribune* and the *Minneapolis Star*. Between 1968 and 1969, the newspapers featured a total of twenty-three articles on police brutality against Indigenous people, of which only three did not directly refer to AIM. The newspapers reported sympathetically on AIM, framing police brutality and the Indian Patrol mostly around civil rights rather than militancy. Birong, "The Influence of Police Brutality on the American Indian Movement's Establishment in Minneapolis, 1968–1969," 79–85.

171. Harold GoodSky interview in: Cohen, "Indian Patrol," 72.

172. Molly Ivins, "Indian Group's 1$^{st}$ Anniversary Called 'Miracle,'" *Minneapolis Tribune*, March 3, 1969.

173. Cohen, "Indian Patrol," 121.

174. Cohen, "Indian Patrol," 196.

175. Cohen, "Indian Patrol," 194ff, 230ff; League, *Police and the Community*, 17.

176. Cohen, "Indian Patrol," 201–204.

177. Cohen, "Indian Patrol," 205–208; League, *Police and the Community*, 17.

178. Cohen, "Indian Patrol," 209–210; Harold GoodSky interview in Cohen, "Indian Patrol," 72; League, *Police and the Community*, 17; Means, *Where White Men Fear to Tread*, 163–164.

179. Cohen, "Indian Patrol," 208–209.

180. Cohen, "Indian Patrol," 121; Cohen, "The Indian Patrol in Minneapolis," 779.

181. Cohen, "Indian Patrol," 224.

182. AIM's claim of twenty-two arrest-free weekends following the start of the patrol is hard to substantiate. Indian Patrollers took drunk people off the street, thereby eliminating this need for arrests. Police officers avoided some of the Indigenous neighborhoods in order to reduce confrontations with Indian Patrollers. Further, police continued to make arrests, many in nonpublic areas (for a discussion, see Cohen, "Indian Patrol," 212–218). However, a report by the league found an improvement of Indigenous-police relations (League, *Police and the Community*, 17). See also Banks, *Ojibwa Warrior*, 64; Banks, "The Black Scholar Interviews: Dennis Banks," 29–30; Bellecourt, *Thunder Before the Storm*, 56ff; Pacifica Radio Archives, "Carter Camp, History and Philosophy of AIM."

183. Cohen, "Indian Patrol," 225–226.

184. Pacifica Radio Archives, "Carter Camp, History and Philosophy of AIM."

185. Cohen, "Indian Patrol," 49. This does not obscure the fact that throughout the organization's existence, a significant number of its members and supporters remained non-Indigenous.

186. Edgar R. Trexler, "Lutherans and American Indians: A Confrontation," in *Christian Century*, September 16, 1970, 1103–1105.

187. Vine Deloria, *God Is Red*, 47–48.

188. For a discussion of the various contributions to AIM see: Davis, *Survival Schools*, 102–103, 105–106, 113, 153, 180, 183–185, 192. Dewing, *Wounded Knee II*, 21–24, 29; Trimbach and Trimbach, *American Indian Mafia*, 60.

189. For an overview, see Davis, *Survival Schools*, 53–97.

190. Davis, *Survival Schools*, 93–96.

191. Davis, *Survival Schools*, 67–91.

192. Davis, *Survival Schools*, 130–168.

193. Davis, *Survival Schools*, 140–145.

194. Davis, *Survival Schools*, 130–145.

195. Erll, *Memory in Culture*, 95–112.

196. Davis, *Survival Schools*, 127–172.

197. Davis, *Survival Schools*, 142–145.

198. Davis, *Survival Schools*, 127–172.

199. Quoted from Matthiessen, *In the Spirit of Crazy Horse*, 36. Journalist Peter Matthiessen's book should be read with caution due to its multiple factual errors surrounding chronology, places, names, and incidents.

200. Davis, *Survival Schools*, 137.

201. Banks, *Ojibwa Warrior*, 28.

202. Davis, *Survival Schools*, 145–146.
203. Bonney, "The Role of AIM Leaders," 212–214, 220.
204. John E. Peterson, "Indian Revolt Financed by Government Grant," *Detroit News*, March 25, 1973; Davis, *Survival Schools*, 153f; personal interview, Sonja Schiele.
205. Davis, *Survival Schools*, 154; Schierle, *Funktion einer Survival School*, 139f.
206. Schierle, *Funktion einer Survival School*, 131; personal interview, Sonja Schierle.
207. Davis, *Survival Schools*, 155.
208. Davis, *Survival Schools*, 142–151, 158–168; Bellecourt, *Thunder Before the Storm*, 108.
209. Davis, *Survival Schools*, 154–157.

## Chapter 3. "We Became Warriors Again": Recasting Race, Gender, and Nation, 1970–1973

1. Kipp, *Viet Cong*, 95–106.
2. Burnette and Koster, *The Road to Wounded Knee*, 47.
3. William Blair, "500 Indians Seize U.S. Building After Scuffle with Capital Police," *New York Times*, November 2, 1972.
4. Crow Dog, *Crow Dog*, 173–175; Brave Bird, *Lakota Woman*, 88–90; Banks, *Ojibwa Warrior*, 138–142; Means, *Where White Men Fear to Tread*, 231–234; Burnette and Koster, *Road to Wounded Knee*, 206–215.
5. Kipp, *Viet Cong*, 99–105.
6. Akwesasne Notes, *BIA*.
7. Connell, "Globalization, Imperialism, and Masculinities," 75–77, 78–79, 81.
8. Connell, "Globalization, Imperialism, and Masculinities," 81 (for retraditionalization), 78–79 (for radicalization).
9. Nobbs, "History, Colonisation," 269–273.
10. Cohen, "Indian Patrol," 48; Bonney, "Role of AIM Leaders," 212.
11. Bonney, "Role of AIM Leaders," 213.
12. See Bonney, "Role of AIM Leaders," 215.
13. Means, *Where White Men Fear to Tread*, 152–153.
14. Weyler, *Blood of the Land*, 42.
15. James G. Abourezk Papers, Russell Means, interviewed by James Abourezk, May 7, 1991, transcript, 17, Archives and Special Collections, University Libraries, University of South Dakota, Vermillion, South Dakota.

16. Means, *Where White Men Fear to Tread*, 148.
17. Russell Means interviewed by James Abourezk, 21.
18. Means, *Where White Men Fear to Tread*, 153. For a comparable experience, see Bellecourt, "Penthouse Interview: Vernon Bellecourt," 59.
19. Banks, *Ojibwa Warrior*, 95.
20. Crow Dog, *Crow Dog*, 163–165; Banks, *Ojibwa Warrior*, 95–104.
21. Crow Dog, *Crow Dog*, 159–168; Banks, *Ojibwa Warrior*, 95–104.
22. Crow Dog, *Crow Dog*, 164; Johnson, Nagel, Champagne, "American Indian Activism and Transformation," 284–292.
23. Crow Dog, *Crow Dog*, 159, 164.
24. Bellecourt, "Birth of AIM," 376.
25. Reinhardt, *Ruling Pine Ridge*, 159.
26. Reinhardt, *Ruling Pine Ridge*, 160.
27. Reinhardt, *Ruling Pine Ridge*, 160. Dennis Banks quoted in Crow Dog, *Crow Dog*, 177.
28. Reinhardt, *Ruling Pine Ridge*, 159–163, 164–188.
29. Baylor, "Modern Warriors," 72–128.
30. Crow Dog, *Lakota Woman*, 79–80.
31. Reinhardt, *Ruling Pine Ridge*, 159–163.
32. Crow Dog, *Crow Dog*, 164.
33. Crow Dog, *Crow Dog*, 164.
34. Busacca, *Seeking Self-Determination*, 65–69, 113–114.
35. Bellecourt, *Thunder Before the Storm*, 94.
36. Bellecourt, *Thunder Before the Storm*, 94.
37. Baylor, "Modern Warriors," III.
38. Tim Giago, "Mount Rushmore Seen Through Native Eyes," *Huffington Post*, May 25, 2011.
39. Lame Deer, *Lame Deer, Seeker of Visions*, 91.
40. Banks, *Oijbwa Warrior*, 110.
41. Schwarz, *Fighting Colonialism*, 24–25.
42. CBS News Segment, September 2, 1970.
43. Banks, *Ojibwa Warrior*, 111–113; Means, *Where White Men Fear to Tread*, 174–178; Anonymous: "Mourning Indians Dump Sand on Plymouth Rock," *New York Times*, November 26, 1970.
44. Bellecourt, *Thunder Before the Storm*, 94.
45. Nagel, *American Indian Ethnic Renewal*, 130–141, 190–212.
46. Studi, "Conversations with Wes Studi."
47. For a comparative, Hawaiian perspective, see Tengan, "Re-Membering Panala'au," 42f.

48. Personal interview, Clyde Bellecourt.

49. Cornell, *Return of the Native*, 139.

50. Lee, "Singing for People," 61–74; Johnson, "We Were All Wounded at Wounded Knee," 92–106.

51. According to CBC News, Sainte-Marie is not from the Piapot First Nation in Saskatchewan, Canada, but was born to a white couple in Boston, Massachusetts. Apparently, Sainte-Marie has been falsely claiming Indigenous ancestry for decades and utilized those claims to take opportunities and honors for herself that instead belong to First Nations, Inuit, and Métis people. While Sainte-Marie's Indigenous heritage is dubious, her support for Native Americans seems to be authentic. Geoff Leo, Roxanna Woloshyn, and Linda Guerriero, "Who Is the Real Buffy Sainte-Marie?", CBC News October 27, 2023, https://www.cbc.ca/newsinteractives/features/buffy-sainte-marie (last accessed January 28, 2024).

52. Rader, *Engaged Resistance*. See also Kim, "We Have Always Had Many Voices," 271–301.

53. Bonney, "Role of AIM Leaders," 218–222.

54. Cohen, "Indian Patrol," 46, 48.

55. Bonney, "Role of AIM Leaders," 218.

56. Smith and Warrior, *Like a Hurricane*, 127.

57. Bonney, "Role of AIM Leaders," 218–219; Kelly, *Rhetoric of Red Power*, 16–17.

58. Kipp, *Viet Cong*, 97.

59. Kolst, "National Symbols as Signs of Unity and Division," 676–701.

60. Connell, "Globalization, Imperialism, and Masculinities," 81.

61. Richard Gibson, "AIM Digs in Against 'the System,'" *Minneapolis Tribune*, October 16, 1971.

62. Young Bear and Theisz, *Standing in the Light*, 155–157; Means, *Where White Men Fear to Tread*, 197; Banks, *Ojibwa Warrior*, 118.

63. Means, *Where White Men Fear to Tread*, 197; Means, "Raymond Yellow Thunder," 229–231.

64. Means, "Raymond Yellow Thunder," 229–230. See also Means, *Where White Men Fear to Tread*, 197.

65. Busacca, *Seeking Self-Determination*, 113.

66. Young Bear, *Standing in the Light*, 155–157; Banks, *Ojibwa Warrior*, 118.

67. Young Bear, *Standing in the Light*, 157.

68. Young Bear, *Standing in the Light*, 156.

69. Johnson, *We Hold the Rock*, 9.

70. Valaskakis, *Indian Country*, 43.
71. Nagel, *American Indian Ethnic Renewal*, 191.
72. Akwesasne Notes, *BIA*, 26.
73. Kipp, *Viet Cong*, 99.
74. Crow Dog, *Lakota Woman*, 76f.
75. Compare with the Black civil rights movement: Wendt, "They Finally Found Out That We Really Are Men," 543–564.
76. Busacca, *Seeking Self-Determination*, 106–108.
77. Busacca, *Seeking Self-Determination*, 70–71, 107–108; Cornell, *Return of the Native*, 154.
78. Kipp, "The Eagles I Fed Who Did Not Love Me," 218.
79. Scholars have explored some connections between AIM and the BPP. See Jeffries, Dyson, and Jones, "Militancy Transcends Race," 4–30; Siddons, "Red Power and the Black Panther," 2–31; Castle, "Black and Native American Women's Activism"; Churchill and Vander Wall, *Agents of Repression*; Cronin, "The American Indian Movement and the Black Panther Party Compared"; Chastang, "Reclaiming Identity"; Karua, "Black and Native Visions of Self-determination," 77–98.
80. Nagel, *American Indian Ethnic Renewal*, 130–131.
81. Kelly, *The Rhetoric of Red Power*, 70–78.
82. Siddons, "Red Power and the Black Panther," 2–31.
83. Chastang, *Reclaiming Identity*, 107ff.
84. Couture, *American Indian Movement*, 58; personal interview, Pat Bellanger, June 24, 2013; personal interview, Dennis Banks.
85. Akwesasne Notes, *BIA*, 15; Akwesasne Notes, *Voices*, 97.
86. Nagel, *American Indian Ethnic Renewal*, 130; Siddons, "Red Power and the Black Panther," 2–31.
87. Bellecourt, *Thunder Before the Storm*, 49.
88. Bellecourt, *Thunder Before the Storm*, 49–50.
89. Davis, *Survival Schools*, 42–51.
90. Bonney, "The Role of AIM Leaders," 213, 220–222.
91. Burnette and Koster, *Road to Wounded Knee*, 209.
92. Fowler, *Shared Symbols, Contested Meanings*, 192.
93. Bonney, "The Role of AIM Leaders," 220–222.
94. Busacca, *Seeking Self-Determination*, 58, 202.
95. Smith and Warrior, *Like a Hurricane*, 138.
96. Dewing, *Wounded Knee II*, 29; Bonney, "Role of AIM Leaders," 220–222.
97. Littlemoon, *They Called Me Uncivilized*, 71–72.

98. Littlemoon, *They Called Me Uncivilized*, 71–78.
99. Littlemoon, *They Called Me Uncivilized*, 73–78.
100. Mihesuah, *Indigenous American Women*, 81–112.
101. Dewing, *Wounded Knee II*, 29.
102. Banks, *Ojibwa Warrior*, 63.
103. Banks, *Ojibwa Warrior*, 63; Means, *Where White Men Fear to Tread*, 163; Cohen, "Indian Patrol," 212.
104. Banks, *Ojibwa Warrior*, 63.
105. Banks, *Ojibwa Warrior*, 63–64.
106. Banks, *Ojibwa Warrior*, 116, 121–125; Means, *Where White Men Fear to Tread*, 211–212; 217–218; Burnette and Koster, *Road to Wounded Knee*, 197.
107. Wendt, "They Finally Found Out that We Really Are Men," 544.
108. Wendt, "They Finally Found Out that We Really Are Men," 544, 553, 559, quote on p. 553.
109. Wendt, "They Finally Found Out that We Really Are Men," 553–559.
110. Wideman, "Russell Means," 70.
111. Wideman, "Russell Means," 70.
112. Wideman, "Russell Means," 70.
113. Means, *Where White Men Fear to Tread*, 217.
114. A case in point are the connections between Indigenous and Welsh nationalists that began after 1973. Rennard, "Cyd-Safiad (Standing Together)"; Rennard, "We're Still Here," 167–182; Rennard, "Becoming Indigenous."
115. Cohen, "Indian Patrol," 48.
116. Personal interview, Pat Bellanger, June 20, 2013.
117. Huck, "Renegates: The Second Battle of Wounded Knee," 6.
118. Studi, "Conversations with Wes Studi."
119. Late 1971 through summer 1972 saw the violent deaths of Bunky Ferris (Hoopa), Raymond Yellow Thunder (Oglala Lakota), Leroy Shenandoah (Onondaga), Philip Celaya (Papago), and Richard Oakes (Mohawk). They were all victims of racial violence. Another Indigenous man, Elijah Leaureaux (Ojibwe), ended up dead after an argument with a white man. In early 1971, Hank Adams (Sioux Assiniboine) was shot and seriously wounded by a white assailant. See Burnette and Koster, *Road to Wounded Knee*, 135–139.
120. Deloria, *Behind the Trail of Broken Treaties*, 46; Crow Dog, *Crow Dog*, 171; Crow Dog, *Lakota Woman*, 83ff.
121. Banks, *Ojibwa Warrior*, 116. Magnuson, *Raymond Yellow Thunder*, 136.

122. Magnuson, *Raymond Yellow Thunder*, 139.

123. Banks, *Ojibwa Warrior*, 116.

124. Banks, *Ojibwa Warrior*, 116.

125. Means, *Where White Men Fear to Tread*, 215–218.

126. Vizenor, *Tribal Scenes*, 54. For the incident, see also Deloria, *Behind the Trail of Broken Treaties*, 44–45; Vizenor, "Dennis at Wounded Knee," 57; Vizenor, *The People Named the Chippewa*, 35.

127. Banks, *Ojibwa Warrior*, 121–125.

128. Anonymous: "AIM to Take No More Abuse from Any One," *Shannon County News*, May 19, 1972, 1, 6.

129. Burnette and Koster, *Road to Wounded Knee*, 197.

130. Means, *Where White Men Fear to Tread*, 211–212; Burnette and Koster, *Road to Wounded Knee*, 197.

131. Engle, *Thunder on the Prairie*, 57.

132. Kipp, *Viet Cong*, 102; James G. Abourezk Papers, John Trudell, interviewed by James Abourezk, July 18, 1980, transcript, 24–28, Archives and Special Collections, University Libraries, University of South Dakota, Vermillion, South Dakota; personal interview, Laura Waterman Wittstock.

133. Chris Bald Eagle interviewed by Reine Kram and Karen Northcott, April 7, 1974, transcript, signature 152.B11.2F, box 3, Wounded Knee Legal Defense/ Offense Records, Minnesota Historical Society Manuscripts Collection; Bernice White Hawk interviewed by Karen Nortcott, June 1976, transcript, signature 152.B11.3B, box 3, WKLDOC Records, MHSMC.

134. Means, *Where White Men Fear to Tread*, 240, 247–248.

135. J. L. Schmidt: "Firebombing, Militants Linked," *Scottsbluff Star-Herald*, January 16, 1972; Joyce Ware, "Court Binds over Five Men," *Scottsbluff Star-Herald*, January 19, 1973; J. L. Schmidt, "Justice Department Official Heads for SB," *Scottsbluff Star-Herald*, January 16, 1972.

136. Chris Bald Eagle interview; Bernice White Hawk interview.

137. Lorelei Means interviewed by Gail, March 31, 1974, transcript, signature 152.B11.2F, box 3, WKLDOC Records, MHSMC; Griffin Film transcript, film indexes, signature 152.B.11.3B, box 3, WKLDOC Records, MHSMC.

138. Crow Dog, *Crow Dog*, 166; Magnuson, *Raymond Yellow Thunder*, 138.

139. Means, *Where White Men Fear to Tread*, 209–212; Banks, *Ojibwa Warrior*, 121–125.

140. Weston, *Native Americans in the News*, 136–146.

141. Baylor, "Media Framing," 241.

142. Baylor, "Media Framing," 241.
143. Burnette and Koster, *Road to Wounded Knee*, 196–197.
144. Dennis Banks, "A Composite Speech Taken from the Narrative of 'The Longest War' by Dennis Banks," in Akard, *Wocante Tinza*, 183.
145. Bonney, "Role of AIM Leaders," 214.
146. Baylor, "Modern Warriors," III.
147. Castile, *To Show Heart*, 117–146.
148. Burnette and Koster, *Road to Wounded Knee*, 202.
149. Baylor, "Modern Warriors," 206.
150. Heppler, *Framing Red Power*, 7.
151. Crow Dog, *Lakota Woman*, 88.
152. Crow Dog, *Lakota Woman*, 88.
153. Baylor, "Modern Warriors," 179–182, 187; Busacca, *Seeking Self-Determination*, 2, 89, 96–98, 136–148; Richardson, *Constructing Two Cultural Realities*, 177–180; Butler, *Check Your Local Listings*, 219–228; Bruce D'Arcus, *The Wounded Knee Occupation*.
154. Baylor, "Media Framing," 244.
155. Baylor, "Media Framing," 249.
156. Baylor, "Media Framing," 244.
157. Schwarz, *Fighting Colonialism*, 25.
158. Deloria, *Playing Indian*. See also Nagel and Clark, "White Men, Red Masks," 112–126; King, *Unsettling America*, 27–42.
159. Clark and Nagel, "White Men, Red Masks," III, 125–126. Tengan and Markham, "Performing Polynesian Masculinities in Football."
160. Schwarz, *Fighting Colonialism*, 9, 13.
161. Baylor, "Modern Warriors," 179; Baylor, "Media Framing," 244–245; Schwarz, *Fighting Colonialism*, 25–28.
162. Baylor, "Modern Warriors," 179; Baylor, "Media Framing," 244.
163. Baylor, "Media Framing," 248–251; Baylor, "Modern Warriors," 190.
164. Usbeck, "Selling the Natural-Born Warrior." See also Schwarz, *Fighting Colonialism*, 25ff.
165. Gerald Vizenor recounts one incident in 1972 when AIM leaders barred an Indigenous woman, Bonnie Wallace (Ojibwe) from a room with television news reporters, because "the militants did not want her light face tones shown on television news reports." See Vizenor, *The Everlasting Sky*, 56.
166. Schwarz, *Fighting Colonialism*, 16.
167. Bonney, "Role of AIM Leaders," 212–214; Davis, *Survival Schools*, 42–51.

168. Bonney, "Role of AIM Leaders," 214–222.

169. Castile, *To Show Heart*, 117–146; Busacca, *Seeking Self-Determination*, 10, 88–135; Brady, "The Occupation of Wounded Knee," 17–31; Heppler, *Framing Red Power*, 73.

170. Schwarz, *Fighting Colonialism*, 16.

171. Crow Dog, *Lakota Woman*, 76f.

172. Reeser, *Masculinities in Theory*, 81–90.

173. Busacca, *Seeking Self-Determination*, 96–98.

174. Vasalakis, *Indian Country*, 39ff.

175. Smith and Warrior, *Like a Hurricane*, 138.

176. Border town civil rights activism occurred from late February through May 1972 as well as from late January through late February 1973.

177. Reinhardt, *Ruling Pine Ridge*, 159–163.

178. Hixon, *American Settler Colonialism*, 113–165, 185–200. For ongoing struggles, see Dewing, *Wounded Knee II*, 1–36; Hammer, "Race and Perception," 29–30, 33–34.

179. Bell, *Relating Indigenous and Settler Identities*, 25–57; Veracini, *Settler Colonialism*, 104ff.

180. Lazarus, *Black Hills*; Grua, *Surviving Wounded Knee*; Ostler, *The Lakotas and the Black Hills*.

181. Reinhardt, *Ruling Pine Ridge*, 146–150; Dewing, *Wounded Knee II*, 29–34; Magnuson, *Raymond Yellow Thunder*, 129–156; Engle, "Thunder on the Prairie," 42–69; Hammer, "Race and Perception."

182. Dewing, *Wounded Knee II*, 40–46.

183. For a brief overview of these confrontations see Dewing, *Wounded Knee II*, 37–51.

184. Estes, "Border Towns, Colonial Logics of Violence"; Estes, "Common Sense Anti-Indianism: Border Town Violence in Rapid City, S.D."

185. For photos of these signs, see Crow Dog, *Lakota Woman*, 43–50, 60–61, 79–81; Means, *Where White Men Fear to Tread*, 196–197, 239–242.

186. For a definition of anti-Indianism, see Cook-Lynn, *Anti-Indianism in Modern America*, X.

187. For South Dakota, see McEldowney, *Where We're At*; South Dakota Advisory Committee, *Liberty and Justice for All*; South Dakota Advisory Committee, *Native Americans in South Dakota*. For Nebraska, see Mason, "You Can Only Kick So Long," 70–76. For Montana, North Dakota, and South Dakota, see Montana-North Dakota-South Dakota Joint Advisory Committee, *Indian Civil Rights Issues*.

188. Innes and Anderson, "Introduction," 5ff.

189. Reinhardt, *Ruling Pine Ridge*, 126–129; Magnuson, *Raymond Yellow Thunder*, 11–24, 37–61.

190. Anonymous, "Protest Autopsy of Indian," *Sioux City Journal*, March 9, 1972.

191. Sam Thorson, "Autopsy Shows Slain Indian Not Mutilated," *Lincoln Star*, March 10, 1972; Anonymous, "Indian's Body Not Mutilated," *Omaha World Herald*, March 10, 1972; Anonymous, "Second Autopsy Shows First Report Accurate," *Scottsbluff Star-Herald*, March 10, 1972.

192. Anonymous, "Gordon Brothers Sent to State Penal Complex," *Scottsbluff Star-Herald*, August 26, 1972.

193. For balanced views read Dewing, *Wounded Knee II*, 29–33; Reinhardt, *Ruling Pine Ridge*, 126–129; Warrior and Smith, *Like a Hurricane*, 112–126. For a major discussion of the distortions, see Magnuson, *Raymond Yellow Thunder*, 155.

194. Anonymous, "Sheridan County Attorney Refutes Rumors on Indian's Death," *Scottsbluff-Star Herald*, March 4, 1972.

195. Anonymous, "Yellow Thunder Death 'Example of Racism,'" *Omaha World-Herald*, March 4, 1972.

196. Magnuson, *Raymond Yellow Thunder*, 135ff.

197. Magnuson, *Raymond Yellow Thunder*, 137.

198. Ed Meagher, "Death of Yellow Cloud [sic] Stirs Sioux to Join Militants in Battle," *LA Times*, March 20, 1972.

199. Meagher, "Death of Yellow Cloud."

200. Richard LaCourse, "Part I: Yellow Thunder, Violent Death of a Silent Man"; Richard LaCourse, "Part II: Boycott as a Human Rights Tool"; Richard LaCourse, "Part III: Sensitizing the Community," undated, in Stanley Lyman Papers, box 4, folder 16, Marriott Library, University of Utah, Salt Lake City, UT.

201. LaCourse, "Part II: Boycott as a Human Rights Tool."

202. Magnuson, *Raymond Yellow Thunder*, 139–146.

203. Magnuson, *Raymond Yellow Thunder*, 153f.

204. Banks, *Ojibwa Warrior*, 116; Crow Dog, *Crow Dog*, 165; Ed Meagher, "Death of Yellow Cloud [sic] Stirs Sioux to Join Militants in Battle," *LA Times*, March 20, 1972.

205. Anonymous, "Tears for Crazy Horse," *Shannon County News*, March 17, 1972, 8.

206. Young Bear, *Standing in the Light*, 155–157; Means, *Where White Men Fear to Tread*, 197; Banks, *Ojibwa Warrior*, 118.

207. LaCourse, "Part III: Sensitizing the Community."

208. See *The FBI Files On The American Indian Movement And Wounded Knee*, ed. Rolland Dewing (Frederick, MD: University Publications of America, 1986), File 100-462483, Volume 13-Bulky Part 2, 1973 (192 pp), Reel 7, 36–47, 83–65; Anonymous, "Red Ribbon and all Indian Grand Jury," *Shannon County News*, March 17, 1972, 6; Means, *Where White Men Fear to Tread*, 204–208; Banks, *Ojibwa Warrior*, 117–118.

209. Quoted in Weyler, *Blood of the Land*, 49.

210. Crow Dog, *Crow Dog*, 168.

211. Nagel and Clark, "White Men, Red Masks," 111; Nagel, "Nation," 398–399.

212. Means, *Where White Men Fear to Tread*, 197–198; Banks, *Ojibwa Warrior*, 117; Crow Dog, *Lakota Woman*, 80–82. For theoretical discussions see Nagel, "Masculinity and Nationalism," 248–261; Nagel, "Nation," 401–408.

213. White resistance to the Indigenous Rights Struggle in the American West paralleled the Black civil rights struggle in the Deep South. Estes, *I Am a Man!*, 39–59, see particularly pages 46–48.

214. Estes, *I Am a Man!*, 40.

215. Estes, *I Am a Man!*, 40–41. The various social movements for change—the civil rights movement, women's movement, gay liberation, and Indigenous activism, among others—provided a front assault on the traditional way white men had defined their manhood; see Kimmel, *Manhood in America*, 189–210.

216. Means, *Where White Men Fear to Tread*, 197–198. See also Banks, *Ojibwa Warrior*, 117.

217. McEldowney, *Where We're At*; South Dakota Advisory Committee, *Liberty and Justice for All*.

218. The American Indian Movement regarded South Dakota every bit as racist as the American South. See Means, *Where White Men Fear to Tread*, 195ff, 242f; Banks, *Ojibwa Warrior*, 117ff, 147ff; Crow Dog, *Crow Dog*, 180; Crow Dog, *Lakota Woman*, 116ff; Burnette and Koster, *Road to Wounded Knee*, 135ff.

219. Tim Giago, "The Man Who Saved Rapid City," *Huffington Post*, November 25, 2013.

220. Calvin Kentfield, "A Letter from Rapid City," *New York Times Magazine*, April 15, 1973, 88.

221. Kentfield, "A Letter from Rapid City," 88; Banks, *Ojibwa Warrior*, 147–149; Means, *Where White Men Fear to Tread*, 196–198, 242; Crow Dog, *Lakota Woman*, 80–82.

222. For the most balanced accounts of the Bad Heart Bull case, see

Dewing, *Wounded Knee II*, 40ff; Smith and Warrior, *Like a Hurricane*, 183ff.

223. For a copy of the arrest record, see Stanley Lyman collection box 6, folder 16.

224. Anonymous, "AIM Calling to Custer Rights Day," *Rapid City Journal*, January 31, 1973.

225. Warrior and Smith, *Like a Hurricane*, 183.

226. Anonymous: "Custer Focal Point for Indian Rights Day," *Custer County Chronicle*, February 1, 1973.

227. Hammer, "Race and Perception," 43–48.

228. Elliot, *Custerology*, 2ff.

229. Crow Dog, *Crow Dog*, 182.

230. Hammer, "Race and Perception," 46.

231. Joan Hathaway, interviewed by Earl Hausle, July 25, 1973, South Dakota Oral History Center, Institute of American Indian Studies, University of South Dakota, Vermillion, South Dakota, American Indian Research Project [henceforth AIRP] 806, 2.

232. Banks, *Ojibwa Warrior*, 152.

233. *The War in South Dakota* transcript, film indexes, signature 152.B.11.3B, WKLDOC Records, MHSMC; *The War In South Dakota*, WKLDOC Records, videotape signature 146.E.9.2F, MHSMC.

234. *The War in South Dakota* (videotape).

235. Cy Griffin film, WKLDOC Records, "Custer Reels 1 & 2," signature 146.E.9.2F; Griffin film transcript.

236. CBS News, transcript, film indexes, signature 152.B.11.3B, WKLDOC Records, MHSMC; Griffin film and film transcript.

237. Hammer, "Race and Perception," 1.

238. Anonymous, "This Happened on February 6, 1973," *Custer County Chronicle*, February 8, 1973.

239. Hobart Gates/Ernst Pippin, interviewed by Mari Sandoz, undated, transcript, Mari Sandoz Collection, University of Nebraska, Lincoln; Ernest Peppin, interviewed by Karen Northcott, January 4, 1974, transcript, signature 152.B11.3B, box 3, WKLDOC Records, MHSMC; Dick Bahnon, interviewed by Karen Northcott, January 3, 1974, transcript, signature 152.B11.3B, box 3, WKLDOC Records, MHSMC.

240. Cy Griffin Film; Lyn Gladstone, "Gates Outlines Basis for Manslaughter Charge in Death," *Rapid City Journal*, February 7, 1973.

241. The immediate trigger of the Custer courthouse riot has remained a source of debate. For a discussion, see Hammer, "Race and Perception," 22.

242. Anonymous, "Violence to Custer City," *Custer Weekly*, February 7, 1973.

243. Rios, "David Seals, Interviews with Thelma Rios."

244. Lyn Gladstone, "Confrontation First, Then Everything Broke Loose," *Rapid City Journal*, February 7, 1973.

245. *We Shall Remain: Wounded Knee* (documentary).

246. Anonymous, "Violence to Custer City," *Custer Weekly*, Feb. 7, 1973

247. Jacob Loafer Jr., interviewed by Gail, October 6, 1974, transcript, signature 152.B11.3B, box 3, WKLDOC Records, MHSMC.

248. Edgar Bear Runner interview, March 29, 1974, transcript, signature 152.B11.3B, box 3, WKLDOC Records, MHSMC.

249. *We Shall Remain: Wounded Knee.*

250. Edgar Bear Runner interview.

251. Lyn Gladstone, "Confrontation First, Then Everything Broke Loose," *Rapid City Journal*, February 7, 1973; Anonymous, "Indians Face Variety of Charges," *Rapid City Journal*, February 7, 1973; Anonymous, "3 Indians, 8 Officers Reported Hurt," *Rapid City Journal*, February 7, 1973; Anonymous, "This Happened February 6, 1973," *Custer County Chronicle*, February 8, 1973.

252. Hammer, "Race and Perception," 58–78.

253. Anonymous, "Participants of Confrontation Cautiously Assess Situation," *Rapid City Journal*, February 7, 1973.

254. John Donnan, interviewed by Earl Ausle, July 25, 1973, South Dakota Oral History Center, Institute of American Indian Studies, University of South Dakota, Vermillion, South Dakota, AIRP 1000.

255. Gene Reese, interviewed by Earl Ausle, July 25, 1973, South Dakota Oral History Center, Institute of American Indian Studies, University of South Dakota, Vermillion, South Dakota, AIRP 681.

256. *The War in South Dakota.*

257. Anonymous, "Violence Flares in City; 16 Hurt, 40 Arrested," *Rapid City Journal*, February 10, 1973.

258. Calvin Kentfield, "A Letter from Rapid City," *New York Times Magazine* (April 15, 1973), 82, 86, 87, 88, 94, 95 (here, 86–87); Bob Lee, "Indian Demonstration in Sturgis Peaceful," *Sturgis Tribune*, February 14, 1973.

259. Means, *Where White Men Fear to Tread*, 158; Bellecourt, *Thunder Before the Storm*, 87–94.

260. Faye Gaillard, "Indians Demand Reform Bureau Reforms," *Akwesasne Notes* vol. 3, no. 8 (October/November 1971): 4; Means, *Where*

*White Men Fear to Tread*, 191f; Burnette and Koster, *Road to Wounded Knee*, 57, 170f.

261. Bellecourt, *Thunder Before the Storm*, 92.

262. Burnette and Koster, *Road to Wounded Knee*, 197.

263. These organizations were the National Indian Brotherhood (Canada), the Native American Rights Fund, the American Indian Movement, the National Indian Youth Council, the National Council on Indian Work, the National Indian Leadership Training, and the American Indian Comm. on Alcohol and Drug Abuse. Akwesasne Notes, *BIA*, 2.

264. Akwesasne Notes, *BIA*, 2–3; Wilkins, ed., *The Hank Adams Reader*, 11–15, 89–145.

265. Akwesasne Notes, *BIA*, 63–90.

266. Deloria, *Behind the Trail of Broken Treaties*, 53.

267. Nagel, *American Indian Ethnic Renewal*, 168.

268. Smith and Warrior, *Like a Hurricane*, 146–153.

269. Burnette and Koster, *Road to Wounded Knee*, 207; Akwesasne Notes, *BIA*, 17; Personal interviews, Pat Bellanger and Laura Waterman Wittstock.

270. LaCourse, "In the Caravan's Wake," 14–21.

271. Crow Dog, *Crow Dog*, 173–175; Crow Dog, *Lakota Woman*, 88–90; Banks, *Ojibwa Warrior*, 138–142; Means, *Where White Men Fear to Tread*, 231–234; Burnette and Koster, *Road to Wounded Knee*, 206–215.

272. Crow Dog, *Crow Dog*, 174.

273. Kipp, *Viet Cong*, 102; Treuer, "Seven Days in November," 100.

274. Kipp, *Viet Cong*, 103.

275. Akwesasne Notes, *BIA*, 13.

276. Akwesasne Notes, *BIA*, 13.

277. Akwesasne Notes, *BIA*, 19.

278. Kipp, *Viet Cong*, 103.

279. Kipp, *Viet Cong*, 103.

280. Burnette and Koster, *Road to Wounded Knee*, 208.

281. Banks, *Ojibwa Warrior*, 137; Akwesasne Notes, *BIA*, 14.

282. Banks, *Ojibwa Warrior*, 137–138; Burnette and Koster, *Road to Wounded Knee*, 211–212.

283. Burnette and Koster, *Road to Wounded Knee*, 208.

284. Akwesasne Notes, *BIA*, 15.

285. Banks, *Ojibwa Warrior*, 138.

286. Heppler, "Framing Red Power," 40–59.

287. Heppler, "Framing Red Power," 52; Busacca, "Seeking Self-Determination," 77–78.

288. Heppler, *Framing Red Power*, 70–71; Busacca, "Seeking Self-Determination," 77–78.

289. Means, *Where White Men Fear to Tread*, 234; Studi, "Conversations with Wes Studi."

290. Banks, *Ojibwa Warrior*, 137.

291. Akwesasne Notes, *BIA*, 20.

292. Means, *Where White Men Fear to Tread*, 233.

293. Banks, *Ojibwa Warrior*, 142.

294. Banks, *Ojibwa Warrior*, 142; Means, *Where White Men Fear to Tread*, 234; Burnette and Koster, *Road to Wounded Knee*, 214; Hearings Before the Subcommittee on Indian Affairs, *Seizure and Occupation of the Bureau of Indian Affairs Headquarters Building*, [henceforth BIA Hearing], 85, 89.

295. Schieffelin, "Performance and the Cultural Construction of Reality," 707–724.

296. Peteet, "Male Gender and Rituals of Resistance," 32.

297. Banks, *Ojibwa Warrior*, 139.

298. Burnette and Koster, *Road to Wounded Knee*, 212.

299. Crow Dog, *Lakota Woman*, 89.

300. Burnette and Koster, *Road to Wounded Knee*, 212.

301. Kipp, *Viet Cong*, 104.

302. Crow Dog, *Crow Dog*, 173–174; Crow Dog, *Lakota Woman*, 89.

303. Crow Dog, *Lakota Woman*, 89; Burnette and Koster, *Road to Wounded Knee*, 211; Means, *Where White Men Fear to Tread*, 233.

304. Akwesasne Notes, *BIA*, 13.

305. Nagel, "Masculinity and Nationalism," 243; Beynon, *Masculinities and Culture*, 43–47.

306. Taylor, *Contesting Constructed Indian-ness*, 54.

307. Compare this to Hawaii and New Zealand, where Indigenous people sought to counter racialized and gendered perceptions. See Tengan and Markham, "Performing Polynesian Masculinities," 2412–2414, 2421–2423; Tengan, "(En)gendering Colonialism," 246–250; Hokowhitu, "Tackling Māori Masculinity"; Hokowhitu, "Death of Koro Paka."

308. For one such account, see Nagel, "Nation," 398–399.

309. Banks, *Ojibwa Warrior*, 142.

310. Banks, *Ojibwa Warrior*, 141–143; Means, *Where White Men Fear to Tread*, 232–235; Burnette and Koster, *Road to Wounded Knee*, 213–215; Crow Dog, *Lakota Woman*, 89–90; BIA Hearing, 85, 89.

311. Akwesasne Notes, *BIA*, 19.

312. Akwesasne Notes, *BIA*, 18–22.

313. Messner, *Politics of Masculinities*, 75–76.
314. Bellecourt, *Thunder Before the Storm*, 94. See also Banks, *Ojibwa Warrior*, 136.
315. Banks, *Ojibwa Warrior*, 136.
316. Anonymous, "BIA Occupation Ends, 'Trail of Broken Treaties' to Continue," *Nishawbe News* 3, no. 3 (1972).
317. Smith and Warrior, *Like a Hurricane*, 179.
318. Akwesasne Notes, *BIA*, 26f.
319. Smith and Warrior, *Like a Hurricane*, 165.
320. Akwesasne Notes, *BIA*, 30–31, 91; Deloria, *Behind the Trail of Broken Treaties*, 58; BIA Hearing, 9–10. See also Anonymous, "Damage to BIA Third Heaviest Ever in U.S.," *Washington Post*, November 11, 1972, A2; Anonymous, "Indians: Drums Along the Potomac," *Newsweek*, November 20, 1972, 27.
321. Akwesasne Notes, *BIA*, 91.
322. Akwesasne Notes, *BIA*, 27, 40–41, 42–44.
323. Akwesasne Notes, *BIA*, 58–59, 93–94. For Black and Indigenous nationalism and civil rights in the Deep South, see Tyson, *Radio Free Dixie*; Lowery, *Lumbee Indians in the Jim Crow South*; Bates, *The Other Movement: Indian Rights and Civil Rights in the Deep South*.
324. On the aftermath of the occupation, see Akwesasne Notes, *BIA*, 30–62.
325. Burnette and Koster, *Road to Wounded Knee*, 218.
326. Burnette and Koster, *Road to Wounded Knee*, 216.
327. Studi, "Conversations with Wes Studi."
328. BIA Hearing, 16.
329. BIA Hearing, 54. Other government officials echoed the same sentiment, for example, Louis Bruce, Commissioner of Indian Affairs (BIA Hearing, 60–61), and Frank Carlucci, Deputy Director of Management and Budget (BIA Hearing, 83–87).
330. Ramirez, "Race, Tribal Nation, and Gender," 20–40.
331. Mihesuah, *Indigenous American Women*, 159–171; Castle, "Black and Native American Women's Activism," 89–96; Jaimes and Halsey, "American Indian Women," 331–334; Waterman Wittstock, "Native American Women in the Feminist Milieu," 373–376. See also Ramirez, "Race, Tribal Nation, and Gender," 22–40.
332. Castle, "Black and Native American Women's Activism," 93.
333. Brave Bird, *Ohitika Woman*, 58–59.
334. Note that M. Annette Jaimes/Marie Anna Jaimes Guerrero

(Juaneño/Yaqui), Theresa Halsey (Standing Rock Sioux), and Laura Tohe (Diné) have drawn heavy criticism for claiming that the feminist movement's concerns for civil rights and tribal sovereignty were irreconcilable. They claim that feminism contradicted Indigenous females' concerns, ignored traditional understandings of gender and sexuality, and ultimately undermined the collective Indigenous rights to tribal sovereignty. Apparently, AIM's male leadership drew upon this line of reasoning. Barker, *Critically Sovereign*, 20f; Barker, "Indigenous Feminisms," 12–13. See also Jaimes and Halsey, "American Indian Women," 334; Guerrero, "Civil Rights versus Sovereignty," 101–121; Tohe, "There Is No Word for Feminism in My Language," 103–110.

335. Nickel and Fehr, *In Good Relation*; Barker, *Critically Sovereign*; Green, *Making Space*; Huhndorf et al., *Indigenous Women and Feminism*.

336. Personal interview, Laura Waterman Wittstock.

337. Elizabeth Castle's dissertation remains unpublished. Troy Johnson has relied on an unpublished doctoral manuscript. Johnson, *Red Power*, 69–70.

338. For example, see Mihesuah, *Indigenous American Women*, 41–61.

339. Stern, *Loud Hawk*, 112.

340. Messner, *Politics of Masculinities*; Nagel, "Nation"; Nagel, "Masculinity and Nationalism."

341. Messner, *Politics of Masculinities*, 70–80.

342. Jaimes and Halsey, "American Indian Women," 311.

343. Quoted in Jaimes and Halsey, "American Indian Women," 314.

344. Quoted in Jaimes and Halsey, "American Indian Women," 314.

345. Castle, "Black and Native American Women's Activism," 86.

346. Couture, *American Indian Movement*, 56.

347. Mihesuah, *Indigenous American Women*, 108, 163. See also Crow Dog, *Lakota Woman*, 69.

348. Crow Dog, *Lakota Woman*, 78.

349. Crow Dog, *Lakota Woman*, 68–69.

350. Crow Dog, *Lakota Woman*, 68–69, 78, 131, 138, 191–192; Mihesuah, *Indigenous American Women*, 164.

351. Quoted in Antell, *American Indian Women Activists*, 170f.

352. Emily Langer, "Russel Means Dies at 72," *Washington Post*, October 22, 2012.

353. Robert D. McFadden, "Dennis Banks, American Indian Civil Rights Leader, Dies at 80," *New York Times*, October 30, 2017; Barker, "Indigenous Feminisms," 13.

354. Barker, "Indigenous Feminisms," 13; Mihesuah, *Indigenous American Women*, 10.
355. Castle, "Black and Native American Women's Activism," 86.
356. Mihesuah, *Indigenous American Women*, 164.
357. O'Sullivan, "We Worry About Survival," 20.
358. Means, *Where White Men Fear to Tread*, 265; O'Sullivan, "Informing Red Power," 974. For another example of Means' sexist attitude, see Matthiessen, *In the Spirit of Crazy Horse*, 124.
359. Vizenor, "Dennis at Wounded Knee," 55.
360. Barker, "Indigenous Feminisms," 12–13.
361. Mihesuah, *Indigenous American Women*, 164.
362. Mihesuah, *Indigenous American Women*, 108, 163.
363. Means, *Where White Men Fear to Tread*, 265.
364. Wideman, "Russell Means," 71–73; Means, *Where White Men Fear to Tread*, 536–538.
365. Crow Dog, *Lakota Woman*, 5.
366. Innes and Anderson, *Indigenous Men and Masculinities*, 11, 15.
367. Innes and Anderson, *Indigenous Men and Masculinities*, 11.
368. Davis, *Survival Schools*, 31–51; Voigt, "Between Powerlessness and Protest."
369. Crow Dog, *Lakota Woman*, 69.
370. Crow Dog, *Lakota Woman*, 191–192.
371. Mihesuah, *Indigenous American Women*, 168; hooks, *Feminist Theory*, 70.
372. Mihesuah, *Indigenous American Women*, 170.
373. Crow Dog, *Lakota Woman*, 78.
374. Kimmel, *Manhood in America*, 189–210.
375. Kipp, *Viet Cong*, 105–106.
376. Crow Dog, *Lakota Woman*, 68–69, 78, 131, 138, 191–192; Mihesuah, *Indigenous American Women*, 164.
377. Quoted from an interview with an unnamed activist. Matthiessen, *In the Spirit of Crazy Horse*, 50–51.
378. Matthiessen, *In the Spirit of Crazy Horse*, 84.
379. Castle, "Black and Native American Women's Activism," 86.
380. Castle, "Black and Native American Women's Activism," 86, 96; Jaimes and Halsey, "American Indian Women at the Center of Indigenous Resistance in Contemporary North America," 332; Mihesuah, *Indigenous American Women*, 162–171.
381. Castle, "Black and Native American Women's Activism," 86–88.

382. Mihesuah, *Indigenous American Women*, 163–164; Smith, "Native American Feminism," 118; Castle, "Black and Native American Women's Activism," 91–94; Jaimes and Halsey, "American Indian Women," 331–334.
383. Jaimes and Halsey, "American Indian Women," 332.
384. Huhndorf et al., *Indigenous Women and Feminism*, 2.
385. Susan Braudy, "'We Will Remember' Survival School," *Ms. Magazine*, July 1976, 94.
386. O'Sullivan, "We Worry About Survival," 17.
387. Messner, *Politics of Masculinities*, 72ff.
388. Messner, *Politics of Masculinities*, 97f.

## Chapter 4. Warriors for a Nation at Wounded Knee, 1973

1. Akwesasne Notes, *Voices*, 22.
2. Akwesasne Notes, *Voices*, 22.
3. Akwesasne Notes, *Voices*, 22.
4. Akwesasne Notes, *Voices*, 22.
5. For an account of the takeover of Wounded Knee, see Anonymous, "Oglalas Liberate Wounded Knee," *Akwesasne Notes* 5, no. 2 (Spring 1973): 12.
6. Camp, "War Stories and Wounded Knee 1973," 10a.
7. Camp, "Wounded Knee Memories."
8. Carroll, *Medicine Bags*, 162.
9. Holm, *Strong Hearts*, 176–179; Carroll, *Medicine Bags*, 163–172.
10. Clara Sue Kidwell, "Foreword," in Reinhardt, *Ruling Pine Ridge*, xv–xix; Castile, *To Show Heart*, 129–133.
11. Reinhardt: "A Crude Replacement: The Indian New Deal, Indirect Colonialism, and Pine Ridge Reservation," 1–56; Taylor, *The New Deal and American Indian Tribalism*.
12. Reinhardt, *Ruling Pine Ridge*, 19–41.
13. Reinhardt, *Ruling Pine Ridge*, 19–41 (on tribal governance). To the present day, Indigenous identity continues to be measured by blood quantum (Wilkens and Stark, *American Indian Politics*). On Pine Ridge, the Indigenous population of mixed heritage can be regarded as a culturally cross-bred colonized elite that acted as an intermediary between the white "colonizer" and the Indigenous "colonized." Reservation politics were predominantly male-oriented and can be categorized as complicit (mixed-blood, assimilated) or resistance masculinities (full-blood,

traditional). See Reinhardt, *Ruling Pine Ridge*, 30–33, 88–96; Hokowhitu, "Producing Elite Indigenous Masculinities."

14. Reinhardt, *Ruling Pine Ridge*, 88–96, 102–103, 211.
15. Reinhardt, *Ruling Pine Ridge*, 13, 209.
16. Kidwell, "Foreword," in Reinhardt, *Ruling Pine Ridge*, xvii–xviii.
17. Akwesasne Notes, *Voices*, 14–21.
18. For an overview, see Reinhardt, *Ruling Pine Ridge*, 129–188.
19. Anonymous, "On the Trail to Wounded Knee," Akwesasne Notes 5, no. 2 (Early Spring 1973): 11. For Wilson's far reaching political powers, see Wounded Kee Hearing, 30–37, 251–252, 124–125, 142.
20. Stanley Lyman, "Memorandum from Superintendent Pine Ridge to Area Director, Aberdeen Area, November 22, 1972 (9pp.)," Stanley Lyman Papers, box 5, folder 33.
21. Akwesasne Notes, *Voices*, 20–21.
22. Akwesasne Notes, *Voices*, 31–32.
23. Reinhardt, *Ruling Pine Ridge*, 161.
24. US Congress, Senate, Hearings Before the Subcommittee on Indian Affairs of the Committee on Interior and Insular Affairs, *Occupation of Wounded Knee: The Causes and Aftermath of the Wounded Knee Takeover*, Ninety-Third Congress, June 16, 1973 Pine Ridge, South Dakota, and June 17, 1973 Kyle, South Dakota (Washington, DC: US Government Printing Office 1974) [Henceforth Wounded Knee Hearing], 251–256, 311.
25. Carroll, *Medicine Bags*, 163–164.
26. Anderson, *The Movement and the Sixties*, 407–408.
27. James G. Abourezk Papers, Bill Hall, interviewed by James Abourezk, September 11, 1980, transcript, 4–32, Archives and Special Collections, University Libraries, University of South Dakota, Vermillion; Akwesasne Notes, *Voices*, 24; Churchill and Vander Wall, *Agents of Repression*, 194–195.
28. Dewing, *Wounded Knee II*, 60–62; Anonymous, "Army Tested Civil Disturbance Plan at Wounded Knee, Memos Show," *New York Times*, December 2, 1975. See also Trimbach and Trimbach, *American Indian Mafia*, 101, 106–112, 117, 128–130, 142–143, 151–153, 568; Churchill and Vander Wall, *Agents of Repression*, 143–144, 195; Churchill and Vander Wall, *COINTELPRO Papers*, 243–244.
29. For military hardware deployed to Wounded Knee, see Weyler, *Blood of the Land*, 80–81; Churchill and Vander Wall, *Agents of Repression*, 194–197; Anonymous, "Garden Plot—'Flowers of Evil,'" *Akwesasne Notes* 7, no. 5 (Early Winter 1975): 6–7.

30. Dewing, *Wounded Knee II*, 104.
31. Churchill and Vander Wall, *Agents of Repression*, 195.
32. James G. Abourezk Papers, Madonna Thunder Hawk, interviewed by James Abourezk, July 18, 1980, transcript, 12, Archives and Special Collections, University Libraries, University of South Dakota, Vermillion.
33. Akwesasne Notes, *Voices*, 41.
34. Weyler, *Blood of the Land*, 80.
35. Anonymous, "Thursday, March 22, 1973," *Akwesasne Notes* 5, no. 2 (Spring 1973): 43.
36. Means, "I Wanna Wear That Uniform."
37. *We Shall Remain: Wounded Knee*.
38. Akwesasne Notes, *Voices*.
39. Akwesasne Notes, *Voices*.
40. Carroll, *Medicine Bags*, 166–172; Holm, *Strong Hearts*, 176–179.
41. Al Cooper and Tony Bush give estimates of 100 to 150 Native veterans. Russell Means gives a number of seventy-five Native veterans from World War I, World War II, Korea, and Vietnam. Personal interviews, Al Cooper and Tony Bush; Linderman, "Gallery Interview," 42; Carroll, *Medicine Bags*, 167.
42. Akwesasne Notes, *Voices*, 194. See Ken Tiger in *We Shall Remain: Wounded Knee*.
43. Personal interview, Al Cooper.
44. Kenneth Tilsen, "A Question of Sovereignty and Freedom," *Akwesasne Notes* 5, no. 2 (Spring 1973): 5. See also Akwesasne Notes, *Voices*, 194ff.
45. Personal interview, George Lamont.
46. Carroll, *Medicine Bags*, 167.
47. Robert Anderson, "The Second Battle of Wounded Knee," in Robert Anderson Papers, box 1, folder 3, page 6 (of 12), Center for Southwest Research, University of New Mexico at Albuquerque, New Mexico.
48. The description of the defenses come from various sources, including articles, maps, pictures, and film footage. Akwesasne Notes, *Voices*, 71 and 207 (maps); 41, 70, 76, 80, 208, 210, 223 (pictures); Crow Dog, *Crow Dog*, 190ff. See also: Holm, *Strong Hearts*, 177f; Carroll, *Medicine Bags*, 166f. Various documentaries thematize the Wounded Knee takeover, including *A Tattoo on My Heart* and *We Shall Remain: Wounded Knee*.
49. Lyman, O'Neill, Lyman, and McKay, *Wounded Knee 1973*, 23–25.
50. Carroll, *Medicine Bags*, 166–167.
51. Kipp, *Viet Cong*, 131.

52. Akwesasne Notes, *Voices*, 41; Anonymous, "Sunday, March 4, 1973 Everybody Can Go Home," *Akwesasne Notes* 5, no. 2 (Spring 1973): 20; Zimmerman, *Airlift*, 151.

53. Holm, *Strong Hearts*, 177; Zimmerman, *Airlift*, 165–166. See also Akwesasne Notes, *Voices*, 217; Kipp, "The Eagles I Fed Who Did Not Love Me," 219.

54. Kipp, *Viet Cong*, 128.

55. Personal interview, Bob Anderson. See also Anderson, "The Second Battle of Wounded Knee," 7.

56. Anderson, "The Second Battle of Wounded Knee," 6.

57. Banks, *Ojibwa Warrior*, 177. See also Crow Dog, *Crow Dog*, 196.

58. Holm, *Strong Hearts*, 171–175.

59. Kipp, "The Eagles I Fed Who Did Not Love Me," 213.

60. Carroll, *Medicine Bags*, 172.

61. Quoted from *A Good Day to Die* (documentary).

62. Akwesasne Notes, *Voices*, 194, 196.

63. Akwesasne Notes, *Voices*, 197.

64. Akwesasne Notes, *Voices*, 196.

65. Akwesasne Notes, *Voices*, 198.

66. Akwesasne Notes, *Voices*, 194, 197.

67. Akwesasne Notes, *Voices*, 197.

68. The Ken Tiger, Bob Anderson, and Bobby Onco interviews are printed in Akwesasne Notes, *Voices*, 194–201.

69. Kipp, *Viet Cong*, 126f.

70. Burnette and Koster, *Road to Wounded Knee*, 234–235; James Parsons, "Wounded Knee: Why?" *Minneapolis Tribune*, March 18, 1973.

71. Akwesasne Notes, *Voices*, 194–201.

72. Personal interview, Madonna Thunder Hawk.

73. Personal interview, Bob Anderson.

74. Hunt, *The Turning*, 171.

75. Means, *Where White Men Fear to Tread*, 271.

76. Personal interview, Bob Anderson.

77. Owen Luck, "A Witness at Wounded Knee."

78. Zimmerman, *Airlift*; James G. Abourezk Papers, Bill Zimmerman, interviewed by James Abourezk, September 8, 1980, Archives and Special Collections, University Libraries, University of South Dakota, Vermillion.

79. Crow Dog, *Crow Dog*, 164.

80. Carroll, *Medicine Bags*, 170.

81. Personal interview, Tony Bush.

82. Personal interview, Tony Bush.
83. Personal interview, Tony Bush.
84. Kipp, "The Eagles I Fed Who Did Not Love Me," 219.
85. Kipp, "The Eagles I Fed Who Did Not Love Me," 221.
86. Littlemoon, *They Called Me Uncivilized*, 73.
87. Enloe, *Bananas*, 93.
88. Grua, *Surviving Wounded Knee*.
89. The Wounded Knee massacre has produced its own historiography. For a starting point, see Greene, *American Carnage*; Grua, *Surviving Wounded Knee*; Ostler, *The Plains Sioux and U.S. Colonialism*, 338–360. For Indigenous perspectives, see Greene, *All Guns Fired at One Time*; Coleman, *Voices of Wounded Knee*; and Flood, *Lost Bird of Wounded Knee*.
90. Dee Alexander Brown, *Bury My Heart at Wounded Knee: An Indian History of the American West* (New York: Bantam Books, 1971).
91. Grua, *Surviving Wounded Knee*.
92. The Wounded Knee Trading Post was owned by Clive and Agnes Gildersleeve since 1934. In 1968, it changed into the hands of Jan and James A. Czywczynski, the Gildersleeve's daughter and her husband. Under them, exploitative business practices and spiritual degradation of the grace site reached another level. Reinhardt, *Ruling Pine Ridge*, 193–202.
93. Schwarz, *Fighting Colonialism*, 31f.
94. Schwarz, *Fighting Colonialism*, 31.
95. Tengan, *Native Men*, 11–14.
96. Nagel, "Masculinity and Nationalism"; Nagel, "Nation"; Enloe, *Bananas*, 83–124; Yuval-Davis, *Gender and Nation*, 2.
97. Akwesasne Notes, *Voices*, 76–77.
98. Gibbon, *The Sioux*, 127–130; Hassrick, *The Sioux*, 15–25.
99. For women's sodalities, see Powers, *Oglala Women*, 25–27, 73–74, 86–87, 139.
100. Powers, *Oglala Women*, 87.
101. Meadows, *Military Societies*, 1–13.
102. Meadows, *Military Societies*, 212–215.
103. Meadows, *Military Societies*, 8.
104. Meadows, *Military Societies*, 9.
105. Meadows, *Military Societies*, xii.
106. Carroll, *Medicine Bags*, 170.
107. Akwesasne Notes, *Voices*, 60–64.
108. Akwesasne Notes, *Voices*, 61–62.
109. Carter Camp, "War Stories."

110. Carroll, *Medicine Bags*, 162.

111. Quote from: Anonymous, "Oklahoma Indian Activist Carter Camp Dies At Age 72," in: *Tulsa World*, January 3, 2014, http://www.tulsaworld.com/obituaries/nationalobits/oklahoma-indian-activist-carter-camp-dies-at-age/article_4e9563be-3c0a-58b9-aa51-fd05e121d3be.html (last accessed April 20, 2024).

112. Akwesasne Notes, *Voices*, 76ff.

113. Holm, *Strong Hearts*, 45–46.

114. Akwesasne Notes, *Voices*, 77.

115. Akwesasne Notes, *Voices*, 76ff.

116. Talbert, "The Resurgence of Ethnicity Among American Indians," 367.

117. James G. Abourezk Papers, Stan Pottinger, interviewed by James Abourezk, August 22, 1980, transcript, 7–25, Archives and Special Collections, University Libraries, University of South Dakota, Vermillion.

118. Anonymous, "Frank Clearwater Mortally Wounded As U.S. Forces Fire On Oglalas Gathering Food," *Akwesasne Notes* 5, no. 3 (Summer 1973): 15; Anonymous, "Justice Dept. Admits Refusal to Negotiate," *Akwesasne Notes* 5, no. 3 (Summer 1973): 18.

119. Stan Pottinger, interviewed by James Abourezk, 7.

120. Bill Hall, interviewed by James Abourezk, 18.

121. Stan Pottinger, interviewed by James Abourezk, 14–15.

122. Stan Pottinger, interviewed by James Abourezk, 27.

123. Bill Hall, interviewed by James Abourezk, 30.

124. Anonymous, "Sunday, March 18, 1973—It Means Total Capitulation," *Akwesasne Notes* 5, no. 2 (Spring 1973): 40.

125. Personal interview, Bob Anderson.

126. Akwesasne Notes, *Voices*, 79–80.

127. Akwesasne Notes, *Voices*, 80.

128. Quoted from *A Tattoo on My Heart* (documentary).

129. Quoted from *A Tattoo on My Heart* (documentary).

130. Carroll, *Medicine Bags*, 168.

131. Crow Dog, *Crow Dog*, 203.

132. Personal interviews, Al Cooper and Bob Anderson.

133. Carroll, *Medicine Bags*, 168–169.

134. Personal interview, Bob Anderson.

135. Crow Dog, *Crow Dog*, 197f; Crow Dog, *Lakota Woman*, 144ff.

136. Luck, "A Witness at Wounded Knee, 1973," 339–340, 343.

137. Akwesasne Notes, *Voices*, 76.

138. Hassrick, *The Sioux*, 96–100; Holm, "Patriots and Pawns," 355f.
139. Talbert, "Resurgence of Ethnicity," 368.
140. Camp, "When in the Course of Human Events," 45–46.
141. Camp, "An interview With Carter Camp."
142. Nagel, *American Indian Ethnic Renewal*, 247–248, 258–261.
143. Reeser, *Masculinities in Theory*, 171ff.
144. Reeser, *Masculinities in Theory*, 171–199.
145. Schwarz, *Fighting Colonialism*, 31.
146. Nagel, "Masculinity and Nationalism," 247–248; Nagel, "Nation," 400–401. See also Anderson, *Imagined Communities*; Hobsbawm and Ranger, *The Invention of Tradition*.
147. Reeser, *Masculinities in Theory*, 177ff.
148. Nagel, "Masculinity and Nationalism," 247–248.
149. For a key primary source, see Akwesasne Notes, *Voices*, 55–58, 76, 81, 130–132, 161ff.
150. Akwesasne Notes, *Voices*, 54–64.
151. Eddie Benton-Benai, "Interview with Eddie Benton, Director, St. Paul American Indian Movement On March 14, 1973," File 176–2404, Section 8, March 21–24, 1973, in *The FBI Files on the American Indian Movement and Wounded Knee*, ed. Rolland Dewing (Frederick, MD: University Publications of America, 1986), Reel 21, 145.
152. Wounded Knee Hearing, Statement of Louis Bad Wound, 233.
153. Anonymous, "Friday, May 3, 1973," *Akwesasne Notes* 5, no. 3 (Summer 1973): 27; Lyman, *Wounded Knee*, 89ff. Compare with the statement of Louis Bad Heart Wound, Wounded Knee Hearing, 233.
154. Reinhardt, *Ruling Pine Ridge*, 5f.
155. Wounded Knee Hearing, 234–235.
156. Akwesasne Notes, *Voices*, 55, 64.
157. Akwesasne Notes, *Voices*, 65–87.
158. Akwesasne Notes, *Voices*, 67.
159. Akwesasne Notes, *Voices*, 81.
160. Personal interview, Al Cooper.
161. Carroll, *Medicine Bags*, 154–158.
162. Akwesasne Notes, *Voices*, 81.
163. Means, *Where White Men*, 9–22.
164. Akwesasne Notes, *Voices*, 96–97.
165. Anonymous, "Interview with Eddie Benton," 142–148.
166. Noriyuki, "The Women of Wounded Knee."
167. For example, see Akwesasne, *Voices*, 153–174.

168. John Adams, interviewed by James Abourezk. September 12, 1980, transcript, 16–17. James G. Abourezk Papers, Archives and Special Collections, University Libraries. University of South Dakota.

169. Akwesasne Notes, *Voices*, 53ff.

170. Tengan, *Native Men*, 11–14.

171. Akwesasne Notes, *Voices*, 89.

172. Personal interview, Robert Anderson. See also Crow Dog, *Lakota Woman*, 145.

173. Sayer, *Ghost Dancing the Law*, 220f.

174. Carter Camp, interviewed for PBS, *We Shall Remain: Wounded Knee.*

175. Connell, *Masculinities*, 61.

176. Reeser, *Masculinities in Theory*, 91–92.

177. Reeser, *Masculinities in Theory*, 91–118.

178. Castile, *To Show Heart*, 133.

179. For body-reflexive practices, see Connell, *Masculinities*, 61; Tengan, *Native Men Remade*, 17, 87–89, 151, 186. For ritual process see van Gennep, *The Rites of Passage*; Turner, *The Ritual Process*.

180. Reeser, *Masculinities in Theory*, 91–118.

181. Anonymous, "A Suspenseful Show of Red Power," *Time*, March 19, 1973, 16.

182. Fixico, *Call for Change*, 17–40; Holm, Pearson, Chavis, "Peoplehood," 13–15.

183. Crow Dog, *Crow Dog*, 203; Crow Dog, *Lakota Woman*, 145; Akwesasne Notes, *Voices*, 104ff.

184. Walker, *Lakota Belief and Ritual*, 78–79, 83–84, 100, 104–105, 243 (*inípi*), 60–61, 153–154 (*yuwipi*).

185. Ostler, *The Plains Sioux*, 169–193.

186. Nagel, *American Indian Ethnic Renewal*, 158ff, esp. 170–173

187. Crow Dog, *Crow Dog*, 195, 203. For a study on Indigenous women at Wounded Knee, see Voigt, "Warrior Women."

188. Akwesasne Notes, *Voices*, 22–32; Jaimes and Halsey, "American Indian Women," 311–314.

189. Personal interview, Bob Anderson.

190. Akwesasne Notes, *Voices*, 14–32.

191. Akwesasne Notes, *Voices*, 31.

192. Banks, *Ojibwa Warrior*, 160.

193. Enloe, *Bananas*, 87.

194. Mihesuah, *Indigenous American Women*, 119.

195. Mihesuah, *Indigenous American Women*, 119.
196. Crow Dog, *Lakota Woman*, 138.
197. Crow Dog, *Lakota Woman*, 131.
198. Mihesuah, *Indigenous American Women*, 163.
199. hooks, *Feminist Theory*, 70.
200. Burnette and Koster, *Road to Wounded Knee*, 230–231.
201. Whitehead, *Men and Masculinities*, 71.
202. Means, *Where White Men Fear to Tread*, 265.
203. Means, *Where White Men Fear to Tread*, 265.
204. Mihesuah, *Indigenous American Women*, 164.
205. McClintock, "Family Feuds," 61–80.
206. Yuval-Davis, *Gender and Nation*, 4.
207. Akwesasne Notes, *Voices*.
208. Nagel, "Masculinity and Nationalism," 253; Scott, *Weapons of the Weak*; Hart, "Engendering Everyday Resistance," 93–121.
209. Akwesasne Notes, *Voices*, 201.
210. Messner, *Politics of Masculinities*, 73.
211. Enloe, *Bananas*, 31.
212. Regina Brave interview.
213. Akwesasne Notes, *Voices*, 161ff, 165, 201.
214. Akwesasne Notes, *Voices*, 201.
215. Akwesasne Notes, *Voices*, 201.
216. Madonna Thunder Hawk, "Madonna Thunder Hawk on Wounded Knee."
217. Regina Brave interview.
218. Stands in Timber and Liberty, *Cheyenne Memoirs*, 181–190.
219. Regina Brave interview.
220. Jaimes and Halsey, "American Indian Women," 316.
221. Medicine, "Warrior Women," 267–277.
222. DeMallie, "Male and Female in Traditional Lakota Culture," 242.
223. Lakota women veterans claim that there were female warrior sodalities among the Lakotas. Madonna Thunder Hawk states that there were four warrior societies among Lakota women. Jaimes and Halsey, "American Indian Women," 316, 337n2. The Lakota Women Warriors' website has been taken down (website).
224. Medicine, "Warrior Women," 274.
225. McKegney, *Maculindians*, 2ff.
226. Personal interview, Bob Anderson.
227. Kunkin, "The Legal Case for Wounded Knee."

228. Kunkin, "The Legal Case for Wounded Knee."
229. Regina Brave interview.
230. Personal interview, Bob Anderson.
231. Regina Brave interview.
232. Regina Brave interview.
233. Regina Brave interview.
234. Regina Brave interview.
235. Regina Brave interview.
236. Madonna Thunder Hawk and Choach Means, interviewed by Elizabeth Castle.
237. Thunder Hawk and Means interview.
238. Jaimes and Halsey, "American Indian Women."
239. Thunder Hawk, "Madonna Thunder Hawk on Wounded Knee."
240. Regina Brave interview.
241. Eric Konigsberg, Who Killed Anna Mae?" *New York Times*, April 25, 2014.
242. Konigsberg, "Who Killed Anna Mae."
243. Weston, *Native Americans in the News*, 117–118; Wells, "Television News Coverage," 53; Abourezk, "From Red Fears to Red Power," 14, 49; Schmidt, "An Examination of Local Newspaper Photographs of the Wounded Knee Occupation," 72ff.
244. Anonymous, "Raid At Wounded Knee," in *Time*, March 12, 1973, 37; Anonymous, "The Siege of Wounded Knee," in *Newsweek* March 19, 1973, 22–23; Bob Wiedrich, "Guerilla Theater at Wounded Knee," *Chicago Tribune*, April 12, 1973; Huck, "Renegades: The Second Battle of Wounded Knee"; Collins, "Showdown at Wounded Knee"; Collier, "Wounded Knee: The New Indian War."
245. Valaskakis, *Indian Country*, 39.
246. McKiernan, "The Media," 9.
247. Valaskakis, *Indian Country*, 36.
248. Schultz, "Bamboozle Me Not at Wounded Knee," 56.
249. Burnette and Koster, *Road to Wounded Knee*, 229.
250. McKiernan, "The Media," 8.
251. McKiernan, "The Media," 9.
252. For a discussion of newspaper reporting and sympathies toward AIM, the federal government, or tribal leadership, see Brady, "The Occupation of Wounded Knee," 174–181.
253. Barry McKiernan, "Wounded Knee," 3. See also Means, *Where White Men Fear to Tread*, 270; Banks, *Ojibwa Warrior*, 162–163; Crow Dog,

*Crow Dog*, 191–192; Crow Dog, *Lakota Woman*, 127, 136; Camp, "Wounded Knee Memories."

254. Burnette and Koster, *Road to Wounded Knee*, xi, 194.

255. Means, *Where White Men Fear to Tread*, 268.

256. The poll is reprinted in Akwesasne Notes, *Voices*, 6; Anonymous, "American Public Support for Independent Oglala Nation," *Akwesasne Notes* 5, no. 3 (Summer/June 1973): 6; Talbot, *Roots of Oppression*, 65. Another poll conducted by the *Minneapolis Tribune* with six hundred adults in Minnesota was less sympathetic. Only 26 percent stated the occupation was justified, 61 percent disagreed, and 13 percent had no opinion. Anonymous, "61% Say Wounded Knee Takeover Not Justified," *Minneapolis Tribune*, May 6, 1973, 11B.

257. Quoted in Akwesasne Notes, *Voices*, 6.

258. Quoted in Akwesasne Notes, *Voices*, 6.

259. Segal, "American Indian Movement,"211–217; Dewing, "South Dakota Newspaper Coverage," 49.

260. Castile, *To Show Heart*, 133.

261. Schwarz, *Fighting Colonialism*, 24–33; Deloria, *Playing Indian*.

262. Quoted in Crow Dog, *Crow Dog*, 200.

263. Means, *Where White Men Fear to Tread*, 262.

264. Means, *Where White Men Fear to Tread*, 271.

265. For the mines and grenade launcher, see Crow Dog, *Lakota Woman*, 135, 137; Crow Dog, *Crow Dog*, 194–195. A slightly different account comes from Banks. Banks, *Ojibwa Warrior*, 176. For mines, the heavy machine gun, and the RPG, see Means, *Where White Men Fear to Tread*, 280–281.

266. Burnette and Koster, *Road to Wounded Knee*, 249.

267. Means, *Where White Men Fear to Tread*, 280.

268. Means, *Where White Men Fear to Tread*, 281.

269. Anderson, "The Second Battle of Wounded Knee," 6.

270. Banks, *Ojibwa Warrior*, 176.

271. Baylor, "Modern Warriors," 173–174; Busacca, "Seeking Self-Determination," 158; Streb, "Rhetoric of Wounded Knee II," 213ff.

272. Baylor, "Modern Warriors," 179–180.

273. Brady, "The Occupation of Wounded Knee," 175–176; Busacca, "Seeking Self-Determination," 138–139. See also Anonymous, "Trap at Wounded Knee," *Time*, March 26, 1973, 6; Schwarz, *Fighting Colonialism*, 24–33.

274. Desmond Smith, "Media Coup D'Etat," *Nation* 216, no. 26 (June 25, 1973): 807.

275. Smith, "Media Coup D'Etat," 808.
276. Smith, "Media Coup D'Etat," 808.
277. Schultz, "Bamboozle," 48; Burnette and Koster, *Road to Wounded Knee*, 230; Crow Dog, *Lakota Woman*, 134.
278. Anonymous, "Trap at Wounded Knee." See also Schultz, "Bamboozle," 55; Hickey, "Was the Truth Buried."
279. Anonymous, "Trap at Wounded Knee." See also Hickey, "Was the Truth Buried."
280. Anonymous, "Letters," *Time*, April 9, 1973, 4.
281. Schultz, "Bamboozle," 48.
282. Crow Dog, *Crow Dog*, 194.
283. Anonymous, "The Siege of Wounded Knee," *Newsweek*, March 19, 1973, 23.
284. Crow Dog, *Lakota Woman*, 139ff; Crow Dog, *Crow Dog*, 199ff; Banks, *Ojibwa Warrior*, 175ff; Means, *Where White Men Fear to Tread*, 262, 270ff.
285. Busacca, "Seeking Self-Determination," 160–196.
286. Vizenor, *Tribal Scenes and Ceremonies*, 52.
287. Vizenor, "Dennis at Wounded Knee," 54–55.
288. Vizenor, "Dennis at Wounded Knee," 55–56.
289. For a general discussion, see Usbeck, "Selling the Natural-Born Warrior."
290. Usbeck, "Selling the Natural-Born Warrior," 177.
291. Baylor, "Modern Warriors," 179–180; Busacca, "Seeking Self-Determination," 158.
292. Akwesasne Notes, *Voices*, 240–244.
293. Dewing, *Wounded Knee II*, 99, 119f.
294. Activist accounts state that Frank Clearwater was either of Cherokee ancestry (Crow Dog, *Lakota Woman*, 142–143; Crow Dog, *Crow Dog*, 205–207; Means, *Where White Men Fear to Tread*, 292) or of mixed Apache/Cherokee ancestry (Banks, *Ojibwa Warrior*, 200–202). The FBI claimed that the man's real name was Frank Clear, that he was of Irish, not Indigenous, heritage, and that he had been a US Army deserter during World War II. See Trimbach and Trimbach, *American Indian Mafia*, 376; Akwesasne Notes, *Voices*, 202–203.
295. Burnette and Koster, *Road to Wounded Knee*, 247–248; Akwesasne Notes, *Voices*, 232–233.
296. Churchill and Vander Wall, *Agents of Repression*, 196.
297. Akwesasne Notes, *Voices*, 245–261.

298. Roos, Smith, Langley, and McDonald, "The Impact of the American Indian Movement on the Pine Ridge Reservation," 89–99.
299. Littlemoon, *They Called Me Uncivilized*, 73.
300. Littlemoon, *They Called Me Uncivilized*, 73–78.
301. Churchill and Vander Wall, *COINTELPRO Papers*, 249ff; Churchill and Vander Wall, *Agents of Repression*, 175ff.
302. Nagel, *American Indian Ethnic Renewal*, 173–175.
303. Cornell, *Return of the Native*, 8; Kidwell, "Introduction," in Reinhardt, *Ruling Pine Ridge*, xix; Nagel, *American Indian Ethnic Renewal*, 187ff.
304. Lazarus, *Black Hills, White Justice*; Grua, *Surviving Wounded Knee*; Ostler, *The Lakotas and the Black Hills*.
305. Akwesasne Notes, *Voices*, 34; Akwesasne Notes, *BIA*, 63–90.
306. Akwesasne Notes, *Voices*, 258.
307. Akwesasne Notes, *Voices*, 249–258.
308. Wounded Knee Hearing, 166, 179.
309. Wounded Knee Hearing, 174.
310. Wounded Knee Hearing, 174.
311. Wounded Knee Hearing, 208.
312. Akwesasne Notes, *Voices*, 54–64.
313. Wounded Knee Hearing, 141, 148.
314. Lazarus, *Black Hills, White Justice*, 309.
315. Akwesasne Notes, *Voices*, 53ff.
316. Reinhardt, *Ruling Pine Ridge*, 202ff.
317. Carroll, *Medicine Bags*, 172.
318. Carroll, *Medicine Bags*, 171–172; Alfred and Lowe, "Warrior Societies in Contemporary Indigenous Communities."
319. Alfred and Lowe, "Warrior Societies in Contemporary Indigenous Communities."

## Chapter 5. Reinventing Warriorhood and Nationalist Struggle after 1973

1. Wounded Knee Legal Defense/Offense Committee, "The Opening Statements of Russell Means and Dennis Banks in U.S. vs Russell Means and U.S. vs Dennis Banks, Feb. 12, 1974" (St. Paul, MN: WKLDOC 1974), 7, WKLDOC Records, signature 147.I.5B, box 46, MHSMC.

2. For various contexts of colonial domination, see Enloe, *Ethnic Soldiers*, 23–49; Hokowhitu, "Taxonomies of Indigeneity"; Hokowhitu, "Haka"; Tengan, "(En)gendering Colonialism"; Tengan and Markham,

"Performing Polynesian Masculinities"; Camacho and Monnig, "Uncomfortable Fatigues."

3. Sneider, "Complementary Relationships," 66–72.
4. Innes and Anderson, "Introduction," 11.
5. Churchill and Vander Wall, *COINTELPRO Papers*, 235, 256, 306.
6. Churchill and Vander Wall, *COINTELPRO Papers*; Churchill and Vander Wall, *COINTELPRO Papers*; Trimbach and Trimbach, *American Indian Mafia*; Stern, *Loud Hawk*; Talbot, *Roots of Oppression*; Johansen and Maestas, *Wasi'chu*; Sayer, *Ghost Dancing the Law*. See also Hearings Before the Subcommittee to Investigate the Administration of the Internal Security Act and Other Internal Security Laws of the Committee on the Judiciary, *Revolutionary Activities Within the United States, The American Indian Movement*; Dewing, ed., *The FBI Files on the American Indian Movement and Wounded Knee*.
7. Churchill and Vander Wall, *COINTELPRO Papers*, 253–254; Sayer, *Ghost Dancing the Law*, 3.
8. Churchill and Vander Wall, *Agents of Repression*, 255.
9. Sayer, *Ghost Dancing*, 11.
10. US Commission on Civil Rights, *Events Surrounding Recent Murders*, 1–2.
11. Ward Churchill and Vander Wall arrive at a lower number of killed in the *COINTELPRO Papers* and a higher number in *Agents of Repression*. Churchill and Vander Wall, *COINTELPRO Papers*, 249; Churchill and Vander Wall, *Agents of Repression*, 175. For the number of women and children killed, see Jaimes and Halsey, "American Indian Women," 328.
12. Federal Bureau of Investigation, *Report for Pine Ridge Indian Reservation*.
13. According to his findings, there were no more than ten deaths directly related to the clashes between AIM and GOON members; the rest, he claimed, were "due to domestic violence, drugs, and alcohol-related mayhem." Tim Giago, "AIM Members' Infighting Makes All Indians Look Bad," *Albuquerque Journal*, March 4, 1994, A15.
14. Mihesuah, *Indigenous American Women*, 9–13, 115–142.
15. Adding to the conspiracy theory that Anna Mae Aquash's murder was engineered through the FBI's Counter Intelligence Program (COINTELPRO) was the fact that the pathologist reported frostbite as cause of death and, instead of fingerprinting her, sent her severed hands to Washington, DC, for identification. A second autopsy revealed that the first, cursory autopsy had somehow missed the gunshot wound to her head. See Hendricks, *Unquiet Grave*. Ward Churchill, a proponent of the FBI

conspiracy theory, should be read with care. Churchill, *Agents of Repression*, 206–211.

16. Mihesuah, *Indigenous American Women*, 9–13, 115–142; Trimbach and Trimbach, *American Indian Mafia*.

17. *New York Times* journalist Eric Konigsberg claims that several women who participated in the takeover of Wounded Knee—the "Pie Patrol," consisting of Madonna Thunder Hawk, Lorelei DeCora, and Thelma Rios, among others, all of whom had close ties to AIM's leaders—were implicated in Aquash's murder, charges that have since been denied by Thunder Hawk and DeCora. In 2010, Rios pleaded guilty to the kidnapping of Aquash and received a five-year sentence, most of which was commuted due to poor health. The article goes on to claim that Thunder Hawk and DeCora knew about the unsolved murder of yet another AIM activist: Ray Robinson, a Black civil rights activist who joined the occupation of Wounded Knee and was killed by fellow AIM members. Konigsberg, "Who Killed Anna Mae."

18. Churchill and Vander Wall, *Agents of Repression*, 175; Churchill and Vander Wall, *COINTELPRO Papers*, 262f.

19. Jaimes and Halsey, "American Indian Women," 328.

20. Bruce Johansen and Robert Maestas have made a compelling case in comparing the death ratio on Pine Ridge, the result of physical repression of Indigenous resistance, to that in Chile three years after the military coup that disposed President Allende in 1973. Johansen and Maestas, *Wasi'chu*, 83ff; Churchill and Vander Wall, *Agents of Repression*, 184.

21. Churchill and Vander Wall, *COINTELPRO Papers*, 231ff; Churchill and Vander Wall, *Agents of Repression*, 177ff, 181ff.

22. Quoted in David Weir and Lowell Bergmann, "The Killing of Anna Mae Aquash," *Rolling Stone*, April 7, 1977, 55.

23. Quoted in Weir and Bergmann, "The Killing of Anna Mae Aquash," 55.

24. Churchill and Vander Wall, *COINTELPRO Papers*, 268–269.

25. Stern, *Loud Hawk*.

26. Vander Wall, "A Warrior Caged," 306.

27. Churchill and Vander Wall, *Agents of Repression*; Churchill and Vander Wall, *COINTELPRO Papers*; Stern, *Loud Hawk*; Talbot, *Roots of Oppression*; Johansen and Maestas, *Wasi'chu*.

28. Bancroft and Waterman Wittstock, *We Are Still Here*, 91f.

29. Robbins, "Self-Determination and Subordination," 106–107.

30. Robbins, "Self-Determination and Subordination," 106–107.

31. Tóth, *From Wounded Knee to Checkpoint Charlie*, 141–167.
32. Robbins, "Self-Determination and Subordination," 107.
33. Rennard, "We're Still Here," 167–182.
34. Tóth, *From Wounded Knee to Checkpoint Charlie*, 71–116.
35. Quoted in Robbins, "Self-Determination and Subordination," 107.
36. Anonymous, "Red Man's International Warrior Society," mimeographed leaflet, undated (after May 9, 1973), Roger A. Finzel Papers, box 1 folder 8, Center for Southwest Research, University of New Mexico at Albuquerque, NM. See also Alfred and Lowe, "Warrior Societies," 11.
37. The painting featured images similar to those in Louis Hall's "Great Red Man's International Warrior Society" from December 1973. Yet another version of that image was painted in the Holocaust Museum at Wounded Knee, page 275.
38. Anonymous, "A Voice from AIM," 12.
39. Noriyuki, "The Women of Wounded Knee"; Thunder Hawk, "Madonna Thunder Hawk on Wounded Knee."
40. Jaimes and Halsey, "American Indian Women," 329.
41. Quoted in Antell, "American Indian Women Activists," 170f.
42. Means, "Women of All Red Nations," 51f.
43. Jaimes and Halsey, "American Indian Women," 329; Castle, "The Original Gangster," 275–278; Winona LaDuke, "Words from Indigenous Women's Network Meeting," *Akwesasne Notes* 17, no. 6 (Early Winter 1985): 8–9; Anonymous, "Women of all Red Nations (WARN)," *Akwesasne Notes* 10, no. 5 (Winter 1978): 15.
44. Noriyuki, "The Women of Wounded Knee."
45. O'Sullivan, "Informing Red Power," 968–973.
46. O'Sullivan, "Informing Red Power," 965–966, 973.
47. O'Sullivan, "Informing Red Power."
48. O'Sullivan, "Informing Red Power," 974.
49. Means, *Where White Men Fear to Tread*, 374–375, 378.
50. Bellecourt, *Thunder Before the Storm*, 117–118.
51. O'Sullivan, "Informing Red Power," 974.
52. Morgensen, *Spaces Between Us*, 93–104.
53. Nickel and Fehr, *In Good Relation*; Barker, *Critically Sovereign*; Green, *Making Space*; Huhndorf et al., *Indigenous Women and Feminism*.
54. These armed confrontations included the six-month occupation of state-owned land by Mohawk warriors at Moss Lake, New York, in 1974; the five-week armed takeover of the abandoned Alexian Brotherhood novitiate by a dozen members of the Menominee Warrior Society with AIM

support in Gresham, Wisconsin, in 1975; an eight-day occupation of the Fairchild factory on the Navajo Reservation in New Mexico in 1975; and two short-lived takeovers of the Yankton Sioux Industries Plant in Wagner, South Dakota, both in 1975. Nagel, *American Indian Ethnic Renewal*, 173–175; Johnson, Nagel, and Champagne, "American Indian Activism and Transformation," 307–308.

55. Nagel, *American Indian Ethnic Renewal*, 164, 175–178; Cornell, *Return of the Native*, 188, 202–213.

56. See *Akwesasne Notes* 10, no. 3 (Summer 1978) issue on "The Longest Walk."

57. Maluca van den Bergh and John Walsh, "The Longest Walk," *American Indian Journal* (September 1978): 17–30; Anonymous, "A Backlash Stalks the Indian," *Business Week*, September 11, 1978, 153, 156, 159, 160; Peter Monkres, "The Longest Walk, An Indian Pilgrimage," *Christian Century* (April 5, 1978): 350–352; Anonymous, "An Indian 'Nation' Is Gaining Unity, Respect—And Results," *U.S. News and World Report*, February 25, 1978, 60–61; Anonymous, "Indians March Toward Self-Rule," *U.S. News and World Report*, March 27, 1978, 72–74; Anonymous, "U.S. Indians: On Legal Trail-And Winning," *U.S. News and World Report*, May 26, 1978, 52–53.

58. Personal interview, Steven Naganashe Perry.

59. Chee, "The Longest Walk."

60. Longest Walk Washington Office, "Longest Walk Manifesto, Affirmation of Sovereignty of the Indigenous People of the Western Hemisphere," July 22, 1978 (28pp) in National Museum of the American Indian, National Congress of American Indians (NCAI), box 449, folder 24.

61. Johnson, Nagel, Champagne, "American Indian Activism and Transformation," 308.

62. Shelly Davis, "Split in AIM Leads to Charges," *News from Indian Country* (mid-January 1994): 1–3; Giago, "AIM Members' Infighting."

63. Anonymous, "AIM Leader, Clyde Bellecourt, Shot and Critically Wounded at Rosebud Res," *Akwesasne Notes* 5, no. 5 (Early Autumn 1973): 8.

64. Stern, *Loud Hawk*; Churchill and Vander Wall, *Agents of Repression*; Churchill and Vander Wall, *COINTELPRO Papers*; Trimbach and Trimbach, *American Indian Mafia*.

65. Konigsberg, "Who Killed Anna Mae."

66. Churchill and Vander Wall, *Agents of Repression*; Churchill and Vander Wall, *COINTELPRO Papers*; Talbot, *Roots of Oppression*; Johansen and Maestas, *Wasi'chu*; Trimbach and Trimbach, *American Indian Mafia*.

67. For an objective account, see Magnuson, *Wounded Knee 1973*.

68. Magnuson, *Wounded Knee 1973*, 47–50, 66–67, 74–76, 80–81, 131–133. For conflictual standpoints, see Churchill and Vander Wall, *Agents of Repression*; Trimbach and Trimbach, *American Indian Mafia*.

69. Dewing, *Wounded Knee II*, 167–176; Bellecourt, *Thunder Before the Storm*, 265–287; Means, *Where White Men Fear to Tread*, 432–441.

70. Stripes, "A Strategy of Resistance," 87–101; Reed, "Old Cowboys," 79–80.

71. Stripes, "A Strategy of Resistance," 90.

72. Plummer, "Hearing His Own Drum," 63.

73. Dennis Banks Interview, UO Today.

74. Anonymous, "Oklahoma Indian Activist Carter Camp Dies at Age 72," *Tulsa World*, January 3, 2014.

75. Bellecourt, *Thunder Before the Storm*, 259–264.

76. Means, *Where White Men Fear to Tread*; Bellecourt, *Thunder Before the Storm*; Banks, *Ojibwa Warrior*; Bancroft and Waterman Wittstock, *We Are Still Here*; Crow Dog, *Crow Dog*; Crow Dog, *Lakota Woman*; Brave Bird, *Ohitika Woman*; Kipp, *Viet Cong*. For documentaries, see *We Shall Remain: Wounded Knee*; *A Tattoo on My Heart*; *A Good Day to Die*; *Trudell*; *From Wounded Knee to Standing Rock: A Reporter's Journey*; *Taking AIM*; *Warrior: The Life of Leonard Peltier*; and *Hanta Po*.

77. See the American Indian Movement Interpretative Center, https://aimcollection.org (last accessed April 12, 2024).

78. Kipp, "The Eagles I Fed Who Did Not Love Me," 217, 223f.

79. Currey, "Wes Studi."

80. Nagel, *American Indian Ethnic Renewal*, 187ff.

81. Nagel, *American Indian Ethnic Renewal*, 158–212.

82. Nagel, *American Indian Ethnic Renewal*, 187–205.

83. Nagel, *American Indian Ethnic Renewal*, 190–198.

84. For example, see Tengan, *Native Men Remade*, 54.

85. Nagel, *American Indian Ethnic Renewal*, 10ff, 190ff, 194ff.

86. Nagel, *American Indian Ethnic Renewal*, 91ff.

87. Smith, *Decolonizing Methodologies*, 143–164; Tengan, *Native Men*, 57.

88. Nagel, *American Indian Ethnic Renewal*, 197.

89. Sneider, "Complementary Relationships," 66–72.

90. Sneider, "Complementary Relationships," 72–76.

91. Castile, *To Show Heart*, 147–180; Cornell, *Return of the Native*, 208–213.

92. Castile, *Taking Charge*, 36ff; Castile, *To Show Heart*, 73ff.

93. Wilkins and Stark, *American Indian Politics*, 87f.
94. Cornell, *Return of the Native*, 209.
95. Wilkins and Stark, *American Indian Politics*, 116ff; Castile, *To Show Heart*, 178–180; Castile, *Taking Charge*.
96. Steinman, "Settler Colonial Power," 1073–1130; Champagne, "From First Nations to Self-Government," 1672–1693.
97. Everson, *Red Power, White Discourse*, 8.
98. For the poll, see chapter 4, footnote 260.
99. Simpson and Yinger, "Techniques for Reducing Prejudice," 145–175.
100. Everson, *Red Power, White Discourse*, 23, 48–49.
101. Everson, *Red Power, White Discourse*, 22, 48–49.
102. Hutchinson, *Dynamics of Cultural Nationalism*, 16.
103. Banks and Ninham, *Remembering Wounded Knee* (Part 4).
104. *Warrior Societies* (documentary).
105. *Warrior Societies* (documentary).
106. Means, *Where White Men Fear to Tread*, 553.
107. Bellecourt, "American Indian Movement," 74; Charles Kills Enemy, interviewed by Herbert T. Hoover, May 14, 1973, AIRP 892, South Dakota Oral History Center, Institute of American Indian Studies, University of South Dakota, Vermillion.
108. AIM Interpretative Center and International Indian Treaty Council, ed., *American Indian Movement*, 3. The text is almost identical to an interview given by Charles Kills Enemy (AIRP 892).
109. Fowler, *Shared Symbols, Contested Meanings*, 155, 192.
110. Camp, "For Our Uncle, Wallace Black Elk," 5.
111. Nagel, *American Indian Ethnic Renewal*, 166–178.
112. See oral interviews in *A Tattoo on My Heart* (documentary).
113. Quoted from *A Tattoo on My Heart* (documentary).
114. Quoted from *A Tattoo on My Heart* (documentary).
115. Quoted from *A Tattoo on My Heart* (documentary).
116. Innes and Anderson, "Introduction," 4.
117. Quoted from *A Tattoo on My Heart* (documentary).
118. Quoted from *A Tattoo on My Heart* (documentary).
119. Personal interview, Gary Rowland.
120. Foster, "Joining the American Indian Movement."
121. Studi, "Oscar-winning Cherokee Actor."
122. Banks, *Remembering Wounded Knee* (Part 4).
123. Madonna Thunder Hawk and Phyllis Young, interviewed by Elizabeth Castle.

124. For an in-depth discussion of Indigenous women, feminism, tribalism, and activism, see Mihesuah, *Indigenous American Women*, 159–171.

125. Madonna Thunder Hawk and Phyllis Young interview.

126. Regina Brave interview.

127. *Warrior Women* (documentary); Castle, "The Original Gangster"; Castle, "Keeping One Foot in the Community."

128. Press conference Dennis Banks and Clyde Bellecourt, July 29, 2013.

129. The AIM Interpretative Center has not materialized yet; and aside from a defunct website, there was little information available online; last accessed April 12, 2024: https://aimcollection.org/pressroom/.

130. Tengan, *Native Men*, 66–67, 74–78.

131. King, "Imperial Recollections."

132. Morgensen, "Cutting to the Roots," 38.

133. Erll, *Memory in Culture*, 101–105.

134. Connerton, "Seven Types of Forgetting," 59–71.

135. Nagel, *American Indian Ethnic Renewal*, 9–12.

136. Camp, "War Stories"; Camp, "For Our Uncle"; Camp, "Wounded Knee Memories."

137. Camp, "War Stories."

138. Camp, "War Stories."

139. Camp, "War Stories."

140. Camp, "War Stories."

141. Camp, "War Stories."

142. Camp, "War Stories."

143. Camp, "War Stories."

144. Camp, "War Stories."

145. Camp, "War Stories."

146. Camp, "War Stories."

147. Camp, "War Stories."

148. Means, *Where White Men Fear to Tread*, 287–293.

149. Banks, *Ojibwa Warrior*, 209–213.

150. Camp, "War Stories."

151. Anonymous, "AIM Leader, Clyde Bellecourt, Shot and Critically Wounded at Rosebud Res.," *Akwesasne Notes* 5, no. 5 (Early Autumn 1973): 8.

152. Camp, "War Stories."

153. Camp, "War Stories."

154. Camp, "War Stories."

155. Camp, "War Stories."

156. Camp, "War Stories."

157. Carter, "For Our Uncle."
158. Carter, "For Our Uncle."
159. Carter, "For Our Uncle."
160. Carter, "For Our Uncle."
161. Anonymous, "Wounded Knee Occupation Force Warriors, Medicine Man, Make Statements During Their Trials," *Akwesasne Notes* 7, no. 3 (Summer 1975): 13.
162. Anonymous, "Wounded Knee Occupation."
163. A small body of work has explored the interplay between Indigenous masculinity, military service, and the commemoration of martial valor. For more general studies on Indigenous military service, perspectives on martial valor and hero-making, see Sonja John, "From Warrior to Soldier"; Voigt, "Race, Masculinity, and Martial Valor"; Roberts, "War, Masculinity, and Native Americans."
164. Personal interview, Nick Leading Fighter.
165. Personal interview, Alfred Theodore Boneshirt Whiting.
166. Personal interview, Alfred Theodore Boneshirt Whiting.
167. Personal interview, Fritz Wallace Eagle Shield.
168. Personal interview, Errol Brown Eyes.
169. Personal interview, Laura Waterman Wittstock.
170. Personal interview, Laura Waterman Wittstock.
171. Personal interview, Laura Waterman Wittstock.
172. Personal interview, Richard Kirkie.
173. Personal interview, George Lamont.
174. Personal interview, George Lamont.
175. See Elliot, "Indian Patriots on Last Stand Hill," 987–1015, especially 1004; Elliot, *Custerology*, 54–56; Schmittou and Logan, "Fluidity of Meaning."
176. Personal interview, George Lamont.
177. Personal interview, Tyrone Apple.
178. Personal interview, Terry Quilt.
179. Personal interview, Gary Rowland.
180. Personal interview, Gary Rowland.
181. Personal interview, Gary Rowland.
182. Personal interview, Gary Rowland.
183. Personal interview, Gary Rowland.
184. Personal interview, Gary Rowland.
185. This interview was conducted in 2013 when Whiteclay, Nebraska, was serving alcohol to reservation residents on Pine Ride, South Dakota,

where alcohol is banned and alcohol-related problems are rampant. In 2017, the four liquor stores in Whiteclay were denied license renewals.

186. The Wounded Knee Museum was in operation in 2013 but was out of service when the author visited again in 2019.

187. Camp, "Wounded Knee Memories."
188. Dewing, *Wounded Knee II*, 172.
189. Bellecourt, *Thunder Before the Storm*, 315.
190. *Warrior Societies* (documentary).
191. *Warrior Societies* (documentary).
192. Bellecourt, *Thunder Before the Storm*, 146.
193. Bellecourt, *Thunder Before the Storm*, 259–264.
194. Means, *Where White Men Fear to Tread*, 541.
195. Banks, *Ojibwa Warrior*, 209.
196. Shortly after her death in October 2022, Sacheen Littlefeather was exposed for fabricating her Indigenous identity. Maria Louise Cruz, better known as Sacheen Littlefeather was not Apache, as she claimed, but had Mexican roots. At the center of the Littlefeather controversy are fundamental questions about what it means to be Native American. Jacqueline Keeler, "Sacheen Littlefeather Was a Native American Icon. Her Sisters Say She Was an Ethnic Fraud," *San Francisco Chronicle*, October 25, 2022, https://www.sfchronicle.com/opinion/openforum/article/Sacheen-Littlefeather-oscar-Native-pretendian-17520648.php (last accessed April 22, 2024).

197. Banks, *Remembering Wounded Knee* (Part 5).
198. Stumbo, "A World Apart," 10.
199. Sayer, *Ghost Dancing*, 225.
200. Sayer, *Ghost Dancing*, 301.
201. Stumbo, "A World Apart," 18.
202. Quoted in Jaimes and Halsey, "American Indian Women," 329.
203. Smith and Warrior, *Like a Hurricane*, 269ff.
204. Means, *Where White Men Fear to Tread*, 540; Banks, *Ojibwa Warrior*, 360; Bellecourt, *Thunder Before the Storm*, 315–318. See also: Jeremy Schneider, "From Wounded Knee to Capitol Hill, The History, Achievements and Legacy of the American Indian Movement," *Indian Nation* 3, no. 1 (April 1976).

205. Vizenor, "Confrontation or Negotiation," 380.
206. Nagel, *American Indian Ethnic Renewal*.
207. Fixico, *Indian Resilience*, 148.
208. Dewing, *Wounded Knee II*, 176.

209. This remembering and commemorating occurred within the material, social, and mental dimension of memory culture. See Erll, *Memory in Culture*, 95–112.

210. Hall, *Warrior's Handbook*.

211. Louis Hall, *A.I.M., Red Man's Great International Warrior Society*, painting 1973.

212. Clyde Bellecourt, "A.I.M. 10th Anniversary Poster," *Survival News*, undated, in Roger A. Finzel Papers, box 1, folder 2, Center for Southwest Research, University of New Mexico, Albuquerque, New Mexico.

213. Alfred and Lowe, "Warrior Societies."

214. Louis Hall, *A.I.M.*; Alfred and Lowe, "Warrior Societies," 11.

215. Hall, "Warrior Manifesto."

216. Hall, "What Is the Warrior Society." See also Alfred and Lowe, "Warrior Societies," 10–11.

217. Bruce, "We Remember Wounded Knee 1890–1973."

218. Anonymous, "Remember Wounded Knee."

219. Rich, "Remember Wounded Knee," 70–91. For a comparative study of visual representations of Indigeneity at Wounded Knee in 1973 and Standing Rock in 2016 through Indigenous media outlets, see Bordeaux, "The American Indian Movement and the Politics of Nostalgia."

220. Siddons, "Red Power and the Black Panther," 26.

221. Johnson, "We Were All Wounded at Wounded Knee,' 92–106.

222. Lee, "Singing for People," 61–74.

223. Anonymous, "Ometakuyeayasi: Dialogues with Dennis Banks," *Black Hills Monthly Magazine* 2, no. 4 (April 1981): 21, in Kay Cole Papers, box 3, folder 28, Center for Southwest Research, University of New Mexico, Albuquerque.

224. Anonymous, "Ometakuyeayasi: Dialogues with Dennis Banks."

225. Harris, "How Did Colonialism Dispossess?" 165–182.

226. *Powwow Highway* (film); *Thunderheart* (film); *Lakota Woman* (film). See also Reed, "Old Cowboys."

227. *We Shall Remain: Wounded Knee* (documentary); *A Tattoo on My Heart* (documentary); *A Good Day to Die* (documentary); *Trudell* (documentary); *From Wounded Knee to Standing Rock: A Reporter's Journey* (documentary); *Taking AIM* (documentary). See also *Hanta Po* (documentary).

228. *Warrior Women* (documentary).

229. Anna Mae Aquash's life and death has inspired an investigative journalist book, a biography, a documentary, and a theater play and play critique; Hendricksen, *Unquiet Grave*; Brand, *The Life and Death of Anna*

*Mae Aquash*; *Anna Mae Brave-Hearted Woman* (documentary); Nolan, *Annie Mae's Movement* (play); Pettit, "A Legacy of Furious Men" (play critique). For Leonard Peltier, see Messerschmidt, *The Trial of Leonard Peltier*; Peltier, *Prison Writings*; Matthiessen, *In the Spirit of Crazy Horse*. See also *Warrior: The Life of Leonard Peltier* (documentary).

## Conclusion

1. Justin Worland, "What to Know About the Dakota Access Pipeline Protests," *Time*, October 28, 2016, https://time.com/4548566/dakota-access-pipeline-standing-rock-sioux/ (last accessed August 18, 2022); Rebecca Hersher, "Key Moments in the Dakota Access Pipeline Fight," NPR, February 22, 2017, https://www.npr.org/sections/thetwo-way/2017/02/22/514988040/key-moments-in-the-dakota-access-pipeline-fight (last accessed April 12, 2024).

2. Anonymous, "Stand With Standing Rock, Protect Protesters' Rights," *ACLU*, undated, https://www.aclu.org/issues/free-speech/rights-protesters/stand-standing-rock (last accessed April 12, 2024); Brad Plumer, "The Battle over the Dakota Access Pipeline, explained," *Vox*, November 29, 2016, https://www.vox.com/2016/9/9/12862958/dakota-access-pipeline-fight (last accessed April 12, 2024).

3. Christopher Mele, "Veterans Serve as 'Human Shields' for Dakota Pipeline Protesters," *New York Times*, November 29, 2016.

4. Ernest Scheyder and Terray Sylvester, "U.S. Veterans, Tribe Elders Join Forces in Pipeline Protest," in *Reuters*, December 3, 2016; Ernest Scheyder and Terray Sylvester, "Sense of Duty Draws U.S. Veterans to Dakota Pipeline Protest," in *Reuters* December 4, 2016.

5. Estes, *Our History Is the Future*; Estes, *Standing with Standing Rock*.

6. Anonymous, "Empire Files: Fighting At Standing Rock with AIM Founder Dennis Banks," *TeleSUR English*, https://www.youtube.com/watch?v=KqanmctAoLs (last accessed August 18, 2022).

7. Anonymous, "Empire Files: Fighting At Standing Rock with AIM Founder Dennis Banks," *TeleSUR English*, https://www.youtube.com/watch?v=KqanmctAoLs (last accessed August 18, 2022).

8. "Remembering Clyde Bellecourt: Making Sure We Had Money for a Meal on Our Way Home from Standing Rock," *Native News Online*, undated. https://nativenewsonline.net/opinion/remembering-clyde-bellecourt-making-sure-we-had-money-for-a-meal-on-our-way-home-from-standing-rock (last accessed August 18, 2022).

9. Estes, *Our History Is the Future*; Estes, *Standing with Standing Rock*.
10. Friedler, "Get the Hell Off."
11. Carroll, *Medicine Bags*, 171–172; Alfred and Lowe, "Warrior Societies."
12. For example, see Voigt, "Indigenous and non-Indigenous Combat Veterans and the Sweat Lodge (Inipi) Ritual," 103–116.
13. Nagel, *American Indian Ethnic Renewal*, 140, 187–212.
14. AIAN reports 2017 (for 2015), 2015 (for 2013), 2012, 2006. See also Carroll, *Medicine Bags*, 207–222.
15. AIAN reports.
16. Garriott and Barlow, *Police in a Multicultural Society*, 322; Usbeck, "Selling the 'Natural-Born Warrior,'" 175–178.
17. Carroll, *Medicine Bags*, 171. See also Holm, *Strong Hearts*, 179.
18. Alfred and Lowe, "Warrior Societies," 10–22.
19. Alfred and Lowe, "Warrior Societies," 10–22.
20. Alfred and Lowe, "Warrior Societies."
21. Grant and Feimer, "Street Gangs in Indian Country, A Clash of Cultures"; Grant, "Native American Involvement on the Gang Subculture, Current Trends and Dynamics," 5–15; Hailer, *American Indian Involvement in Urban Street Gangs: Invisible or More?*
22. Carney and Stuckey, "The World As the American Frontier," 237–247; Espey, "America and Vietnam: The Indian Subtext."
23. Carroll, *Medicine Bags*, 62–85; King, *Unsettling America*, 28–29.
24. Carroll, *Medicine Bags*, 179–196; Rosier, *Serving Their Country*, 278–282; Elliot, *Custerology*, 273–282.

# Bibliography

### Primary Sources

*Archival Collections*

Archives and Special Collections, University Libraries, University of South Dakota, Vermilion, SD.
    American Indian Research Project
    James G. Abourezk Papers, 1970–1983
Association on American Indian Affairs (AAAIA) Papers, Seeley G. Mudd Library, Princeton University, Princeton, NJ.
Center for Southwest Research, University Libraries, University of New Mexico, Albuquerque, NM.
    Robert L. Anderson American Indian Movement Papers, 1973–2009
    Roger A. Finzel American Indian Movement Papers, 1965–1995
    Kay Cole Papers, 1971–1992
    Carol Sullivan Papers, 1966–2014
Don Doll, S.J. Collection, Special Collections and University Archives, Marquette University, Milwaukee, WI.
Doris Duke Oral History Project, American Indian Historical Research Project, Manuscript Division, Marriott Library, University of Utah, Salt Lake City, UT.

Doris Duke Oral History Project, American Indian Historical Research Project, Center for Southwest Research. Special Collections, University of New Mexico, Albuquerque, NM.

The FBI Files on the American Indian Movement and Wounded Knee, University of Hamburg, Germany.

National Congress of American Indians (NCAI) Files, Cultural Resources Center, National Museum of the American Indian (NMAI), Suitland, MD.

Stanley Lyman Papers, Manuscript Division, Marriott Library, University of Utah, Salt Lake City, UT.

Pacifica Radio Archives, North Hollywood, CA.

South Dakota Vietnam Veterans Oral History Project, South Dakota Historical Society, Pierre, SD.

Wounded Knee Legal Defense/Offense Records, Minnesota Historical Society Manuscripts Collection, St. Paul, MN.

## Newspaper Archival Collections

American Indian Periodicals from the Princeton University Library.

American Indian Periodicals from the State Historical Society of Wisconsin, 1884–1981.

Periodicals by and about North American Indians, 1923–1981.

Underground Press Collection, Library of Congress, Washington, DC.

## Oral Interviews Conducted by the Author

Robert Anderson, American Indian Movement, August 12, 2009.

Tyrone Apple (Lakota), US Army, Vietnam, July 22, 2013.

Patricia Ballenger (Ojibwe), American Indian Movement, June 20 and 24, 2013.

Dennis J. Banks (Ojibwe), American Indian Movement, January 31, 2014.

Clyde Bellecourt (Ojibwe) and Dennis Banks (Ojibwa), American Indian Movement, Press Conference, June 29, 2013.

Clyde Bellecourt (Ojibwe), American Indian Movement, June 15, 2013.

Ed Charging Elk (Lakota), US Army, Vietnam, July 19, 2013.

Allen Cooper, American Indian Movement, August 9, 2009.

Fritz Wallace Eagle Shield (Lakota), US Army, Vietnam, August 23, 2013.

George Lamont (Lakota), US Army, Vietnam, July 22, 2013.

Nick Leading Fighter (Lakota), US Army, Vietnam, July 19, 2013.

William Manard (Lakota), US Army, Vietnam, July 19, 2013.

Steven Naganashe Perry (Ojibwe), US Army, Vietnam, June 14, 2013.
Terry Quilt (Lower Brule), US Marines, Vietnam, July 13, 2013.
Gary Rowland (Lakota), US Army, Post-Vietnam, July 23, 2013.
Carol Sullivan, August 10, 2009.
Sonja Schierle, June 2, 2015.
Madonna Thunder Hawk (Lakota), American Indian Movement, February 12, 2014.
Laura Waterman Wittstock (Seneca), Indigenous Activist, July 6, 2013.
Alfred Theodore Boneshirt Whiting (Lakota), US Navy (Vietnam Era), July 22, 2019.

*Newspapers and Magazines*

*Akwesasne Notes*
*Albuquerque Journal*
*American Opinion*
*Business Week*
*Chicago Tribune*
*Christian Century*
*Collier's Weekly*
*Custer County Chronicles*
*Custer Weekly*
*Detroit News*
*Ebony*
*Huffington Post*
*LA Times*
*Lincoln Star*
*Minneapolis Tribune*
*New York Times*
*New York Times Magazine*
*News From Indian Country*
*Newsweek*
*The Nishnawbe News*
*Omaha World-Herald*
*People*
*Ramparts*
*Rapid City Journal*
*San Francisco Chronicle*
*Scottsbluff Star-Herald*

*Shannon County News*
*Time*
*Tulsa World*
*US News and World Report*
*Washington Post*
*Wichita Daily News*

### Books, Articles, Oral Interviews, and Other Sources

Adams, John. Interviewed by James Abourezk. September 12, 1980. James G. Abourezk Papers, Archives and Special Collections, University Libraries, University of South Dakota.

A.I.M. Interpretative Center and International Indian Treaty Council, eds. *American Indian Movement, Past, Present, and Future.* Minneapolis and San Francisco. Undated.

Akwesasne Notes. *BIA, I'm Not Your Indian Anymore.* 3rd print. Rooseveltown, NY: Akwesasne Notes, 1976.

———. *Voices from Wounded Knee, 1973, In the Words of the Participants.* 3rd ed. Rooseveltown, NY: Akwesasne Notes, 1976.

Anderson, Robert. "The Second Battle of Wounded Knee." Robert Anderson Papers, Collection No. MSS 695, Box 1 Folder 3, Center for Southwest Research, University of New Mexico at Albuquerque, NM.

Anonymous. "Ometakuyeayasi: Dialogues with Dennis Banks." *Black Hills Monthly Magazine* 2, no. 4 (April 1981): 20, 21, 28.

Anonymous. "Remember Wounded Knee." Poster with Bobby Onco. Undated. Library of Congress. Last accessed July 18, 2018. https://www.loc.gov/item/yan1996000165/PP/.

Bancroft, Dick, and Laura Waterman Wittstock. *We Are Still Here: A Photographic History of the American Indian Movement.* St. Paul: Minnesota Historical Society, 2013.

Banks, Dennis. "The Black Scholar Interviews: Dennis Banks." *Black Scholar* 7, no. 9 (June 1976): 28–36.

———. Interviewed by James Abourezk. July 20, 1980. James G. Abourezk Papers, Archives and Special Collections, University Libraries, University of South Dakota.

Banks, Dennis. With Richard Erdoes. *Ojibwa Warrior: Dennis Banks and the Rise of the American Indian Movement.* Norman: University of Oklahoma Press, 2004.

Banks, Dennis, and Dorothy Ninham. *Remembering Wounded Knee*, Parts

1–5, Dennis Banks and Dorothy Ninham, directed by Friends of the American Indian Movement, 2015, accessed July 1, 2020.
- https://www.youtube.com/watch?v=VIUfEXmJhIE (Part 1)
- https://www.youtube.com/watch?v=P4o0VhOxikg (Part 2)
- https://www.youtube.com/watch?v=lXgh1qlSR6E&t=1s (Part 3)
- https://www.youtube.com/watch?v=ToFctSG7PJI (Part 4)
- https://www.youtube.com/watch?v=55mCJpP5-sM (Part 5)

Bellecourt, Clye. Interviewed by James Abourezk. July 20, 1980. James G. Abourezk Papers, Archives and Special Collections, University Libraries, University of South Dakota.

Bellecourt, Clyde, and Jon Lurie. *The Thunder Before the Storm: The Autobiography of Clyde Bellecourt*. Saint Paul: Minnesota Historical Society Press, 2016.

Bellecourt, Vernon. "Penthouse Interview: Vernon Bellecourt." *Penthouse International Magazine for Men* (July 1973): 59–64, 122, 131–132.

———. "American Indian Movement." In *Contemporary Native American Address*, edited by John Maestas, 66–82. Provo, UT: Brigham Young University 1976.

———. "Birth of AIM." In *Native American Testimony, A Chronicle of Indian-White Relations from Prophecy to Present, 1492–2000*, edited by Peter Nabokov, 372–376. New York: Penguin Books, 1999.

Benton-Benai, Eddie. "Interview with Eddie Benton, Director, St. Paul American Indian Movement on March 14, 1973," File 176–2404, Section 8, March 21–24, 1973. In *The FBI Files on the American Indian Movement and Wounded Knee*, edited by Rolland Dewing. Frederick, MD: University Publications of America, 1986. Reel 21, 142–148.

Brave, Regina. Interviewed by Elizabeth Castle, February 17, 2005, accessed July 1, 2020, https://www.youtube.com/watch?v=7ComjbEmt4Y&t=1s.

Brave Bird, Mary, and Richard Erdoes. *Lakota Woman*. New York, NY: Grove Weidenfeld, 1990.

———. *Ohitika Woman*. New York: HarperPerennial, 1993.

Braudy, Susan. "'We Will Remember' Survival School." *Ms. Magazine* (July 1976): 77, 78, 79, 80, 94, 120.

Bruce, Carter. "We Remember Wounded Knee 1890–1973." Poster. Undated. Library of Congress, last accessed July 18, 2018. http://www.loc.gov/pictures/item/2015649244/.

Burnette, Robert, and John Koster. *The Road to Wounded Knee*. New York: Bantam Books, 1974.

Camp, Carter. "History and Philosophy of AIM, Series: The Road to Wounded Knee, No. 3." *KPFA Broadcast*, March 29, 1973. Pacifica Radio Archives, North Hollywood, CA.

———. "When in the Course of Human Events, An Interview with Carter Camp." *Akwesasne Notes* 5, no. 5 (Autumn 1973): 11.

———. "War Stories and Wounded Knee 1973." *News from Indian Country* (March 10, 2003): 10a.

———. "For Our Uncle, Wallace Black Elk." *Country Road Chronicles* (February 29, 2004): 5.

———. Interviewed for PBS "We Shall Remain: Wounded Knee (Episode Five)," *Native American Netroots*. Last accessed April 12, 2024. http://nativeamericannetroots.net/diary/1279.

———. "Wounded Knee Memories." *Native American Netroots*. Undated. Last accessed July 18, 2018. http://nativeamericannetroots.net/diary/1279.

Cannon, Martin J. *Men, Masculinity, and the Indian Act*. Vancouver & Toronto: UBC Press 2019.

Carmichael, Stokely, and Charles V. Hamilton. *Black Power: The Politics of Liberation in America*. New York: Vintage Books, 1967.

Collier, Peter. "Salmon Fishing in America: The Indians vs. The State of Washington." *Ramparts* (April 1971): 36–45.

———. "Wounded Knee: The New Indian War." *Ramparts* 11, no. 12 (June 1973): 25–29, 56–59.

Collins, Paul. "Showdown at Wounded Knee." *Ebony* 28, no. 8 (June 1973): 46, 47, 50, 52, 53, 56.

Crow Dog, Leonard, and Richard Erdoes. *Crow Dog: Four Generations of Sioux Medicine Men*. New York, NY: HarperCollins Publishers, 1995.

Foster, Lenny. "Joining the American Indian Movement," Filmed by Robert Upham, accessed April 12, 2024, https://www.youtube.com/watch?v=5J2s3P0RwtE.

Friedler, Delilah. "Get the Hell Off": The Indigenous Fight to Stop a Uranium Mine in the Black Hills." *Mother Jones*, March/April 2020. https://www.motherjones.com/politics/2020/05/the-black-hills-are-not-for-sale/.

Hall, Bill. Interviewed by James Abourezk, September 11, 1980, James G. Abourezk Papers, Archives and Special Collections, University Libraries, University of South Dakota, Vermillion, SD.

Hall, Louis. *A.I.M., Red Man's Great International Warrior Society*, painting 1973.

———. "What Is the Warrior Society." *Indian Survival Crisis Bulletin* 1 (September 1983). Last accessed July 18, 2018. http://www.louishall.com/newsletters/warrior/1.html.

———. "Warrior Manifesto." *Indian Survival Crisis Bulletin* 2 (October 1983). Last accessed July 18, 2018. http://www.louishall.com/newsletters/warrior/2.html.

———. *Warrior's Handbook*. Undated. Last accessed July 18, 2018. http://www.louishall.com/books/warrior.html.

Hathaway, Joan. Interviewed by Earl Ausle. July 25, 1973. South Dakota Oral History Center, Institute of American Indian Studies, American Indian Research Project 806, University of South Dakota, Vermillion, SD.

Hayes, Jack. "Blood Brothers." *Minneapolis-St. Paul Magazine*, March 1996, 50–53, 80–89, 250.

Hickey, Neil. "Was the Truth Buried at Wounded Knee? (Four Part Series)." *TV Guide*, December 1–22, 1973.

Huck, Susan L. M. "Renegades: The Second Battle of Wounded Knee." *American Opinion*, May 1973, 1–14.

Ickes, Harold L. "Indians Have a Name for Hitler." *Collier's Weekly*, January 15, 1944, 58.

Johnson, Troy, ed. *You Are on Indian Land! Alcatraz Island, 1969–1971*. Los Angeles: American Indian Studies Center, University of California, 1995.

———. *Alcatraz, Indian Land Forever*. Los Angeles: American Indian Studies Center, University of California, 1994.

Josephy, Alvin M., Joane Nagel, and Troy Johnson. *Red Power: The American Indians' Fight for Freedom*. 2nd ed. Lincoln: University of Nebraska Press, 1999.

Kills Enemy, Charles. Interviewed by Herbert T. Hoover, May 14, 1973. American Indian Research Project, AIRP 892. South Dakota Oral History Center, Institute of American Indian Studies, University of South Dakota, Vermillion, SD.

Kipp, Woody. *Viet Cong at Wounded Knee: The Trail of a Blackfeet Activist*. Lincoln: University of Nebraska Press, 2004.

———. "The Eagles I Fed Who Did Not Love Me," *American Indian Culture and Research Journal* 18, no. 4 (1994): 213–232.

Kunkin, Art. "The Legal Case for Wounded Knee, An Interview with Carter Camp and Mark Lane." *Los Angeles Free Press*, June 6–24, 1973.

LaCourse, Richard. "In the Caravan's Wake: An Unstable Status Quo." *Legislative Review* 2 (November 1, 1972): 14–21.
Lame Deer, John Fire, and Richard Erdoes. *Lame Deer, Seeker of Visions*. New York: Pocket Books, 1994.
Leach, Gary (Colville/Sioux). Interviewed by Irene Silentman and Anna Boyd, February 5, 1970. Doris Duke Oral History Project, American Indian Historical Research Project, Transcript Tape 453, Center for Southwest Research. Special Collections. University of New Mexico, Albuquerque, NM.
Linderman, Lawrence. "Gallery Interview: Indian Leader Russell Means." *Gallery* (August 1973): 38, 39, 41, 42, 61, 62, 128, 132, 133, 134.
Littlemoon, Walter, with Jane Ridgway. *They Called Me Uncivilized: The Memoir of an Everyday Lakota Man from Wounded Knee*. Bloomington, IN: iUniverse, 2009.
Longest Walk Washington Office. "Longest Walk Manifesto, Affirmation of Sovereignty of the Indigenous People of the Western Hemisphere." July 22, 1978 (28pp.). National Museum of the American Indian, National Congress of American Indians (NCAI), Box 449, Folder 24.
Luck, Owen. "A Witness at Wounded Knee, 1973." *Princeton University Library Chronicle* 67, no. 2 (Winter 2006): 330–358.
Lyman, Stanley David, Floyd A. O'Neill, Susan K. Lyman, and Susan McKay. *Wounded Knee 1973*. Lincoln: University of Nebraska Press, 1991.
McKiernan, Barry. "The Impact: A Firsthand Review." *Minnesota Leader* 1, no. 3 (December 30, 1974): 12.
———. "The Media." *Minnesota Leader* 1, no. 3 (December 30, 1974): 8–11.
———. "Notes from a Day at Wounded Knee." *Minnesota Leader* 1, no. 3 (December 30, 1974): 6–7.
———. "The Trial." *Minnesota Leader* 1, no. 3 (December 30, 1974): 4–5, 11.
———. "Wounded Knee: A Firsthand Review." *Minnesota Leader* 1, no. 3 (December 30, 1974): 1–3, 11.
Means, Bill. "I Wanna Wear That Uniform." Extended interviews by Emily Kunstler and Sarah Kunstler for the documentary *William Kunstler, Disturbing the Universe*. Produced and directed by Emily Kunstler and Sarah Kunstler. Disturbing the Universe, Independent Television Service, 2010. Last accessed July 15, 2018. http://www.pbs.org/pov/disturbingtheuniverse/extended-interviews/3/.
Means, Lorelei DeCora. "Women of All Red Nations." In *Red Power: The*

*American Indians' Fight for Freedom*, 2nd ed., edited by Alvin M. Josephy, Joane Nagel, and Troy Johnson, 51–52. Lincoln: University of Nebraska Press, 1999.

Means, Russell. Interviewed by James Abourezk. May 7, 1991 (Transcript). James G. Abourezk Papers. Archives and Special Collections. University Libraries. University of South Dakota.

———. "Raymond Yellow Thunder." In *We, The People of Earth and Elders Volume II*, edited by Serle L. Chapman, 229–232. Missoula, MO: Mountain Press Publishing, 2000.

Means, Russell, and Marvin J. Wolf. *Where White Men Fear to Tread: The Autobiography of Russell Means*. New York: St. Martin's Press, 1995.

Nolan, Yvette. *Annie Mae's Movement*. Toronto: Playwrights Union of Canada, 1999.

Peltier, Leonard. *Prison Writings, My Life Is My Sundance*. New York, NY: St. Martin's Griffin, 1992.

Plummer, William. "Hearing His Own Drum." *People* (December 10, 1992): 63–64, 68, 70.

Pottinger, Stan. Interviewed by James Abourezk, August 22, 1980, transcript, James G. Abourezk Papers, Archives and Special Collections, University Libraries, University of South Dakota, Vermillion, SD.

Rios, Thelma. "David Seals, Interviews with Thelma Rios." January 10, 2004. John Graham Defense Committee. Last accessed April 12, 2024. http://www.grahamdefense.org/20040110seals.htm.

Roubideaux, Thomas L. *South Dakota Vietnam Veterans Oral History Project*. South Dakota Historical Society, Pierre, SD.

Schultz, Terry. "Bamboozle Me Not at Wounded Knee." *Harper's* 246, no. 1477 (June 1973): 46–48, 53–56.

Smith, Desmond. "Media Coup D'Etat." *Nation* 216, no. 26 (June 25, 1973): 806–809.

Stands in Timber, John, and Margot Liberty. *Cheyenne Memoirs*, 2nd ed. New Haven, CT: Yale University Press, 1967.

Steiner, Stan. *The New Indians*. New York: Delta Book, 1968.

Studi, Wes. "Oscar-Winning Cherokee Actor Wes Studi on His Culture, His Work, and the Award of a Lifetime," CBC Radio News, interview by Rosanna Deer Child, undated. Last accessed April 12, 2024, https://www.cbc.ca/player/play/1630072387808.

———. "Conversations with Wes Studi," *SAG-AFTRA Foundation*, March 22, 2019, last accessed April 12, 2024, https://www.youtube.com/watch?v=eLW7WFw4xU4&t=1630s.

Stumbo, Bella. "A World Apart, Russell Means and Dennis Bank, Back at Wounded Knee." *Los Angeles Times Magazine* 2, vol. 24 (June 15, 1986): 10–21.

Thunder Hawk, Madonna. Interviewed by James Abourezk. July 18, 1980. James G. Abourezk Papers, Archives and Special Collections, University Libraries, University of South Dakota.

———. "Madonna Thunder Hawk on Wounded Knee." Extended interviews by Emily Kunstler and Sarah Kunstler for the documentary *William Kunstler, Disturbing the Universe*. Produced and directed by Emily Kunstler and Sarah Kunstler. Disturbing the Universe, Independent Television Service, 2010. Last accessed July 15, 2018. http://www.pbs.org/pov/disturbingtheuniverse/extended-interviews/9/.

Thunder Hawk, Madonna, and Choach Means. Interviewed by Elizabeth Castle, February 2, 2005, accessed July 1, 2020, https://www.youtube.com/watch?v=t-2Rmjdmg2Q&t=5s.

Thunder Hawk, Madonna, and Phyllis Young. Interviewed by Elizabeth Castle, January 27, 2005, accessed July 1, 2020, https://www.youtube.com/watch?v=CjcyKnmcXxI.

Treuer, Robert. "Seven Days in November." *Washingtonian* (May 1978): 74–78, 96–101.

Trudell, John. Interviewed by James Abourezk. July 18, 1980. James G. Abourezk Papers, Archives and Special Collections, University Libraries, University of South Dakota.

Young Bear, Severt, and R. D. Theisz. *Standing in the Light: A Lakota Way of Seeing*. Lincoln: University of Nebraska Press, 1994.

Walker, James R. *Lakota Society*. Edited by Raymond DeMallie. Lincoln: University of Nebraska Press, 1982.

———. *Lakota Belief and Ritual*, Edited by Raymond DeMallie and Elaine A. Jahner. Lincoln: University of Nebraska Press, 1991.

Westermeyer, Joseph J. "Indian Powerlessness in Minnesota." *Society* 10, no. 3 (March/April 1973): 45–47, 50–52.

Whitebird, Francis. *South Dakota Vietnam Veterans Oral History Project*. South Dakota Historical Society, Pierre, SD.

Wideman, John Edgar. "Russell Means." *Modern Maturity Magazine* 38, no. 5 (September/October 1995): 68–79.

Wounded Knee Legal Defense/Offense Committee. "The Opening Statements of Russell Means and Dennis Banks in U.S. vs Russell Means and U.S. vs Dennis Banks, Feb. 12, 1974." WKLDOC Records, Signature 147.I.5B, Box 46, MHSMC, St. Paul, MN.

Zimmerman, Bill. *Airlift to Wounded Knee.* Chicago: Swallow Press, 1976.

Zimmerman, Bill. Interviewed by James Abourezk. September 8, 1980. James G. Abourezk Papers, Archives and Special Collections, University Libraries, University of South Dakota.

## Government Documents and Official Papers

Alfred, Taiaiake, and Lana Lowe. "Warrior Societies in Contemporary Indigenous Communities." Paper prepared for the Ipperwash Inquiry. May 2005. Last accessed April 12, 2024. https://www.attorneygeneral.jus.gov.on.ca/inquiries/ipperwash/policy_part/research/index.html.

Department of Veterans Affairs, *American Indian and Alaska Native Veterans: 2015 American Community Survey,* August 2017, 24pp.

———. *American Indian and Alaska Native Veterans: 2013 American Community Survey,* May 2015, 25pp.

———. *American Indian and Alaska Native Service Members and Veterans,* September 2012, 28pp.

———. *American Indian and Alaska Native Veterans: Lasting Contributions,* September 2006, 21pp.

Harkins, Arthur M, and Richard G. Woods. *Attitudes of Minneapolis Agency Personnel toward Urban Indians.* Minneapolis, MN: University of Minnesota, Training Center for Community Programs, December 1968.

Federal Bureau of Investigation. *Report for Pine Ridge Indian Reservation, South Dakota, Accounting for Native American Deaths Pine Ridge Indian Reservation, South Dakota.* Report of the Federal Bureau of Investigation Minneapolis Division, May 2000. Last accessed April 12, 2024, https://www.fbi.gov/minneapolis/about-us/history-1/copy_of_report-for-pine-ridge-indian-reservation-south-dakota.

Grant, Christopher. "Native American Involvement on the Gang Subculture, Current Trends and Dynamics." Community Corrections Institute, Bureau of Justice Assistance, Office of Justice Programs, US Department of Justice, July 2013, 5–15. Last accessed April 12, 2024, http://www.communitycorrections.org/images/publications/NAInvolveinGangs-Trends.pdf. Website has been moved to here: https://storage.googleapis.com/night-fox-clients-storage/communitycorrections.org/publications/files/5cf1609d761a38.07207337.pdf.

League of Women Voters of Minneapolis. *Indians in Minneapolis.* Minneapolis, MN: April 1968.

———. *The Police and the Community.* Minneapolis, February 1971.

———. *The Police and the Community: A Second Look*. Minneapolis, March 1976.

McEldowney, Mary Ellen. *Where We're At: Statistical Report on Status of Minorities and Women in South Dakota*. Division of Human Rights, Department of Commerce and Consumer Affairs, South Dakota: August 1973.

Minnesota Advisory Committee to the US Commission on Civil Rights. *Bridging the Gap: The Twin Cities Native American Community*. St. Paul, MN, January 1975.

Montana-North Dakota-South Dakota Joint Advisory Committee to the US Commission on Civil Rights, *Indian Civil Rights Issues in Montana, North Dakota, South Dakota*. Washington, DC: Government Printing Office, 1974.

*Official Report of the Nineteenth Annual Conference of Charities and Correction* (1892), 46–59. Reprinted in Richard H. Pratt, "The Advantages of Mingling Indians with Whites," in *Americanizing the American Indians: Writings by the "Friends of the Indian" 1880–1900* (Cambridge, MA: Harvard University Press, 1973), 260–271.

South Dakota Advisory Committee to the US Commission on Civil Rights, *Liberty and Justice for All*. Washington, DC: Government Printing Office, October 1977.

———. *Native Americans in South Dakota: An Erosion of Confidence in the Justice System*. Washington, DC: Government Printing Office, March 2000.

US Commission on Civil Rights. *Events Surrounding Recent Murders on the Pine Ridge Reservation in South Dakota*. Rocky Mountain Regional Office, Denver, March 3, 1976.

US Congress, House of Representatives, Hearings Before the Subcommittee on Indian Affairs of the Committee on Interior and Insular Affairs. *Seizure and Occupation of the Bureau of Indian Affairs Headquarters Building*. Held in Washington, DC, December 4 and 5, 1972, 92nd Congress. Washington, DC: US Government Printing Office, 1972.

US Congress, Senate, Hearings Before the Subcommittee on Indian Affairs of The Committee on Interior and Insular Affairs, *Occupation of Wounded Knee, The Causes and Aftermath of the Wounded Knee Takeover*. 93rd Congress, June 16, 1973, Pine Ridge, S.D. and June 17, 1973, Kyle, S.D. Washington, DC: US Government Printing Office, 1974.

US Congress, Senate, Hearings Before the Subcommittee to Investigate the Administration of the Internal Security Act and Other Internal

Security Laws of the Committee on the Judiciary, *Revolutionary Activities Within the United States, The American Indian Movement*. 94th Congress, 2nd Session, April 6, 1976. Washington, DC: US Government Printing Office 1976.

### Documentaries, Films, and News Segments

*Anna Mae Brave-Hearted Woman*. Directed, produced, and written by Lan Brookes Ritz, DVD 1979/2009.

CBS News Segment, September 2, 1970, accessed April 12, 2024, https://www.youtube.com/watch?v=3Wd1uLgV7mc&t=1s.

Cy Griffin film, WKLDOC Records, "Custer Reels 1 & 2," signature 146.E.9.2F.

Dennis Banks Interview. *UO Today*. Interview 488. Oregon Humanities Center. University of Oregon. Last accessed April 12, 2024, https://www.youtube.com/watch?v=MKzlq_-PxYo.

*A Good Day to Die: Dennis Banks and the American Indian Movement*. Produced and directed by David Mueller and Lynn Salt. Kino Lorber Films, 2010.

*Incident at Oglala*. Directed by Michael Apted. Miramax Films, 1992.

*Hanta Po, All of My Relations: An Historical Photographic Essay on the American Indian Movement, 1968–2006*. By AIM photographer Dick Bancroft. St. Paul, MN, DVD, undated.

*Lakota Woman: Siege at Wounded Knee*. Directed by Frank Pierson. Turner Films, made for TV with video release, 1994.

*A Tattoo on My Heart: The Warriors of Wounded Knee 1973*. Produced and directed by Charles Abourezk and Breet Lawlor. Badland Films, 2004.

*Powwow Highway*. Directed by Joanelle Nadine Romero and Jonathan Wacks. Handmade Films/Warner Brothers, 1989.

*Taking AIM: The Story of the American Indian Movement*. Directed by Lucas Langworthy. DVD, 2010.

*Thunderheart*. Directed by Michael Apted. Tristar Pictures, 1992.

*Trudell*. Directed by Heather Rae. Appaloosa Pictures and Balcony Releasing, 2005.

*The War In South Dakota*. WKLDOC Records, videotape signature 146.E.9.2F, MHSMC.

*Warrior: The Life of Leonard Peltier*. Directed by Suzie Baer. Shenandoah Film Productions, 1991.

*Warrior Societies*. Directed by Ryan Slater. Meeches Video Productions, 2007.

*Warrior Women.* Directed by Christina King and Elizabeth Castle. Vision Maker Media and ITVS, 2019.

*We Shall Remain: Wounded Knee* (Episode Five). Produced and directed by Stanley Nelson. Public Broadcasting Service, DVD, 2009.

*From Wounded Knee to Standing Rock: A Reporter's Journey.* Produced and directed by Kevin McKiernan. Video Project, 2019.

## Secondary Sources

### Books and Articles

Adams, David Wallace. *Education for Extinction: American Indians and the Boarding School Experience, 1875–1928.* Lawrence: University Press of Kansas, 1995.

Akard, William Keith. "Wocante Tinza: A History of the American Indian Movement." PhD diss., Ball State University, 1987.

Allen, Paula Gunn. *The Sacred Hoop: Recovering the Feminine in American Indian Traditions.* Boston: Beacon Press, 1986.

Anderson, Benedict. *Imagined Communities: Reflections on the Origin and Spread of Nationalism.* London: Verso, 2006.

Anderson, Kim. *A Recognition of Being: Reconstructing Native Womanhood.* Toronto, Ont.: Second Story Press, 2000.

Anderson, Kim, and Robert Alexander Innes. *Indigenous Men and Masculinities: Legacies, Identities, Regeneration.* Winnipeg: University of Manitoba Press, 2015.

Anderson, Terry. *The Movement and the Sixties: Protest from Greensboro to Wounded Knee,* rev. ed. New York: Oxford University Press, 1995.

Antell, Judith A. "American Indian Women Activists." PhD diss., University of Berkeley, 1990.

Antone, Bob. "Reconstructing Indigenous Masculine Thought." In *Indigenous Men and Masculinities: Legacies, Identities, Regeneration,* edited by Robert Alexander Innes and Kim Anderson, 21–37. Winnipeg: University of Manitoba Press, 2015.

Arvin, Maile, Eve Tuck, and Angie Morrill. "Decolonizing Feminism: Challenging Connections between Settler Colonialism and Heteropatriarchy." *Feminist Formations* 25, no. 1 (Spring 2013): 8–34.

Axtell, James. "Ethnohistory: An Historian's Viewpoint." *Ethnohistory* 26 (Winter 1979): 1–13.

Balibar, Etienne. "The Nation Form: History and Ideology." *Review* 13, no. 3 (Summer 1990): 329–361.

Banerjee, Sikata. *Make Me a Man: Masculinity, Hinduism, and Nationalism in India*. New York: SUNY, 2005.

———. *Muscular Nationalism: Gender, Violence, and Empire in India and Ireland*. New York: New York University Press, 2012.

Baringer, Sandra K. "Indian Activism and the American Indian Movement, a Bibliographical Essay." *American Indian Culture and Research Journal* 21, no. 4 (1997): 217–250.

Barker, Joanne. *Sovereignty Matters, Locations of Contestation and Possibility in Indigenous Struggles for Self-Determination*. Lincoln: University of Nebraska Press, 2005.

———. "Indigenous Feminisms." In *Oxford Handbook of Indigenous People's Politics*, edited by José Antonio Lucero, Dale Turner, and Donna Lee VanCott, DOI: 10.1093/oxfordhb/9780195386653.013.007, 1–25.

Barker, Joanne, ed. *Critically Sovereign, Indigenous Gender, Sexuality, and Feminist Studies*. Durham, NC: Duke University Press, 2017.

Barrett, Frank J. "The Organizational Construction of Hegemonic Masculinity: The Case of the U.S. Navy." In *The Masculinities Reader*, edited by Stephen Whitehead and Frank J. Barrett, 77–99. Cambridge, UK: Polity, 2001.

Barsh, Russel Lawrence. "American Indians in the Great War." *Ethnohistory* 38, no. 3 (1991): 276–303.

Basso, Matthew, Laura McCall, and Dee Garceau-Hagen. *Across the Great Divide: Cultures of Manhood in the American West*. New York: Routledge, 2001.

Bates, Denise E. *The Other Movement: Indian Rights and Civil Rights in the Deep South*. Tuscaloosa: University of Alabama Press, 2012.

Baylor, Timothy John. "Modern Warriors: Mobilization and Decline of the American Indian Movement (AIM), 1968–1979." PhD diss., University of North Carolina at Chapel Hill, 1994.

———. "Media Framing of Movement Protest: The Case of American Indian Protest." *Social Science Journal* 33, no. 3 (1996): 241–255.

Bell, Avril. *Relating Indigenous and Settler Identities: Beyond Domination; Identity Studies in the Social Sciences*. New York: Palgrave Macmillan, 2014.

Berkhofer, Robert F. *The White Man's Indian: Images of the American Indian from Columbus to the Present*. New York: Random House, 1978.

Bernstein, Alison R. *American Indians and World War II: Toward a New Era in Indian Affairs*. Norman: University of Oklahoma Press, 1991.

Beynon, John. *Masculinities and Culture*. Philedlphia, PA: Open University, 2002.

Billig, Michael. *Banal Nationalism*. London: Sage, 1995.
Birong, Christine. "The Influence of Police Brutality on the American Indian Movement's Establishment in Minneapolis, 1968–1969." MA thesis, University of Arizona, 2009.
Blansett, Kent. *A Journey to Freedom: Richard Oakes, Alcatraz, and the Red Power Movement*. New Haven, CT: Yale University Press, 2018.
Bonney, Rachel A. "The Role of AIM Leaders in Indian Nationalism." *American Indian Quarterly* 3, no. 3 (1977): 209–224.
Bordeaux, Clementine. "The American Indian Movement and the Politics of Nostalgia: Indigenous Representations from Wounded Knee to Standing Rock," *International Journal of Communications* 16 (2022), 4636-4658.
Bourque, Susan C., and Joan W. Scott. "Introduction: The Concept of Gender." *Deadalus* 116, no. 4 (Fall 1987): 21–30.
Brady, Miranda Jean. "The Occupation of Wounded Knee: Press Coverage of the American Indian Movement." MS thesis, San Jose State University, 2003.
Brand, Johanna. *The Life and Death of Anna Mae Aquash*. Toronto: James Lorimer and Company Publishers, 1978.
Braun, Sebastian Felix. "Building on Native Sovereignty: From Ethic Membership to National Citizenship." In *Native American Nationalism and Nation Re-Building: Past and Present Cases*, edited by Simone Poliandri, 93–122. Albany: State University of New York Press, 2016.
Breuilly, John. *Nationalism and the State*. Manchester: Manchester University Press, 1982.
Britten, Thomas A. *American Indians in World War I: At Home and at War*. Albuquerque: University of New Mexico Press, 1997.
Brown, David. "Are There Good and Bad Nationalisms?" *Nations and Nationalism* 5, no. 2 (April 1999): 281–302.
———. "The Ethnic Majority: Benign or Malign?" *Nations and Nationalism* 14 (2008): 768–788.
Brown, Lester B. *Two Spirit People: American Indian, Lesbian Women and Gay Men*. New York: Haworth Press, 1997.
Brunette, Pauline. "The Minneapolis Urban Indian Community." *Hennepin County History* 49, no. 1 (Winter 1989/90): 4–15.
Bruyneel, Kevin. *The Third Space of Sovereignty: The Postcolonial Politics of U.S.-Indigenous Relations*. Minneapolis: University of Minnesota Press, 2007.

Burt, Larry W. *Tribalism in Crisis: Federal Indian Policy, 1953–1961*. Albuquerque: University of New Mexico Press, 1982.
Busacca, Jeremy. "Seeking Self-Determination: Framing, the American Indian Movement, and American Indian Media." PhD diss., Claremont Graduate University, 2007.
Butler, Monica Lynnette. "Check Your Local Listings: Indigenous Representation in Television." PhD diss., Arizona State University, Tempe, AZ, 2008.
Butler, Judith. *Gender Trouble: Feminism and the Subversion of Identity*. Routledge Classics. New York: Routledge, 2006.
Cahill, Cathleen D. *Federal Fathers and Mothers: A Social History of the United States Indian Service, 1869–1933*. Chapel Hill: University of North Carolina Press, 2011.
Cahn, Edgar S. *Our Brother's Keeper: The Indian in White America*. Washington, DC: New Community Press, 1969.
Calhoun, Craig. *Nations Matter: Culture, History, and the Cosmopolitan Dream*. London: Routledge, 2007.
Camacho, Keith L., and Laurel A. Monnig. "Uncomfortable Fatigues: Chamorro Soldiers, Gendered Identities, and the Question of Decolonization in Guam." In *Militarized Currents: Toward a Decolonized Future in Asia and the Pacific*, edited by Setsu Shigematsu and Keith L. Camacho, 147–179. Minneapolis: University of Minnesota Press, 2010.
Carney, Zoe, and Mary E. Stuckey. "The World as the American Frontier: Racialized Presidential War Rhetoric." *Southern Communication Journal* 80, no. 3 (July–August 2015): 163–188.
Carpio, Myla Vicenti. *Indigenous Albuquerque*. Lubbock: Texas Tech University Press, 2011.
Carroll, Al. *Medicine Bags and Dog Tags: American Indian Veterans from Colonial Times to the Second Iraq War*. Lincoln: University of Nebraska Press, 2008.
Castile, George Pierre. *To Show Heart: Native American Self-Determination and Federal Indian Policy, 1960–1975*. Tucson: University of Arizona Press, 1998.
———. *Taking Charge: Native American Self-Determination and Federal Indian Policy, 1975–1993*. Tucson: University of Arizona Press, 2006.
Castle, Elizabeth. "'Keeping One Foot in the Community': Intergenerational Indigenous Women's Activism from the Local to the Global (and Back Again)." *American Indian Quarterly* 27, nos. 3 & 4 (Summer & Fall 2003): 840–861.

———. "Black and Native American Women's Activism in the Black Panther Party and the American Indian Movement." In *Visions and Voices, American Indian Activism and the Civil Rights Movement*, edited by Kurt Peters and Terry Strauss, 85–99. New York: Albatros Press, 2009.

———. "'The Original Gangster': The Life and Times of Red Power Activist Madonna Thunder Hawk." In *The Hidden 1970s: Histories of Radicalism*, edited by Dan Berger, 267–284. New Brunswick, NJ: Rutgers University Press, 2010.

Champagne, Duane. "From First Nations to Self-Government: A Political Legacy of Indigenous Nations in the United States." *American Behavioral Scientist* 51 (2008): 1672–1693.

Chastang, Amanda B. "Reclaiming Identity: How the Black Panther Party and the American Indian Movement Challenged External Media Representations Through Self-Representation." MA Thesis. Tulsa: University of Tulsa, 2018.

Chávez, Ernesto. "'Birth of a New Symbol': The Brown Berets' Gendered Chicano National Imaginary." In *Generations of Youth: Youth Cultures and History in the Twentieth Century America*, edited by Joe Austin and Michael N. Willard, 205–222. New York: New York University Press, 1998.

Child, Brenda J. *Boarding School Seasons: American Indian Families, 1900–1940.* Lincoln: University of Nebraska Press, 1998.

Chilisa, Bagele. *Indigenous Research Methodologies.* London: Sage Publications, 2012.

Churchill, Ward, and Jim Vander Wall. *Agents of Repression: The FBI's Secret Wars Against the Black Panther Party and the American Indian Movement.* Boston: South End Press, 1988.

———. *The COINTEPLRO Papers: Documents from the FBI's Secret Wars Against Domestic Dissent.* Boston: South End Press, 1990.

Clark, David Anthony Tyeeme, and Joane Nagel. "White Men, Red Masks: Appropriations of "Indian' Manhood in Imagined Wests." In *Across the Great Divide: Cultures of Manhood in the American West*, edited by Matthew Basso, Laura McCall, and Dee Garceau-Hagen, 109–130. New York: Routledge, 2001.

Clarkin, Thomas. *Federal Indian Policy in the Kennedy and Johnson Administrations, 1961–1969.* Albuquerque: University of New Mexico Press, 2001.

Cobb, Daniel M. "Talking the Language of the Larger World: Politics in Cold War (Native) America." In *Beyond Red Power: American Indian*

*Politics and Activism since 1900*, edited by Daniel Cobb and Loretta Fowler, 161–177. Santa Fe, NM: School for Advanced Research, 2007.

———. *Native Activism in Cold War America: The Struggle for Sovereignty*. Lawrence: University Press of Kansas, 2008.

Cobb, Daniel M., Sarah Berger, and Lily Skopp, "'A Sickness that has Grown to Epidemic Proportions': American Indian Anti- and Decolonial Thought During the Long 1960s." *Comparative American Studies, An International Journal* 17, no. 2 (2020): 199–223.

Cobb, Daniel M., and Loretta Fowler. *Beyond Red Power: American Indian Politics and Activism since 1900*. Santa Fe, NM: School for Advanced Research, 2007.

Cohen, Fay G. "The Indian Patrol in Minneapolis: Social Control and Social Change in an Urban Context." PhD diss., University of Minnesota, 1973.

———. "The Indian Patrol in Minneapolis: Social Control and Social Change in an Urban Context." *Law and Society Review* 7, no. 4 (Summer 1973): 779–786.

———. "The American Indian Movement and the Anthropologist: Issues and Implications of Consent." In *Ethics and Anthropology, Dilemmas in Fieldwork*, edited by Michael A. Rykiewich and James P. Spradley, 81–94. New York: John Wiley & Sons, 1976.

Coleman, William S. E. *Voices of Wounded Knee*. Lincoln: University of Nebraska Press, 2000.

Connell, Raewyn. *Masculinities*. Cambridge: Polity Press, 1995.

———. *The Men and the Boys*. Cambridge: Polity Press, 2000.

———. "The Social Organization of Masculinity." In *The Masculinities Reader*, edited by Stephen Whitehead and Frank J. Barrett, 30–49. Cambridge, UK: Polity, 2001.

———. *Gender*. Cambridge, UK: Polity, 2002.

———. "Globalization, Imperialism, and Masculinities." In *Handbook of Studies on Men and Masculinities*, edited by Michael Kimmel, Jeff Hearn, Raewyn Connell, 71–89. Thousand Oaks, CA: Sage Publications, 2005.

Connell, Raewyn W., and James W. Messerschmidt. "Hegemonic Masculinity: Rethinking the Concept." *Gender and Society* 19, no. 6 (December 2005): 829–859.

Connerton, Paul. "Seven Types of Forgetting." *Memory Studies* 1, no. 1 (2008): 59–71.

Cook-Lynn, Elizabeth. *Anti-Indianism in Modern America: A Voice from Tatekeya's Earth*. Urbana: University of Illinois Press, 2001.
Cornell, Stephen E. *The Return of the Native: American Indian Political Resurgence*. New York: Oxford University Press, 1988.
Cornell, Stephen, and Douglas Hartmann. *Ethnicity and Race: Making Identities in a Changing World*. Thousand Oaks, CA: Pine Forge Press, 1998.
Cornwall, Andrea, and Nancy Lindisfarne, eds. *Dislocating Masculinity: Comparative Ethnographies*. London: Routledge, 1994.
Coulthard, Glen. *Red Skins, White Masks: Rejecting the Colonial Politics of Recognition*. Minneapolis, MN: University of Minneapolis Press, 2014.
Couture, Steven L. "The American Indian Movement: A Historical Perspective." PhD diss., University of St. Thomas, MN, 1996.
Cowger, Thomas. *The National Congress of American Indians: The Founding Years*. Lincoln: University of Nebraska Press, 1999.
Crenshaw, Kimberlé. *Critical Race Theory: The Key Writings That Formed the Movement*. New York: New Press, 1995.
Cronin, Míceál Daniel. "The American Indian Movement and the Black Panther Party Compared: Violence, the State and Social Movements in the USA, 1966 to 1976." NUI Galway: PhD thesis, 2020.
D'Arcus, Bruce. "The Wounded Knee Occupation and the Politics of Scale: Marginal Protest and Central Authority in a Media Age." PhD diss., Syracuse University, 2001.
———. "The Urban Geography of Red Power: The American Indian Movement in Minneapolis-Saint Paul, 1968–70." *Urban Studies* 47, no. 6 (May 2010): 1241–1255.
Danziger, Edmund. *Survival and Regeneration: Detroit's American Indian Community*. Detroit: Wayne State University Press, 1991.
Davis, Julie L. *Survival Schools: The American Indian Movement and Community Education in the Twin Cities*. Minneapolis, MN: University of Minnesota Press, 2013.
Deloria, Philip. *Playing Indian*. New Haven, CT: Yale University Press, 1998.
Deloria, Vine. *Custer Died for Your Sins: An Indian Manifesto*. New York: Avon Publishers, 1969.
———. *Behind the Trail of Broken Treaties: An Indian Declaration of Independence*. Austin: University of Texas Press, 1985.
———. *God Is Red: A Native View of Religion*. Golden, CO: Fulcrum Publishing, 1994.
DeMallie, Raymond. "Male and Female in Traditional Lakota Culture."

In *The Hidden Half: Studies of Plains Indian Women*, edited by Patricia Albers and Bea Medicine, 237–266. Washington, DC: University Press of America 1983.
Demetriou, Demetrakis Z. "Connell's Concept of Hegemonic Masculinity: A Critique." *Theory and Society* 30, no. 3 (June 2001): 337–361.
Dewing, Rolland. "South Dakota Newspaper Coverage of the 1973 Occupation of Wounded Knee." *South Dakota History* 12, no. 1 (1982): 48–64.
———. *Wounded Knee II*. Chadron, NE: Great Plains Network, 1995.
Driskill, Qwo-Li. *Queer Indigenous Studies: Critical Interventions in Theory, Politics, and Literature*. Tucson: University of Arizona Press, 2011.
Dudziak, Mary L. *Cold War Civil Rights: Race and Image of American Democracy*. Princeton, NJ: Princeton University Press, 2022.
Dunlay, Thomas W. *Wolves for the Blue Soldiers: Indian Scouts and Auxiliaries with the United States Army, 1860–90*. Lincoln: University of Nebraska Press, 1982.
Elliott, Michael A. "Indian Patriots on Last Stand Hill." *American Quarterly* 58, no. 4 (December 2006): 987–1015.
———. *Custerology: The Enduring Legacy of the Indian Wars and George Armstrong Custer*. Chicago: University of Chicago Press, 2007.
Elliston, Deborah. "A Passion for the Nation." *American Anthropologist* 31, no. 4 (2004): 606–630.
Enloe, Cynthia H. *Ethnic Soldiers: State Security in a Divided Society*. New York: Penguin, 1980.
———. *Bananas, Beaches and Bases: Making Feminist Sense of International Politics*. 2nd revised ed. Berkeley: University of California Press, 2014.
Erll, Astrid. *Memory in Culture*. Basingstoke: Palgrave Macmillan, 2011.
Espey, David. "America And Vietnam, The Indian Subtext." Last accessed April 12, 2024, http://www.english.upenn.edu/~despey/vietnam.htm.
Estes, Nick. *Our History Is the Future: Standing Rock versus the Dakota Access Pipeline, and the Long Traditions of Indigenous Resistance*. London: Verso, 2019.
———. *Standing with Standing Rock: Voices from the NoDAPL Movement*. Minneapolis: University of Minnesota Press, 2019.
Estes, Steve. *I Am a Man! Race, Manhood, and the Civil Rights Movement*. Chapel Hill: University of North Carolina Press, 2005.
Everson, David W. "Red Power, White Discourse: Privilege Narratives and the American Indian Movement, 1973–2015." PhD diss., University of Notre Dame, Indiana, July 2017.

Ferrante, Joan, and Prince Browne Jr. *The Social Construction of Race and Ethnicity in the United States*, 2nd ed. Upper Saddle River, NY: Prentice Hall, 2001.

Fixico, Donald Lee. *Termination and Relocation: Federal Indian Policy, 1945–1960*. Albuquerque: University of New Mexico Press, 1986.

———. "Ethics and Responsibilities in Writing American Indian History." *American Indian Quarterly* 20 (Winter 1996): 29–39.

———. *The Urban Indian Experience in America*. Albuquerque: University of New Mexico Press, 2000.

———. *Call for Change: The Medicine Way of American Indian History, Ethos, & Reality*. Lincoln: Univerisity of Nebraska Press, 2013.

———. *Indian Resilience and Rebuilding: Indigenous Nations in the Modern American West*. Albuquerque: University of New Mexico Press, 2013.

Flood, Michael, Judith Kegan Gardiner, Bob Pease, and Keith Pringle, eds. *International Encyclopedia of Men and Masculinities*. London, New York: Routledge, 2007.

Flood, Renée Sansom. *Lost Bird of Wounded Knee: Spirit of the Lakota*. New York: Scribner, 2014.

Fowler, Loretta. *Shared Symbols, Contested Meanings: Gros Ventre Culture and History, 1778–1984*. Ithaca, NY: Cornell University Press, 1987.

Franco, Jeré Bishop. "Empowering the World War II Native American Veteran: Postwar Civil Rights." *Wicazo Sa Review* 9, no. 1 (Spring 1993): 32–37.

———. *Crossing the Pond: The Native American Effort in World War II*. Denton: University of North Texas Press, 1999.

Garriott, David E., and Melissa Hickman Barlow. *Police in a Multicultural Society: An American Story*. 2nd ed. Long Grove, IL: Waveland Press, 2010.

Gibbon, Guy E. *The Sioux: The Dakota and Lakota Nations*. Malden, MA: Blackwell Publishers, 2003.

Goldstein, Joshua S. *War and Gender: How Gender Shapes the War System and Vice Versa*. Cambridge: Cambridge University Press, 2001.

Graham, Laura R., and H. Glenn Penny. *Performing Indigeneity: Global Histories and Contemporary Experiences*. Lincoln: University of Nebraska Press, 2014.

Grant, Christopher, and Steve Feimer. "Street Gangs in Indian Country, A Clash of Cultures." *Journal of Gang Research* 14, no. 4 (Summer 2007): 27–53.

Green, Joyce A. *Making Space for Indigenous Feminism*. Nova Scotia: Fernwood Publishing, Zed Books, 2007.

Greene, Jerome A. *All Guns Fired at One Time: Native Voices of Wounded Knee, 1890*. Pierre: South Dakota Historical Society, 2020.
———. *American Carnage: Wounded Knee, 1890*. Norman: University of Oklahoma Press, 2014.
Grua, David W. *Surviving Wounded Knee: The Lakotas and the Politics of Memory*. Oxford: Oxford University Press, 2016.
Guerrero, Marie Anna Jaimes. "Civil Rights Versus Sovereignty: Native American Women in Life and Land Struggles." In *Feminist Genealogies, Colonial Legacies, Democratic Futures*, edited by M. Jaqui Alexander and Chandra Talpade Mohanty, 101–121. New York, NY: Routledge, 1997.
———. "'Patriarchal Colonialism' and Indigenism: Implications for Native Feminist Spirituality and Native Womanism." *Hypatia* 18, no. 2 (Spring 2003): 58–69.
Hailer, Julie Ann. "American Indian Involvement in Urban Street Gangs: Invisible or More?" PhD diss., University of Arizona, 2008.
Hammer, Justin C. "Race and Perception: The 1973 American Indian Movement Protest in Custer, South Dakota." MA thesis, University of South Dakota, 2011.
Harris, Alexandra, and Mark Hirsch, eds. *Why We Serve, Native Americans in the United States Armed Forces*. Washington, DC: National Museum of the American Indian, 2020.
Harris, Cole. "How Did Colonialism Dispossess? Comments from an Edge of Empire." *Annals of the Association of American Geographers* 94, no. 1 (2004): 165–182.
Hart, Gillian. "Engendering Everyday Resistance: Gender, Patronage, and Production in Politics in Rural Malaysia." *Journal of Peasant Studies* 19, no. 1 (1991): 93–121.
Hassrick, Royal B. *The Sioux, Life and Customs of a Warrior Society*. Norman: University of Oklahoma Press, 1964.
Hendricks, Steven. *The Unquiet Grave: The FBI and the Struggle for the Soul of Indian Country* Boston: Da Capo Press, 2007.
Herzberg, Hazel W. *The Search for an American Indian Identity, Modern Pan-Indian Movements*. Syracuse, NY: Syracuse University Press, 1971.
Hewitt, William L. "The Indian Who Never Got Home: The Burial of Sergeant John R. Rice." *Nebraska History* 77 (1996): 12–20.
Higate, Paul, ed. *Military Masculinities: Identity and the State*. Westport, CN: Praeger, 2003.
Hill Collins, Patricia, and Sirma Bilge. *Intersectionality*. Cambridge: Polity, 2016.

Hitchmough, Sam. "Performative Protest and the Lost Contours of Red Power Activism." *Comparative American Studies, An International Journal* 17, no. 2 (2020): 224–237.

Hixon, Walter. *American Settler Colonialism: A History*. New York, NY: Palgrave Macmillan, 2013.

Hobsbawm, Eric J. "Introduction: Inventing Traditions." In *The Invention of Tradition*, edited by Eric J. Hobsbawm and Terence Ranger, 1–14, 23rd ed., Cambridge: Cambridge University Press, 2015.

Hobsbawm, Eric J., and Terence Ranger. *The Invention of Tradition*. 23rd ed. Cambridge: Cambridge University Press, 2015.

Hokowhitu, Brendan. "Māori Masculinity, Post-Structuralism, and the Emerging Self." *New Zealand Sociology* 18, no. 2 (2003): 179–201.

———. "Tackling Māori Masculinity: A Colonial Geneology of Savagery and Sport." *Contemporary Pacific* 16, no. 2 (2004): 259–284.

———. "The Death of Koro Paka: 'Traditional' Māori Patriarchy." *Contemporary Pacific* 20, no. 1 (2008): 115–141.

———. "Producing Elite Indigenous Masculinities." *Settler Colonial Studies* 2, no. 2 (2013): 23–48.

———. "Haka: Colonized Physicality, Body-Logic, and Embodied Sovereignty." In *Performing Indigeneity: Global Histories and Contemporary Experiences*, edited by Laura R. Graham and H. Glenn Perry, 273–304. Lincoln: University of Nebraska Press, 2014.

———. "Taxonomies of Indigeneity." In *Indigenous Men and Masculinities: Legacies, Identities, Regeneration*, edited by Alexander Robert Innes and Kim Anderson, 80–98. Winnipeg: University of Manitoba Press, 2015.

hooks, bell. *Feminist Theory: From Margin to Center*. London: Pluto Press, 2000.

———. *We Real Cool: Black Men and Masculinity*. New York: Routledge, 2004.

Holm, Tom. "Culture, Ceremonialism, and Stress: American Indian Veterans and the Vietnam War." *Armed Forces & Society* 12, no. 2 (Winter 1986): 237–251.

———. "Patriots and Pawns, State Use of American Indians in the Military and the Process of Nativization in the United States." In *The State of Native America: Genocide, Colonization, and Resistance*, edited by M. Annette Jaimes, 345–370. Boston, MA: South End Press, 1992.

———. "PTSD in Native American Vietnam Veterans: A Reassessment." *Wicazo Sa Review* 11, no. 2 (Autumn 1995): 83–86.

———. *Strong Hearts, Wounded Souls: Native American Veterans of the Vietnam War*. Austin: University of Texas Press, 1996.

———. "The Militarization of Native America: Historical Process and Cultural Perception." *Social Science Journal* 34, no. 4 (1997): 461–474.
Holm, Tom, Diane J. Pearson, and Ben Chavis. "Peoplehood, A Model for the Extension of Sovereignty in American Indian Studies." *Wicazo Sa Review* 18, no. 1 (Spring 2003): 7–24.
Holstein, James A., and Jaber F. Gubrium, eds. *Inside Interviewing: New Lenses, New Concerns*. Thousand Oakes: Sage Publications, 2003.
Huhndorf, Cheryl, Shari M. Suzack, Jeanne Peareault, and Jean Barman, eds. *Indigenous Women and Feminism: Politics, Activism, Culture*. Vancouver: UBC Press, 2010.
Hunt, Andrew E. *The Turning: A History of Vietnam Veterans Against the War*. New York: New York University Press, 1999.
Hutchinson, John. *The Dynamics of Cultural Nationalism: The Gaelic Revival and the Creation of the Irish Nation State*. London: Allen & Unwin, 1987.
———. "Cultural Nationalism." In *The History of Nationalism*, edited by John Breuilly, 75–96. Oxford: Oxford University Press, 2013.
Innes, Robert Alexander, and Kim Anderson. *Indigenous Men and Masculinities: Legacies, Identities, Regeneration*. Winnipeg: University of Manitoba Press, 2015.
Iverson, Peter. "American Indians in the Twentieth Century." In *A Companion to the American West*, edited by William Deverell, 329–345. Malden, MA: Blackwell Publishing, 2004.
———. "American Indian History as a Continuing Story." *Historian* 66, no. 3 (Fall 2004): 524–531.
Jackson, Ronald L., and Muarli Balaji, eds. *Global Masculinities and Manhood*. Urbana: University of Illinois Press, 2011.
Jacobs, Sue-Ellen. *Two-Spirit People: Native American Gender Identity, Sexuality, and Spirituality*. Urbana: University of Illinois Press, 2005.
Jaimes, M. Annette, and Theresa Halsey. "American Indian Women at the Center of Indigenous Resistance in Contemporary North America." In *The State of Native America: Genocide, Colonization, and Resistance*, edited by M. Annette Jaimes, 311–344. Boston, MA: South End Press, 1992.
Judson L. Jeffries, Omari L. Dyson, and Charles E. Jones. "Militancy Transcends Race: A Comparative Analysis of the American Indian Movement, the Black Panther Party, and the Young Lords." *Black Diaspora Review* 1, no. 2 (2010): 4–30.
John, Sonja. "From Warrior to Soldier? Lakota Veterans on Military Valor."

In *Warring over Valor: How Race and Gender Shaped American Military Heroism in the Twentieth and Twenty-First Centuries*, edited by Simon Wendt, 165–182. New Brunswick, NJ: Rutgers University Press, 2018.
Johansen, Bruce, and Roberto Maestas. *Wasi'chu: The Continuing Indian Wars*. New York: Monthly Review Press, 1979.
Johnson, Jan. "'We Were All Wounded At Wounded Knee': The Engaged Resistance of Folk and Rock in the Red Power Era." In *Indigenous Pop: Native American Music from Jazz to Hip Hop*, edited by Jeff Berglund, Jan Johnson, and Kimberli Lee, 92–106. Tucson: University of Arizona Press, 2016.
Johnson, Troy. "Roots of Contemporary Native American Activism." *American Indian Culture and Research Journal* 20, no. 2 (1996): 127–154.
———. *We Hold the Rock: The Indian Occupation of Alcatraz, 1969 to 1971*. San Francisco, CA: Golden Gate National Parks Association, 1997.
———. *Red Power: The Native American Civil Rights Movement*. New York: Chelsea House Publishers, 2007.
———. *The American Indian Occupation of Alcatraz Island: Red Power and Self-Determination*. Lincoln: University of Nebraska Press, 2008.
Johnson, Troy R., and John Garvey. "The Government and the Indians: The American Indian Occupation of Alcatraz Island, 1969–1971." In *American Indian Activism: Alcatraz to the Longest Walk*, edited by Troy Jonson, Joane Nagel, and Duane Champagne, 153–185. Urbana: University of Illinois Press, 1997.
Johnson, Troy R., Joanne Nagel, and Duane Champagne, eds. *American Indian Activism: Alcatraz to the Longest Walk*. Urbana: University of Illinois Press, 1997.
———. "American Indian Activism and Transformation, Lessons from Alcatraz." In *Contemporary Native American Communities*, edited by Troy Johnson, 283–314. Walnut Creek, CA: AltaMira Press, 1999.
Kauanui, J. Kēhaulin. "'A Structure, Not an Event': Settler Colonialism and Enduring Indigeneity," *Lateral* 5, no. 1 (2016).
Karua, Mau. "Black and Native Visions of Self-determination." *Critical Ethnic Studies* 3, no. 2 (Fall 2017): 77–98.
Kelly, Casey Ryan. "The Rhetoric of Red Power and the American Indian Occupation of Alcatraz Island (1969–1971)." PhD diss., University of Minnesota, 2009.
Kimmel, Michael S. *Manhood in America: A Cultural History*. 3rd ed. New York: Oxford University Press, 2012.
Kim, Seonghoon. "'We Have Always Had Many Voices': Red Power

Newspapers and a Community of Resistance." *American Indian Quarterly* 39, no. 3 (Summer 2015): 271–301.

King, Richard C. "Imperial Recollections: The Colonial Contexts and Postcolonial Predicaments of Exhibiting Native American Cultures and Histories in the Contemporary United States." PhD diss., University of Illinois at Urbana, 1996.

———. *Unsettling America: The Uses of Indianness in the 21st Century*. New York: Rowman and Littlefield Publishers, 2013.

King, Tiffany Lethabo. *The Black Shoals: Offshore Formations of Black and Native Studies*. Durham, NC: Duke University Press, 2019.

———. "New World Grammars, The 'Unthought' Black Discourses of Conquest." In *Otherwise Worlds: Against Settler Colonialism and Anti-Blackness*, edited by Tiffany Lethabo King, Jenell Navarro, and Andrea Smith. Durham, NC: Duke University Press, 2020.

Klopotek, Brian. "'I Guess Your Warrior Look Doesn't Work Every Time': Challenging Indian Masculinity in the Cinema." In *Across the Great Divide: Manhood in the American West*, edited by Matthew Basso, Laura McCall, and Dee Garceau, 251–274. New York: Routledge, 2001.

Kolst, Pål. "National Symbols as Signs of Unity and Division." *Ethnic and Racial Studies* 29, no. 4 (August 2006): 676–701.

Kotlowski, Dean J. "Alcatraz, Wounded Knee, and Beyond: The Nixon and Ford Administrations Respond to Native American Protest." *Pacific Historical Review* 72, no. 2 (2003): 201–227.

Kovach, Margaret. *Indigenous Methodologies: Characteristics, Conversations, and Contexts*. Toronto: University of Toronto Press, 2009.

Krouse, Susan Applegate. "What Came Out of the Takeovers: Women's Activism and the Indian Community School of Milwaukee." *American Indian Quarterly* 27, nos. 3 & 4 (summer/fall 2003): 533–547.

———. *North American Indians in the Great War*. Lincoln: University of Nebraska Press, 2007.

Kýrová, Lucie, and György Ferenc Tóth. "Red Power at 50: Re-Evaluations and Memory." *Comparative American Studies, An International Journal* 17, no. 2 (2020): 107–116.

LaDuke, Winona, and Sean Aaron Cruz. *The Militarization of Indian Country*. East Lansing: Michigan State University Press, 2013.

LaGrand, James. *Indian Metropolis: Native Americans in Chicago, 1945–75*. Urbana: University of Illinois Press, 2002.

Lamphere, Louise, Helena Ragon, and Patricia Zavella. *Situated Lives: Gender and Culture in Everyday Life*. New York: Routledge, 1997.

Langston, Donna Hightower. "American Indian Women's Activism in the 1960s and 1970s." *Hypatia* 18, no. 2 (Spring 2003): 114–132.

LaPier, Rosalyn R., and David R. M. Beck. *City Indian: Native American Activism in Chicago: 1893–1934*. Lincoln: University of Nebraska Press, 2015.

Lazarus, Edward. *Black Hills, White Justice: The Sioux Nation versus the United States, 1775 to the Present*. New York: HarperCollins Publishers, 1991.

Lee, Kimberli. "Singing for People: The Protest Music of Buffy Sainte-Marie and Floyd Westerman." In *Indigenous Pop, Native American Music from Jazz to Hip Hop*, edited by Jeff Berglund, Jan Johnson, and Kimberli Lee, 61–74. Tucson: University of Arizona Press, 2016.

Lee, Lloyd L. *Diné Masculinities: Conceptualizations and Reflections*. North Charleston, SC: CreateSpace Independent Publishing Platform, 2013.

Liamputtong, Pranee, and Douglas Ezzy. *Qualitative Research Methods*, 2nd ed. Oxford: Oxford University Press, 2005.

Little, John. "Sioux Warriors and the Vietnam War." *Great Plains Quarterly* 35, no. 4 (Fall 2015): 357–375.

———. "Vietnam Akíčita: Lakota and Dakota Military Traditions in the 20th Century." PhD diss., University of Minnesota, 2020.

Lowery, Melinda Maynor. *Lumbee Indians in the Jim Crow South: Race, Identity and the Making of a Nation*. Chapel Hill: University of North Carolina Press 2010.

Lucero, Nancy. "'Being Indian in the City': Generational Differences in the Negotiation of Native Identity among Urban-Based American Indians." In *Indigenous in the City, Contemporary Identities and Cultural Innovation*, edited by Evelyn Peters and Chris Andersen, 193–215. Vancouver: UBS Press, 2013.

Magnusson, Stew. *The Death of Raymond Yellow Thunder, And Other True Stories from the Nebraska-Pine Ridge Border Towns*, Lubbock: Texas Tech University Press, 2008.

———. *Wounded Knee 1973: Still Bleeding; The American Indian Movement, the FBI, and Their Fight to Bury the Sins of the Past*. Arlington, VA: Court Bridge Publishing, 2013.

Maracle, Lee. *I Am Woman: A Native Perspective on Sociology and Feminism*. 2nd ed. Vancouver, BC: Press Gang Publishers, 1996.

Martinez, David. *Life of the Indigenous Mind: Vine Deloria Jr. and the Birth of the Red Power Movement*. Lincoln: University of Nebraska Press, 2019.

Mason, Dale W. "'You Can Only Kick So Long': AIM Leadership in Nebraska, 1972–1979." *Journal of the West* 23, no. 3 (1984): 70–76.

Matthiessen, Peter. *In the Spirit of Crazy Horse*. New York: Viking Press, 1991.
Mayer, Tamar. *Gender Ironies of Nationalism: Sexing the Nation*. London: Routledge, 2000.
McClellan, E. Fletcher. "The Politics of American Indian Self-Determination, 1958–1975: The Indian Self-Determination and Education Assistance Act of 1975." PhD diss., University of Tennessee, 1988.
McClintock, Anne. "Family Feuds: Gender, Nationalism and the Family." *Feminist Review* 44 (Summer 1993): 61–80.
———. *Imperial Leather: Race, Gender and Sexuality in the Colonial Contest*. New York: Routledge, 1995.
McDowell, Linda, Esther Rootham, and Abby Hardgrove. "Precarious Work, Protest Masculinity, and Communal Regulation: South Asian Young Men in Luton, UK." *Work, Employment, and Society* 28, no. 6 (2014): 847–864.
McKegney, Sam. *Carrying the Burden of Peace: Reimagining Indigenous Masculinities Through Story*. Tucson: University of Arizona Press, 2021.
———. *Masculindians: Conversations About Indigenous Manhood*. East Lansing: Michigan State University Press, 2014.
McKenzie-Jones, Paul. *Clyde Warrior, Tradition, Community, and Red Power*. Norman: University of Oklahoma Press, 2015.
Meadows, William. "Honoring Native American Code Talkers." *American Indian Culture and Research Journal* 35, no. 3 (2011): 1–36.
———. *Kiowa, Apache, and Comanche Military Societies: Enduring Veterans, 1800 to the Present*. Austin: University of Texas Press, 1999.
———. *The Comanche Code Talkers of World War II*. Austin: University of Texas Press, 2002.
Medicine, Beatrice. "'Warrior Women': Sex Role Alternatives for Plains Indian Women." In *The Hidden Half: Studies of Plains Indian Women*, edited by Beatrice Medicine and Patricia Albers, 267–280. Washington, DC: University Press of America, 1983.
Mencarelli, James, and Steve Severin. *Protest: Red, Black, Brown Experience in America*. Grand Rapids: Eerdmans Publishing, 1975.
Mertens, Donn, Fiona Cram, and Bagele Chilisa. *Indigenous Pathways into Social Research: Voices of a New Generation*. New York: Routledge, 2013.
Messerschmidt, James W. *Masculinities and Crime: Critique and Reconceptualization of Theory*. Lanham, MD: Rowman and Littlefield Publishers, 1993.

Messerschmidt, Jim. *The Trial of Leonard Peltier*. Boston: South End Press. 1983.

Messner, Michael A. *Politics of Masculinities, Men in Movements*. Thousand Oaks, CA: Sage, 1997.

Mihesuah, Devon A. *Indigenous American Women: Decolonization, Empowerment, Activism*. Lincoln: University of Nebraska Press, 2003.

Miller, Douglas K., *Indians on the Move, Native American Mobility and Urbanization in the Twentieth Century*. Chapel Hill: University of North Carolina Press, 2019.

Morgan, David. "Class and Masculinity." In *Handbook of Studies on Men and Masculinities*, ed. Michael S. Kimmel, Jeff Hearn, and Raewyn Connell, 165–177. Thousand Oaks, CA: Sage Publications, 2005.

Morgensen, Scott Lauria. *Spaces between Us: Queer Settler Colonialism and Indigenous Decolonization*. Minneapolis: University of Minnesota Press, 2011.

———. "Theorizing Gender, Sexuality, and Settler Colonialism: An Introduction." *Settler Colonial Studies* 2, no. 2 (2012): 2–22.

———. "Cutting to the Roots of Colonial Masculinity." In *Indigenous Men and Masculinities: Legacies, Identities, Regeneration*, edited by Robert Alexander Innes and Kim Anderson, 38–61. Winnipeg: University of Manitoba Press, 2015.

Morrell, Robert, and Sandra Swart. "Men in the Third World: Postcolonial Perspectives on Masculinity." In *Handbook of Studies on Men and Masculinities*, edited by Michael Kimmel, Jeff Hearn, Raewyn Connell, 90–113. Thousand Oaks, CA: Sage Publications, 2005.

Nagel, Joane. "American Indian Ethnic Renewal: Politics and the Resurgence of Identity." *American Sociological Review* 60, no. 6 (1995): 947–965.

———. *American Indian Ethnic Renewal: Red Power and the Resurgence of Identity and Culture*. New York: Oxford University Press, 1996.

———. "Nation." In *Handbook of Studies on Men and Masculinities*, edited by Michael Kimmel, Jeff Hearn, Jeff and Raewyn Connell, 397–413. Thousand Oaks, CA: Sage Publications, 2005.

———. "Masculinity and Nationalism: Gender and Sexuality in the Making of Nations." *Ethnic and Racial Studies* 21, no. 2 (2010): 242–269.

———. "American Indian Ethnic Renewal: Red Power and the Resurgence of Identity and Culture." *American Sociological Review* 60, no. 6 (December 1996): 947–965.

Nelson, Jennifer. *Women of Color and the Reproductive Rights Movement*. New York: New York University Press, 2003.

Nickel, Sarah, and Amanda Fehr, eds. *In Good Relation: History, Gender,*

*and Kinship in Indigenous Feminism*. Winnipeg: University of Manitoba Press, 2020.
Nobbs, Jade M. "History, Colonisation." In *International Encyclopedia of Men and Masculinities*, edited by Michael Flood, Judith Kegan Gardiner, Bob Pease, and Keith Pringle, 269–273. London: Routledge, 2007.
Ogbar, Jeffrey O. G. *Black Power, Radical Politics and African American Identity*. Baltimore, MD: Johns Hopkins University Press, 2004.
Omi, Michael, and Howard Winant. *Racial Formation in the United States: From the 1960s to the 1990s*, 2nd ed. New York: Routledge, 1994.
Orlando, Joan Weibel. *Indian Country, L.A.: Maintaining Ethnic Community in Complex Society*, 2nd ed. Urbana, Chicago: University of Illinois Press, 1999.
Ostler, Jeffrey. *The Lakotas and the Black Hills: The Struggle for Sacred Ground*. New York: Penguin Books, 2010.
———. *The Plains Sioux and U.S. Colonialism from Lewis and Clark to Wounded Knee*. Cambridge: Cambridge University Press, 2004.
O'Sullivan, Meg Devlin. "'We Worry About Survival': American Indian Women, Sovereignty, and the Right to Bear and Rise Children in the 1970s." PhD diss., University of North Carolina, 2007.
———. "Informing Red Power and Transforming the Second Wave: Native American Women and the Struggle Against Coerced Sterilization." *Women's History Review* 25, no. 6 (2016): 965–982.
Parman, Donald Lee. *Indians and the American West in the Twentieth Century: The American West in the Twentieth Century*. Bloomington: Indiana University Press, 1994.
Peteet, Julie. "Male Gender and Rituals of Resistance in the Palestinian Intifada: A Cultural Politics of Violence." *American Ethnologist* 21, no. 1 (1994): 31–49.
Peters, Evelyn, and Chris Andersen, eds. *Indigenous in the City: Contemporary Identities and Cultural Innovation*. Vancouver: UBC Press, 2013.
Pettit, Alexander. "A Legacy of Furious Men: The American Indian Movement and Anna Mae Aquash in Plays by Tomson Highway, E. Donald Two-Rivers, Yvette Nolan, and Bruce King." *Studies in American Indian Literatures* 27, no. 2 (Summer 2015): 29–61.
Piché, Allison. "Imprisonment and Indigenous Masculinity: Contesting Hegemonic Masculinity in a Toxic Environment." In *Indigenous Men and Masculinities: Legacies, Identities, Regeneration*, edited by Robert Alexander Innes and Kim Anderson, 197–213. Winnipeg: University of Manitoba Press, 2015.

Poliandri, Simone. *Native American Nationalism and Nation Re-Building: Past and Present Cases*. Albany, NY: State University of New York Press, 2016.

Powers, Marla N. *Oglala Women: Myth, Ritual, and Reality*. Chicago: University of Chicago Press, 1986.

Price, Catherine. *The Oglala People, 1841–1879: A Political History*. Lincoln: University of Nebraska Press, 1996.

Prucha, Francis Paul. *The Great Father: The United States Government and the American Indians*. Abridged ed. Lincoln: University of Nebraska Press, 1986.

Pyke, Karen D. "Class-Based Masculinities: The Interdependence of Gender, Class, and Interpersonal Power." *Gender and Society* 10, no. 5 (October 1996): 529–549.

———. "What Is Internalized Racial Oppression and Why Don't We Study It? Acknowledging Racism's Hidden Injuries." *Sociological Perspectives* 53, no. 4 (2010): 551–572.

Rader, Dean. *Engaged Resistance: American Indian Art, Literature, and Film from Alcatraz to the NMAI*. Austin: University of Texas Press, 2011.

Ramirez, Renya. *Native Hubs: Culture, Community, and Belonging in Silicon Valley and Beyond*. Durham, NC: Duke University Press, 2007.

———. "Race, Tribal Nation, Gender, a Native Feminist Approach to Belonging." *Meridians: Feminism, Race, Transnationalism* 7, no. 2 (2007): 22–40.

Reed, T. V. "Old Cowboys, New Indians, Hollywood Frames the American Indian Movement." *Wicazo Sa Review* 16, no. 2 (Autumn 2001): 75–96.

Reeser, Todd W. *Masculinities in Theory: An Introduction*. Malden, MA: Wiley-Blackwell, 2010.

Reinhardt, Akim D. "A Crude Replacement: The Indian New Deal, Indirect Colonialism, and Pine Ridge Reservation." *Journal of Colonialism and Colonial History* 6, no. 1 (Spring 2005): 1–56.

———. *Ruling Pine Ridge: Oglala Lakota Politics from the IRA to Wounded Knee*. Lubbock: Texas Tech University Press, 2007.

Rennard, Kate. "Cyd-Safiad (Standing Together): The Politics of Welsh and American Indian Rights' Movements, 1960s–Present." PhD diss., University of Minnesota, August 2012.

———. "We're Still Here: Memory and Commemoration in the Alliance between the American Indian Movement and Welsh Nationalists."

*Comparative American Studies, An International Journal* 17, no. 2 (2020): 167–182.

———. "Becoming Indigenous: The Transnational Networks of the American Indian Movement, Irish Republicans, and Welsh Nationalists," NAIS 8, no. 2 (Fall 2021): 92–124.

Rich, Elizabeth. "'Remember Wounded Knee': AIM's Use of Metonymy in 21st Century Protest." *College Literature* 31, no. 3 (Summer 2004): 70–91.

Richardson, Ione Mavis. "Constructing Two Cultural Realities: Newspaper Coverage of Two American Indian Protest Events." PhD diss., University of Minnesota, 2005.

Richter, Daniel K. "Whose Indian History?" *William and Mary Quarterly* 50 (1993): 379–393.

Rifkin, Mark. *When Did Indians Become Straight? Kinship, the History of Sexuality, and Native Sovereignty*. New York: Oxford University Press, 2011.

———. *The Erotics of Sovereignty: Queer Native Writing in the Era of Self-Determination*. Minneapolis: University of Minnesota Press, 2012.

———. *Settler Common Sense: Queerness and Everyday Colonialism in the American Renaissance*. Minneapolis: University of Minnesota Press, 2014.

Rizzo, Tracey, and Steven Gerontakis. *Intimate Empires: Body, Race, and Gender in the Modern World*. Oxford: Oxford University Press, 2016.

Robbins, Rebecca. "Self-Determination and Subordination: The Past, Present, and Future of American Indian Governance." In *The State of Native America, Genocide, Colonization, and Resistance*, edited by M. Annette Jaimes, 87–122. Boston, MA: South End Press, 1992.

Roberts, Kathleen Glenister. "War, Masculinity, and Native Americans." In *Global Masculinities and Manhood*, edited by Ronald L. Jackson and Murali Balaji, 141–160. Urbana: University of Illinois Press, 2013.

Robinson, Edward J. "Hey Uncle, Uncle Sam!: American Indian GIs and Veterans and Red Power Activism in the Era of the Vietnam War." MA thesis, Canterbury Christ Church, 2016.

Roesch, Claudia. *Macho Men and Modern Women: Mexican Immigration, Social Experts, and Changing Family Values in the 20th Century United States*. Berlin: De Gruyter Oldenbourg, 2015.

Roos, Philip D., Dowell H. Smith, Stephen Langley, and James McDonald. "The Impact of the American Indian Movement on the Pine Ridge Reservation." *Phylon* 41, no. 1 (1980): 89–99.

Rosello, Mireille. *Declining the Stereotype: Ethnicity and Representation in French Cultures*. Dartmouth: University Press of New England, 1998.

Rosenthal, Gabriele. "Biographical Research." In *Qualitative Research Practice*, edited by Clive Seale, Giampietro Gobo, Jaber F. Gubrium, David Silverman, 48–64. London: Sage Publications, 2006.

Rosenthal, Nicolas G. "Beyond the New Indian History: Recent Trends in the Historiography on the Native Peoples of North America." *History Compass* 4/5 (2006): 962–974.

———. *Reimagining Indian Country: Native American Migration and Identity in Twentieth-Century Los Angeles*. Chapel Hill: University of North Carolina Press, 2012.

Rosier, Paul C. *Serving Their Country: American Indian Politics and Patriotism in the Twentieth Century*. Cambridge, MA: Harvard University Press, 2009.

———. "'They Are Ancestral Homelands': Race, Place, and Politics in Cold War Native America." *Journal of American History* 92, no. 4 (2006): 1300–1326.

Sabo, Kupers. "Gender and the Politics of Punishment." In *Prison Masculinities*, edited by Donald F. Sabo, Terry Allen Kupers, and Willie James London, 3–18. Philadelphia, PA: Temple University Press, 2001.

Sayer, John William. *Ghost Dancing the Law: The Wounded Knee Trials*. Cambridge, MA: Harvard University Press, 1997.

Schieffelin, Edward. "Performance and the Cultural Construction of Reality." *American Ethnologist* 12, no. 4 (1985): 707–724.

Schierle Sonja. *Funktion einer Survival School für Städtische Indianer, Heart of the Earth Survival School, Indian: Alternativschule In Minneapolis, Minnesota*. Wiesbaden: Steiner Verlag, 1981.

Simpson, George Eaton, and J. Milton Yinger. "Techniques for Reducing Prejudice: Changing the Situation." In *Psychology and Race*, edited by Peter Watson, 145–175. New York: Routledge, 2017.

Schmidt, Anne. "An Examination of Local Newspaper Photographs of the Wounded Knee Occupation of 1973." MA thesis, University of Nebraska at Omaha, 2000.

Schmittou, Douglas A., and Michael H. Logan. "Fluidity of Meaning: Flag Imagery in Plains Indian Art." *American Indian Quarterly* 26, no. 4 (2002): 559–604.

Schwarz, Maureen Trudelle. *Fighting Colonialism with Hegemonic Culture: Native American Appropriation of Indian Stereotypes*. Albany: State University of New York Press, 2013.

Scott, James. *Weapons of the Weak: Everyday Forms of Peasant Resistance*. New Haven, CT: Yale University Press 1985.

Scott, Joan W. "Gender: A Useful Category of Historical Analysis." *American Historical Review* 91, no. 5 (1986): 1053–1075.

———. "Unanswered Questions." *American Historical Review* 113, no. 5 (December 2008): 1422–1430.

Segal, Michaly Dror. "The American Indian Movement: The Potential of a Counter-Narrative." PhD diss., University of Pennsylvania, 2000.

Shigematsu, Setsu, and Keith L. Camacho. *Militarized Currents: Toward a Decolonized Future in Asia and the Pacific*. Minneapolis: University of Minnesota Press, 2010.

Shipway, Martin. *Decolonization and Its Impact: A Comparative Approach to the End of the Colonial Empires*. Malden, MA: Blackwell, 2008.

Shoemaker, Nancy. "Urban Indians and Ethnic Choices: American Indian Organizations in Minneapolis, 1920–1950." *Western Historical Quarterly* 19, no. 1 (1988): 431–447.

———. *Negotiators of Change: Historical Perspectives on Native American Women*. New York: Routledge, 1995.

Shreve, Bradley Glenn. *Red Power Rising: The National Indian Youth Council and the Origins of Native Activism*. Norman: University of Oklahoma Press, 2011.

Siddons, Louise. "Red Power and the Black Panther, Radical Imagination and Intersectional Resistance at Wounded Knee." *American Art* 35, no. 2 (Summer 2021): 2–31.

Silliman, Stephen W. "The 'Old West' in the Middle East: U.S. Military Metaphors in Real and Imagined Indian Country." *American Anthropologist* 110, no. 2 (June 2008): 237–247.

Sinha, Mrinalini. *Colonial Masculinity: The "Manly Englishman" and the "Effeminate Bengali" in the Late Nineteenth Century*. Manchester: Manchester University Press, 1995.

Smith, Andrea. *Conquest: Sexual Violence and American Indian Genocide*. Cambridge, MA: South End Press, 2005.

———. "Native American Feminism, Sovereignty and Social Change." *Feminist Studies* 31, no. 1 (Spring 2005): 116–132.

Smith, Linda Tuhiwai. *Decolonizing Methodologies: Research and Indigenous Peoples*. 2nd ed. London: Zed Books, 2012.

Smith, Paul Chaat, and Robert Allen Warrior. *Like a Hurricane: The Indian Movement from Alcatraz to Wounded Knee*. New York, NY: New Press, 1996.

Smith, Sherry L. *Hippies, Indians, and the Fight for Red Power*. Oxford: Oxford University Press, 2012.

Sneider, Leah. "Complementary Relationships: A Review of Indigenous Gender Studies." In *Indigenous Men and Masculinities, Legacies, Identities, Regeneration*, edited by Robert Alexander Innes and Kim Anderson, 62–79. Winnipeg: University of Manitoba Press, 2015.

Sorkin, Alan L. *The Urban American Indian*. Lexington, MA: Lexington Books, 1978.

Spotted Eagle, Brook. "The Brave Heart Society: An Oral History of Indigenous Women's Society." MA thesis, University of Montana, 2013.

Steinman, Erich. "Settler Colonial Power and the American Sovereignty Movement: Forms of Domination, Strategies of Transformation." *American Journal of Sociology* 117, no. 4 (January 2012): 1073–1130.

Stern, Kenneth. *Loud Hawk: The United States Versus the American Indian Movement*. Norman: University of Oklahoma Press, 1994.

Stoler, Laura Ann. "Carnal Knowledge and Imperial Power: Gender, Race, and Morality in Colonial Asia." In *Gender at the Crossroads of Knowledge: Feminist Anthropology in the Postmodern Era*, edited by Michaela Di Leonardo, 51–101. Berkeley: University of California Press, 1991.

———. "Making Empire Respectable: The Politics of Race and Sexual Morality in Twentieth-Century Colonial Cultures." In *Situated Lives: Gender and Culture in Everyday Life*, edited by Louise Lamphere, Helena Ragon, and Patricia Zavella, 373–399. New York: Routledge, 1997.

Straus, Terry, and Grant P. Arndt, eds. *Native Chicago*. Chicago: Native Chicago Independent Press, 1998.

Streb, Edward Justin. "The Rhetoric of Wounded Knee II: A Critical Analysis of Confrontational and 'Media Event' Discourse." PhD diss., Northwestern University, 1979.

Streets, Heather. *Martial Races: The Military, Race, and Masculinity in British Imperial Culture, 1857–1914*. New York: Palgrave, 2004.

Strega, Susan, and Leslie Brown. *Research as Resistance: Revisiting Critical, Indigenous, and Anti-Oppressive Practices*. Toronto: Canadian Scholars Press, 2015.

Stripes, James. "A Strategy of Resistance: The 'Actorvism' of Russell Means from Plymouth Rock to the Disney Studio." *Wicazo Sa Review* 14, no. 1 (Spring 1999): 87–101.

Summers, Martin. *Manliness and Its Discontents: The Black Middle Class and the Transformation of Masculinity, 1900–1930*. Chapel Hill: University of North Carolina Press, 2004.

Swain, Jon. "Masculinities in Education." In *Handbook of Studies on Men and Masculinities*, edited by Michael Kimmel, Jeff Hearn, Raewyn Connell, 213–230. Thousand Oaks, CA: Sage Publications, 2005.

Taiaiake, Alfred. *Peace, Power, and Righteousness: An Indigenous Manifesto*. Oxford: Oxford University Press, 1999.

Talbert, Carol. "The Resurgence of Ethnicity Among American Indians: Some Comments on the Occupation of Wounded Knee." In *Ethnicity in the Americas*, edited by Henry Frances, 365–384. The Hague, Paris: Mouton Publishers, 1976.

Talbot, Steve. *Roots of Oppression: The American Indian Question*. New York: New York International Publishers, 1981.

Tate, Michael. "Red Power, Government Publications and the Rising Indian Activism of the 1970s." *Government Publications Review* 8, A (1981): 499–518.

———. "From Scout to Doughboy: The National Debate over Integrating American Indians into the Military, 1891–1918." *Western Historical Quarterly* 17, no. 4 (October 1986): 417–437.

Taylor, Graham. *The New Deal and American Indian Tribalism: The Administration of the Indian Reorganization Act, 1934–45*. Lincoln: University of Nebraska Press, 1980.

Taylor, Michael. *Contesting Constructed Indian-Ness: The Intersection of the Frontier, Masculinity, and Whiteness in Native American Mascot Representations*. Lanham, MD: Lexington Books, 2013.

Tengan, Ty P. Kāwika. "(En)Gendering Colonialism: Masculinities in Hawai'i and Aotearoa." *Cultural Values* 6, no. 3 (2002): 239–256.

———. *Native Men Remade: Gender and Nation in Contemporary Hawai'i*. Durham, NC: Duke University Press, 2008.

———. "Re-Membering Panala'au: Masculinities, Nation, and Empire in Hawai'i and the Pacific." *Contemporary Pacific* 20, no. 1 (2008): 27–53.

———. "The Return of Kū? Remembering Hawaiian Masculinity, Warriorhood, and Nation." In *Performing Indigeneity: Global Histories and Contemporary Experiences*, edited by Laura R. Graham and H. Glenn Perry, 206–246. Lincoln: University of Nebraska Press, 2014.

Tengan, Ty P. Kāwika, and Jesse Makani Markham. "Performing Polynesian Masculinities in American Football: From 'Rainbows to Warriors.'" *International Journal of the History of Sport* 26, no. 16 (December 2009): 2412–2431.

Thomas, Robert K. "Colonialism, Classic and Internal." *New University Thought* 6 (1966–1967): 34–43.

Thompson, Alistair. "The Voice of the Past: Oral History." In *The Oral History Reader*, 3rd ed., edited by Robert Perks and Alistair Thompson, 33–39. London: Routledge 2006.

Thompson, Paul, and Joanna Bornat. *The Voice of the Past, Oral History*. Oxford: Oxford University Press, 2017.

Tohe, Laura. "There Is No Word for Feminism in My Language." *Wicazō Ša Review* 15, no. 2 (2000): 103–110.

Tóth, György Ferenc. *From Wounded Knee to Checkpoint Charlie: The Alliance for Sovereignty between American Indians and Centra Europeans in the Late Cold War*. Albany: State University of New York Press, 2017.

Townsend, Kenneth William. *World War II and the American Indian*. Albuquerque: University of New Mexico Press, 2000.

Thrush, Coll. *Native Seattle: Histories from the Crossing Over Place*. Seattle: University of Washington Press, 2007.

Trimbach, Joseph H., and John M. Trimbach. *American Indian Maffia: An FBI Agent's True Story About Wounded Knee, Leonard Peltier, and the American Indian Movement (AIM)*. Denver, CO: Outskirts Press, 2008.

Tully, James. "The Struggles of Indigenous People for and of Freedom." In *Political Theory and the Rights of Indigenous Peoples*, edited by Duncan Ivison, Paul Patton, and Wil Sanders. Cambridge: Cambridge University Press, 2000.

Turner, Victor. *The Ritual Process, Structure and Anti-Structure*. Aldine de Gruyter: New York, 1969.

Tyson, Timothy B. *Radio Free Dixie, Robert F. Williams and the Roots of Black Power*. Chapel Hill: University of North Carolina Press, 1999.

Usbeck, Frank. "Selling the Natural-Born Warrior." In *Selling Ethnicity and Race, Consumerism and Representation in Twenty-First-Century America*, edited by Gabriele Pisarz-Ramirez, Frank Usbeck, Anne Grob, and Maria Lippold, 175–193. Wissenschaftlicher Verlag Trier, 2006.

———. "Fighting Like Indians: The 'Indian Scout Syndrome' in U.S. And German War Reports During World War II." In *Visual Representations of Native Americans: Transnational Contexts and Perspectives*, edited by Carsten Fitz, 125–143. Heidelberg: Winter, 2012.

Valaskakis, Gail Guthrie. *Indian Country: Essays on Contemporary Native Culture*. Waterloo, Ontario, Canada: Wilfried Laurier University Press, 2005.

Van Deburg, William L. *New Day in Babylon: The Black Power Movement and American Culture, 1965–1975*. Chicago: University of Chicago Press, 1993.

van Gennep, Arnold. *The Rites of Passage*. University of Chicago Press: Chicago, 1961.
Vander Wall, Jim. "A Warrior Caged." In *The State of Native America, Genocide, Colonization, and Resistance*, edited by M. Annette Jaimes, 291–310. Boston, MA: South End Press, 1992.
Veracini, Lorenzo. *Settler Colonialism: A Theoretical Overview*. Houndmills, Basingstoke, NY: Palgrave Macmillan, 2010.
Viola, Herman J. *Warriors in Uniform: The Legacy of American Indian Heroism*. Washington, DC: National Geographic, 2008.
Vizenor, Gerald. *Tribal Scenes and Ceremonies*. Minneapolis: Nodin Press, 1976.
———. "Dennis at Wounded Knee." *American Indian Quarterly* 7, no. 2 (Spring 1983): 51–65.
———. *The People Named the Chippewa, Narrative Histories*. Minneapolis: University of Minnesota Press, 1984.
———. "Confrontation or Negotiation." In *Native American Testimony: A Chronicle of Indian-White Relations from Prophecy to Present, 1492–2000*, edited by Peter Nabokov, 376–380. New York, NY: Penguin Books 1999.
———. *The Everlasting Sky: Voices of the Anashinabe People*. St. Paul: Minnesota Historical Society Press, 2000.
Voigt, Matthias André. "'Fighting for Their Freedom at Home': Native American Vietnam Veterans in the Red Power Movement, 1969–1973." In *War Veterans and the World after 1945, Cold War Politics, Decolonization, Memory*, edited by Ángel Alcalde and Xosé M. Núñez Seixas, 83–99. London: Routledge, 2018.
———. "Race, Masculinity, and Martial Valor: Native American Veterans from WWI to Vietnam and Beyond." In *Warring over Valor: How Race and Gender Shaped American Military Heroism in the Twentieth and Twenty-First Centuries*, edited by Simon Wendt, 79–95. Philadelphia, PA: Temple University Press, 2018.
———. "Indigenous and non-Indigenous Combat Veterans and the Sweat Lodge (Inipi) Ritual: War-related Trauma, Ceremony, and Transformation." In *War and Trauma in Past and Present: An Interdisciplinary Collection of Essays*, edited by Chiara Manghi, Mareike Spychala, Lina Stempel, 103–116. Wissenschaftlicher Buchverlag: Trier, 2019.
———. "Between Powerlessness and Protest: Indigenous Men and Masculinities in the Twin Cities and the Emergence of the American Indian Movement." *Settler Colonial Studies* 11, no. 2 (2021): 221–241.
———. "Warriors for a Nation: The American Indian Movement,

Indigenous Men, and Nation-building at the Takeover at Wounded Knee in 1973." *American Indian Culture and Research Journal* 45, no. 2 (2021): 1–38.

———. "Warrior Women: Indigenous Women, Gender Relations, and Sexual Politics Within the American Indian Movement and at Wounded Knee." *American Indian Culture and Research Journal* 46, no. 3 (2023): 101–130.

Waetjen, Thembisa. "The Limits of Gender Rhetoric for Nationalism: A Case Study from Southern Africa." *Theory and Society* 30, no. 1 (February 2001): 121–152.

———. *Workers and Warriors: Masculinity and the Struggle for Nation in South Africa*. Urbana: University of Illinois Press, 2004.

Waterman Wittstock, Laura. "Native American Women: Twilight of a Long Maidenhood." In *Comparative Perspectives of Third World Women: The Impact of Race, Sex, and Class*, edited by Beverly Lindsay, 207–228. New York: Praeger, 1989.

———. "Native American Women in the Feminist Milieu." In *Contemporary Native American Address*, edited by John Maestas, 373–376. Provo, UT: Brigham Young University Publications, 1976.

Wells, Natalie P. "Television News Coverage of the America Indian Occupation of Wounded Knee, South Dakota: An Analysis of Network Broadcasts, February–May 1973." MA thesis, San Francisco State University, 1982.

Wendt, Simon, and Pablo Dominguez Andersen, eds. *Masculinities and the Nation in the Modern World: Between Hegemony and Marginalization*. New York: Palgrave Macmillan, 2015.

Wendt, Simon, ed. *Warring over Valor: How Race and Gender Shaped American Military Heroism in the Twentieth and Twenty-First Centuries*. Philadelphia, PA: Temple University Press, 2018.

———. "'They Finally Found Out That We Really Are Men': Violence, Non-Violence, and Black Manhood in the Civil Rights Era." *Gender and History* 19, no. 3 (November 2007): 543–564.

Wengraf, Tom. *Qualitative Research Interviewing: Biographic Narrative and Semi-structured Methods*. Los Angeles: Sage, 2012.

West, Candace, and Don Zimmerman. "Doing Gender." *Gender and Society* 1, no. 2 (1987): 125–151.

Weston, Mary Ann. *Native Americans in the News: Images of Indians in the Twentieth-Century Press*. Westport, CT: Greenwood Press, 1996.

Weyler, Rex. *Blood of the Land: The Government and Corporate War against First Nations*, rev. ed. Philadelphia, PA: New Society Publications, 1992.
White, Bruce. "The American Indian as Soldier, 1890–1919." *Canadian Review of American Studies* 7 (Spring 1976): 15–25.
———. "The American Army and the Indian." In *Ethnic Armies, Polyethnic Armed Forces from the Time of the Habsburgs to the Age of Superpowers*, edited by N. F. Dreisziger, 69–88. Waterloo, Ontario: Wilfried Laurier University Press, 1990.
Whitehead, Stephen. *Men and Masculinities: Key Themes and New Directions*. Cambridge, UK: Polity, 2002.
Whitehead, Stephen, and Frank J. Barret. *The Masculinities Reader*. Cambridge, UK: Polity, 2001.
Wilkins, David E. *The Hank Adams Reader: An Exemplary Native Activist and the Unleashing of Indigenous Sovereignty*. Golden, CO: Fulcrum Publishing, 2011.
Wilkens, David E., and Heidi Kiiwetinepinesiik Stark. *American Indian Politics and the American Political System*. Lanham, MW: Rowman and Littlefield Publishers, 2017.
Wilson, Shawn. *Research Is Ceremony: Indigenous Research Methods*. Halifax: Fernwood Publishing, 2008.
Wolfe, Patrick. "Settler Colonialism and the Elimination of the Native." *Journal of Genocide Research* 8, no. 4 (2006): 387–409.
———. "Structure and Event: Settler Colonialism and the Question of Genocide." In *Empire, Colony, Genocide: Conquest, Occupation, and Subaltern Resistance in World History*, edited by A. Dirk Moses, 82–101. Oxford: Berghahn Books, 2008.
Xaba, Thokozani. "Masculinity and Its Malcontents: The Confrontation Between 'Struggle Masculinity' and 'Post Struggle Masculinity' (1990–1997)." In *Changing Men in Southern Africa*, edited by Robert Morrell, 105–124. Pietermaritzburg: University of Natal Press, 2001.
Yuval-Davis, Nira. *Gender & Nation*. Thousand Oaks, CA: Sage Publications, 1997.
Yuval-Davis, Nira, and Floya Anthias. *Woman-Nation-State*. New York: St. Martin's Press, 1989.
Zissu, Erik M. "Conscription, Sovereignty, and Land: American Indian Resistance During World War I." *Pacific Historical Review* 64, no. 4 (November 1995): 537–566.

*Websites and Blogs*

*ACLU*

American Indian Movement Interpretative Center. Last accessed July 18, 2018. http://www.aim-ic.org/ and https://www.facebook.com/AIM InterpretiveCenter/.

*CBS News*

Chee, April. "The Longest Walk: Activism and Legislation in Indian Country." July 1, 2016. Nation Museum of the American Indian (NMAI). Last accessed July 18, 2018, http://blog.nmai.si.edu/main/2016/07/the-longest-walk-activism-and-legislation-in-indian-country.html.

Currey, Richard. "Wes Studi: At the Edge of Courage," *VVA Veteran* (March/April 2015), last accessed April 12, 2024, http://vvaveteran.org/35-2/35-2_wesstudi.html.

Estes, Nick. "Border Towns, Colonial Logics of Violence." Posted December 17, 2012, last accessed April 12, 2024, https://oldwars.wordpress.com/2012/12/17/border-towns-colonial-logics-of-violence/.

———. "Common Sense Anti-Indianism: Border Town Violence In Rapid City, S.D." Posted February 6, 2014, last accessed July 18, 2018, https://oldwars.wordpress.com/2014/02/06/common-sense-anti-indianism-border-town-violence-in-rapid-city-sd/.

International Indian Treaty Council. "Declaration of Continuing Independence by the First International Indian Treaty Council at Standing Rock Sioux Indian Country." Last accessed July 18, 2018. https://www.iitc.org/about-iitc/the-declaration-of-continuing-independence-june-1974/.

The Lakota Women Warriors, last accessed September 14, 2022, http://www.lakotawomenwarriors.org/.

Noriyuki, Duane. "The Women of Wounded Knee." Undated. Last accessed April 12, 2024, http://www.dickshovel.com/lsa21.html.

*Native News Online* (News Outlet)

*NPR* (News Outlet)

*Reuters* (News Agency)

*Vox* (News Outlet)

Vukelich, James. "Ojibwe Word of the Day: Ogichidaa, Ogichidaakwe: A Warrior, a Veteran, a Ceremonial Headman or Woman," last accessed April 12, 2024, https://www.youtube.com/watch?v=yxMvqqn_B-A.

# Index

Abernathy, Ralph, 213
Abourezk, James, 181, 220
Adam, David Wallace, 80
Adams, Hank, 142, 327n119
Adams, John, 194–195
*Akwesasne Notes* (Indigenous newspaper), 116, 151, 193, 196, 206
Alcatraz Island, 4, 6, 28–29, 61, 116, 233–234, 271, 313n193
alcohol use, 85–86, 89–90
Alfred, Taiaiake, 294
alienation, from tribal traditions, 68, 80, 83–84, 87, 91–92, 100–101, 159–160
Alliance, Nebraska (protest), 104, 123
American Civil Liberties Union (ACLU), 280
American Horse, 132
American Indian Cultural Folklore Group, 88
American Indian Movement (AIM)
activism overview of, 104
agenda of, 105, 117, 242–243; 3–4, 16, 62, 72, 79, 101, 107, 116, 130–141, 142, 191–196, 220, 229–230, 245, 260, 278, 286
alliances with other movements, 121, 157, 230, 281–282
American flag usage at, 113, 171, 258, 278, 285
as anti-intellectual, 119–120
armed self-defense in, 119–126
Black Panther Party (BPP) influence on, 115–116
Bureau of Indian Affairs (BIA) takeover and, 287
chauvinism in, 158, 203, 210
Christian churches as enemy of, 97–98
colonialism excuse in, 159
confrontation politics of, 108–109
criticism of, 117–119, 154, 218–219, 265–267
cultural alliance with reservation traditionalists, 107–108, 130, 163, 167, 243
and cultural disconnect, 10, 105–106
cultural memory of, 247–253, 292–293
as cultural or spiritual movement, 117, 240, 242
demands at Wounded Knee, 220–220

American Indian Movement (AIM) (*cont.*)
  demographics of, 72, 316n34
  division within, 249–253
  documentaries and films regarding, 277
  empowerment through protest activism, 110, 112
  experiences of powerlessness and, 70–73, 79–93
  factions of, 126
  Federal Bureau of Investigation (FBI) and, 227, 229
  financial support for, 98, 230, 322n186, 323n204
  and formative experiences and expressions of Indigenous men, 79–93
  Fort Laramie Treaty and, 230
  gender relations in, 155–163
  gender roles and sexism in, 5, 9–10, 91, 159, 163, 203, 232
  growth of, 3–4
  Guardians of the Oglala Nation (GOON) and, 228
  identity politics, 26, 104–119, 129, 247
  ideology of, 112, 115, 285–286
  Independent Oglala Nation (ION) and, 183–191
  Indian Patrol and, 71, 93–98
  Indian Patrol and Indigenous-police relations, 321–322n182, 321n170
  Indigenous Vietnam veterans' participation in, 10–11, 82–83, 168–181, 288–290
  Indigenous women in, 155–163, 290–292
  International Indian Treaty Council (IITC) and, 229–230
  as International Warrior Society, 229–231, 277–278
  Interpretive Center of, 237, 248
  lack of culturally appropriate behavior of, 118–119
  and Lakota culture, 24, 107–108
  leadership of, 9–10, 73
  leadership of, after 1973, 235–237
  legacy of, 255, 262–266, 292–293
  logo of, 112–113
  long-term impact in South Dakota and Minnesota of, 239
  media (*see* media)
  militancy of, 117, 126–127
  militant manhood and visual self-representation, 121–122
  military service and, 82–83, 168–181, 288–290
  as modern warriors, 2–3, 11, 20, 24–27, 62, 66, 87, 103, 104–119, 128–130, 145–146, 148–152, 163–164, 175–176, 179–181, 213, 221–222
  moral righteousness of, 245
  motivations for joining, 60
  nationalist symbols of, 112, 113, 114, 134
  nationalist warrior masculinity and, 25, 166, 175–176, 283–284
  as neo-traditionalists, 24, 79, 107–108, 117, 130, 167
  nonviolence in, 119–126
  occupation tactic of, 109
  origin of, 3, 62, 68, 70–71, 87–88
  overview of, 3–15, 71, 74, 101, 282–288
  painting regarding, 266–269
  Pan-Indian consciousness and, 43–44
  performance of warriorhood, 11, 20, 25, 126–130, 145–155, 163, 198–201, 211–218
  photo exhibition of, 247–248
  protest masculinity, 23, 26, 68–69, 73, 79, 83–84, 92–93, 93–98, 101, 283, 284
  protest tactics of, 109, 126–127
  Red Power movement and, 62
  revolutionary culture of, 111–119
  savage reactionary image of, 11
  as a self-help organization, 72
  self-perception as warriors, 129
  sexual politics in, 155–163

slogan of, 112
song of, 113
and spirituality, 106–107, 112, 244–246, 255, 261, 267
Stillwater Prison and, 87–88
Ten Point Program of, 116
Twenty-Point proposal, 142
uniform of, 114–115, 121–122
Vietnam Veterans' perspective regarding, 253–261
viewpoints regarding, 106–107
as warrior society, 166, 183–191, 197–201, 213, 221–222
Wounded Knee takeover and, 220, 286, 293
"American Indian Movement" (Louis Hall), 266–269, 275
American Indian Religious Freedom Act, 239
American male identity, breadwinning and, 84
Andersen, Pablo Dominguez, 12
Anderson, Benedict, 17
Anderson, Bob, 175, 179, 201, 208
Anderson, Kim, 12, 91, 159–160
Anderson, Robert, 196
Apple, Tyrone, 259
Applegate Krouse, Susan, 8
Aquash, Anna Mae, 8, 221, 228, 235, 277, 278, 353n15. *See also* Pictou-Aquash, Anna Mae
Archambault, David, II, 280
Arikaras, 82–83
Arlington National Cemetery, 142–143
assimilation, 38–41, 42–43, 73, 85, 91–92, 167, 308–309n99
Augustana College, Sioux Falls, South Dakota, 104
authenticity, defined, 69

Bad Heart Bull, Wesley, 131, 136, 287
Balaji, Murali, 31
Bancroft, Dick, 248
Banerjee, Sikata, 305n29
Banks, Dennis
background of, 72–74, 114

Black Panthers and, 94, 95
on Bureau of Indian Affairs (BIA) takeover, 146–147, 148–149, 152, 153
at Cass Lake Reservation, 123
chauvinism of, 157, 159, 203
Church clergy and, 98
on confrontational style of AIM, 126–127
criticism against other AIM leaders, 161
criticism of, 158, 159, 232, 256–257
on Custer, South Dakota protest, 137, 138
cultural alienation of, 73–74, 106
death of, 236
efforts to bridge cultural disconnect, 106–107
founding of AIM, 72–74, 86
formative experiences, 80–81, 99, 89–90, 91–93, 82–83, 87–89
on Gordon protest, 122–124
and impacting news media, 146–147
Independent Oglala Nation (ION) and, 192
on Indigenous Rights Struggle, 271
leadership of, 74, 236
"Longest Walk" and, 233
on NoDAPL protests, 281
on nonviolence, 119
at photo exhibition, 247–248
photo of, 74, 195
reputation of, 157–158
on self-defense, 122–126
on survival schools, 99
Wounded Knee leadership trial, 225, 227
on Wounded Knee takeover, 210, 216, 241–242, 251, 263–264
Barnett, Don, 136
Battle of Little Bighorn (1876), 138, 206, 258
American flag, capture of, 258
Custer Battle National Monument, Montana (protest), 276
Battle of the Rosebud (1876), 207

Battle of Wounded Knee (1890). *See* Wounded Knee (1890) massacre
Baylor, Timothy, 11, 126, 127, 128
Bear Runner, Edgar, 139
Bear Runner, Oscar, 243
Bellanger, Pat, 94, 121–122, 155
Bellecourt, Clyde
  achievements of, 265
  AIM Interpretive Center and, 237, 248
  background of, 72–73
  on Black Panther Party (BPP), 94–96, 116–117
  on Bureau of Indian Affairs (BIA) takeover, 153
  chauvinism of, 157
  church clergy and, 98
  confrontation politics of, 108–109, 110
  criticism of, 158, 250–251
  death of, 236
  founding of AIM, 70
  formative experiences, 73, 80–81, 85, 90, 91–93, 88–89, 85, 90
  and impacting news media, 146–147
  on NoDAPL protests, 281
  painting to, 266
  at photo exhibition, 247–248
  photo of, 74–75, 145, 153
  as role model, 96
  shooting by Carter Camp, 234
  on sterilization, 233
  on survival schools, 99
  toxic masculinity of, 158, 236–237
  on Wounded Knee takeover, 251, 262, 263
Bellecourt, Vernon, 73, 87, 107, 228, 236, 250
Benton-Benai, Eddie, 72, 76, 88, 192, 194, 262–263
Berry, Marion, 145
BIA (Floyd Crow Westerman), 113
Big Foot
  Holocaust Museum, 276
  Memorial Ride, 261
  Wounded Knee (1890), 276
Bissonette, Gladys, 202
Bissonette, Pedro, 272, 278
Black civil rights movement, 44, 203
  "massive resistance" and White Citizen Councils, 135
  rhetoric of manhood, 134–135
Black Elk, Nicolas, 252
Black Elk, Wallace, 189, 195, 199–200, 252
Black Hills, South Dakota, 109
*Black Panther* newsletter, 116
Black Panther Party (BPP)
  and armed self-defense, 120–121
  *Black Panther* newsletter, 116
  Black Patrol, 94, 95–96
  connections to AIM, 94–96, 115–117, 326n79
  and gender relations within, 160–162
  and model of manhood, 95–96
  and police brutality, 95–96
  and Ten-Point Program, 115–116, 121
  in Twin Cities, MN, 94–96
  in Oakland, CA, 94
  and white support, 239
Black Power
  ideology, 95, 116, 314n225
  and Red Power, 115–116, 270
Blansett, Kent, 15–16
boarding schools, 37–38, 42, 46, 79–81, 80, 92
  Hampton Institute, Virginia, 37
  Haskell School, Kansas, 37
body/bodily practices/physicality
  body building, 305n29
  body-reflexive practice, 198, 200–201
  at Bureau of Indian Affairs protest, 151–152
  and nation, 151–152, 197–201
  ritual performance, 148
  ritual practices, 51–52, 64, 66, 148–149, 183, 197, 198, 199–201, 238, 240–241, 248, 287, 288
  at Wounded Knee takeover, 197–201
Bonney, Rachel, 88, 92, 126
border towns, 130–141, 163, 286–287
  bias in, 132
  *See also specific locations*

bourgeois family, as model family, 34–35
Brando, Marlon, 213, 264
Braun, Felix, 36
Brave, Regina, 206, 208, 209, 210, 246–247, 282
Brave Bird, Mary. *See* Crow Dog, Mary
Brave Hearted Women's Society, 206, 207
Brave Woman (Buffalo Calf Road Woman), 207
Brightman, Lehman, 109, 233
Britten, Thomas, 56
Brown, Bill, 217
Brown, Dee, 182
Brown Berets, 315n14
Brown Eyes, Errol, 255
Bruyneel, Kevin, 35
Buffalo Calf Road Woman (Brave Woman), 207
Bureau of Indian Affairs (BIA)
　authority of, 305–306n37
　control of, 33–34
　guardian-warden relationship and, 306–307n53
　and (Indigenous) incompetence, 33–34
　and identity (blood quantum, ancestry), 33–34
　as oversight agency, 36
　in painting Wounded Knee Holocaust Museum), 272, 273, 274
　paternalism, 33–34
　performing warriorhood at takeover of, 141–155
　takeover of BIA field offices, 141
　takeover of BIA headquarters, 142, 102–103, 124, 127, 130, 141–155, 163, 287
Burnette, Robert, 117, 142, 145, 149, 154, 203, 212, 221
Burnt First Nation (Canada), 294
"Bury My Heart at Wounded Knee" (Sainte-Marie), 270
Busacca, Jeremy, 129–130
Bush, Tony, 180

Camacho, Keith L., 47
Camp, Carter
　on (AIM) warrior society, 190, 242–243, 278, 290
　on colonial oppression, 253
　as cultural warrior, 236–237
　death of, 236
　on Independent Oglala Nation (ION), 252
　on Indigenous warriors, 250–253
　on Indigenous women's involvement, 231
　leadership of, 73, 173–174, 186
　photo of, 145, 195
　shooting of Clyde Bellecourt, 234–235
　on warriorhood, 253
　on warrior societies, 185–186
　on Wounded Knee takeover, 165–166, 173–174, 197, 208, 215, 242–243, 249, 251–252, 262
　writings of, 249
Camp, Craig, 252
Camp, Yellow Thunder (protest), 235
Cannon, Martin J., 13
capitalism, 35
Carlisle Indian School, Pennsylvania, 37
Carmichael, Stokely, 116, 145
Carroll, Al, 11, 47–48, 49, 166, 173, 179, 185, 189, 223, 224, 294
Carter, Bruce, 269–270
Case, Francis, 181
Cass Lake Reservation, Minnesota (AIM convention, protest), 123–124, 126, 161
Castle, Elizabeth, 8, 156, 161–162
Catches, Pete, 252
Celaya, Philip, 327n119
ceremony, 51–52, 200
　sweat lodge *(inípi)*, 51, 189, 198–199, 200, 244–245, 252
　Sun Dance, 200, 241, 244–245
　*yuwipi*, 200
Chamorro men (Guam), 47
Champagne, Duane, 6

Charging Elk, Ed, 48–49
chauvinism, 5, 9–10, 91, 158, 203, 210, 232
Chavis, Ben, 16
Cheyennes, 82–83, 207
Chicanos, 124
Chips, Godfrey, 126
Christianity, in settler colonialism, 32
citizenship, 36, 53
    Citizenship Act, 53
    *Ex Parte Green*, 53
    Nationality Act of 1940, 53
    Snyder Act, 53
City Hill, South Dakota (protest), 138
civic nationalism, 17–18
civil rights
    civil rights, Black, 44–45, 64, 98, 135
    civil rights, Indigenous, 35–36, 41, 44–45, 64, 130–141
Clearwater, Frank, 219, 272, 275, 278, 351n294
Cobb, Daniel, 7
Cohen, Fay, 72, 97, 112
Colburn, Wayne, 187–188
Cold War, 45
Coler, Ronald, 229
colonial
    ambivalence, 15, 25, 33, 46, 47, 128, 305n34
    attitudes towards Indigenous people, 31–34, 46–47
    mimicry, 15, 25, 128
colonial imagery
    of Indigenous lands, 33
    of Indigenous men, 32
    of Indigenous women, 33
colonialism, 20, 31, 46, 168–181, 243, 306n45
    colonialism excuse, 159
    colonization, 34–42
    complicity/resistance to, 15, 68, 98, 115, 288, 305n34
    heteropatriarchy and, 30
    internal colonialism, 37
    and white supremacy, 32
    *See also* settler colonialism
colonized Indigenous elite, 46, 223, 304–305n29
compensation, under termination policy, 38
commemorating/remembering (AIM), 247–253, 292–293
Connell, Raewyn, 18–19, 69, 197–198
Cooper, Al, 173
Cornell, Stephen, 7–8
counting coup, 190
Crazy Horse, 109, 130, 138, 261
criminal justice system, 86–89, 93–94
Crow Dog, Leonard
    at BIA (Bureau of Indian Affairs) takeover, 148–149, 151
    cultural practices of, 124–126, 148–149, 151, 180, 189, 198–200
    on Custer, South Dakota, 137
    death of, 236
    in exhibition, 271, 276
    in faction, 126
    on Gordon, Nebraska protest, 134
    influence of on AIM, 107–108
    leadership of, 180, 189, 252
    photo of, 78–79, 195, 199, 276
    as spiritual/cultural advisor to AIM, 107–108, 124–126, 148–149, 151, 180, 189, 198–199, 252
    at Wounded Knee, 180, 189, 198–199
Crow Dog, Mary, 108, 114–115, 127, 129, 157–158, 159, 160–161, 202–203
Crows, 82–83
cultural
    adaptation, 20, 66, 73, 160, 242
    authenticity, 64, 70–71
    borrowing, 24, 79
    conformity, 41, 73, 160
    cultural/ethnic renewal, 6, 11–12, 29, 42–44, 52, 61–65, 66, 103, 110, 192, 197, 200, 237, 247, 262–263, 284, 285, 287, 288, 292
    hybridity, 15, 20, 31

integrity, 4, 26, 66, 101, 230
invention/reinvention, 20–21, 40–41, 66, 71, 113, 115, 243
  memory, 130–131, 181–182, 248–249
  nationalism, 64
  racial capital, 11, 20, 128, 135, 215, 218, 286
  reappropriation, 11, 113, 126–130, 163, 295
  renaissance, in Indian Country, 12, 121, 237–247, 255–256, 278, 292–293
  revitalization, 4, 6, 62, 64, 66, 98, 105, 181–182, 196–197, 238–241, 262, 263, 265, 272, 287–288
cultural warriors, 237–247
Custer, George Armstrong, 137, 258
Custer, South Dakota (protest), 104, 124, 131, 136–141
Custer Battlefield National Monument, Montana (protest), 276
Czywczynski, Jan and James A., 344n92

Dakota Access Pipeline (DAPL), 279–282
Dauki, Horace, 252
Davis, Angela, 116, 169, 213
Davis, Julie, 6, 8, 91–92, 100
"Declaration of Continuing Independence of the Sovereign Native American Indian Nations," 230
decolonization, 30, 44, 63, 231–233, 238, 248
DeCora Means, Lorelei, 155, 157, 194, 210, 232, 354n17
Deegan, Charles, 72
Deere, Phillip, 252
defensive othering, 81
Deloria, Philip, 21, 128
Deloria, Vine, Jr., 7, 64, 65, 111, 142
DeMallie, Raymond, 207
Demetriou, Demetrakis Z., 19
dependency theory, 47–48

Dewing, Rolland, 117
Donahue, James, 88
double colonization, 10, 91, 162, 232

Eagle Shield, Fritz Wallace, 255
education
  alternative (survival schools), 98–101
  colonial (boarding school education), 42, 46, 73, 79–81, 82, 92
empire-building, masculinity and femininity in, 30
engaged resistance, 112
Enloe, Cynthia, 181, 204, 206
Erll, Astrid, 248–249
Esgenoopetitj Rangers, 294
Estes, Steve, 135
ethnic
  ethnic/cultural pride, 4, 16, 25, 29, 40, 72, 74, 92, 101, 105, 110, 112, 114, 115, 121, 114, 129, 145, 197, 200, 222, 223, 243, 265, 285, 292–293
  nationalism, 17–18
ethnocentrism, 17, 46, 192, 200
ethnohistory, 21
Eubanks, Matthew, 94
Everson, Davis W., 239
*Ex Parte Green*, 53

Fairchild factory, New Mexico, 356n54
Fanon, Frantz, 65
Farge, Peter La, 111
fashion, cultural, 114–115
Federal Bureau of Investigation (FBI), 227, 228, 229, 235
  and Counter-Intelligence-Program (COINTELPRO), 4, 6, 235, 353n15
Federal Indian policies
  allotment, 36, 38, 41, 200
  assimilation, 38–41, 42–43, 73, 85, 91–92, 167, 308–309n99
  compensation, 38
  relocation program, 38–41, 42–44, 83–84, 90, 284–285

Federal Indian policies (*cont.*)
  self-determination, 63, 238–239
  termination policy, 36–37, 38–39, 41, 61, 90, 108, 238–239, 284–185
feminism
  Indigenous women's concerns versus Western, 155, 162, 233, 337–338n334
  women of color and feminism, 162
Ferris, Bunky, 327n119
fish-in movement, 7, 60–61
Fixico, Donald, 16, 22–23, 61, 62, 85, 264–265
flag, adversary nature of, 113
Fools Crow, Frank, 252
Fort Laramie Treaty, 168, 219, 224, 230
Foster, Lenny, 189, 244, 245
Free, Bob, 217
Frizzell, Kent, 195

Gates, Hobart, 138
gender
  bias, in border towns, 132
  and nation-building, 18
  as performative, 20–21
  relational nature of, 25
  and settler colonialism, 29–34, 34–42
  stereotypes, 32–34
  survival schools and, 98–100
  theorizing, 15–23
  *See also* Indigenous men/masculinity; Indigenous women
General Service Administration (GSA), 154
Ghost Dance, 181, 196, 201, 288
Giago, Tim, 228
Gilbert, Madonna. *See* Thunder Hawk, Madonna
Gildersleeve, Clive and Agnes, 344n92
Goings, Milo, 179, 189–190
GoodSky, Harold, 72
Gordon, Nebraska (protests), 104, 113, 122, 131, 133–134, 163, 287
government restraint, 154–155

Graham, John, 228
grassroots organizing (by AIM), 315–316n31
Gravy, Wavy, 145
Great White Father, 34, 99
Grimm, Lloyd, 219
Guardians of the Oglala Nation (GOON), 167, 169, 228
Guevara, Che, 65
Gunn Allen, Paula, 158, 232
Guthrie Valaskakis, Gail, 211

hair, cultural symbolism of, 114
Hall, Bill, 187–188
Hall, Louis
  AIM painting, 230–231, 266–269, 272, 275, 278
  writings, 266, 269
Halsey, Theresa, 8, 207, 228
Hammer, Justin, 137
Hampton Institute, Virginia, 37
Haskell School, Kansas, 37
Hawaii, settler colonialism responses in, 305n34
Hayes, Ira, 55–56, 143
Heard, Harvey, 188
Heart of the Earth Survival School, 100
hegemonic masculinity, 12, 19, 305n29
Hill, David, 138, 139
Hitchmough, Sam, 7
Hobsbawm, Eric, 20
Ho Chi Minh, 65
Hokowhitu, Brendan, 13, 32, 69–70
Holder, Stan, 173–174, 180, 186, 187–188, 189–190, 252, 290
Holm, Tom, 11, 16, 34, 47–48, 50, 166, 173
Holocaust Museum at Wounded Knee, 271–277
hooks, bell, 203
Hornik-Camp, Casey, 186
Hot Springs, South Dakota (protest), 104, 131
House Concurrent Resolution 108, 38
Hutchinson, John, 63–64, 240

Ickes, Harold, 54
identity, Indigenous, 43, 340n13
IdleNoMore movement (Canada), 281
incarceration, 86–87, 93–94
Independent Oglala Nation (ION)
  bodily practices and, 197–201
  brotherhood in, 194
  bureaucracy of, 193
  citizenship of, 193–194
  community-building efforts of, 194–195
  cultural renewal/revitalization and, 196–197, 197–201, 242–246
  declaration of, 1, 166, 192, 223
  declaration of and setup of warrior society, 1, 166, 183–191, 223
  form of governance, 192–193, 221–222, 223
  gendering of, 191–211
  as imagined nation, 194, 224, 288
  inclusiveness of, 194
  and ION warrior society, 183–191
  male bodies and, 197–201
  as masculine/masculinist project, 191–192, 200–202, 204, 206, 211, 223, 224, 269–270, 281, 287, 291
  moral regeneration and, 196–197
  nationalist elements of, 192
  national reclamation and, 196–197
  and Western/Indigenous nation-building concepts, 191–196, 221–222
  overview of, 183–191, 249
  peoplehood (or Lakota-ness), 194–196, 222
  setup of, 221–222
  support for, 194, 239
Indian Act (Canada), 13–14
Indian Centers, 43
Indian Child Welfare Act, 233
Indian Claims Commission, 38
Indian Community School, 8–9
Indian Health Board, 316n31
Indian Health Services (IHS), 232–233
Indian Memorial, 259

Indian New Deal, 38, 42
Indian Patrol, 71, 93–98, 101, 115–116, 119
Indian Reorganization Act (IRA), 166
Indian scout syndrome, 34, 55
Indian Self-Determination and Education Assistance Act, 238–239
*Indian's Friend*, 54
"Indians playing Indian" themes, 21, 77, 128, 129, 146, 215, 216, 218, 236, 240–241, 286
Indian Wars, 32–33, 146
Indigeneity, 30, 42–52
  and essentialism, 69
Indigenous family, 35
Indigenous masculinity studies, 12–13
Indigenous men/masculinity
  adherence to dominant norms and ideals, 25, 91, 100–101, 159–160, 291
  alcohol use by, 85–86
  alienation of, 68, 80, 83–84, 87, 91–92, 100–101, 159–160
  authenticity and, 69–70
  and the body, 151–152, 197–201
  chauvinism and, 9, 91
  colonial images of, 32–34
  colonizing of, in the United States, 34–42
  conforming to hegemonic ideals by, 10, 41, 91, 159–160
  construction of, 10, 13, 41–42
  defined, 41–42, 66
  demands of, 4–5
  emasculation/powerlessness, 32–33, 47, 70–73, 79–93, 222–223, 238, 282
  feminizing of, 32–33
  formative experiences, 73–93
  as hypovirile/hypervirile, 32–33
  impact of colonialism, 41–42, 91, 159–160
  as incompetent, 32–33, 306n45
  as infantilized, 32–33, 306n45

Indigenous men/masculinity (*cont.*)
    and the military, 45–61, 82–83
    physicality of, 32, 151–152, 197–201
    as political prisoners, 55, 87, 272, 274
    as power gender, 9
    in Red Power era, 2–3
    in statistics, 40, 41–42
Indigenous militarization, 46–48
Indigenous mobility, 308n88
Indigenous people
    connection to homeland, 309n109
    colonizing of, 34–42
    hair symbolism to, 114
    legal status, of Indigenous people, 35
    stereotypes of, 31–35, 46
    values of, 118
    writings, music, and films regarding, 111–112
Indigenous renaissance/renewal, 237–247, 292–293
Indigenous Rights Struggle, 45, 135, 225–226, 239, 245–246, 266, 270–271
Indigenous-settler colonial relations, 30–31, 237–247
Indigenous women
    activism of, 5, 8–10, 14, 18, 25, 155–157, 164, 281–282
    in American Indian Movement (AIM), 155–163, 201–211, 290–292
    colonial images of, 33
    double colonization of, 10, 91, 162, 232
    and feminism, 155, 162, 233, 337–338n334
    gender relations and, 9, 155–163
    grassroots activism of, 9–10, 155–157, 164, 201–202, 231, 233, 281–282
    invisibility of in AIM, 9, 155
    and male chauvinism, 158, 203, 210
    in NoDAPL protesting, 281–282
    in Red Power Movement, 8–9, 91, 155, 210
    self-determination, sovereignty, and decolonization of, 231–233
    sexual politics and, 155–163
    status positions of in urban context, 84
    sterilization of, 232–233
    traditional (pre)reservation roles, 183, 207–208
    at Wounded Knee takeover, 201–211, 223–224, 246–247, 290–292
    writings regarding, 8, 9
Innes, Robert Alexander, 12, 91, 159–160
integration of Native Americans into settler society, 36–37
internalized oppression, 81, 88, 91, 160
International Indian Treaty Council (IITC), 229–230, 277
intratribal conflict, 166–169
invention/reinvention of traditions, 20
Iwo Jima Memorial, 143

Jackson, Ronald, 31
Jaimes, Annette M., 228
Jaimes, M. Annette, 8, 207
Japanese, insults against, 83
Johansen, Bruce, 354n20
John, Sonja, 50
Johnson, Troy, 6
Jones, Paul McKenzie, 7
Jumping Bull compound (shootout), 4, 229, 235

Kelly, Casey Ryan, 64
Kelly, Pat, 175
Kent State University, 28
Kidwell, Clara Sue, 167
Kills Enemy, Charles, 242
Killsright, Joe Stuntz, 229
King, Matthew, 220, 252
Kipp, Woody
    activism of, 237
    on Bureau of Indian Affairs (BIA) takeover, 102–103, 143, 144
    on cultural pride, 112
    on racism, 115
    on revolutionary culture, 114
    on Russell Means, 161

on the US military, 82, 83
on warriorhood, 151
on Wounded Knee takeover, 174, 175, 176, 177–178, 180
Kirkie, Richard, 257
Konigsberg, Eric, 354n17
Korean War, 46, 52–61
Kunstler, William, 227
Kýrová, Lucie, 7

Lakotas
   colonial oppression of, 200
   connection of American Indian Movement (AIM) to, 24, 106–108, 285
   Fort Laramie Treaty and, 182
   male and female sodalities of, 183–185, 206–208
   military service and, 48–52, 52–56, 56–61
   subjugation of, 181–182
   understandings of warriorhood, 24
   Wounded Knee symbolism to, 181–182
Lame Deer, John, 109
Lamont, Buddy, 219, 252, 272, 275, 278
Lamont, George, 173, 258, 259
Lamont, Lawrence "Buddy," 219
Lane, Mark, 227
Langston, Donna Hightower, 8
Lazarus, Edward, 221
Leach, Gary, 28–29
Leading Fighter, Nick, 254
League of Women Voters (LWV), 71, 94, 320n143
Leaureaux, Elijah, 327n119
Legal Rights Center, 316n31
legal status, of Indigenous people, 35
Listiguj Rangers, 294
Little Earth Housing Project, 316n31
Littlefeather, Sacheen, 263–264
Littlemoon, Walter, 117, 181
logic of elimination, 30
The "Longest Walk" (demonstration), 4, 6, 233–234
Looking Cloud, Arlo, 228
Lou Harris poll, 212, 239

Lowe, Lana, 294
Lucero, Nancy, 43
Luck, Owen, 179
Lutheran churches, 98
Lyons, Oren, 194

machismo, 69, 85
Madrid, Rocky, 179
Maestas, Robert, 354n20
manhood rhetoric, 134–135
Manifest Destiny, 31
manliness, contested meanings of, 130–141
Māori masculinity, 305n34
Mao Tse-Tung, 65
marginalized masculinity, 12, 19, 304–305n29
martial race ideology
   in British colonial India, 306n41
   and Western perceptions of Indigenous men, 34, 46
Marx, Karl, 65
Muscular Christianity, 31
masculine militancy, 121–122
masculinity
   Black masculinity, 95–96, 116, 120–121
   and the body, 151–152, 197–201
   colonial, 31–32, 34–35, 304–305n29
   complicit, 19, 37, 46, 223, 304–305n29
   hegemonic masculinity, 12, 19, 30–34
   hybrid bloc of, 19
   Indigenous masculinity defined, 41–42, 66
   marginalized masculinity, 19
   and nationalism, 18, 29–34, 34–42, 183, 191–192
   nationalist warrior masculinity, 25, 166, 175–176, 283–284
   protest masculinity, 23, 26, 68–69, 73, 79, 83–84, 92–93, 93–98, 101, 283, 284
   reservation, 166–168
   in resistance movements, 10, 30, 183, 191–192

masculinity (*cont.*)
  social classes and, 68–69
  theorizing, 15–23
  warrior masculinity, 105
  *See also* Indigenous men/masculinity
Mayflower II replica (protest), 104, 110
McClintock, Anne, 204
McCloud, Janet, 162
McKegney, Sam, 13, 35
McKiernan, Kevin Barry, 212
Meadows, William, 47–48, 185
Means, Bill, 67–68, 134, 145, 169, 189, 235, 244
Means, Lorelei DeCora, 155, 157, 194, 210, 232, 354n17
Means, Russell
  achievements of AIM, 263, 264
  acting career of, 235–236
  background of, 105–106
  on Bureau of Indian Affairs (BIA) takeover, 147–148
  at Cass Lake Reservation, 123
  chauvinism of, 203
  confrontation approach to, 126–127, 147
  on colonialism, 159
  criticism of, 158, 250, 257, 264
  as cultural nationalist, 242
  on Custer, South Dakota protest, 138
  death of, 236
  in exhibition, 271
  on female-male balance, 158
  on the Ghost Dance, 196
  on Gordon, Nebraska protest, 135
  on Indigenous Rights Struggle, 225–226, 263, 264
  leadership of, 73
  leadership of, after 1973, 235–236
  on manhood, 220, 225–226
  and media, 127, 147, 153, 215–217, 233
  on murder of Yellow Thunder, 132–133
  on other AIM leaders, 105–106, 264
  photo of, 77, 150–151, 153, 195, 276
  at Plymouth Rock protest, 67
  reputation of, 157–158, 161
  on self-defense, 121
  on sterilization, 233
  at Wounded Knee leadership trial, 225–227
  on Wounded Knee takeover, 215–216, 221, 251
  Yellow Thunder Camp of, 235
media
  bias, 126–130, 146
  coverage of AIM protests, 5, 9, 11, 109, 113, 126–130, 163, 227, 264, 265, 284, 286
  coverage at BIA takeover, 146–148
  coverage at Wounded Knee takeover, 211–218
  and invisibility of Indigenous women, 9, 153, 156, 158–159, 202–204, 210–211, 291
  savviness, 240–241, 264, 285
medicine bags, 194
medicine way of understanding, 16, 22–23
memory
  and AIM, 247–253, 282–283
  and historical amnesia/denial, 130–131
  and survival schools, 98–100
  theorizing, 248–249
  and Wounded Knee, 181–182
Menominee Warrior Society, 355–356n54
Messerschmidt, James W., 87–88
Messner, Michael, 152–153
Mihesuah, Devon Abbott, 8, 91, 158
Mi'kmaq Warriors, 294
  Mi'kmaq Warrior Society, 294
military service
  cultural traditions and, 49–50, 51–52
  draft for (Vietnam War), 53
  homecoming experience following, 55–56, 58–60
  hybrid patriotism and, 48–49, 283
  impact of, 82–83, 92
  Indian scout syndrome, 34, 54, 55
  masculine culture in, 82–83
  motivations for service, 45, 47–52

(national) integration/segregation
  debate, 52–53
 reinventing Indigeneity through,
  45–52
 roles in, 53–54
 statistics regarding, 45–46
 understanding
 warrior recognition from, 283
 *See also* veterans (Indigenous);
  *specific conflicts*
military veterans. *See* veterans
  (Indigenous)
Mills, Douglas K., 40
Mills, Sidney, 61
Minneapolis, Minnesota. *See* Twin
  Cities, Minnesota
*Minneapolis Tribune* (newspaper), 96,
  112–113
Miskito people (Nicaragua), 235
Mitchell, George, 72, 89–90, 154
mobility, Indigenous, 308n88
Mohawk Warrior Society, 267, 294
Momady, N. Scott, 111
Monnig, Laurel A., 47
Morgan, Fred, 89–90
Morgensen, Lauria, 79
Morton, Rogers, 154
Moss Lake, New York, 355–356n54
Mount Rushmore, South Dakota
  (occupations), 104, 109
movement culture, 111–119
Moves Camp, Ellen, 201–202

Nagel, Joan, 30
Nagel, Joane, 6, 8, 17, 73, 192, 308–
  309n99
nation, defined, 17
National Congress of American
  Indians (NCAI), 56, 63
National Council of Churches
  (NCC), 195
National Indian Youth Council
  (NIYC), 7, 63
nationalism
 and the body, 151–152, 197–201
 civic, 17–18

cultural, 63–64, 240, 249
 elements of, 192
 ethnic, 17–18
 gender and, 19–20, 29–42, 183,
  191–192, 204–207
 heteropatriarchy and, 30
 in Indian Country, 3–15
 imagined communities, 17
 masculinity and, 18, 29–34, 34–42,
  183, 191–192
 political nationalism, 63, 240
 race and, 19–20, 29–42
 struggle, after 1973, 227–237
 theorizing, 15–23
 Vietnam veterans' perspective
  regarding, 253–261
nationalist struggle, remembering and
  commemorating of, 247–277,
  283–284
nationalist symbolism, 111–119
nationalist warrior masculinity, 25,
  166, 175–176, 283–284
Nationality Act of 1940, 53
National Organization of Women
  (NOW), 162
nation-building, 17, 18, 191–196
Native Americans. *See* Indigenous
  men/masculinity; Indigenous
  people; Indigenous women
*News From Indian Country*
  (newspaper), 249
New Zealand, settler colonialism
  responses in, 305n34
Ninham, Dorothy, 240
Nixon, Richard, 147
NoDAPL protests, 279–282
nonviolence in AIM, 119–126
nuclear family model, 35

Oakes, Richard, 327n119
Oglala Civil Rights Council
  (OSCRO), 167, 201
Oglala Lakotas, 167. *See also* Lakotas
Ojibway Warrior Society, 294
Ojibwe, 24, 103, 124
Omi, Michael, 37

Onco, Robert Charles (Bobby), 174–175, 177, 256, 269–270
oral history, 21–22
O'Sullivan, Meg Devlin, 9
*oyate omniciye*, 193

paintings, heroizing warriors and anti-colonial struggle through, 266–270
Pan-Indianism, 42, 43–44
paternalism, of US government, 33–34, 221
Pearson, Diane, 16
Peltier, Leonard, 229, 277, 278
peoplehood, 16–17, 43, 44
performance (bodily) theorizing, 20
Pictou-Aquash, Anna Mae, 8, 221, 228, 235, 277, 278, 353n15. *See also* Aquash, Anna Mae
Piegan (Blackfeet), 207
Pine Ridge, South Dakota
  alcohol and, 360n185
  demographics of, 340n13
  intratribal conflict on, 166–168
  massacre on, 181
  photo of, 241
  physical violence on, 227–228
  political repression on, 227–228
  and reservation masculinities, 166–168
  shootout at Jumping Bull compound at, 4, 229, 235
  and tribal governance, 166–168
  *See also* Wounded Knee takeover
Plains Indians, 43–44, 184–185, 190, 206–207
Plains Wars, 33
Plymouth, Massachusetts, 105, 110
police, 86–89, 93–94, 95–96, 119, 121–122, 318n102, 320n143, 321n170
police brutality. *See* police
political status, of Indigenous people, 35–36
political warriors, 227–237
Poor Bear, Enos, 178
Poor Bear, Webster, 178, 244

Poor People's March, 63
postcolonialism, 15
Potter, Jack, 168
Pottinger, Stan, 187, 188
powerlessness, 32–33, 47, 70–73, 79–93, 222–223, 238, 282
Pratt, Richard, 37
Pretendian
  Littlefeather, Sacheen, 263–264, 361n196
  Sainte-Marie, Buffy, 111, 270, 325n51
protesting
  as catalyst, 45
  causes of, 4
  getting in your face approach of, 108
  heroizing warriors and anti-colonial struggle at protest sites, 271–277
  list of, 104
  militarization of, 124–125
  protest masculinity, 23, 26, 68–69, 73, 79, 83–84, 92–93, 93–98, 101, 283, 284
  radicalization of, 104–130
  warrior recognition from, 283–284
  *See also* masculinity

queer/Two-Spirit people studies, 14, 35
Quilt, Terry, 259–260

race, 15–23, 98–100
racial bias, 55, 84–85, 93–94, 101, 131–132, 202
racial conflict, in border towns, 130–141
Rader, Dan, 112
radicalization
  defined, 104–105, 108
  masculine warriorhood and, 110–111
  nationalist symbolism and, 111–119
  nonviolence and armed self-defense in AIM and Black Panthers, 119–126
  overview of, 104–105, 163
  political, 104–130
  of protest activism, 108–110
  revolutionary culture and, 111–119
  warrior masculinity and, 105

Ramirez, Reyna, 309n109
Rancher's Association (RA), 169
Rapid City, South Dakota (protests), 104, 131, 137
reappropriation, cultural, 126–130
Redbone, 111, 270
Red Cloud, 276
Red Cloud, Charlie, 252
Redner, Russ, 252
Red Power, 15–16, 63, 64
Red Power movement
   American Indian Movement (AIM) and, 3, 62, 104, 265–266
   Black Power movement as compared to, 64–65, 115–116, 120
   causes of, 42–43, 45, 79
   and culture, 111–112
   decline of, 233–235
   demands, 4
   defined, 7, 15–16, 63–64
   and gender, 4–5, 249, 282
   influences on, 120
   legacy of, 6–7, 237–238, 292–293
   moral righteousness of, 245
   organizations in, 5–6
   overview of, 2–3, 4–5, 61–65
   Pan-Indian consciousness and, 42
   and Indigenous renaissance, 237–239, 292–293
   slogans of, 114
   studies regarding, 6
   veterans' involvement in, 11
   waves of, 7
   writings regarding, 7–8
   women in, 8–9, 91, 155, 210
Red Wing State Training School, 80–81
Reese, Gene, 140
Reinhardt, Akim, 107, 193
relocation program, 38–41, 284
remasculinization, 104, 201, 222–223, 284
renewal, revitalization, and remasculinization in Indigenous men, 3, 23, 104–130, 222–223, 239–240, 284
reservation masculinities, 166–168
reservations
   as internal colonies, 37
   overview of, 37
retraditionalization
   defined, 104
   militarization and, 124–125
   nationalist symbolism and, 111–119
   nonviolence and armed self-defense in AIM and Black Panthers, 119–126
   and radicalization in Indigenous men, 104–130
   renewal, revitalization, and remasculinization and, 3, 23, 104–130, 222–223, 239–240, 284
   revolutionary culture and, 111–119
   warrior masculinity and, 105
revolutionary culture, nationalist symbolism and, 111–119
Rice, John, 55, 143
Rich, Elizabeth, 270
Rifkin, Mark, 35
Rios, Thelma, 139, 354n17
ritual, 51–52, 64, 66, 148–149, 183, 197, 198, 199–201, 238, 240–241, 248, 287–288
Road Woman, Buffalo Calf (Brave Woman), 207
Robeson County, North Carolina, 154
Robinson, Perry Ray, 235, 354n17
Rosen, Ron, 179
Rosier, Paul, 48
Roubideau, Jim, 139, 169
Roubideaux, Ramon, 195, 220–221
Roubideaux, Thomas, 49–50
Rowland, Gary, 244–245, 260–261, 271

Sainte-Marie, Buffy, 111–112, 270, 325n51
savage reactionary image, 128
Sayer, John William, 196, 227
Scenic, South Dakota, 133
Schierle, Sonja, 100
Schultz, Terri, 211–212
Schwarz, Maureen Trudelle, 11, 21, 127, 128, 182

Scottsbluff, Nebraska (protest), 131
Second Treaty of Fort Laramie
    (1868), 221
self-defense, armed, 119–126
self-determination, 61, 63, 231–233
self-governance, 239
settler colonialism
    and Christianity, 32
    definition, 29–34, 34–42, 306n45
    Hawaiian responses to, 305n34
    Indigenous responses to in Canada,
        267–269, 294
    Indigenous-settler colonial relations
        (USA), 237–247
    and logic of elimination, 30
    Māori responses to, 305n34
    New Zealand responses to, 305n34
    and reinventing Indigeneity, 42–45,
        45–52, 52–61, 61–66
    and westward expansion, 31
Seventh Cavalry Regiment, 181
seventies superskins, 117
sexism, male, 5, 9–10, 91, 159, 163,
    203, 232
sexual revolution, 160–161
Sheep Mountain, North Dakota
    (protest), 104
Shenandoah, Leroy, 327n119
Shreve, Bradley, 7, 16
Siddons, Louise, 270
Sinha, Mrinalini, 32
Sitting Bull, 130, 181, 276
Six Nations Iroquois Confederacy, 194
Smith, Desmond, 216
Smith, Paul Chaat, 6, 136, 154
Sneider, Leah, 63
Snyder Act, 53
social classes, masculinity construction
    and, 68–69
social hierarchies, 85–86
Society of American Indians (SAI), 62
Sohappy, Sergeant, 61
songs, heroizing warriors and anti-
    colonial struggle through, 266–270
South Dakota, racial conflict in, 135–
    136. *See also specific locations*

sovereignty, 16–18, 29–31, 35–36,
    63, 65, 195–196, 219–222, 224,
    230–233, 233–234, 239–240, 242,
    280–281
Special Operations Group (SOG), 168
spirituality, warriorhood and, 107
Spock, Benjamin, 145
Standing Rock Indian Reservation
    (protest), 279–282
Steiner, Stan, 111
stereotyping, 105, 127–128, 218, 295
sterilization of Indigenous women,
    232–233
Stern, Kenneth, 156
Stillwater Prison, 87–88
street gangs, 293–295
Studi, Wes, 50–51, 57–58, 60, 110, 122,
    154, 237, 245–246
Sturgis, South Dakota (protest), 104, 131
Sun Dance (ceremony), 108, 142, 241,
    244–245
survival schools, 6, 71, 98–100, 101,
    115–116
syncretism, 31, 51, 310n137
sweat lodge *(inípi)* ceremony, 200

Tachikawa Airfield, 82
Talbert, Carol, 187, 190
Tenfingers, Luke, 252
Tengan, Ty, 13
Ten-Point Program (American Indian
    Movement), 116
Ten-Point Program (Black Panther
    Party), 121
termination policy, 38, 284
Thanksgiving (protest) in Plymouth
    Rock, Mass, 67, 104, 110, 126
Thanksgiving Play (protest), 105, 110
Thomas, Robert K., 37
Thunderbird, Margo, 211
Thunder Hawk, Madonna, 8, 57, 155,
    162–163, 178, 210, 354n17
Tiger, Ken, 173, 176–177, 252
TigerSwan, 280–281
*tiospaye*, 192–193, 195, 207, 222
Tóth, György, 7

Trail of Broken Treaties (ToBT) (protest), 4, 103, 141–155, 142
treaty rights, 35–36
tribal governance, 37, 166–168, 220–221
(modern) tribal warriors, 293–295
Trudell, John, 154, 229, 236, 264
Truman, Harry, 55
Twenty Points position paper, 142
Twin Cities, Minnesota
　American Indian Movement (AIM) in, 71, 105
　conditions in, 84–87, 89–90, 93, 283
　criminal justice system in, 86–89
　drinking culture, 89–90
　grassroots organizing, 315–316n31
　Indigenous community grievances in, 71
　urban Indigenous community of, 93
　police brutality in, 93–94, 96
　protest masculinity emergence in, 68–69, 83–84, 92, 93–98, 101, 283
　racial bias in, 84–85, 93
　social hierarchies in, 85–86
　survival schools in, 71, 98–100
　urban experience, 39–41, 84–87, 89–90, 93
　urban relocation to, 39–40, 43, 83–84
　white bureaucracy of, 93
Twin Cities Naval Air Station, Minneapolis, Minnesota (takeover), 104
Two-Spirit/LGBTQ people, 14, 35

"U.N. Declaration on the Rights of Indigenous People," 230
United Native Americans (UNA), 109
urbanization, 38–41, 43
urban relocation, 38–41, 83–84, 92–93
Usbeck, Frank, 21
US Commission on Civil Rights, 228

Vander Wall, Jim, 229
veterans (Indigenous)
　as activists, 29
　on AIM (American Indian Movement), 11, 253–261
　bond of, 179–180
　on nationalism, 253–261
　new directions of, 293–295
　on warriorhood, 253–261
　as warriors, 2
　at Wounded Knee takeover, 168–181, 260–261
　writings regarding, 11
Vietnam Veterans Against War (VVAW), 178
Vietnam War
　betrayal following, 178–179
　double discrimination following, 60
　draft, 53
　homecoming experience following, 58–60
　hybrid patriotism and, 48–49
　Indigenous service in, 45–46, 48–52, 56–61, 288–290
　and Indigenous motivations for military service, 48–52
　protest against, 28
　questioning regarding, 83
　racial dimensions of, 57–58
　and Sixties Movements, 28–29, 56–61, 67–68, 170
　Wounded Knee takeover as compared to, 168–181, 188–189, 212, 213, 223
Vizenor, Gerald, 123, 158–159, 218
Voigt, Matthias, 8

Waetjen, Thembisa, 18
Wallace, Bonnie, 94, 329n165
Warner, Volney, 168–169
Warrior, Robert Allen, 6, 136, 154
warrior construct (of AIM members)
　battle honors, 129
　bodily practices, 197–201
　challenge of by women, 25, 224, 291–292
　contradictions of, 290
　confluence of currents of warriorhood, 11, 175–176, 223, 284, 288
　and counting coup, 189–190

warrior construct (of AIM members) (*cont.*)
  development of, 282–288
  functions of, 25
  heroizing of, 266–277
  nature of, 105, 284
  performance of warriorhood, 11, 20, 25, 126–130, 145–155, 163, 198–201, 211–218
  political, 227–237
  radicalization and, 110–111
  remembering and commemorating of, 247–277, 282–283
  self-perception as modern warriors, 2, 126–130, 183–191, 226
  social dynamics regarding, 286
  spirituality and, 107
  at takeover of Bureau of Indian Affairs (BIA), 141–155
  traditional protective spiritual medicine, 148–151 (at BIA takeover), 124–126 (at Gordon), 180–181, 189, 199–201 (at Wounded Knee)
  Vietnam Veterans' perspective regarding, 253–261, 288–290
  at Wounded Knee takeover and, 183–191, 247–253
warrior masculinity after 1973, transforming, 227–237
warrior society/-ies
  in Canada, 224, 267, 269, 294
  female sodalities during pre-reservation times, 183, 206–208
  male sodalities during pre-reservation times, 183–185, 190
  at Wounded Knee, 183–191, 213, 223
warriors/warriorhood
  American culture and, 295
  colonial discourse on, 32–34, 46–47
  new directions for, 293–295
  through military service, 2, 46–52, 52–61
  (traditional) understandings of, 24–25
warrior women
  and women's reference to cultural traditions, 206–208
  at Wounded Knee, 201–211
Waterman Wittstock, Laura, 155–156, 248, 256–257
weapons of the weak, 15
Weather Underground, 121
Wendt, Simon, 12, 120
"We Remember Wounded Knee" woodcut, 269
West Coast Okiijida, 294
Westerman, Floyd Crow, 89–90, 111, 113–114
Westermeyer, Joseph C., 84
"We Were All Wounded at Wounded Knee" (Redbone), 270
White Citizen Councils, 135
Whiteclay, Nebraska, 360n185 (protest)
White Crow, Jay, 94
white feminist movement, 162–163
White Oak, Oklahoma (AIM convention), 161
white segregationists and rhetoric of manhood, 135
white supremacy, 32
Whiting, Alfred Theodore Boneshirt, 254–255
Williams, Jack, 229
Williams, Jim, 145
Wilson, Richard, 167
Winant, Howard, 37
Winter Dam, Lac Courte Oreilles, Wisconsin (takeover), 104, 110
Wolfe, Patrick, 30
Women of All Red Nations (WARN), 232, 292
World War I, 46, 52–61, 54, 305n34
World War II, 42, 44–45, 46, 52–61, 54, 305n34
Wounded Knee (1890)
  and "a dream of revitalization," 182, 192
  and connection to 1973, 1–2, 178, 192, 196, 249, 262, 269–272, 276, 278, 288

and Ghost Dance, 181, 196
massacre, 1, 170, 181, 184
ongoing injustice, 181–182
symbolism of, 181–183, 192
Wounded Knee, South Dakota, 165, 174, 181–182, 192, 197, 223, 288
Wounded Knee leadership trials, 227
Wounded Knee Legal Defense/Offense Committee (WKLD/OC), 227
Wounded Knee Holocaust Museum, 271–277
Wounded Knee takeover (1973)
American Indian Movement (AIM) and, 220, 286, 293
artwork regarding, 269–270
Black Panther Party (BPP) and, 116
bodily practices and, 197–201
caravan to, 165–166
casualties of, 219
cause of, 131, 167
confronting US hegemony at, 218–222
cultural practices at, 199–200
cultural pride and dignity in, 243–244
cultural renewal and, 197–201
defenses/defensive strategy, 171–177
declaration of ION and setup of warrior society, 1, 166, 183–191, 223
demands, 220
end of, 218–219
in exhibition, 271–272
federal response to, 313n193
fighting US colonialism at, 168–181
Fort Laramie Treaty and, 219, 224
gendered nation-building at, 191–211, 223
and Ghost Dance, 189, 196, 200–201, 288
government response to, 168–169
guerilla theater and guerilla warfare in, 211–218
hostages in, 170
impact of, 218–222

Independent Oglala Nation (ION) and, 183–191, 197–201
Indigenous women's participation in, 201–211, 223–224, 246, 291–292
intratribal conflict and, 166–168
life following, 118
male bodies and, 197–201
media coverage of, 211–218
media's warriors at, 211–218
military hardware at, 168–169, 215, 341n29
moral regeneration and, 196–197
nationalist warrior masculinity and, 25, 166, 175–176, 283–284
and national reclamation, cultural revitalization, and moral regeneration, 196–197
and nation-building concepts (Indigenous/Western), 191–211
negotiations at, 170, 220
overview of, 1, 4, 165–166
parallels to Vietnam, 168–169, 173, 175, 177–178, 189
photo of, 170, 171–172, 184, 213, 214
public support of (Lou Harris poll), 212, 239
purpose of, 168, 221
(re)asserting political sovereignty at, 218–222
reclaiming Indigeneity at, 218–222
spiritual guidance at, 252
Standing Rock protest as compared to, 281
symbolism of, 197, 219–220, 222–224, 240, 244, 251–252, 262, 271
tribal sovereignty and, 220
un-Indigenous behavior of urban AIM activists during, 117–118
veterans at, 168–181, 260–261
Vietnam Veteran participation in, 289–290
warriorhood and, 223, 251–252
warrior society and, 183–191
warrior women at, 201–211
weaponry at, 174–175, 212, 215–216

Wounded Knee Trading Post, 182, 193, 219, 344n92

Xaba, Thokozani, 69
XIT, 111

Yankton Sioux Industries Plant, Wagner, South Dakota, 356n54
Yellowtail, Robert, 55
Yellow Thunder, Raymond
  controversy surrounding murder, 132
  Gordon, Nebraska (protest), 122–123, 131, 132–135
  murder, 113
  murder, compared to Wesley Bad Heart Bull, 136
  Yellow Thunder camp (protest), 235
Young, Phyllis, 246
Young Bear, Severt, 113
Young Horse, Floyd, 147, 149, 151
Young Lords, 121, 315n14
Yuval-Davis, Nira, 204
*yuwipi* ceremony, 200

Zigrossi, Norman, 228–229

Milton Keynes UK
Ingram Content Group UK Ltd.
UKHW020422030924
447802UK00014B/689/J